The Fall of the Bell System

The Fall of the Bell System

A Study in Prices and Politics

PETER TEMIN

with

LOUIS GALAMBOS

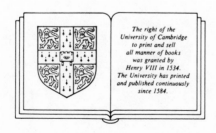

The right of the
University of Cambridge
to print and sell
all manner of books
was granted by
Henry VIII in 1534.
The University has printed
and published continuously
since 1584.

Cambridge University Press

Cambridge

New York   New Rochelle   Melbourne   Sydney

Published by the Press Syndicate of the University of Cambridge
The Pitt Building, Trumpington Street, Cambridge CB2 1RP
32 East 57th Street, New York, NY 10022, USA
10 Stamford Road, Oakleigh, Melbourne 3166, Australia

First published 1987
Reprinted 1988 (twice)

Printed in the United States of America

Library of Congress Cataloging-in-Publication Data
Temin, Peter.
The fall of the Bell system.
Includes index.
1. American Telephone and Telegraph Company –
Reorganization – History. 2. Telephone – United States –
History. I. Galambos, Louis. II. Title.
HE8846.A55T44   1987   384.6′065′73   87-10293
ISBN 0 521 34557 X

British Library Cataloging in Publication data applied for.

For my daughters,
Elizabeth and Melanie,
the next generation of
telephone users

Contents

viii   *Contents*

Tables, figures, and plates

Preface

Rumors started to circulate on the morning of Friday, January 8, 1982, that a settlement had been reached in the government's antitrust suit against the American Telephone and Telegraph Company. Trading was halted in AT&T's stock at midmorning, and at noon William Baxter, the Assistant Attorney General for Antitrust, and Charles L. Brown, the chairman of AT&T's board, held a press conference. They announced that the rumors were indeed correct. The case had been settled.

The agreement followed lines that Baxter had advocated. The Bell Operating Companies, which furnished local telephone service for most of the country, were to be divested from AT&T, which would retain its ownership of Western Electric and Bell Labs and would continue to provide long distance service. The Bell System, which had formed the backbone of American telephone service for a century, would no longer exist. No single company would be able to exercise the sort of end-to-end responsibility that AT&T had long held for most telecommunications in the United States.

The complex process of divestiture would take two years to complete; the new industry structure came into being at the start of 1984. The immediate effect on consumers was expected to be negative, and it was. Repairs – already becoming more difficult to obtain because of FCC decisions – became even more expensive and harder to arrange. Was the problem in the telephone (either your property or AT&T's) or the telephone lines (the local telephone company's responsibility)? Everyone's mailbox filled up with incomprehensible messages about something called "equal access." (Most people, it turned out, simply did not want to choose a long distance carrier.) Then local rates began to rise – not as fast or as far as had been predicted early in 1982 in the aftermath of the press conference, but visibly nonetheless. The effect on business customers was less clear-cut. After some initial confusion, large businesses found themselves better placed to reduce costs and obtain services tailored to their needs. Small businesses had mixed results. Although today divestiture seems to be generally approved by people close to telecommunications (either as suppliers or as large customers), most consumers seem to dislike the change.

Their irritation – if recent surveys are a guide – appears to be growing as the problems with residential service persist.

How did it happen? Did AT&T dig its own grave? Or was the giant firm caught in a policy web from which divestiture seemed the only escape? Were the steps leading to divestiture an orderly process of public policy formation? Was the choice a consensus solution? Surely this story can tell us much about the way our government functions: about business – government relations, about the role of big business in our society, and about the manner in which our largest corporations respond to change. We may also learn from this saga whether divestiture was the best remedy for the real and imagined telecommunications problems existing at the end of the 1970s. The narrative that follows deals in detail with each of these matters, and proposes answers to each of these questions. It provides as well a carefully documented account – based on public sources, interviews, and private company records – of how the divestiture unfolded. Although the heart of the book is a narrative, some background is presented in the first chapter, where telephone pricing and particularly the much misunderstood "separations" process are explained. Prices may seem arcane to some readers, but they played a central role in the history of U.S. telecommunications policy; they deserve to be understood more fully than they were by most of the participants.

This book had its origin in the desire of Mr. Brown to commission a scholarly history of the breakup of the Bell System, a book that would serve as a point of reference for other studies. With a keen sense of history, Brown thought that the best time to record the story was while the participants themselves could still recall it. AT&T would sponsor the study and provide access to its officers and papers, but it would not interfere with the views expressed by the author. Brown wanted an outsider to write the story, albeit with information from insiders.

I was intrigued. I had written books about the history of the American economy, but never before had I been offered the opportunity to see developments in the economy and public policy from inside a functioning corporation. This seemed an unusual and promising opportunity. The event itself – the end of the Bell System – was important and dramatic enough to provide an intriguing history. The opportunity to tell this story by drawing upon sources inside AT&T, as well as public documents, meant that I would have a good shot at unraveling the mysteries surrounding the turmoil in telecommunications in the 1970s and 1980s – turmoil that ultimately let to AT&T's surprising last-minute settlement of the antitrust case. The story would, I knew, be complex, but I decided that it could be told fully and fairly if I had help from many of the people who had lived through it. I had previously done some work for AT&T in connection with the government's antitrust suit against the company.

Even though the research I did—on the early regulation of the Bell System—was not used directly in the trial, some of it provided a starting point for a scholarly article, and I had already been thinking about further telecommunications research. From the start Louis Galambos, Professor of History at Johns Hopkins, was designated by AT&T as editor of the book. After he and I talked with Mr. Brown, we were commissioned to undertake the study.

In the following months of research and writing, AT&T was as good as its word. The firm gave us access to documents and people; and although they provided staff assistance and comments on the accuracy of my factual material, they remained removed from the book's editorial content. To the extent that AT&T's sponsorship gave me access to many people from the former Bell System who have influenced my views, this aspect of the origins of the book has affected the product. But this is, after all, the usual process in any scholarly endeavor. Galambos and I also talked with many people outside the System who were not sympathetic to it. I have heard many views of the events recorded here. To further the reader's understanding of how I synthesized these views, I have indicated the sources for the accounts drawn from interviews. I would like to believe that this is the same book I would have written had it been supported by an independent agency. The views expressed here are my own.

Throughout the research and writing of the book, I have received much assistance and cooperation from persons both inside and outside AT&T. I have acknowledged Louis Galambos's able assistance by placing his name on the title page. The firm's support for this project provides an important example for other companies and for scholars concerned with the role of business in modern society. In addition, and of utmost importance, was the assistance of all those who took the time to share their experiences with us. Present and past employees of AT&T, congressional and FCC staff members, Justice Department lawyers, AT&T's competitors—all told their versions of these events, providing the kind of source material about which most historians can only dream. This study was greatly enhanced by their cooperation and openness in sharing their experiences and views with us. I thank them and those who commented on the manuscript for their help; they and others are named in the Acknowledgments.

I also wish to thank the institutions—especially MIT—that provided the time and the place for writing. I received a sabbatical leave from MIT during 1985–6, during which I was the Pitt Professor of American History and Institutions at Cambridge University. Elected a Fellow of St. John's College, Cambridge, I was welcomed by the university and the college into a setting that is both beautiful and stimulating. I could not have found a better locale for writing. I owe a particular debt to the Master and Fellows of St. John's, who made a visiting American feel very much at home in the ongoing life of the college. Johns Hopkins University, where Louis Galambos teaches, also provided considerable support.

It is doubly fitting that this book should be published by Cambridge University Press. Voluminous research notes and scattered early drafts were transformed into a book at Cambridge University by the holder of a professorship endowed by the Press.

Peter Temin

Cambridge, Massachusetts
April 1987

Acknowledgments

This book involved the assistance of many people. AT&T greatly appreciates their time and effort and especially the spirit of cooperation in which it was given. The contributions of many of them are noted elsewhere in the book, but some special acknowledgments are in order here.

AT&T was most fortunate to have two accomplished scholars working together on the project. The author, Peter Temin, waded through great reams of information, conducted many hours of interviews, patiently reviewed or listened to each of the multitude of comments, explanations, and suggestions, and evaluated and translated it all into a coherent, meaningful story. The issues and events leading to the divestiture agreement are complex and many-sided. That they appear here clearly, in straightforward exposition, insightfully analyzed, is a tribute to Peter Temin's diligence, perception, and ability as a first-rate scholar.

Another first-rate scholar, Louis Galambos, was with the project from the beginning, designated as the editor. His experience in the history of business was an important asset throughout, as he carried out much of the basic research in AT&T files and archives. Literally "turning the pages" in box after box of records, Galambos was able to greatly shorten the research process by advising us what records to seek out from company files and archives. He participated with Peter Temin in all but three of the interviews, eventually carrying out several himself while Temin was in England. His editing role, which at our request became that of an advisor to AT&T and colleague to the author, began with early drafts. His advice on sharpening the themes allowed Temin to focus early on the analysis and on carrying out the rewriting. Both his editing and his expert advice contributed importantly to the shape of the final product.

The corporate archive staff was given administrative responsibility for the project by AT&T. It provided logistical support to the author and editor in locating records, assisted in identifying people to be interviewed and in making the needed arrangements, produced and distributed the manuscript through its various versions, and assisted with the research and annotation. Robert Garnet, himself the author of a book about AT&T's early history, provided assistance with research into the corporate reorganizations of the 1970s and 1980s. His advice on these and related corporate matters was especially helpful. Laraine Antes handled all the word processing and record keeping, and managed the process of preparing and distributing the seemingly endless drafts and redrafts over the course of several years. We all repeatedly tested the endurance and patience of this assistant extraordinaire, but she never faltered. Linda Straub and Shirley Steiner gave enthusiastic and skillful assistance in tracking down and polishing the footnote references, and Mary Jane Kelly helped with formating the legal citations; if the citations are useful to other scholars, it is largely because of their timely interventions. Ralph Swinburne found needed documents among the mammoth files left over at AT&T from the government's antitrust suit. Much needed advice in handling various project arrangements was furnished by Gerry Murphy. Alan Gardner assisted in the manuscript preparation, and Linda Lee and Vera Robinson cheerfully helped with numerous secretarial chores. As project manager, I worked closely with the author and editor and managed the AT&T staff operation. The efforts and cooperation of all, especially Peter Temin and Louis Galambos, through sometimes trying circumstances and tight schedules are greatly appreciated.

Others who contributed include Henry Trout, who graciously guided Temin and Galambos through an AT&T toll office containing a class 4 switch and a yellow line on the floor (see Chapters 6 and 7). Graduate students Harry Foster, Kenneth Lipartito, and Katherine Simonds and undergraduate Jonathan Gruber provided able research assistance to Peter Temin at an early stage in the project. Sharon Widomski provided timely assistance to Louis Galambos.

Many people read the manuscript at various times, and their comments helped Peter Temin to improve the accuracy and clarity of the story. We appreciate the attention they gave a long and heavy typescript. Helpful assistance or comment was received from James Armstrong, Edward Block, Henry Boettinger, Charles Brown, Alfred Chandler, Donald Coleman, James DeBois, Edward Goldstein, Mel Horwitch, William Letwin, Richard Levine, Robert Lloyd, Arch McGill, Ted Miller, James Olson, Alfred Partoll, Victor Pelson, Brian Savin, Bernard Strassburg, Morris Tanenbaum, Howard Trienens, Richard Vietor, Alvin von Auw, John Zeglis, and several others.

Finally, the guidance and unwavering patience of Frank Smith and Russell Hahn at Cambridge University Press is particularly appreciated. Working with them has been a great pleasure.

Robert G. Lewis
American Telephone and Telegraph Co.
June 1, 1987

Note on sources

I have drawn on a wide range of sources in writing this history, and I have tried to document these sources as completely as possible to help later investigators. Three kinds of information that sometimes pose problems for bibliographers play a large role in this book. With these problems in mind, I will briefly describe the problematical sources and the conventions I have adopted to refer to them.

The voluminous public record of AT&T's regulatory and legal struggles provides a unique window into the development of telecommunications policy. These documents are, however, often hard for the nonspecialist to locate and retrieve. I have given the legal reference (intelligible to any legal librarian) in the footnotes. Since these references typically give no clue to the general reader about the nature of the document, I have preceded the legal reference with the normal historical citation descriptive of the source.

This study, in addition, relied heavily on internal AT&T records to show the evolution of ideas, policies, and organizational structures within the Bell System. These documents include public and internal speeches, letters, memorandums, documents discovered in antitrust suits, and management reports that were written in the course of AT&T's long and at times convoluted internal deliberations. Any committee report or memorandum not otherwise identified is an internal AT&T document. Where they have been discovered or published, I have given a reference. The other documents are in the AT&T Corporate Archives.

Finally, Louis Galambos and I conducted many interviews with the participants in this history, persons within the Bell System and other businesses and those in various branches of the government. Nearly all of these interviews were recorded and transcribed. They were then edited by the various interviewees. The edited transcripts are in AT&T's Corporate Archives, and each citation refers to the page numbers of the final draft of the transcript. A list of the people interviewed follows. Those individuals not identified below appear in the text and index.

G. Ashley (AT&T, general attorney)   M. Baudhuin (AT&T, public
D. Aylward   affairs)

W. Baumol
W. Baxter
G. Bell
E. Block
H. Boettinger
T. Bolger
C. Brown
R. Carr
W. Cashel
J. Clendenin (BellSouth, president)
E. Crosland
J. deButts
W. Ellinghaus
G. Epstein (FCC, chief of Common Carrier Bureau)
F. Fielding
J. Fox
H. Geller
B. Gilmer
F. Gluck
E. Goldstein
R. Gradle
W. Grimes (House Judiciary Committee, staff)
D. Guinn
C. Hugel
C. Jackson
J. Kilpatric
R. Levine
R. Lilley
S. Litvack
R. Lumb (AT&T, public affairs)
A. McGill
W. McGowan
M. McGuire (AT&T, public affairs)
R. McLean

H. Moulton
J. Nellis (House Judiciary Committee, general counsel)
B. Owen
A. Partoll
D. Perkins (AT&T Board of Directors)
D. Procknow (AT&T Technologies, president)
I. Ross (AT&T Bell Laboratories, president)
J. Rosse (Stanford University, professor of economics)
W. Sharwell
H. Shooshan
D. Staley
B. Strassburg
W. Stump (AT&T, federal regulatory matters)
H. Symons (Rep. Timothy Wirth's staff, counsel)
M. Tanenbaum
M. Tiffany (Senate Judiciary Committee, antitrust counsel)
H. Trienens
B. Tunstall
L. Van Deerlin
P. Verveer (U.S. Department of Justice, attorney)
A. von Auw
J. Weber
W. Weiss
K. Whalen
W. White (Senate Commerce Committee, senior counsel)
B. Wunder
J. Zeglis

Introduction

The forces that would break apart the mighty Bell System within fifteen years were already visible in 1970 to those who cared to look. No one, however, could have known how these forces would interact to produce AT&T's divestiture on January 1, 1984. Action could be seen, reaction only imagined. Two discussions at meetings of the time reveal the knowledge of these forces that existed at the start of the 1970s. One took place in a public professional meeting. The other occupied a regularly scheduled gathering of Bell System executives. The two episodes reveal differing aspects and perceptions of the emerging telecommunications "problem" – and some of the ideas and forces that would interact to determine its resolution.

The first interchange took place at a meeting of antitrust lawyers in the spring of 1970. Howard Trienens, a partner in Sidley and Austin, the giant Chicago law firm that handled much of AT&T's federal regulatory business, moderated a panel of distinguished lawyers that included Commissioner Kenneth Cox from the Federal Communications Commission (FCC) and Professor William Baxter from the Stanford Law School. Trienens opened a brief discussion of competition in telecommunications by responding to Cox's description of the FCC's recent decision to allow Microwave Communications, Inc. (MCI), then a tiny new company, to sell private line services (i.e., telecommunication services that did not go through Bell's national switched network) between Chicago and St. Louis. Trienens asserted that the MCI decision did not involve the issue of competition squarely because the new firm had applied to the FCC for permission to offer a new, low-quality service unobtainable from the Bell System. The FCC had agreed, arguing that MCI and the Bell System would appeal to different customers. Trienens therefore postulated a hypothetical condition in which MCI built a microwave system between Chicago and St. Louis comparable in quality to the Bell System. It would be able to charge lower rates for the same services offered by the Bell System because it was not subject to the Bell System's nationwide rate averaging.

How should the established carrier respond? Trienens argued that it should be able to compete, that is, lower its price in response to the new competitor. "Otherwise," the lawyer said, there would not be competition; there would be "allocation of markets." But, continued Trienens,

1

"This is where I fall off the sled." What would happen if the Bell System responded to the new entrant by lowering its rates enough to drive it out of business? The entrant would have raised money from "a lot of innocent investors," built physical facilities, and contributed to the campaigns of congressmen. It would be, in short, "somebody that has got to be protected." The FCC would be forced to create a regulatory scheme to protect the entrant, lowering existing carrier rates a little, but not as much as they would be lowered with unregulated competition. Merging the actual FCC decision and his hypothetical one, Trienens asked, why do we not face up to the implications of our current policies?

Baxter replied "from the economist's point of view." He denied Trienens's assumption that investors were innocent. He asserted that if entrants knew that the established carrier was allowed to drive them out again, they would not enter. "There may be several companies that make mistakes and come in and get burned, because the common carriers cut prices . . . and chase them back out," Baxter continued. "That is the worst thing that can happen and that is no tragedy." This "worst case" would occur where a natural monopoly exists and the established carrier has lower costs than any entrant. If there is no natural monopoly, then the established carrier would not have a cost advantage over an entrant and would be unable to drive the new firm out. In this more favorable case, there would be no problem. Baxter looked forward to the opportunity to discover which case applied to the telephone network.[1]

Both discussants saw clearly that the FCC's policy would confront the Bell System with problems of competition and agreed that the System should have the right to respond. But the two lawyers foresaw very different reactions to AT&T's response. Baxter anticipated a world in which the Bell System and its competitors would struggle over the market for telecommunications services on the basis of relative costs. Trienens, by contrast, foresaw a political contest that would involve far more than simple price competition. His worst case was not a few business failures but the allocation of markets designed to prevent these failures.

Regulatory events of the 1960s had begun to suggest which view was more accurate, but the full answer would come only as the growth of competition in telecommunications and the debate over prices accelerated in the next decade. This discussion near the start of the process was noteworthy not only because it posed sharply one of the primary issues of

---

[1]The characterization of Baxter's point of view as that of an economist was provided by another moderator. See panel discussion at the Eighteenth Annual Spring Meeting of the American Bar Association, "The Role of Competition in Transportation and Communications," *Antitrust Law Journal*, Vol. 39, 1970, pp. 487–9.

public debate, but also because these two gifted lawyers would meet again eleven years later on opposite sides of the government's antitrust suit against AT&T – a suit in which the Justice Department challenged the legality of Bell's responses to competition. Trienens and Baxter would negotiate the suit's resolution.

The second discussion took place at the semiannual Presidents' Conference of the Bell System in the fall of 1971. While the presidents of the nineteen Bell Operating Companies were preparing to attend the meeting, they had each received a surprising teletype message. The Presidents' Conferences normally were held at a sunny resort, where the presidents met with the men from 195 Broadway (AT&T's corporate headquarters in New York) to plan and coordinate the vast Bell System. Working in the morning and playing tennis or golf in the afternoon, the executives maintained the personal bonds that were an integral aspect of doing Bell's business. But three weeks before this conference, the presidents were notified that its location had been changed from a comfortable California resort to a Chicago-area hotel selected by the president of the Illinois Bell Telephone Company: Charles L. Brown.

No one could mistake the Arlington Park Towers for a resort. There was no tennis, no golf. There would, in any case, be no time to enjoy sports; the presidents had assembled for serious business. H.I. Romnes, chairman of AT&T's board and its chief executive officer (CEO), acknowledged the obvious. "We meet," he said, "in somewhat less elegant surroundings than usual, and the opportunities for recreation . . . appear somewhat limited." Romnes went on to explain the sudden change in the conference's venue. The Bell System had "given not much more than lip service to what most businesses take for granted is the starting point of all corporate strategy": making money. Instead, the giant utility had based its strategy on "an appraisal of the public's communications requirements and what it would take to meet them." Faithful to its role as steward of the nation's telephone network, the Bell System had worked for close to a century to keep ahead of the public's demand for service. Network engineers like Romnes were the high priests of this religion, the initiated who could design the measures needed to fulfill the System's chosen mission. In pursuit of this goal, the Bell System's 1 million employees sold $17 billion worth of services a year by 1970, as shown in Tables 1 and 2.

It was an article of faith within the Bell System that caring for the public would allow it to earn the return to which it was entitled under regulation. Romnes said that he did not want to give "the impression that our faith is wavering," but it clearly was. The System was receiving a "lesser and lesser rate of return on every new dollar invested." It could not afford the "luxury" of long-run discussions among the presidents – symbolized by

The fall of the Bell System

Table 1. *Bell System revenue and earnings (millions of dollars)*

	Revenue	Net income[a]	Return on average total capital(%)
1950	3,262	472	6.07
1955	5,297	815	6.76
1960	7,920	1,568	7.69
1965	11,062	2,212	7.59
1970	16,955	3,257	7.51
1975	28,927	5,518	7.99
1980	50,709	10,010	9.87

[a]Before interest deductions.
Source: Bell System Statistical Manual 1950–1981, AT&T, Comptroller's-Accounting Division, June 1982, pp. 102, 106.

Table 2. *Bell System employees (thousands)*

	AT&T and Bell Operating Companies	Western Electric	Bell Labs	Total
1950	523	73	6	602
1955	616	120	10	746
1960	580	143	12	736
1965	612	169	15	795
1970	773	215	17	1005
1975	770	153	16	939
1980	848	174	22	1044

Source: Bell System Statistical Manual 1950–1981, June 1982, p. 702

the absence of more tangible luxuries at the conference as well – in its need to reverse this alarming trend.[2]

The financial news was indeed bleak. AT&T's earnings per share, which had risen sharply in the early 1960s, had fallen just as sharply toward the end of the decade. The price of AT&T's stock had followed suit, and the market-to-book ratio (the ratio of the market value of the firm's stock to its book value) had fallen from close to 2.0 early in the decade to less than 1.0 (see Figure 1). AT&T had continued to pay dividends, as it had throughout the Great Depression of the 1930s. Its stock was the most widely held in the world. But investors were losing faith in the Bell System's ability to

[2]H.I. Romnes, "Opening Remarks," Presidents' Conference, Chicago, Illinois, November 8–9, 1971.

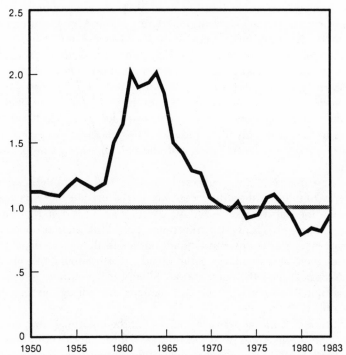

Figure 1. Ratio of market price to book equity per share of AT&T common stock, 1950–1983. (Source: *Bell System Statistical Manual 1950–1981*, June 1982, p. 410, and AT&T Treasury Department, General Reference Binder, March 1984, p. B106.)

earn an adequate and growing rate of return. The System seemed out of touch with its environment at the close of the turbulent 1960s.[3]

The problems were not only financial. The Bell System's reputation as the best telecommunications network in the world had been tarnished by a series of service failures over the previous few years. Overloaded switching equipment in New York City broke down in 1969, stranding much of the financial community and isolating businesses. This highly visible interruption of service had called into question the Bell System's ability to set and police its own standards of service.

The service failures also symbolized the more basic problem of maintaining the Bell System's technical preeminence. Bell Labs had long been a leader in the discovery of new technology. Its research during and after the Second World War in microwave radio and then transistors had made

[3]See, e.g., "The Outlook for AT&T: Effects of Federal Action," *U.S. News & World Report*, February 5, 1968, pp. 62–4.

this technology accessible to other firms that were emerging as the Bell System's rivals. As the electronics markets grew and telecommunications came to involve more electronics, Western Electric – the System's manufacturing arm – was finding it increasingly difficult to maintain its historical position as the dominant producer of telecommunications equipment. But if Western Electric could not be counted on to be the low-cost supplier, how were the operating companies to procure their terminals and switches? What kinds of changes at Western Electric and Bell Labs were needed to keep up with the rapidly evolving market? Was government support for Western's integration with the Bell Operating Companies still justified?

As if in response to these concerns, the FCC had begun in the previous few years to allow competition not only in the private line services discussed by the antitrust lawyers, but also in parts of the market for telephone equipment. The FCC's new policy posed the same problems here that Baxter and Trienens had defined, although they were expressed in terms of technical standards rather than prices. Should the operating companies beat back the competition? Should they continue to behave in the traditional, careful Bell System manner, as befitted an established public utility?

Even though Chicago was at the center of the emerging competition in private line services and Brown of Illinois Bell was on the front line of the competitive battle, no answers to these difficult questions were forthcoming at the Chicago Presidents' Conference. Romnes had summoned the "Bell System management to take charge of its own future." But instead of leading the charge, he expressed his hope that the operating company presidents, "when you get back home, will inspire your own colleagues to the quest for right answers that will insure a sound future for the Bell System."[4]

The future direction of the company was no more visible than the scope of competition in telecommunications. The Bell System had attained the goal stated early in the century by AT&T's legendary president, Theodore Vail: to provide every household with a telephone connected to every other telephone. "Universal service" having been achieved, it was not at all clear where the System should go. Individual operating companies were beginning to stir, but the System as a whole lacked headway. The Bell style of organization that had worked so well to provide telephone service for over half a century did not seem to provide a framework for firm action from 195 Broadway in this time of crisis.

Unhappily, the Bell System lacked time to contemplate its strategic and

[4]H.I. Romnes, "Closing Remarks," Presidents' Conference, Chicago, Illinois, November 8–9, 1971.

structural problems. The tide of competition was beginning to run more rapidly, and the risk of foundering on economic, regulatory, or legal rocks was increasing day by day. In the late 1950s, after a previous storm of controversy, the Bell System had reached an apparently safe harbor, but the evolution of finances, technology, and public policy had forced it into the parlous straits of 1970–1. The decisions made within the company in the next few years would interact with an evolving public debate to enlarge and intensify that crisis throughout the decade. Every branch of the federal government would be involved. And the consequences of the widening controversies would shape the choices faced by Charles Brown, by then AT&T's CEO, a decade after the cheerless Chicago Presidents' Conference – choices that would spell the fall of the Bell System.

The web of problems faced by public officials and by AT&T's managers were only dimly seen at the start of the 1970s. It has become clear since then, however, that the critical decisions of the early 1970s had their origins not only in the immediate problems of the time but also in the long history of AT&T and its relations with the government. Over the years, AT&T had struck a variety of bargains with different levels of government and with different federal agencies to create the peculiar framework in which Bell System managers moved. In addition, the System – which included by the 1970s 1 million employees, more than the population of many countries today – had acquired a strong internal culture that conditioned its managers' every move. Growing conflict between a rapidly changing regulatory and commercial environment and Bell's resilient traditions would leave the Bell System's leaders facing less and less attractive possibilities as the 1970s progressed. Out of this conflict would arise a new public policy toward telecommunications and a new corporate strategy for AT&T.

The following pages chronicle the widening conflict from its antecedents before 1970 to its climax in the early 1980s. This account emphasizes three aspects of the process of change within AT&T and in the various public forums. First, the conflict was cumulative. Actions taken at one time created or increased forces – typically due to enticing gaps between prices and costs – that would force other decisions in the years ahead. Paradoxically, however, the internal logic of this process was not visible to most of its participants. They tended to view each action in isolation and each force as autonomous. It is one task of history to put these actions and forces together to provide a synthesis that is in essence more complete than the contemporary perceptions.

Second, the process was dominated by changing ideology, not changing technology. It was ideas, not things, that urged on the actors at critical points in the contests over telecommunications policy and AT&T's organization. The debate between Baxter and Trienens foreshadowed this aspect of the crisis.

Third, the interaction between AT&T's strong internal culture and hierarchy, on the one hand, and the federal government's loose structure, on the other, would be a critical element in the story. AT&T was out of touch with the political process in the 1970s, and its attempted interventions would have unexpected consequences. To a considerable extent, the firm's interventions would be dictated by events within AT&T that were largely hidden from the outside world. A critical question for the giant firm would be whether it could change its perceptions, goals, and organization fast enough to keep pace with the rapidly evolving political and economic processes of that decade. The 1971 Presidents' Conference did not hold out much hope that it could.

I

Setting the stage

The regulated monopoly

The Bell System of 1971 was distinguished not only by its size and the problems it faced, but also by the unique relationships it had established over almost a century of dealing with state and federal governments. (For AT&T's size, see Table 3.) The System had grown initially in the midst of turmoil over the rise of modern corporate enterprise, contemporary with the emergence of state regulation and the creation of the Interstate Commerce Commission (ICC), AT&T's first federal regulator. But for a nation accustomed to small enterprises, the size and power of the modern corporation were difficult to accept. Many Americans at the turn of the century were unhappy with the prospect of regulation; they questioned whether giant firms like AT&T should be allowed to exist, regulated or not. This view gave rise to the Sherman Antitrust Act, passed shortly after the formation of the ICC. Congress in effect told the federal executive that it should either regulate or prosecute monopolies. But Congress did not indicate how that choice was to be made. Instead of locating the decision in a single office, it was left to be made through bargains and implicit understandings between federal and state regulatory agencies and the Department of Justice.

AT&T soon confronted this crucial ambiguity in public policy. Although the company moved adroitly to fashion a compromise that preserved its position as a regulated monopoly, it continued to be at risk that its performance would not satisfy one or more of the government bodies with which it dealt and that the bargains it made would begin to unravel. The process began shortly before the First World War when Theodore Vail's policy of acquiring independent telephone companies hit an antitrust snag. The U.S. Attorney General questioned whether this policy was as consistent with antitrust law as it was with efficient performance. He filed a suit against AT&T, alleging that the telephone company had violated the Sherman Act by acquiring a small long distance company in the Pacific Northwest. AT&T successfully bargained for peace with the Justice Department. The suit was resolved by a consent decree – AT&T's first – and an out-of-court agreement with the Justice Department embodied in a letter

9

Table 3. *The largest U.S. corporations in 1970*

Company	Assets[a]	Net income[a]	No. of employees[b]
AT&T (incl. Western Electric)	53.3	2.5	1,000
Standard Oil (N.J.)	19.2	1.3	143
General Motors	14.2	.6	700
Ford	9.9	.5	432
IBM	8.5	1.0	269
General Electric	6.3	.3	397

[a]Billions of dollars.
[b]Thousands.
Source: Fortune, May 1971, pp. 172–3, 200–201.

from Nathan Kingsbury, a vice president of AT&T, to the Attorney General (known ever after as the Kingsbury Commitment).[1]

AT&T agreed to stop buying competing telephone companies and to connect them to its long distance lines – a sharp reversal of Vail's previous policy. It also agreed to sell its holdings in Western Union, the first of many agreements in which AT&T was asked to preserve Western Union as an independent supplier of communications services. Even with its new policies, however, AT&T would be tolerated by the federal government only so long as it followed special rules of behavior. In effect, the Kingsbury Commitment stated that the telephone company would bear watching because it was operating at the limit of what the antitrust laws would allow. AT&T would continue to live close to that legal line for the next seventy years.

Although President Woodrow Wilson congratulated the Attorney General and AT&T for reaching the 1913 understanding, the Kingsbury Commitment did not maintain competition in interstate telephone service.[2]

[1]American Telephone and Telegraph Company, *1910 Annual Report,* p. 21; *US v. AT&T,* No. 6082, U.S. Dist. Ct., Dist. of Oregon, *Original Petition,* July 24, 1913; Nathan C. Kingsbury to James C. McReynolds, December 19, 1913 (Kingsbury Commitment); *US v. AT&T,* No. 6082 (D. Or. 1914) (Decree).
[2]President Woodrow Wilson to James C. McReynolds, December 19, 1913. The agreement promised more than it could deliver. The Kingsbury Commitment as written precluded *any* AT&T purchase of a telephone company, and the Attorney General felt the need to clarify the agreement in his annual report for 1914. He argued that no barrier was intended for the achievement of monopoly in the provision of local telephone service; rival telephone companies in a given locality could consolidate under the agreement even if one of them was a Bell company. But, in a remark that foreshadowed the *Modification of Final Judgment* two-thirds of a century later, the Attorney General imposed the condition on any purchase that "the consolidated company will make connections with all long distance interstate lines and thereby preserve competition in interstate communication." This policy is known now as "equal access." *Report of the Attorney General,* 1914, p. 14; see also Roger Shale, Assistant Attorney General, "Memorandum re American Telephone & Telegraph Company's Commitment," November 12, 1919.

The legal guidelines lost their crispness in the interpretation, allowing AT&T considerable freedom of action. The focus of public policy also shifted with the onset of World War I from the preservation of competition to the achievement of efficiency. As the antitrust movement of the Progressive era subsided, relations between corporate enterprise and American society improved for a time; although never on as secure a basis as they had been before the rise of the large corporate combine, business-government relations also became far more cordial. One measure of this new mood was the 1921 legislation that gave the ICC the power to exempt AT&T from the antitrust laws for the purpose of acquiring other telephone companies. Of the 234 independent companies purchased under the ICC's jurisdiction, the Bell System acquired 223. Changing circumstances had nullified this important part of the Kingsbury Commitment.[3]

With the onslaught of the Great Depression, however, cooperation once again gave way to conflict between the corporation and American society. In this context, Congress passed the Communications Act in 1934, creating the Federal Communications Commission and spelling out its mission. The FCC's primary responsibility was to regulate radio and, later, TV broadcasting, but it was charged also with so-called common carrier activities, notably telephony. The Communications Act stated that its purpose in this area was "to make available, so far as possible, to all the people of the United States a rapid, efficient, Nationwide, and worldwide wire and radio communication service with adequate facilities at reasonable charges."[4] Defining reasonable charges more precisely, the act incorporated a prohibition on discrimination from the 1887 Interstate Commerce Act, pronouncing "any unjust or unreasonable discrimination in charges" to be "unlawful."[5] The twin pillars of telephone regulation under the FCC were to be universal service and nondiscriminatory rates.

When Congress passed the new law, the Bell System was providing

[3]The Postmaster General operated the telephone system in 1918–19 and explicitly encouraged the consolidation of competing systems into one national system. *Act of Congress Covering Taking Over of Wires*, Pub. Resolution No. 38, 40 Stat. 904, 1918; President's Proclamation Taking Over Telephone and Telegraph Systems, July 22, 1918; Postmaster General, Bulletin No. 2, Order No. 1783, "Order Assuming Possession and Control," August 1, 1918; Bulletin No. 3, "Consolidation of Competing Telephone Systems," August 7, 1918, in *Government Control and Operation of Telegraph, Telephone and Marine Cable Systems, August 1, 1918 to July 31, 1919* (Washington, D.C.: GPO, 1921), pp. 45–6, 62–3.
The Willis-Graham Act, passed in 1921, overrode the Kingsbury Commitment, and in 1922 AT&T was granted explicit permission to reacquire the firm whose purchase had prompted the antitrust suit. *Willis-Graham Act*, ch. 20, 42 Stat. 27, 1921; *US v. AT&T*, No. 6082 (D. Or. 1922) (order modifying Decree). For the other acquisitions, see ICC Finance Dockets, 1921–34.
[4]73rd Congress, 2nd Session, S. 3285, *Communications Act of 1934*, ch. 652, 48 Stat. 1064, 1934 (codified as amended at 47 U.S.C. 151 §1, 1937).
[5]Ibid., §202. Many other parts of the ICA were incorporated into the Communications Act as well.

The fall of the Bell System

virtually all of the long distance telephone service in the country and most of the local service. Local calls were handled by the 18 principal Bell Associated Operating Companies joined together by AT&T's Long Lines (long distance service) and its General Departments at 195 Broadway, New York City.[6] A large variety of independent telephone companies still operated in particular localities, but they too were linked to each other and to the national network through the Bell System. AT&T's ownership of the Bell Operating Companies was known as the System's "horizontal" integration, and Congress was willing in 1934 to accept this dimension of AT&T's powerful monopoly as long as it was regulated effectively by state and federal agencies.

This tolerance did not extend to the company's "vertical" integration – its ownership of Western Electric and the Bell Telephone Laboratories. This aspect of the system dated from 1881, when Bell had purchased Western Electric. Faced with the need to protect a patent monopoly for a simple instrument, Bell's leaders had determined from the first that all legal telephones should be owned and leased by the company. Anyone else owning a phone was thus in violation of Bell's patents. The company did not adopt this policy because there were joint costs in the supply of telephone service and telephone sets. Quite the contrary. It was precisely because it was so easy for anyone to make telephone sets that Bell could never hope to police licenses for their manufacture. But although this decision had solved one problem, it had created another. Demand was expanding rapidly, and even before 1881 the Bell Company had struggled to supply all of the telephones used by its customers; understandably, it leaped at the opportunity to buy Western Electric, a leading manufacturer of electrical products. As Western Electric was merged further into the Bell System over the next generation, the manufacturing firm also began to provide a way to ensure a high degree of technological uniformity among the Bell Operating Companies.[7]

AT&T added other businesses to its basic telephone operation over the years, but in 1925, when Walter Gifford began his long tenure as presi-

[6]New England Telephone and Telegraph Company, Southern New England Telephone Company, New York Telephone Company, New Jersey Bell Telephone Company, Bell Telephone Company of Pennsylvania, Diamond State Telephone Company, Chesapeake & Potomac Telephone Companies, Southern Bell Telephone and Telegraph Company, Ohio Bell Telephone Company, Cincinnati & Suburban Bell Telephone Company, Michigan Bell Telephone Company, Indiana Bell Telephone Company, Wisconsin Telephone Company, Illinois Bell Telephone Company, Northwestern Bell Telephone Company, Southwestern Bell Telephone Company, Mountain States Telephone and Telegraph Company, Pacific Telephone and Telegraph Company (American Telephone and Telegraph Company, *1934 Annual Report*, p. 11).
[7]George D. Smith, *The Anatomy of a Business Strategy: Bell, Western Electric, and the Origins of the American Telephone Industry* (Baltimore: The Johns Hopkins University Press, 1985), p. 158.

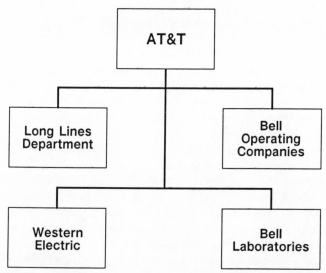

Figure 2. Predivestiture Bell System

dent of the firm (its CEO in those days), he set about bringing order into what had become an increasingly diverse collection of activities. He sold AT&T's international operations to ITT and its broadcasting facilities to NBC. Ventures into movies and TV lasted only a little while longer. Gifford joined the research and development activities in the Engineering Department of AT&T and in Western Electric to form a new organization: the Bell Telephone Laboratories. Bell Labs rapidly became recognized as one of the premier research institutions in the country, and over the years its scientists collected an impressive number of Nobel prizes. With Western Electric, it was identified within the Bell System as the primary source of the business's vitality. The Bell Operating Companies were the arms of the Bell System; Western Electric and Bell Labs were its legs (see Figure 2).[8]

But in the second year of the New Deal, amid widespread public distress about the inner workings of American capitalism, Congress was unsure that the Bell System needed legs like these to be an effective public utility. The original draft of the Communications Act gave the new regulatory commission jurisdiction over the contracts between AT&T and its subsidiaries, Western Electric in particular. "Charges have been made," the bill's sponsor said on the floor of the Senate, "that there is a tremendous spread of profit between the cost to the Western Electric of manufacturing the equip-

[8]American Telephone and Telegraph Company, *1926 Annual Report*, p. 13; *1925 Annual Report*, p. 15; *1924 Annual Report*, p. 18.

14 The fall of the Bell System

ment and the prices paid by the operating companies." The results included both high profits on manufacturing and an inflated rate base for operations.[9]

AT&T's Gifford objected to the proposed extension of regulation on the grounds that FCC control of AT&T's internal contracts would wreck the telephone business (foreshadowing the arguments that would be used in the 1970s to oppose further congressional initiatives). His views seem to have carried great weight with Congress.[10] The congressional committee replaced its broad grant of authority over AT&T's internal contracts with a mandate to the FCC to study the contracts and report back to Congress on whether further legislation was needed.[11]

The FCC study, completed in 1939, gave substance to congressional concern about Western Electric's prices.[12] With the U.S. entry into World War II, this problem was tabled, but after the war the Justice Department asked the general counsel for the FCC's investigation to draw up an antitrust complaint against the Bell System. The complaint alleged that AT&T and Western Electric had conspired to monopolize the

[9]Rate regulation of telephones and other utilities allows a reasonable rate of return on invested capital. The rate base of the Bell System, as the stock of invested capital is called, included telephones and other equipment purchased by regulated telephone operating companies from Western Electric—which was not regulated. High Western Electric prices meant high manufacturing profits; a larger rate base meant larger profits in operations as well.

Excerpts of the debate on S. 3285, 73rd Congress, 2nd Session, May 15, 1934, in Memorandum of Federal Communications Commission as Amicus Curiae, US v. AT&T, CA No. 74–1698, U.S. Dist. Ct., Dist. of Columbia, December 30, 1975.

[10]Communications Act of 1934, 47 U.S.C. 151 §215, 1937.

[11]The new commission took its mandate seriously and initiated a thorough study of the Bell System. Completed five years later, the almost 700-page study surveyed the history, structure, and operation of the telephone network. It has provided the source material for many books about the Bell System, which frequently share the report's critical tone toward AT&T.

76th Congress, 1st Session, House, Report of the Federal Communications Commission on the Investigation of the Telephone Industry in the United States, 1939; John Sheahan, "Integration and Exclusion in the Telephone Equipment Industry," Quarterly Journal of Economics, Vol. 70 (May 1956), pp. 249–69; Gerald W. Brock, The Telecommunications Industry (Cambridge, Mass.: Harvard University Press, 1981); N.R. Danielian, A.T.& T.: The Story of Industrial Conquest (Reprint, 1939, New York: Arno Press, 1974).

[12]The FCC's report noted that Western's prices have "an appreciable influence on the cost of telephone service." The authors of the report went on to say that these prices "bear no reasonable relation to the indicated cost of manufacture." More discipline was needed here, as well as with Long Lines, but the report's authors argued against using regulation for this task. They asserted that the Bell System's natural monopoly did not extend to equipment manufacture; Western's monopoly of the Bell System's market for equipment was the result of AT&T's patent monopoly. Competition, therefore, was a more effective form of discipline for Western's prices than regulation. The report's authors supported amending the Communications Act to require the Bell System to license its patents to competing manufacturers. 76th Congress, 1st Session, House, Report of the Federal Communications Commission on the Investigation of the Telephone Industry in the United States, 1939, pp. 579–89.

market in telephone equipment, excluded other manufacturers and sellers of equipment from the market, and earned monopoly profits for the conspirators. The Department of Justice filed the complaint in 1949, directing its suit at Western Electric. It asked the court to separate Western Electric from the Bell System and to divide it into three competing units. The remaining Bell System would be required to buy its equipment by competitive bidding.[13]

AT&T mobilized its resources to fight the suit and succeeded in preserving its vertical integration. Then as now, AT&T refused to contemplate life without its manufacturing capability. Critical support for the company came from the Defense Department, which recalled Bell's service in the Second World War and valued Western Electric's management of the Atomic Energy Commission's Sandia Laboratories. Then too, the nation opted for a more conservative brand of leadership in 1952. The new Eisenhower administration saw its role in the political economy as preserving and strengthening corporate capitalism, not breaking up a firm that appeared to be both efficient and essential to the national security. The government terminated the suit by a 1956 Consent Decree that, in the words of the Attorney General, promised "no real injury" to AT&T.[14] The decree required the company to license its patents, a measure that seemed at the time to have little impact, since the market for telephone equipment made with these patents was not open to competition. It restricted Western Electric to manufacturing only equipment of the sort used in telephony and limited the Bell System to "furnishing common carrier communications services." These services were defined to be "communications services and facilities, other than message telegram service, the charges for which are subject to public regulation under the Communications Act of 1934."[15] This requirement too seemed to be of little consequence, since Walter Gifford had drawn AT&T back from its interwar ventures into radio, motion pictures, and TV.

The Bell System had its hands full just trying to furnish communications services in the postwar era of economic expansion. There had been 2 million unfilled orders for new telephones – the largest number in Bell's history – at the close of World War II. As this backlog was eliminated during the next decade, the number of telephones in service doubled.[16]

---

[13]*US* v. *Western Electric Co.*, CA No. 17–49, U.S. Dist. Ct., Dist. of New Jersey, *Complaint*, January 14, 1949.

[14]U.S. Attorney General Herbert Brownell as quoted in T. Brooke Price, AT&T, vice president and general counsel, memo, March 3, 1954, in 86th Congress, 1st Session, House, Committee on the Judiciary, *Report of Antitrust Subcommittee on Consent Decree Program of the Department of Justice* (Celler Report), January 30, 1959, pp. 53–4.

[15]*US* v. *Western Electric Co.*, CA No. 17–49, *Final Judgment*, 1956 Trade Cas. ¶68,246 (D. N.J. 1956).

[16]*Bell System Statistical Manual 1920–1964*, Business Research Division, Comptroller's Department, AT&T, April 1965, pp. 504, 518.

Horace Moulton, AT&T's general counsel, seemed quite content as he proclaimed that, "as long as grass grows and water runs, . . . we are under a prohibition from expanding outside the regulated fields."[17] As Moulton's statement suggests, AT&T was pleased with the decree. There was no hint at this time that the boundary between the regulated services that AT&T could offer and the unregulated activities from which it was barred would prove hard to specify in succeeding decades. The new bargain between the Bell System and the government looked promising. Although the 1956 decree had left some Justice Department lawyers bitter and congressmen suspicious, there was every reason to believe that this accommodation between public authority and the nation's largest business would endure at least as long as the Kingsbury Commitment had.

Indeed, seen from the vantage point of the late 1950s, the Bell System had admirably fulfilled the mission set out so many years before by Theodore Vail. He had embraced state regulation as a way of extending Bell's nationwide monopoly of the telephone network, and his successors also had accepted federal regulation, a strategy that seemed confirmed by the 1956 Consent Decree. Vail had defined "universal service"–a telephone in every home connected to every other telephone in the country–as the Bell System's primary goal. That too had been largely accomplished by the mid-1950s. In 1956 over 70 percent of American households had telephones, connected by AT&T's long distance service to all others, an accomplishment unequaled throughout the world. In the United States, for every 100 persons there were 34 telephones, compared to only 13 in the United Kingdom and fewer than 10 in France and Germany.[18]

AT&T, of course, had grown exceedingly large in attaining these goals. It was without question the largest company in the world, measured by the size of its assets (see Table 3). AT&T also had employees in every state and every congressional district and could muster substantial political power. But it was, in the eyes of its leaders, a benevolent giant. In the words of Walter Gifford, the Bell System's very size imposed "an unusual obligation" on the company to provide adequate, dependable service: "The only sound policy . . . is to continue to furnish the best possible telephone service at the lowest cost consistent with financial safety." Indeed, the available evidence suggests that, over the long term, AT&T came very close to adhering to the standard Gifford proclaimed. It was a

[17]85th Congress, 2nd Session, House, Committee on the Judiciary, Antitrust Subcommittee, "Consent Decree Program of the Department of Justice," Hearings, Serial No. 9, Testimony of Horace P. Moulton, April 1, 1958, p. 2104.
[18]Only in Scandinavia and in some tiny countries did the availability of telephone service even approach Bell's U.S. standard. *Bell System Statistical Manual 1920–1964*, p. 504; AT&T, *The World's Telephones*, January 1, 1956.

Theodore N. Vail, president of AT&T from 1885 to 1887 and 1907 to 1919.

well-behaved public utility, with a powerful corporate culture framed in terms of service and technological progress.[19]

It had to be. Only its best behavior could shield the largest regulated monopoly in the world from attack–and even that might not be enough. To deliver this performance, AT&T's leaders over the years had devised numerous ways to maintain coherence and give direction to the huge Bell System. Vail had introduced a model organization for the Bell Operating Companies in 1909 that lasted for over half a century. The companies were organized along functional lines, with three main departments: Plant, Traffic, and Commercial. Since each department contained people with similar skills and training, this style of organization facilitated internal communication and promoted operational efficiency. The similarity of format allowed communication between the General Departments at AT&T and the operating companies and between the companies themselves. Further communication was provided by conferences of specialists and committee meetings and, most importantly, by the semiannual Presidents' Conferences, such as the one outside Chicago in the fall of 1971. These conferences and more frequent one-day meetings were needed because the Bell System was technologically integrated but highly decentralized in a political and managerial sense. Control over senior management appointments throughout the System was in the hands of AT&T, but the executives of the operating companies ran their own organizations and dealt with their regulatory agencies independently.[20]

Although AT&T was responsible for financing Long Lines and coordinating the Bell System's overall needs, each operating company raised its own debt capital. The traditional budgetary procedure was for the operating companies to notify AT&T of their need for new capital, the equity portion of which was supplied by AT&T. The General Departments would comment on, but seldom change, the projections. This decentralized style of financial planning, with its centripetal flow of information, was highly successful so long as the regulatory environment facing the Bell System remained relatively stable. Not until the late 1960s did the types of problems that surfaced at the 1971 Presidents' Conference begin to develop within the System.

Tri-Company Councils were formed in the 1950s to provide engineering coordination. The councils, consisting of representatives from AT&T, Western Electric, and Bell Labs, managed the development of new prod-

---

[19]Walter S. Gifford, "A Statement of Policy of the American Telephone and Telegraph Company," address to the NARUC, October 20, 1927.
[20]Each company paid a license contract fee of approximately one percent of its revenues to support AT&T's General Departments. Robert W. Garnet, *The Telephone Enterprise: The Evolution of the Bell System's Horizontal Structure, 1876–1909* (Baltimore: The Johns Hopkins University Press, 1985); Alvin von Auw, *Heritage & Destiny: Reflections on the Bell System in Transition* (New York: Praeger Publishers, 1983).

ucts and services. They were, however, coordinating bodies, not command or line organizations; they left the separate managements of Western Electric and Bell Labs with a great deal of freedom to chart their own course. So long as they performed successfully – as they clearly did – they could retain a high degree of autonomy. Over the years following 1925, Bell Labs, jointly owned and financed by AT&T and Western Electric, became the primary source of new technology incorporated into the Bell System and was mainly responsible for determining where it was used.

The Bell System worked spectacularly well. Telephone service became progressively cheaper, more available, and more automatic. Long distance service was extended across the country. Dial phones replaced operators. Coaxial cables and – after the Second World War – microwave radio transmission were introduced. Scientists at Bell Labs invented the transistor and many types of lasers. Much of the solid state electronic technology that transformed telephony into telecommunications came out of Bell Labs and was implemented first by the Bell System. This record of relentless technological improvement was the glue that held together AT&T's various accommodations with the state and federal governments.[21]

Separations

One of the most critical compromises in the pattern of accommodations between AT&T and its varied governmental overseers involved the dedication of Bell's technology to the furtherance of universal service. This particular bargain was struck by AT&T, the FCC, and state regulators while the Justice Department was actually negotiating with the telephone company over the terms of the 1956 Consent Decree. At that time, state regulators, the FCC, and the Bell System were also negotiating changes in the allocation of costs – changes that in effect would enable the benefits of new technology to be reflected in local rates. The resultant structure of telephone prices would have a decisive impact on the future of telecommunications, an effect that would unfortunately be misunderstood by most of the participants and observers of the debates over telecommunications policy in the 1970s and 1980s.

The confusion centered on the "separations" process, a formula or procedure that was used to determine costs (and thus prices) and that had

[21]M.D. Fagen, ed., *A History of Engineering and Science in the Bell System: The Early Years, 1875–1925* (N.p.: Bell Telephone Laboratories, 1975); M.D. Fagen, ed., *A History of Engineering and Science in the Bell System: National Service in War and Peace, 1925–1975* (N.p.: Bell Telephone Laboratories, 1978); G. Schindler, ed., *A History of Engineering and Science in the Bell System: Switching Technology, 1925–1975* (N.p.: Bell Telephone Laboratories, 1982).

originated in World War II. Between 1939 and 1942, the number of telephone messages carried by Long Lines had shot up from 60 to 114 million.[22] Long Lines' profits naturally had risen too, and the FCC had asked AT&T to show cause why its interstate rates should not be reduced. Walter Gifford promptly and indignantly responded that the Bell System was engaged with the government in fighting the war. AT&T was struggling to handle the increased volume of war-related traffic; it was advertising to convince the public to call less often. Lower rates would encourage people to call more frequently. "I fail to see," Gifford concluded, "how by any stretch of the imagination a reduction in long distance rates will help win the war."[23]

Gifford's unanswerable question presented the FCC with a dilemma: how to reduce Long Lines' profits without reducing its rates. The search for an answer carried the investigation into the theoretical marshland of determining how to separate activities between *inter*state and *intra*state jurisdictions. Many toll calls were interstate and subject to federal regulation; local telephone service and toll calls within states were subject to state jurisdiction. But the costs of interstate and intrastate services somehow had to be separated to allow the regulators to determine the rate of return that would be allowed in each jurisdiction.

This task was complicated by the existence of two ways to conceptualize the telephone network: "board-to-board" and "station-to-station." Arcane as these theories may seem to be, they were at the heart of the telecommunications policy debates in the 1970s and 1980s, and must be understood if the controversies and implications of the various policy decisions made during those years are to be untangled. A simple explanation is necessary. A "board" is a toll switch that connects the local telephone exchange with the toll network. "Station" is the generic term for a telephone set or what we call a telephone. In the station-to-station theory, toll calls go from the calling telephone (station) to the receiving telephone. In the board-to-board theory, by contrast, all activity within the local exchange is considered local activity; the toll call goes only from one switch (board) connecting the local exchange with the toll network to another switch.

The two concepts are illustrated in Figure 3, which shows two local exchanges, for San Francisco and Boston. Two telephones, that is, individual stations, are shown in each exchange. Each station is connected to its respective toll board, and the two toll boards are connected to each other through the national telephone network. Calls within each exchange (SF1

[22]*Bell System Statistical Manual 1920–1964*, p. 1204.
[23]FCC, *Order*, FCC Docket 6468, "Rates and Charges for Communication Services Furnished by its Long Lines Department," November 20, 1942; Statement of Walter S. Gifford, November 21, 1942, AT&T Information Department; AT&T, *Motion of Respondent for Continuance*, FCC Docket 6468, December 1, 1942.

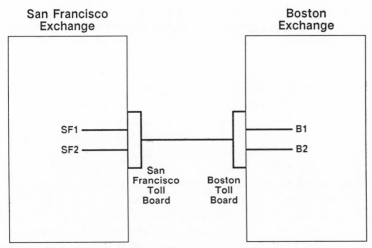

Figure 3. Exchange–station and board connections.

to SF2, for example) are considered local in both theories, but interexchange calls (like one from SF1 to B1) are treated differently. In the station-to-station theory, the entire call is considered a toll call. In the board-to-board theory, only that part of the call that goes between the two boards is considered toll; the portion of the call between SF1 and the San Francisco toll board and between B1 and the Boston toll board is considered to be local service.

The board-to-board theory is harder to explain, but its costs are relatively simple to calculate. The Bell System was organized as local operating companies with a separate long distance carrier. The local companies were legally distinct from AT&T's Long Lines; they were regulated by different commissions (state regulators), and they had separate accounts. Telephone bills always distinguished between toll and local calls, and it was a simple matter to relate the revenue from interstate toll calls to Long Lines' costs. This traditional AT&T procedure was an expression of board-to-board thinking; it assumed that the relevant costs of interstate toll calls were those incurred by Long Lines in going from board to board.

Station-to-station accounting is far more difficult to calculate. The problem is that some way has to be found to separate the portion of the costs of the local exchange that can be related to toll calls from the costs resulting from local exchange service. The questions of whether to do this and how to do it were raised frequently in early rate proceedings, but they were not so much answered as ignored.[24]

[24]James W. Sichter, "Separations Procedures in the Telephone Industry: The Historical Origins of a Public Policy," Harvard University Program on Information Resources Policy, Publication p-77–2, Cambridge, Mass., January 1977.

This quandary found its way to the Supreme Court in 1930 in *Smith* v. *Illinois Bell*. The issue before the Court was whether the rates ordered by the Illinois state commission were "confiscatory" – that is, too low to allow the company a reasonable return on its investment – under the Fourteenth Amendment. Illinois Bell used board-to-board accounting to argue that the rates were too low; the state commission argued that on the basis of station-to-station accounting, the rates were reasonable and lawful.

Pointing to the "indisputable fact" that exchange property – telephones and local lines – was used for both interstate and intrastate service, the Court concluded that board-to-board accounting would make local rates too high. The local rates would include part of the costs properly attributable to interstate long distance service. In the Court's words: "It is obvious that, unless an apportionment is made, the intrastate service to which the exchange property is allocated will bear an undue burden – to what extent is a matter of controversy."[25] Calculations of intrastate rates therefore had to be based on station-to-station accounting, although state regulatory commissions were not constrained by this decision to use any specific method in setting those rates. The result of the Court's argument was that an arrow from the Bell System's quiver had been broken. Local Bell Operating Companies could no longer use board-to-board accounting as the basis for arguing that intrastate rates were so low as to be confiscatory.[26]

Drawing on the Supreme Court's decision, the FCC decided late in 1942 to resolve its wartime dilemma by simply requiring AT&T to replace its board-to-board with station-to-station accounting. This would increase Long Lines' costs by adding charges for the cost of capital used in completing interstate calls through the equipment of the local operating company. Long Lines' profits would fall. The costs of the local telephone companies that had to be covered by local (intrastate) rates also would fall because

---

[25]*Smith* v. *Illinois Bell Tel. Co.*, 282 U.S. 133 at 151, 1930. This case shows that regulatory lags are a result of our legal system, not of recent technology. The Illinois Commerce Commission attempted to reduce the telephone rates charged by the Illinois Bell Telephone Company beginning in 1921. The Commission ordered the rates reduced in 1923, but the order was appealed. The new rates did not go into effect until 1934, by which time an expenditure of $2.5 million was required to refund $19 million to Illinois Bell's customers. The issue twice reached the Supreme Court, which first affirmed and then largely negated the need to use the station-to-station theory in evaluating telephone rates.

[26]James W. Sichter, "Separations Procedures in the Telephone Industry: The Historical Origins of a Public Policy;" Peter Temin and Geoffrey Peters, "Cross Subsidization in the Telephone Network," *Willamette Law Review*, Vol. 21, (Spring 1985), pp. 199–223.

As it turned out, the Court upheld the rates set by the state commission when the case returned to it a second time. The Court took issue the second time around with Illinois Bell's depreciation allowances. The result was to make the new station-to-station rates essentially the same as the old board-to-board rates. The Court's initial decision seemed to have established a principle that would have no effect at all on telephone rates. The Bell System continued to set its rates on board-to-board principles, with only occasional objections by state regulators. *Lindheimer* v. *Illinois Bell Tel. Co.*, 3 F. Supp. 595 (N.D. Ill. 1933), *aff'd*, 292 U.S. 151, 1934.

part of the local capital stock would be shifted to the interstate (toll) jurisdiction. Local rates could fall, encouraging universal service. Separating interstate and intrastate costs along station-to-station lines solved the immediate problems of Long Lines' profits and wartime demand, as well as the long-standing problem of jurisdiction posed by *Smith* v. *Illinois Bell*. It was an opportunity too good to be missed. The chairman of the FCC suggested to Gifford that they get together and agree on "a cooperative approach" to these problems. They and their staffs met several times in January 1943. AT&T, in keeping with its tradition of compromising with public authority, agreed to use station-to-station accounting in setting telephone rates.[27]

But this particular agreement created a new problem even as it solved an old one. There was, alas, no simple and natural way to distribute local capital costs between local and long distance services under the station-to-station model. The Supreme Court had noted that this allocation was a "matter of controversy." Many of the costs of the local plant do not vary with use; the assignment of these costs to particular services is therefore completely arbitrary. As a result, an elaborate mechanism had to be constructed over the next few years to calculate this vital allocation. The Bell Operating Companies collected revenue and the Bell System organized its internal accounts on a board-to-board basis. It then separated its costs and capital stock – hence the term "separations" – into intrastate and interstate categories along station-to-station lines, calculated the revenue requirements of the two parts of the separated capital stock, and divided the revenues received between Long Lines and the local telephone operating companies (both Bell and independent) in accordance with these revenue requirements. Using a procedure taken from the railroads, the expenses of the local exchange plant were divided between interstate and intrastate jurisdictions on the basis of relative use, measured by what was called "subscriber line use," or SLU. The whole process was called the "separations" process. Its procedures were embodied by 1947 in a complex *Separations Manual* that – as revised – has been the bible of this private-public process ever since.[28]

[27]James Lawrence Fly, FCC, to Walter S. Gifford, December 18, 1942; Keith S. McHugh, AT&T, vice president, "Memorandum of Discussion with Commissioners Walker, Wakefield and Durr in Re Docket 6468, Washington, D.C., January 6, 1943"; McHugh to all associated company presidents, announcing understandings reached with the FCC on Long Lines rate case, January 20, 1943; McHugh to FCC Commissioner Paul A. Walker, confirming an agreement reached by telephone January 20, 1943.

[28]The *Separations Manual* actually divided the station-to-station expenses of interstate telephone service into traffic-sensitive and non-traffic-sensitive portions. The local companies' traffic-sensitive expenses of supplying interstate service could be calculated directly, and they were compensated out of interstate revenues. Then the non-traffic-sensitive expenses were allocated to intrastate and interstate use on the basis of relative use or SLU, defined as the time the local plant was used for interstate calls divided by its total time in use. The

The FCC appeared to be wedded to a formula based on SLU in 1950 when it began a new inquiry into interstate rates. AT&T, acting in the spirit of the 1943 agreement, proposed an alteration of the *Separations Manual* that would have shifted more of the local telephone plant into the interstate rate base. The National Association of Railroad and Utility Commissioners (NARUC – now the National Association of Regulatory Utility Commissioners) strongly supported the AT&T plan. There was an increasing gap between the rates charged by Long Lines and the rates charged by Bell Operating Companies for comparable intrastate calls (and even for some interstate calls handled by multistate companies like Pacific Telephone). The state regulators worried about this "toll rate disparity," which had continued to grow as local rates rose in the postwar inflation. Larger separations payments would provide the opportunity for state regulators to lower intrastate rates and reduce the toll rate disparity.[29] But the FCC resisted the proposed change. It was, the Commission said, inconsistent with *Smith v. Illinois Bell:* "Its adoption would have the effect of introducing an arbitrary method whereby interstate services subject to Federal jurisdiction would, in effect, be subsidizing services beyond that jurisdiction."[30]

The FCC had raised the specter of "cross-subsidization," a vision that would haunt telecommunications debates for an entire generation. As the FCC used this term in 1950, it referred to deviations from SLU. The simple counting of interstate and total minutes required by SLU admittedly has a certain attractiveness. But in fact there is no natural way to allocate the joint costs of the local plant to different uses, particularly since a major part of the expenses are not traffic sensitive. Neither SLU nor any other method is intrinsically more correct than any other. No cost-based definition of cross-subsidization is more correct than any other.[31] Under board-to-board accounting, any division of revenue is a cross-subsidy flow-

revenue requirement of the local plant allocated to interstate use was paid from interstate revenues. There were, then, two deductions from the payments to Long Lines from the operating companies, one for traffic-sensitive expenses and one for the revenue requirement of the non-traffic-sensitive capital. The sum of these deductions was known as "separations charges." *Separations Manual*, October 1947; see also *Recommended Report and Order of FCC-NARUC Joint Board on Jurisdictional Separations*, FCC Docket 18866, "Separations Procedures," October 27, 1970, 26 FCC 2d 248; *NARUC-FCC Separations Manual* incorporated into Part 67 of the Commission Rules, 47 CFR 67.

[29] *Message Toll Telephone Rates and Disparities*, report of the NARUC-FCC Toll Rate Subcommittee, July 1951. The change would also allow AT&T to increase its earnings by transferring some of the Bell System's capital to interstate jurisdiction, where the FCC allowed higher rates of return than most states.

[30] Paul A. Walker to Matt L. McWhorter, October 18, 1950.

[31] John R. Meyer et al., *The Economics of Competition in the Telecommunications Industry* (Cambridge, Mass.: Oelgeschlager, Gunn & Hain, 1980), pp. 3–10; Leland L. Johnson, *Competition and Cross-Subsidization in the Telephone Industry* "R-29–76-RC" (Santa Monica, Calif.: Rand Corp., 1982).

ing from the interstate (toll) jurisdiction to the intrastate (local) jurisdiction. Under the FCC's station-to-station accounting, the definition of cross-subsidy would be arbitrary, and it would vary over time as usage changed.

At that crucial point in framing policy, political forces intruded on a decision that could not be made on economic grounds alone. The needs of war had been replaced by the needs of postwar state commissioners who had powerful friends in Congress. The 1950 convention of NARUC was held in Arizona, the home state of Senator Ernest W. McFarland, the Republican majority leader and chairman of the Senate subcommittee overseeing the FCC. Responding to an appeal from NARUC, McFarland wrote to the FCC, expressing his dismay at the Commission's willingness to "shift the load from the big user to the little user; from the large national corporations which are heavy users of long distance to the average housewife and business or professional man who do not indulge in a great deal of long distance." Noting the growing toll rate disparity, the senator said, "I am not in a position to pass upon the question as to whether the remedy suggested by NARUC is the proper one but I am certain that something should be done – and at once."[32]

The FCC resisted. Holding to its position that SLU allocated as much local plant to interstate use as was warranted by *Smith* v. *Illinois Bell,* the Commission sent back to Senator McFarland a long and detailed history of separations, replete with relevant statistics. The Commission characterized the toll rate disparity as "natural" and claimed that it was fulfilling its legal mandate to regulate interstate rates only. Senator McFarland replied sharply: "I believe that the Commission's six-page reply takes a strictly technical attitude toward the whole problem rather than the broad, constructive viewpoint required by the Communications Act. . . . Frankly, the Commission's reply is disappointing to me and to my colleagues whose interest and concern occasioned my original letter to you."[33]

The FCC bent before the stiff wind blowing from the Hill. The threat of congressional action was more than the commissioners could bear, and they reopened negotiations with AT&T. The resulting revision of the *Separations Manual* shifted enough revenue requirements to interstate operations to justify interstate rate increases in the next two years. These were the first interstate rate increases granted since the creation of the FCC. They also took place while technological progress was reducing the cost of long distance service and rising wages were raising the cost of labor-intensive local services. The toll rate disparity to which Senator McFarland

[32]Ernest W. McFarland to Paul A. Walker, January 30, 1951.
[33]Paul A. Walker to Ernest W. McFarland, February 14, 1951; McFarland to Walker, March 6, 1951.

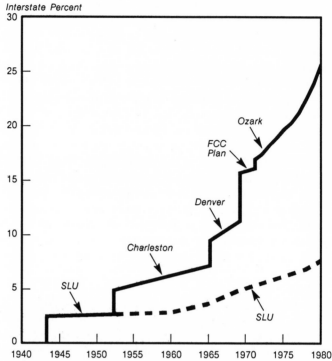

Figure 4. Exchange plant allocated to interstate service, 1940–
1980. Note: Revisions of the *Separations Manual* are generally
named after the location of the NARUC convention in which
they are announced, as indicated here. (Source: FCC Docket
78-72, AT&T Comments, March 3, 1980, p. 94.)

had directed the FCC's attention was sharply reduced; the subsidy that
flowed from long distance to local service was sharply increased.[34]

Long Lines' earnings rose again in 1955, while AT&T was trying to
settle its antitrust suit. The FCC, responding to the desires of state commissioners, negotiated another revision of the *Separations Manual* that
pushed even more revenue requirements into interstate jurisdiction. As
shown in Figure 4, this was only one of several expansions of the separations process. SLU, shown by a dashed line, was left far behind as the

[34]The incentive for operating companies to reduce their costs was also decreased, exacerbat-
ing the contrast in the developing trends of local and long distance costs. FCC, *Order to
Continue Investigation*, FCC Docket 9889, "Investigation of Rates and Charges for Interstate Communications Services," November 21, 1951 (adopting revisions of the *Separations Manual*); *1952 Addendum to the Separations Manual*; FCC Public Notice, "FCC
Announces Proposed Increases and Reductions in Interstate Long Distance Telephone
Rates," January 14, 1952.

Commission, NARUC, and AT&T allocated more and more of the local plant (both Bell and independent) to interstate jurisdiction.

In a sense, the growth of the separations subsidy granted government approval to Bell's horizontal integration in much the same way that the 1956 Consent Decree confirmed the legality of its vertical structure. Regulators could channel the benefits of Bell Labs' new technology to local rates in pursuit of universal service because the Bell System functioned as a unit.[35] It did not matter—or at least it did not seem to matter in the 1950s—that prices and costs for individual services were increasingly diverging. In particular, the board-to-board cost of long distance telephone service was dropping further and further below its price. The toll rate disparity was being replaced by an entrepreneurial price-cost gap. An astute businessman could make a lot of money by recognizing and taking advantage of this difference between prices and costs.

To this volatile economic situation one should add the political dangers evident in this brief review of AT&T's early history. AT&T had been involved with the federal government continuously, from Vail's acceptance of regulation before the First World War to the Consent Decree and modification of separations in the 1950s. But although Vail and his successors had succeeded in creating a unitary network and an organization to run it, the government—never monolithic—had been growing even more divided in its authority and in its goals. Different parts of the government—state regulators, the FCC, Congress, the Justice Department, federal courts, even the Presidents—had their own separate agendas that pressed on the Bell System. The aims of these bodies and the balance of power between them shifted over time. The federal government was torn between its desire to promote competition and its reliance on the Bell System for efficient operation of the national telephone network. Although efficiency was the dominant concern in the mid-1950s, it would not long remain the overriding objective of federal policy.

---

[35]Separations also channeled interstate revenues to independent telephone companies offering local service in many localities. These firms joined with consumers and state regulators to urge expansion of the local subsidy.

II

Competition comes to the Bell System

The great TELPAK controversy

AT&T's difficulties in the late 1950s started slowly, almost symbolically, in a tiny corner of the telephone business: private lines. As the term "private lines" indicates, these were lines *not* connected to the switched telephone network, but rather dedicated to the private use of parties who wanted to communicate frequently over specified pathways (e.g., business customers who had to call their branch offices frequently). The Bell System had provided private lines for large customers for many years, but this minor service earned only about 0.5 percent of the Bell System's total revenue.[1] In November 1956 – shortly after the signing of the Consent Degree – the FCC decided to consider whether the private line business should be changed by allowing microwave systems employing radio frequencies above 890 megahertz to be used by private (i.e., non-Bell) parties. The increased sophistication of radio technology had made microwave radio eminently suitable for private lines. Potential users were asking the Commission for permission to build their own microwave systems instead of using AT&T's facilities.

Prominent among these users were the TV networks. They had grown rapidly in the postwar years, and they were heavy users of point-to-point telecommunications services to transmit their programming before sending it out over the air. A TV signal, after all, contains a lot of information. The FCC was eager to foster the growth of this new form of communication. In fact, the Commission was far more concerned about the growth of broadcasting, which it regulated under Title 3 of the Communications Act, than of point-to-point telecommunications, which it regulated under Title 2. The networks had sought and received FCC permission to construct and operate their own private lines when the Bell System lacked the capacity to carry their signals. And even though FCC policy, by limiting the number of TV channels, made TV broadcasting enormously profitable, the networks wanted permission to reduce their costs by constructing their own private line facilities when they thought that the Bell

[1]*Bell System Statistical Manual 1950–1981*, AT&T, Comptroller's–Accounting Division, June 1982, pp. 203, 206.

System's prices were higher than the costs of an independent private line.[2]

The FCC also was interested in promoting the manufacture of telecommunications equipment. The principal non-Bell manufacturer of microwave equipment was Motorola. This expanding firm had emerged from the Second World War with a nationwide dealer network for the sale of electronic equipment, and its sales had grown by a factor of ten in the decade following 1945. It had developed a microwave relay system in the 1940s for sale to pipelines, railroads, and electric utilities – the types of firms allowed to use microwave radio under existing FCC rules. Since the Consent Decree of 1956 confirmed that Western Electric would continue to supply the Bell System, further growth in Motorola's market would have to take place among users of independent private lines. Motorola wanted to expand that market as much as possible. The firms petitioning the FCC to allow greater use of microwave radio would look largely to Motorola for the equipment they hoped to use; many of their petitions, in all probability, were inspired by their prospective supplier.[3]

Motorola championed the cause of liberalization and emerged as the main opponent of AT&T in the early regulatory proceedings about microwave communications. But Motorola did more than that. Its entry into the FCC's proceedings began a change that would irrevocably alter the nature of the agency's decision-making process. As long as AT&T had been virtually the only common carrier before the Commission, their interactions had consisted largely of informal discussions. (Western Union's presence as the perennial industry invalid had not disturbed this process.) "Continuing surveillance," as the FCC liked to call it, was sufficient to assure the public that the Bell System was being adequately monitored. In any case, common carrier activities were only a minor concern of the Commission. The FCC made no attempt to disentangle the costs for individual Bell System services; it was enough for the agency to ensure that the System as a whole was not making excessive profits.[4] After Motorola entered the controversy, however, the FCC was forced to handle problems on a more formal basis and to examine costs for individual telephone services. Continuing surveillance gave way to formal proceedings.

In 1959 these proceedings yielded results distressing to the telephone company. The FCC decided to allow private microwave systems to be used not only where common carrier services did not exist, that is, in the

[2]See FCC, *Report and Order*, FCC Docket 11164, "Amendment of Part 4 of the Commission's Rules and Regulations Governing Television Auxiliary Broadcast Stations" (Video II), August 4, 1958, 44 FCC 1354.

[3]Motorola Corporation, *Annual Reports*, 1946–59.

[4]Henry Geller, interview, June 20, 1984, pp. 1–3; William R. Stump, interview, November 30, 1984, p. 36.

traditional exceptions, but also more generally. The Commission said that it would authorize a private system wherever common carriers could not or would not provide the user with precisely the services he demanded. Even though it was not stated explicitly, this meant that if a private microwave system was cheaper than the equivalent Bell service, a firm could now use it for that reason alone. The FCC hoped to encourage diversity in communications and to stimulate competition in the equipment market by allowing Motorola and other firms new opportunities to expand their business. Sounding a theme that would reappear in later proceedings, the FCC noted that not all users of communications equipment required the same quality of service. Faced with diverse demands, AT&T had designed the telecommunications network for alternate uses. The Bell System prided itself on the high quality of its service, but, said the FCC, individual users do not all require the same flexibility and should have the option of constructing a single-purpose microwave system. People should be able to choose Fords if they do not want Cadillacs.[5]

AT&T argued that this decision would encourage "cream skimming," that is, the intrusion of independent operations in the most profitable parts of the telephone network. Long Lines' prices for interstate long distance calls were uniform across the country. Wherever one lived or worked, calls traveling the same distance carried the same price. "Nationwide average pricing," as this practice was called, purposely did not take account of cost differences on different routes; the prices did not reflect the costs of the individual service. Customers on low-cost routes were therefore subsidizing those on high-cost routes. Any potential competitor who could choose which routes to serve – that is, any competitor who was not a nationwide common carrier – could simply select the lowest-cost routes, charge lower prices, and take business away from Bell. The competitors would skim the cream off the national telephone network's rate structure.

Cream skimming applied to different qualities of service as well as to different locations. A customer needing only minimal service obviously could be supplied at lower cost than one requiring the more complex, higher-quality offerings of the Bell System. If this user built his own system or was charged a lower price by Bell, he would no longer be subsidizing the high-cost user. This by itself might not be cause for public alarm, but the Bell System would then be forced to raise rates for the high-cost services to replace the cream that had been skimmed off. Responding to this argument, the FCC barred the sharing of private microwave systems; only the biggest customers would be able to use them. But

---

[5]FCC, *Report and Order*, FCC Docket 11866, "Above 890 Mc.," July 29, 1959, 27 FCC 359 at 403–13, *recon. denied*, 29 FCC 825, 1960.

the FCC's decision in *Above 890* nevertheless broke with the basic principles of nationwide averaging and cross-subsidization in the telephone network. It marked the first step down the path to the distressing Presidents' Conference of 1971 – and beyond.

The FCC denied that it was dealing with fundamental issues. It was only setting new policy for a small corner of the telecommunications market, simply cleaning up a regulatory tangle created by a series of specific decisions in previous years. The Commission held to its view that the switched telephone network was a natural monopoly at the same time that it promoted competition in private line communications. It accepted Motorola's calculation that less than 3 percent of AT&T's business was at risk. The FCC appeared to believe that it could build a durable regulatory wall between this natural monopoly island and the competitive sea.[6]

But the FCC's wall was soon breached. As we can see today, the attempt had from the start been doomed to failure. It was inconceivable that the demand for non-Bell service would stay within the bounds outlined by the FCC and Motorola, that is, off the natural monopoly shore. Point-to-point communication and private lines were very useful for large users. But the advantages of tapping the switched network were far greater – and far more attractive economically to Bell's would-be competitors. Sooner or later, independent users of private microwave systems would want to connect their systems with the public switched network. AT&T tried to point out the existence of amphibious creatures, coming ashore to bear their young, but the FCC failed to take the company seriously. Its claims were – the Commission judged – merely self-serving. As it turned out, they also were prescient.

Frederick Kappel, AT&T's chairman of the board and CEO, established an internal task force, the Broadband Planning Group, to examine the implications of the FCC's *Above 890* decision and to develop an appropriate response. The task force estimated that if the Bell System stayed on its current course, it would lose $100 million in annual revenues and would be pressured to connect private microwave systems to the public switched network. Moreover, Henry Boettinger, who headed one of the group's committees, saw the *Above 890* decision as a decisive turning point in FCC policy: "Competitive supply would be substituted

[6]Ibid., 386–9, 408–14. The legal line between common carrier and other services was unclear. The 1956 Consent Decree had defined common carrier services as regulated services under the Communications Act – presumably under Title 2. The FCC had decided to allow entry into private line services, but it had not decided to deregulate this activity. Since microwaves are part of the radio spectrum, the FCC regulated entry under Title 3 of the Communications Act – even if Title 2 no longer applied. The Consent Decree had not recognized this subtlety and regulated activity – under either title – was AT&T activity. Fatefully, the FCC was unable to draw a bright line between AT&T's monopoly common carrier business and the new competitive, private line business.

for the principle of common carrier provision of an important and growing sector of communications."[7] There in microcosm was the central issue that would lead AT&T and the federal government into deeper and deeper conflict over the next two decades.

The Broadband Planning Group recommended TELPAK, a new service which amounted to dramatic reduction in AT&T's rates for private line services, to meet the competition from private microwave systems. The proposed TELPAK tariff was based on the costs that a private user would face if he were building his own system. TELPAK would allow buyers to choose one of four different capacities (ranging from 12 to 240 voice-grade channels) and pay a fixed rate per mile for that capacity, regardless of use. On the low-capacity lines, TELPAK cut prices by about half; on the higher-capacity lines that would be used by the largest customers, the cuts ranged from three-quarters to a whopping seven-eighths.[8]

Any firm that dropped its price by seven-eighths was certain to arouse suspicion. When the company was the largest in the world and the possessor of a near monopoly of telecommunications, this outcome was eminently predictable. Either it was losing money on its new prices or it had been making an exorbitant profit from the old rates. TELPAK looked suspiciously like predatory pricing, a subject bound to draw the ardent attention of both the FCC and the Justice Department.

Was it? Were the new rates predatory in the sense that they were set more to wipe out existing or potential competitors than to cover costs? Like many things in this complex world, it depended on how you viewed it. The debates of the next two decades showed that there were different ways of determining costs and·setting prices, and any individual price would look quite different under different schemes. Much of the confusion that marked regulatory, congressional, and judicial debate about prices and cross-subsidies in fact derived from the lack of agreement on the way prices should be set and costs determined. Perhaps it will help to clarify the matter if we take a few lines now to describe two basic concepts of pricing.

The most familiar procedure leads to what can be called "competitive" prices. These are the prices used by most firms in the economy. They are set on the basis of costs and demand. Costs are hard to calculate in firms using joint facilities to produce many products, and there is no presumption that they are calculated with any precision. (Reasonable people also disagree over the size and price elasticity of demand.) But the conceptual basis for competitive pricing is clear: The relevant costs are incremental costs, the costs of increasing the output at the margin of production. They

[7]*SPCC* v. *AT&T*, CA No. 78–0545, U.S. Dist. Ct., Dist. of Columbia, Defendant's Exhibit S-T-3, Henry M. Boettinger, testimony, June 7, 1982, p. 7, and Defendant's Exhibit S-1568, "Broadband Rate Planning Group Report – September 1960."

[8]FCC, *Tentative Decision*, FCC Docket 14251, "Investigation of TELPAK Tariff," adopted March 18, 1964, 38 FCC 370 at 385–6.

are the marginal costs beloved of economists. In general, prices based on marginal costs generate the largest profits for a firm.

A very different procedure leads to what might be called "regulatory" prices. These are the prices prescribed by regulatory commissions and used by public utilities. They generally are based on average rather than marginal costs, and they are designed to achieve quite different results than competitive prices. Typically, they attempt to approximate the value of service rather than its cost. Applied to the field of telecommunications, regulatory or "value of service" prices had three attributes, all of which were important in the ensuing debates over public policy in this industry.

One of these basic characteristics derived from the nature of rate-of-return regulation. AT&T's Theodore Vail had accepted regulation in the early 1900s as the price of maintaining and extending the Bell System's telephone monopoly. He did so to enable the regulators to satisfy themselves that AT&T was not making excessive profits from its monopoly. A central function of telephone regulation, therefore, was to limit the overall rate of return on the Bell System's invested capital. To do this, the prices were set by "looking backward"; they were based on the historical record of telephone investment. The telephone plant was evaluated at its historical cost. No calculation of marginal costs was needed. The overall return was compared to the total invested capital to derive an average rate of return. Individual rates were set so that they would be "fair" and would avoid "unjust or unreasonable discrimination" (in the words of the Communications Act). They were not based – as competitive prices were – on the cost of the particular service being priced.[9]

The second hallmark of regulatory pricing in telecommunications dated from the First World War. The Postmaster General had supervised the operation of the telephone system during the mobilization and had prescribed uniform national prices for long distance service.[10] Following the armistice, AT&T took control of the network again, but it continued thereafter to set prices on a mileage basis throughout the country. It did so in spite of the fact that costs for long distance service clearly differed between locations – depending on the terrain, the volume of traffic, and other factors. These uniform prices were consistent with the basic concept of nationwide averaging. They created the kinds of opportunities for cream skimming that we have just noted, but that would cause problems for the Bell System only if the industry's regulators allowed competitors to enter and take advantage of the gap between prices and costs on selected routes.

[9]Alfred E. Kahn, *The Economics of Regulation: Principles and Institutions*, Vol. 1 (New York: John Wiley & Sons, 1970–1), chap. 2.

[10]Bulletin No. 22, Toll Rate Schedule, Order No. 2495, December 13, 1918, in *Government Control and Operation of Telegraph, Telephone and Marine Cable Systems, August 1, 1918 to July 31, 1919* (Washington, D.C.: GPO, 1921), pp. 75–81.

The third major attribute of regulatory telephone pricing derived from the separations process discussed in Chapter 1. The spread between the prices and the board-to-board costs of interstate services grew over time as regulators understandably gave in to the desire to keep local service prices down. The growth of separations charges multiplied the opportunities for cream skimming; they created incentives for independent entrepreneurs to offer interstate services along board-to-board lines.

Each of these fundamental characteristics of regulatory prices would have a significant impact on the emerging struggle over competition. The contrast between the backward-looking nature of traditional telephone pricing and the forward-looking nature of competitive pricing was the key feature in the debate over TELPAK. The Bell System's old private line prices were the former; TELPAK was designed to be the latter. Moreover, AT&T's old private line rates were based on nationwide average costs. The costs were aggregate; they were the costs of the system as a whole or of the interstate and intrastate parts of it. The average historical costs of the existing plant as it had accumulated over the years were much higher than the marginal costs of any particular private line.

Private lines were outside the separations process – because they were outside the switched telephone network – but in fact private line tariffs could not deviate too far from the price of ordinary long distance service. Before *Above 890*, AT&T's larger customers – big businesses, TV networks – chose between private lines and switched services; the prices needed to stay roughly in balance. Since the price of switched service was based on average costs, as embodied in the separations process, the price of private line service was indirectly influenced by those average costs and by the separations subsidy.[11]

Above 890 changed the choices offered to the Bell System's customers. They could now opt for a private microwave system totally independent of the Bell System and separations. AT&T had to take that choice into consideration and set new prices for this new context. Low TELPAK rates were the result. But what were the costs of TELPAK services? The company anticipated an expansion of its sales of private line services as a result of the low TELPAK rates. It would be constructing new plant and using new equipment to provide at least part of these services. Albert Froggatt,

---

[11]The local loops used by private lines were assigned totally to the interstate jurisdiction under the separations process. Nevertheless, the FCC ruled in 1961 that consideration would be given to "the competitive interplay among the private line services and between these services and the message classifications" in the determination of private line rates. In AT&T's words: "The essential point is that a balance is struck, based primarily on cost to the customer, between private line and message telephone service." FCC, *Initial Decision*, FCC Docket 11645, "Private Line Charges," July 6, 1961, 34 FCC 244, at 297; FCC, *Final Decision*, FCC Docket 11645, January 28, 1963, 34 FCC 217, at 226; *Comments of AT&T*, FCC Docket 18920, "Specialized Common Carriers," October 1, 1970, p. 65.

AT&T's associate director of engineering economics, argued that TELPAK revenues should be compared with the costs of the new plant and equipment used to provide the new services: "So long as the Telpak rates covered the costs of that additional plant [and equipment], the business we in turn obtained by offering the service would be profitable to the Bell System."[12]

Froggatt was appealing to the theory of competitive pricing. He considered the incremental cost of furnishing the new business generated by TELPAK to be the relevant cost. He was simply using the marginal cost of economics, the appropriate cost for profit-maximizing firms that approximate the economist's ideal of efficient resource allocation. But he was breaking significantly with the regulatory tradition of basing rates on historical nationwide average costs.

TELPAK would ensure that a firm deciding whether to use a Bell private line or construct its own would be faced with roughly equal costs. There would be little room for Motorola or another equipment manufacturer to cut its prices in order to induce firms to choose its equipment. There would not be sufficient profits to justify massive marketing efforts by the equipment suppliers. Under these conditions, some firms would probably choose to build and operate their own private lines – but not many. Consumers, that is, companies using private lines, would be as well off as in any competitive market. This new situation – something close to a competitive equilibrium – would satisfy the FCC's aim of making microwave technology available to large business firms at the lowest possible cost.

There was one catch. TELPAK would leave most of the private line market in AT&T's hands. If the FCC wanted to introduce competitors into this field, as opposed to introducing competitive pricing, then TELPAK would not achieve the agency's goal. But why would the FCC want to do this, since TELPAK would give consumers the lower prices of a competitive market? There are two possible reasons. First, the FCC (like Congress in many of the acts passed during the Great Depression) may have equated the number of competitors with the conditions of competition. The Commission may have wanted multiple suppliers of microwave equipment, independent of the effects on prices. This goal expresses a long-standing confusion between the number of competitors and the extent of competition. Second, the FCC may not have believed that AT&T would maintain the low TELPAK prices once the threat of entry by other equipment suppliers had been turned away. The reasoning in either case involved a concern with the Bell System's great size and market power, and that boded ill for AT&T. Whatever the FCC's motivation – and no clear state-

[12]*US* v. *AT&T*, CA No. 74–1698, U.S. Dist. Ct., Dist. of Columbia, Defendant's Exhibit D-T-207, Albert M. Froggatt, written testimony, November 18, 1981, p. 8.

ments were made – the Commission soon made very clear that it was not pleased with TELPAK.

AT&T's response seemed to surprise the FCC. Bernard Strassburg, soon to become head of its Common Carrier Bureau, had wanted to shake up the telephone company with the *Above 890* decision. The Commission clearly had succeeded, but the response was unexpectedly strong. The proposed TELPAK rates of 1961 were so low that almost no one could be expected to construct a separate, non-Bell microwave system. From the viewpoint of William Melody (an FCC economist in the late 1960s and later a government witness in the antitrust suit against AT&T), "TELPAK was a massive overreaction." Strassburg too thought that the Bell System had overreached itself, and – under the watchful eye of Motorola – the FCC began to take action.[13]

Motorola was hardly a neophyte in FCC dealings. As the primary supplier of mobile radio equipment in the country, it had gone before the Commission to get radio licenses for its customers. When Motorola challenged AT&T's proposed new tariff, it did so on grounds that it knew the FCC could not ignore. TELPAK, asserted Motorola and Western Union – whose own small private line business was threatened by AT&T's low prices – was not compensatory (i.e., it was furnished below costs). It was designed to destroy competition. It was discriminatory. The 1934 Communications Act did not say much about the first two accusations, but it clearly outlawed discriminatory pricing.[14]

The FCC suspended TELPAK for three months, after which it took effect under the law.[15] But the investigation into its legality continued, and the Commission quickly decided that the tariff was discriminatory if it did not cover AT&T's costs. The controversy then came to focus on the calculation of those costs.[16] Although it was perfectly clear to AT&T's Frog-

[13]AT&T introduced several other services, including wide area telephone service (WATS), at flat rates, at the same time. Stump, interview, November 30, 1984, p. 32; Bernard Strassburg, interview, March 27, 1985, pp. 2–6; *US* v. *AT&T*, CA No. 74–1698 (D.D.C.), William H. Melody, testimony, June 8, 1981, Tr. 9387.

[14]*Communications Act of 1934*, 47 U.S.C. 151 §202; Stump, interview, November 30, 1984, p. 37.

[15]Although TELPAK was introduced initially in January 1961, the FCC suspended a modification that AT&T introduced in August in response to an earlier technical objection by Western Union. FCC, *Order* initiating FCC Docket 14251, "Investigation of TELPAK Tariff," September 7, 1961. See FCC, *Tentative Decision*, FCC Docket 14251, adopted March 18, 1964, 38 FCC 370 at 373, for description.

[16]The Commission argued, first, that TELPAK would not be discriminatory if the TELPAK service was functionally different from other private line services. Second, TELPAK would not be unreasonably discriminatory if it provided the same services as other services, but the rate differential arose from different costs. Third, TELPAK service would be sufficiently dissimilar from other private line service to justify different rates, even if the costs were the same, if non-TELPAK customers would benefit from the tariff through retention of otherwise lost revenues or, more precisely, the loss of the surplus of revenues over costs.

AT&T argued that TELPAK service was indeed different and that, even if it was not,

gatt which costs were appropriate, he was uncertain about the FCC's view. He thought that the FCC or its staff might want to use the separations process as a model for the costs in TELPAK. The Commission, in other words, might want to divide the Bell System's aggregate costs by some standard of relative use and not look at the costs of the capital actually involved in the TELPAK business. Froggatt considered that model to be inappropriate, but he decided to develop the historical, station-to-station costs of facilities already in place, which he called "in-plant" costs, as well as the costs of current construction (the ones he felt were correct). Froggatt discussed these issues at the Bell System's Presidents' Conference in October 1960 and with University of Chicago economist Ronald Coase, who supported the use of "current" costs. But Froggatt doggedly furnished the FCC with both sets of figures: the current costs relevant for competitive prices and the in-plant costs pertaining to regulatory prices.[17]

The FCC was startled by all of these numbers. It saw AT&T as obfuscatory, not confused. Using Froggatt's in-plant cost estimates and ignoring the competitive alternative, the FCC decided in 1964 that TELPAK was discriminatory because it did not cover its costs. This made it unlawful under the Communications Act, and the Commission ordered AT&T to file new rates.[18] AT&T appealed the decision, joined by the users of the

AT&T's costs of furnishing it were different from the costs of serving other customers. The FCC rejected both claims. The question then boiled down to the third condition: whether TELPAK imposed a burden on the other users of the telephone network. A decade later, this would become known as "the burden test," associated with the name of William Baumol, economic consultant to AT&T after 1966. (The FCC did not explicitly adopt this test in 1961, referring to it as "the principal argument of AT&T" and using it only in a sample calculation.)

This burden test is more severe than the test that most economists would impose for predatory pricing. As economists typically look at the issue, and as the FCC argued after applying the burden test to TELPAK, the question is whether the price exceeds the relevant costs, that is, whether the rates are "compensatory." In the burden test, not only do the rates have to exceed the cost of the service in question, but the effect of these rates on the provision of other services must be considered. Consequently, if these services divert business from other AT&T services that earn a surplus of revenue over costs, then the gain from this service must outweigh the loss from the other services. In other words, this burden test gives the ratepayers a property right in the surpluses generated by the existing rate structure. FCC, *Tentative Decision*, FCC Docket 14251, March 18, 1964, 38 FCC 370 at 376.

[17]*US* v. *AT&T*, CA No. 74–1698 (D.D.C.), Defendant's Exhibit D-T-207, Albert M. Froggatt, testimony, November 18, 1981, pp. 9–11. Coase was a curious advisor on dealing with the FCC; he had just published an article decrying regulation of the electromagnetic spectrum – the FCC's primary function. He was an advocate of radical, not incremental, change. Ronald H. Coase, "The Federal Communications Commission," *Journal of Law and Economics*, Vol. 2 (October 1959), pp. 1–40.

[18]The FCC compared Motorola's estimates of private microwave costs for TELPAK A and B, the rates to small customers, to AT&T's individual private line rates for the appropriate number of channels. It concluded in 1964 that private microwave systems could not compete with AT&T's normal private line service for these relatively small capacities. It

TELPAK tariff, who insisted that the Commission preserve their access to the favorable rates that had been available since 1961. The political process was opening up, embracing a broader range of participants, just as it had when Motorola had become involved in the *Above 890* case. In the *TELPAK* dispute, the FCC found itself caught between the demands of AT&T's largest customers for low rates and the demands of its would-be competitors for high rates. The results were regulatory chaos, continuing TELPAK rates, and a growing and vocal contingent of TELPAK users.

Meanwhile, AT&T performed a second cost study in response to a new FCC request in 1963 that originated in one of the agency's perennial attempts to protect Western Union from "unfair" competition. The FCC asked AT&T to allocate *book* costs among seven classes of service. Froggatt still regarded book or "in-plant" costs as inappropriate for rate making, but he complied with the Commission's request. "As a matter of practical necessity," he testified, "the principles of the [separations] manual were used as the basis of the seven-way split."[19] Even so, Froggatt furnished the FCC several different allocations of book costs among the various services. The resultant study – known appropriately if enigmatically as the Seven Way Cost Study – showed that the overall rate of return for the seven categories of interstate services was 7.5 percent, but the earned rate of return for TELPAK was only 0.3 percent.[20] AT&T, it seemed, was not making any money on TELPAK. It was, by this reckoning, furnishing this service only to preempt the competition; it was engaging in discriminatory pricing.

AT&T objected to this conclusion. The study's calculations were based on the regulatory approach to pricing. If the FCC was going to allow competition, then surely competitive prices were appropriate. AT&T did its own calculations based on the competitive approach, using incremental or marginal costs, and concluded that TELPAK earned a 5.5 percent return, close to the company's overall interstate figure of 7.5 percent. The difference was reasonable in AT&T's eyes, but the FCC would not budge. Overwhelmed by AT&T's voluminous responses to its requests, the Commission was unwilling to concede that AT&T's calculations were correct.[21]

therefore ruled that TELPAK A and B were not justified by competitive necessity. The rates for larger customers, TELPAK C and D, were left in force while further studies were ordered. FCC, *Tentative Decision*, FCC Docket 14251, March 18, 1964, 38 FCC 370 at 395.

[19]FCC Docket 14650, "Domestic Telegraph Investigation," AT&T Exhibit 90, Albert M. Froggatt, written testimony, December 16, 1965, p. 5.

[20]FCC Docket 14650, AT&T Exhibit 80, "Special Interstate Cost Study," December 16, 1965, pp. 1, 19.

[21]"Telpak Review," August 26, 1965; AT&T brought in an economics expert, James Bonbright of Columbia University, to testify that fully distributed costs were useful for separations but not for rate-making purposes. Arguing that the "cost of service" is only one of several criteria applicable to proper rate making, Bonbright asserted that the Seven Way

The Commission's version of AT&T's rate of return on TELPAK—0.3 percent—would haunt the telephone company for years to come. It appeared to be a clear signal of the company's predatory behavior and would be cited prominently.[22] AT&T's demurs about the Commission's methodology fell on deaf ears; its preferred calculations went unnoticed. The company had responded to the FCC's request in good faith, albeit at great length, while reserving to itself the high ground of methodological disagreement. It had, by this respectful response, given the FCC the ammunition it needed, and the Commission had opened fire.[23]

Unhappily for the cause of intellectual clarity, neither party to the conflict had defined a consistent position. AT&T wanted to act like a competitive firm in defense of its monopoly over telephone services. The FCC, taking the opposite tack, wanted the Bell System to act like a regulated monopoly in a market that the agency had just recently made competitive. As might be expected in such a situation, the debates dragged on for years, generating a long, involved regulatory record and satisfaction for neither party.

AT&T asked William Baumol, professor of economics at Princeton University and a future president of the American Economic Association, to present its case. He showed clearly that AT&T's position had the force of economic theory behind it (the same economic theory that was to provide the rationale behind the growing movement for deregulation in general and competitive telecommunications in particular). But although he could explain why incremental cost pricing was as close to the economist's ideal of marginal cost pricing as one was likely to get and why these prices would provide the same benefits to consumers whether charged by AT&T or its competitors, Baumol was not able to demonstrate how the FCC could ensure that AT&T would continue to charge these prices if the competition was driven away. He could not, in other words, explain away the underlying issue of AT&T's great size and power.[24]

The results were unfortunate for the Bell System. Economist William

Cost Study was "based on principles of measurements that disqualify it as a reliable measure of the profitability of each of the seven categories of service." Fully distributed costs, he said, "arbitrarily apportion shares of total costs, not actual cost in an economically significant sense of that word." FCC Docket 14650, AT&T Exhibit 89, James C. Bonbright, written testimony, December 8, 1965.

[22] Gerald W. Brock, *The Telecommunications Industry* (Cambridge: Mass.: Harvard University Press, 1981), p. 210; Stephen Breyer, *Regulation and Its Reform* (Cambridge: Mass.: Harvard University Press, 1982), p. 305.

[23] Stump, interview, November 30, 1984, pp. 17–19.

[24] See FCC Docket 16258, "Charges for Interstate and Foreign Communications Service," Bell Exhibit 26, William J. Baumol, written testimony, May 31, 1966. For an analysis of the positions taken and their evolution over time, see Louis T. Brewer, "The Development of a Test for Burden: The Evolution of a Practical Application of Economic Analysis," ca. June 1972.

Melody (who had recently joined the FCC staff from Iowa State University) presented the arguments opposing TELPAK. He relied only slightly on economic theory, resting his case on the historical tradition of regulatory pricing. His defense of average cost pricing – increasingly known as "fully distributed cost pricing" – appealed to the regulatory history of the telephone industry.[25] On intellectual grounds Baumol and AT&T may have had the better arguments, but the Commission did not buy them. The FCC was not staffed by economists, nor was it refereeing articles for publication. Strassburg, in particular, was a lawyer interested in making policy.

In the dark, all cats are gray; to Strassburg, all economists looked alike. As he saw it, Melody neutralized Baumol's testimony. Melody gave respectability to the FCC's preferred conclusions and allowed the Commission to avoid facing all of the implications of its actions. Hearings on TELPAK costs continued throughout the 1960s, and even then the problem could not be resolved. Controversies about the rates were still going on throughout the 1970s. The FCC had introduced the thin wedge of competition, and TELPAK had not provided AT&T with a price response that satisfied both its needs and its regulators.[26] TELPAK instead had created a divisive issue that would continue to strain relations between the Bell System and the federal government for several decades, disturbing the underpinnings of the 1956 accommodation.

---

[25]Melody replied to Baumol's argument that the Bell System was more efficient than the entrants by asserting that in that case Bell's average costs, that is, its fully distributed costs, would be less than the entrants' marginal or incremental costs. Therefore, the whole pricing controversy would disappear. This theoretical argument, however, assumed that fully distributed costs were board-to-board costs, when in fact – as a result of separations – they were station-to-station. The relation between fully distributed costs and incremental costs said nothing about the comparative costs of furnishing interstate services. It only revealed that the Bell System was engaged in a far different business from that of the firms attempting to enter various corners of the telecommunications industry. See FCC Docket 16258, FCC Exhibit 52, William H. Melody, written testimony, November 25, 1968.

[26]The question of whether TELPAK was compensatory, that is, whether it covered its costs, was replaced over time by the question of whether it discriminated between customers. The FCC had allowed AT&T to discriminate against small customers in 1964 as a matter of competitive necessity, but it ruled in 1970 that selected TELPAK sharing introduced to preserve Western Union's business discriminated against other small customers. Faced with the choice of allowing unlimited TELPAK sharing – which would transform it into a simple price reduction – and no TELPAK sharing, AT&T chose the latter. When the FCC ruled in 1976 that now even this was illegal discrimination, AT&T tried to cancel the tariff completely. Objections from users generated a court order preserving TELPAK for the existing users until 1985. See Charles Ferris, "Resale and Sharing of Private Line Communications Services: AT&T Restriction and FCC Regulation," *Virginia Law Review*, Vol. 61, 1975, p. 679; Carol L. Weinhaus and Anthony G. Oettinger, "Concepts: Understanding Debates Over Competition and Divestiture," Center for Information Policy Research, Harvard University, June 1985, Appendix A; Jordan Jay Hillman, "Telecommunications Deregulation: The Martyrdom of the Regulated Monopolist," *Northwestern University Law Review*, Vol. 79, 1984–5, pp. 1183–1234; especially pp. 1186–7.

Quickening change

In 1963, Bernard Strassburg became the head of the FCC's Common Carrier Bureau, a post he would hold for a decade. A self-proclaimed New Deal liberal in the tradition of Thurman Arnold, Strassburg had a healthy suspicion of big business. He was also concerned that regulatory agencies like the FCC lacked the resources they needed to control effectively giant firms such as AT&T. In 1955, when the Attorney General had asked the FCC whether it agreed with the Defense Department that divestiture of Western Electric would impair the efficiency of the telephone network, Strassburg had prepared the reply for the Commission. Then head of the Rates and Revenue Branch of the Commission's Telephone Division, Strassburg had argued that although the FCC had the statutory power to regulate Western Electric's prices and profits, the extent of actual regulation was limited sharply by the Commission's resources. In particular, the Commission could not say either that Western Electric could be replaced by a competitive market without cost or that it was earning unreasonable profits. The Commissioners forwarded to the Attorney General the parts of the letter that described the FCC's legal authority – but disingenuously, they excised the parts that revealed the practical limitations of that authority. The letter as sent described a Commission with quite adequate authority. The letter as written described a Commission with severely limited powers over Western Electric.[27]

The FCC's problems were particularly acute because the agency and Strassburg were confronting in AT&T the biggest business in America, a corporation with a virtually exclusive franchise to a market that was expanding rapidly in the 1960s. Little wonder, given his perspective, that Strassburg sought to check AT&T's expansion and to introduce a measure of competition into the Bell System's preserve. He seized the opportunity presented by his bureaucratic position and set out to test his beliefs in the marketplace.[28]

Soon after taking charge of the Common Carrier Bureau, Strassburg instituted an inquiry into the use of computers in telecommunications. The age of computers was just dawning; at that time, only a few people were actively experimenting with new ways to use them in communications, and even fewer were protesting to the agency about the Bell System's performance in this regard. But Strassburg moved out ahead of the

[27]Congressman Celler later castigated the FCC for not formulating standards by which to evaluate AT&T's earnings and for not listening to representations from its staff that the profits were too high. 86th Congress, 1st Session, House, Committee on the Judiciary, *Report of the Antitrust Subcommittee on Consent Decree Program of the Department of Justice* (Celler Report), January 30, 1959, pp. 71–82.
[28]Strassburg, interview, March 27, 1985; Geller, interview, June 20, 1984, pp. 34–5.

specific complaints coming into the Commission in an attempt to formulate a general policy. The problem he had to deal with derived partially from the 1956 Consent Decree. It made no sense to bar AT&T from supplying telephone terminal equipment, also known as "customer premises equipment," for computer users. Under the terms of the decree, however, AT&T could supply this equipment only if it was regulated. But it simply did not make sense to extend regulation to all terminal equipment. A computer with a modem connects to the telephone network. Should it therefore be regulated? Should all computers be regulated? IBM, just bringing out its 360 series of computers, was not amused by that prospect. Nor did the FCC have a logical formula for defining the limits of the regulated monopoly.[29]

The Commission's attention had been directed to this issue by complaints from computer users who could not understand why the Bell System did not immediately reconfigure the entire telephone network to deal with their particular needs. AT&T, taking an equally extreme position, did not want to bother dealing with the myriad demands from this tiny – relative to the Bell System's national market – and obstreperous group of customers.[30]

For somewhat different reasons, AT&T also opposed the request of Thomas Carter of Carter Electronics, Inc., that AT&T permit the use of his acoustical device for relaying mobile radio/telephone messages. The "Carterfone" did not make an electrical connection with the telephone network. With this device, the sound of conversation from an ordinary telephone handset activated the switch of a radio, which then communicated with the user of a mobile radio/telephone. In effect, the Carterfone allowed the mobile radio/telephone to be patched into the Bell System network. AT&T, reaffirming its end-to-end responsibility for the network, refused to permit the innovation to be used. Carter would not, however, be awed by the telephone giant. He sold his device to customers in defiance of the existing tariff. When AT&T discontinued his customers' service, he filed a private antitrust suit against the company. The court decided that regulation under the Communications Act and not prosecution under the Sherman Act was still controlling. It referred Carter's complaint to the FCC under the doctrine of primary jurisdiction.[31]

For Strassburg, this was an excellent opportunity to lend a hand to a small entrepreneur and to make the giant Bell System more responsive to its varied clientele. AT&T argued to the Commission that the Carterfone

[29]FCC, *Notice of Inquiry*, FCC Docket 16979, "Computer Inquiry," adopted November 9, 1966, 7 FCC 2d 11; FCC, *Report and Further Notice of Inquiry*, FCC Docket 16979, adopted May 1, 1969, 17 FCC 2d 587 at 591.

[30]Strassburg, interview, March 27, 1985; Edward M. Goldstein, interview, April 25, 1985, pp. 2, 7–8.

[31]*Carter v. AT&T*, 250 F. Supp. 188, 192 (N.D. Tex. 1966), *aff'd*, 365 F.2d 486 (5th Cir. 1966), *cert. denied*, 385 U.S. 1008, 1967.

should be proscribed because it was not useful and could not be guaranteed to work properly, thus casting blame on the telephone company from customers who could not differentiate between the Carterfone and the Bell System. The device was, AT&T also claimed, manufactured by an unstable firm. In the 1940s and 1950s, tenuous arguments like these had been eaten up by the FCC, but Strassburg no longer found them appetizing in the context of his computer inquiry.[32] He required that AT&T explain exactly how its network would be damaged (not just how customers who used the Carterfone might be inconvenienced) before the agency would prohibit the device. Indeed, the Commission rejected the existing AT&T tariff prohibiting the use of non-Bell equipment for its failure to distinguish between harmful and nonharmful interconnection. The FCC did not deny that AT&T needed to regulate interconnection and to be responsible for network standards. But the agency repudiated AT&T's customary arguments on the grounds that they were imprecise in defining harm. The Commission approved the use of the Carterfone.[33]

Just as this fight between Bell and Strassburg was reaching its climax, AT&T's top management changed. H.I. Romnes, who represented the flowering of the Bell System's engineering tradition, became chairman of AT&T's board and its CEO in 1967. He was a cautious, reflective man who had started his career working on circuit design at Bell Labs before the Great Depression. A brilliant engineer, he had become the architect of nationwide direct distance dialing. After advancing through a series of engineering and then management positions, Romnes had become presi-

[32]The FCC previously had accepted AT&T's argument that a device that could accidentally leave a customer's circuit open was harmful. *Jordaphone Corp.* v. *AT&T* Docket 9383, 18 FCC 644 at 669–70, 1954.

The almost ridiculous case of Hush-A-Phone, a plastic device that connected to the telephone mouthpiece to increase privacy, shows the lengths to which AT&T's argument could be stretched in the 1950s. Even though this nonelectrical device could not conceivably have harmed the telephone network, AT&T argued that it lowered the transmission volume and decreased the quality of telephone service, usurping AT&T's authority and responsibility. The FCC went along with this view, defining AT&T's end-to-end responsibility to include even the way a customer used and spoke into his telephone. End-to-end, one might say, went mouth-to-mouth instead of merely station-to-station.

The Hush-A-Phone Corporation took the FCC's decision to the Court of Appeals, which had little sympathy for the Commission's position. The court noted that the FCC and AT&T "do not challenge the subscriber's right to seek privacy. They say only that he should achieve it by cupping his hand between the transmitter and his mouth and speaking in a low voice." Turning to the tariff in question, the court continued, "To say that a telephone subscriber may produce the result in question by cupping his hand and speaking into it, but may not do so by using a device which leaves his hand free to write or do whatever else he wishes, is neither just or reasonable." Despite this caustic tone, the court stopped short of denying the FCC the role of protecting the telephone network; it argued only that the commission had exceeded its authority in this particular case. *Hush-A-Phone Corp.*, 20 FCC 391, 1955, *order set aside, Hush-A-Phone Corp.* v. *US*, 238 F.2d 266 at 269 (D.C. Cir. 1956), *on remand* 22 FCC 112, 1957.

[33]FCC, *Decision*, FCC Docket 16942, "Carterfone," adopted June 26, 1968, 13 FCC 2d 420.

dent of Western Electric at the end of the 1950s and had moved to AT&T headquarters in 1964.[34]

Shortly after taking his new office, this austere Norwegian-American expressed a surprisingly expansive view of the use of computers in communications and of the impending Carterfone decision. The System's ideal of end-to-end responsibility seemed to move him less than it did Bell's more service-oriented managers. Romnes held the network in almost mystical awe, and he saw abundant new opportunities in a telephone system with a wider variety of terminals at its ends. His concern, as he expressed it in 1967, was merely that the Bell System's "prime responsibility for maintenance" of the network be preserved by the use of "suitable interfaces or buffer devices to keep the attached equipment from affecting other users of the network." Subject to this safeguard, Romnes accepted Strassburg's initiative.[35]

The situation soon threatened, however, to move completely out of AT&T's control. The FCC, in line with the comprehensive approach Strassburg had taken in his computer inquiry, had not restricted its attention solely to the Carterfone. It prepared to declare all of AT&T's existing interconnection tariffs invalid. If the Bell System could not come up with an acceptable alternative before the FCC's order took effect, anyone would be able legally to connect anything to the telephone network. This was not what Romnes had in mind. He appointed a high-level Tariff Review Committee in mid-1967 to devise alternative interconnection tariffs that would protect the system.

The Tariff Review Committee operated in a crisis atmosphere. As engineers responsible for the network, its members were wary of change and of non-Bell outsiders. They advanced scraps of data exposing minor hazards of interconnection as grounds for caution. They clothed their fear of the unknown in specific scenarios for disaster.[36] Cooler heads might well

[34]Romnes fully understood the technical nature of the telephone network. What he did not understand – what his training and experience had not prepared him for – was how to move the mountainous hierarchy he headed. Less than a year of his career had been spent at an operating company; he had never been involved in the service aspect of Bell's operations, nor did he relate well to the business side of the network. He was widely revered as a deep thinker and a man who was thoughtful of others, but he was not a vigorous leader. He lacked charisma. His vice chairman and successor, John deButts, never understood how Romnes had become CEO. John D. deButts, interview, October 25, 1984, pp. 53–4.

[35]H.I. Romnes, "Dynamic Communications for Modern Industry," speech before the American Petroleum Institute, Chicago, Illinois, November 13, 1967; Alvin von Auw, *Heritage & Destiny: Reflections on the Bell System in Transition* (New York: Praeger Publishers, 1983), p. 137.

[36]Edward M. Goldstein, an AT&T engineering director, listed for the committee all of the problems that customer equipment would pose for signaling, switching, and transmission in the network. The central office might not respond to the initiation of a call if the impedance across the line was too high; the call might be charged to a wrong number on multiparty lines; a wrong number might be reached; all digits might not be registered; the connection might be dropped in the middle if the station opened the line for more than half

have recalled that the Bell System had never included all of the devices connected to the network and that there was a long history of terminal interconnection for those who wanted to see it. The independent telephone companies, often quite small and primitive, could be thought of as early private branch exchanges (PBXs). Defense Department equipment on military bases, connected to the network under "letters of military necessity," was used without protective devices. The sound and video equipment of the TV networks, increasingly large customers of the Bell System, generated signals sent directly over the network without evident difficulty. It was possible to argue that these were all special cases in a controlled environment. But they represented extensive experience with terminal interconnection before *Carterfone*–experience that was quite varied and apparently trouble free.[37]

The Tariff Review Committee nevertheless recommended tariffs allowing ancillary equipment–answering machines or computer modems–to be attached to the Bell System "only in connection with special interface equipment provided, installed and maintained by the telephone company."[38] As Strassburg acknowledged later, the idea of a protective connecting arrangement grew out of "the established regulatory culture."[39] It embraced a natural division of responsibility between AT&T and its customers. If these devices were used, the telephone company would not need to tell its customers what they could and could not attach to the network. It would not have to monitor or control what other people were doing; its protective coupling device would simply screen out any harmful signals. The Bell System would know what signals it was getting. The vendors of equipment would know the electrical characteristics of the network they were facing. AT&T would avoid all of the competitive and

a second or if it sent a 2600-Hertz tone through the line. The line might be left open if the station did not properly restore the line to its normal situation, which can require attention from the Bell System's plant forces. One device could cause dial tone delays to other customers.

Customer-provided equipment at the terminating stations might not activate the charging mechanism when it answered, resulting in a free call, or might not properly restore itself to normal so as to be able to receive additional calls, unnecessarily tying up common equipment and possibly requiring special attention from plant personnel. Excessive output levels on one circuit would reduce the quality of the transmission on other circuits. Noise would increase, and noise identifiable as another conversation–"cross-talk," in telephone jargon–would undermine consumers' faith in the privacy of their communication. Edward M. Goldstein, talk presented to the Tariff Review Committee, "Effects on Switching, Signaling and Charging," April 10, 1968. For another similar talk, see *US* v. *AT&T*, CA No. 74–1698 (D.D.C.), Defendant's Exhibit D-7-1, V.N. Vaughan notes.

[37] Robert E. Gradle, interview, November 16, 1984, pp. 12–13.
[38] "Illustrative General Exchange Tariff Covering the Provision of Interfaces for COAM [Customer owned and maintained] Devices," draft, presented at the Tariff Review Committee meeting, April 10, 1968.
[39] *US* v. *AT&T*, CA No. 74–1698 (D.D.C.), Bernard Strassburg, written testimony, October 14, 1981, Tr. 17243.

legal problems attendant on examining the plans or equipment of its customers and competitors.[40]

Romnes announced the new policy at a gathering of company executives on September 5, 1968. He introduced a small, inexpensive device called a "protective coupling arrangement (PCA)" through which equipment owned and maintained by Bell's customers could be connected to the switched network. He proclaimed dryly, "We welcome competition," and emphasized that "our intent is to make interfaces as simple and inexpensive as possible." In fact, he said: "The more the merrier."[41]

AT&T had seized the initiative. Rather than fighting change, as it had in the Carterfone case, the firm had marked off a new area in which the debate over telecommunications policy could take place. Romnes had severely qualified the traditional concept of end-to-end responsibility, curtailing Bell's authority so long as customers were willing to use the PCA.[42]

Romnes made it clear that he was promulgating a new strategy for the Bell System. He stressed the existence of a new era in telecommunications and a new openness in the network. AT&T had set the stage for an expansion in the use of increasingly sophisticated devices connected to the Bell System. It was starting to do for customer equipment what Strassburg was trying to do for computers: setting a general rule for new entrants. It is ironic that in later antitrust suits against AT&T, these tariffs would be assailed for being anticompetitive when they were in fact the telephone company's initial move toward competition.

Protective couplings might not have been attacked so vociferously if AT&T had decided to offer them free to customers, as a matter of right. The company decided instead to charge the owners of independent terminals for the PCAs through which they would be attached to the network. To do anything else, the Tariff Review Committee reasoned, would be to charge the general rate payers the cost of accommodating computer users and others who were experimenting with new kinds of equipment. The committee did not conceptualize the issue as one of protecting the rate payers' network—in which case they might be expected to pay. Nor, of course, did the committee conclude that what was involved was an effort to quiet the Bell System's fears—in which case AT&T should have borne

[40]*US v. AT&T*, CA No. 74–1698 (D.D.C.), Defendant's Exhibit D-T-2, Edward M. Goldstein, written testimony, July 8, 1981, pp. 30–1.
[41]H.I. Romnes, "Connecting with the Telephone Network," talk on video cassette tape, September 5, 1968.
[42]The FCC allowed AT&T's revised tariffs permitting interconnection through a PCA to become effective on January 1, 1969, but noted that it was unable at that time to evaluate the revised tariff fully. The Commission noted that the tariff went beyond its *Carterfone* decision and acknowledged that the question of whether a customer should be able to provide his own network control signaling unit was open. FCC, *Memorandum and Order*, "AT&T 'Foreign Attachment' Tariff Revisions," December 24, 1968, 15 FCC 2d 605.

the cost itself. Even though Carter's initial legal action had been in the form of an antitrust complaint, the group apparently did not consider the antitrust implications of the PCA charge.[43] In light of the company's background and the amount of attention its every action attracted in Washington, D.C., and elsewhere, this latter subject would seem to have cried out for analysis before the fact.

These considerations notwithstanding, Romnes certainly had guided AT&T through an important break with its deepest traditions. Nevertheless, he soon found himself challenged to go ever further down the path to competition under pressure from another fledgling company. Microwave Communications, Inc. (MCI), was even smaller than Carter Electronics; it had neither staff nor finances. It had applied to the FCC in 1963 for permission to build a private microwave line from St. Louis to Chicago. MCI clearly was too small to use this facility itself; it proposed instead to sell capacity to others. Even though the FCC's *Above 890* decision had expressly barred the sharing of microwave systems, MCI proposed to sell its capacity in small units to users having no stake in the facility itself.

MCI's application had advanced slowly through the FCC's approval process while the Commission grappled with *TELPAK*, the *Computer Inquiry*, and *Carterfone*. With nothing to sell, MCI had fallen deeper and deeper into debt while it was appearing before the Commission in an effort to keep its application alive. The debt was under $40,000 in 1968, a tiny amount relative to the borrowings of the Bell System but a large sum for MCI. The company's founders went searching for financial support and came into contact with William McGowan, a flamboyant venture capitalist. McGowan could not believe that any businessman would want to borrow less than $40,000, and he asked why they did not want more. When they replied that their debts were less than $40,000, McGowan realized that he was dealing with innocents unable to plan for the future. Appreciating the value of their idea and their pending application, he took steps to gain control of MCI and began to pump capital into the business. He launched a variety of local MCI companies around the country; they provided him with a source of capital, local support, and the appearance of organizational breadth. By the time the FCC belatedly considered MCI's applications, McGowan was in the telecommunications business.[44]

It would never be the same. AT&T was a magisterial presence at the Commission, studiously correct and accommodating to a fault (as demonstrated by its willingness to supply the FCC with cost estimates it firmly believed were wrong). McGowan, by contrast, was a street fighter, a man

---

[43]Tariff Review Committee Meetings, Vols. I and II.
[44]Larry Kahaner, *On the Line* (New York: Warner Books, 1986), pp. 53–9; *US* v. *AT&T*, CA No. 74–1698 (D.D.C.), William G. McGowan, testimony, Tr. 3577–8; William G. McGowan, interview, September 27, 1985, pp. 6–7.

Bernard Strassburg, chief of the FCC Common Carrier Bureau from 1964 to 1974.

William G. McGowan, chairman of the board and chief executive officer of MCI beginning in 1968. (Photo courtesy of George Kemper.)

who took advantages when they appeared and seldom worried about the rules of combat. Motorola had changed the FCC's procedures by forcing the agency to become more formal. MCI changed them again, bringing a new level of contentiousness and distrust of AT&T to the Commission's proceedings.

McGowan's company wanted permission to compete directly with the Bell System in the sale of particular communications services. In the *Above 890* decision, the FCC had not disturbed AT&T's monopoly over the sale of long distance services. If customers wanted to use a telephone line for only a part of the day or for the length of their phone calls, if they wanted to use just a small amount of service, they were still supposed to go to AT&T. Only those customers large enough to have their own equipment, either alone or with a small group of companies (after 1966), could avoid using the Bell System for their internal communications.[45] AT&T competed for the bulk communications business of these large firms through its TELPAK tariff. Each firm had to decide whether to use the Bell System or its own facility. AT&T, however, was the only seller to firms that wanted to buy services, not facilities. There was only one public network operating under government regulations. *Above 890* encouraged competition outside this network without – or so the Commission stated – disturbing the regulated natural monopoly status of the network itself.

MCI was now proposing to sell access to private lines, not to the switched network. But MCI's private line customers would, of course, want to get messages to and from the private lines. How would they do this? If it was by attaching the private line to the switched network, would MCI then be a customer or a competitor of the Bell System? These issues were raised by McGowan in the course of the FCC hearings even before MCI became AT&T's competitor; that was McGowan's way of convincing the FCC to allow him to become a competitor. He adopted the winning strategy of assuming that his company had somehow been granted approval in principle to compete with AT&T; the only issues, then, were ones of implementation.

McGowan argued that MCI would be offering a new service, that it would tailor its services to the needs of customers, and that it would provide greater flexibility than AT&T would permit. AT&T countered that MCI, like Motorola before it, was simply cream skimming. Far from offering a new service, MCI was charging lower prices for an existing service. McGowan was able to do so, AT&T argued, because his rates were not part of the nationwide average rate structure. AT&T was thus to be doubly disadvantaged – held both to historical costs and to national

[45]Charles Ferris, "Resale and Sharing of Private Line Communications Services: AT&T Restriction and FCC Regulation," *Virginia Law Review*, Vol. 61, 1975, p. 679.

averages – while MCI could use current costs and serve only high-density, low-cost markets like the one between Chicago and St. Louis. To be sure, AT&T had itself begun to discriminate between customers on the basis of size; TELPAK provided low rates to large private line users. MCI now argued that the lower rates should be available to everyone. McGowan would not try to compete with TELPAK for large users; he would offer TELPAK-like rates to small customers.

The Bell System also had the burden of being a very large and established utility. MCI was a struggling upstart. It could expect to gain some support on that basis alone. Moreover, MCI could use lower-quality construction and limited facilities in ways that the Bell System could not. The new firm's crews were nonunion; they were not always careful about getting building permits; they did not build carefully designed structures. In fact, MCI argued that its rural facilities did not even need bathrooms – the technicians could use the fields![46] It is hard to imagine the Communication Workers of America, state commissioners, or the FCC allowing AT&T to adopt similar cost-cutting measures. To the extent that MCI's construction costs were below AT&T's for these reasons, the FCC was being asked to change the structure of the telecommunications industry for only a temporary gain.

To the extent that MCI was offering lower-quality services than the Bell System, of course, McGowan's business was also cream skimming. As with *Above 890*, the cream skimming did not have to be geographic. AT&T argued that MCI aimed to supply only a low-cost route and low-cost customers, that is, those who did not care about quality.

The FCC ignored AT&T's warnings and accepted at face value MCI's claim to be furnishing "interplant and interoffice communications with unique and specialized characteristics." On a four-to-three vote – with the chairman voting against MCI – the FCC found AT&T's "cream skimming argument to be without merit."[47] Strassburg was obviously intrigued by McGowan's arguments. He wanted AT&T to be more flexible, to supply services to smaller units and in greater variety – the same concerns he had expressed in the *Carterfone* hearings. AT&T told him that he was opening a door he would not be able to close. But Strassburg insisted that approv-

[46]Larry Kahaner, *On the Line*, pp. 27, 85–89.
[47]The Commission noted that these new characteristics were not the result of new equipment or technology; MCI would simply allow customers to do things that the Bell System would not. MCI's offering of 2-kilohertz channels is a case in point. The Bell System used 4-kilohertz voice-grade channels as its unit; it had abandoned 2-kilohertz as substandard.

   MCI was allowing customers to subdivide these channels in pursuit of lower prices. The service, of course, would be of lower quality, so low that it is not clear that any 2-kilohertz channels actually were used. MCI's announcement served only to convince the FCC that the aspiring entrant was offering something new.

   FCC, *Decision*, FCC Docket Nos. 16509–19, "Applications of MCI for Construction Permits," adopted August 13, 1969, 18 FCC 2d 953, *recon. denied*, 21 FCC 2d 190, 1970.

ing MCI's application was just an experiment, a chance to try something that might not even work. Wishful thinking led him to ignore the clear signs of danger on that front.[48]

The Commission regarded McGowan's tiny business as a fringe firm rather like Western Union. Strassburg in particular conceptualized the *MCI* proceeding as a very specific one, concerned with a small company and a single line. Nevertheless, the FCC's vote was close. It had required the enthusiasm of the head of the Common Carrier Bureau and of several pro-competition commissioners who strongly favored competitors to get it through. One of these commissioners, Kenneth Cox, participated in the panel discussion between Baxter and Trienens reported in the Introduction. He found his views so close to McGowan's that he left the Commission to work for MCI shortly after the vote. There is no evidence that Cox and McGowan discussed employment before the FCC's vote, but Cox could not have been unaware that his views made him an attractive potential officer of MCI.[49] (AT&T, of course, never hired former regulators.) With only a hair less support, McGowan might never have gotten his fledgling enterprise off the ground.

With this decision in hand, though, MCI's boss quickly advanced on a broad front. He was not about to conduct an academic experiment for Strassburg, to proceed at a stately pace while generating the data needed to evaluate the effect of the Commission's decision on this one specific route. Instead, his affiliated MCI companies immediately flooded the FCC with applications for permission to construct microwave systems for hire all over the country. By mid-1970 the Commission was facing almost 2,000 such requests, most of them coming from MCI companies and another firm, Datran, that aspired to construct a digital data network.

In an unusual move, the FCC decided that it was unable to deal with this aftermath of *Above 890* and *MCI* on a case-by-case basis. The Commission took the initiative in setting out the general issues to be decided. Having dealt with MCI's initial application on highly individual grounds, it then recognized MCI as the forerunner of a class of applicants and approved the applications from the class as a whole under the title of *Specialized Common Carriers*.[50] Consistent with its regulatory tradition,

[48]*Initial Decision of Hearing Examiner Herbert Sharfman*, FCC Docket Nos. 16509–19, October 17, 1967, 18 FCC 2d 979, at 1006; Stump, interview, November 30, 1984, pp. 33–4.

[49]*MCI v. AT&T*, No. 74 C 633, U.S. Dist. Ct., Northern Dist. of Illinois, Eastern Division, Deposition of Kenneth A. Cox, February 6, 1978.

[50]FCC, *First Report and Order*, FCC Docket 18920, "Specialized Common Carriers," June 3, 1971, 29 FCC 2d 870, *aff'd sub nom. Wash. Util. & Trans. Comm'n v. FCC*, 513 F.2d 1142 (9th Cir. 1975), *cert. denied*, 423 U.S. 836, 1975. *Specialized Common Carriers* therefore was classified as rulemaking rather than adjudication. Strassburg's views prevailed nonetheless. See *US v. AT&T*, CA No. 74–1698 (D.D.C.), Defendant's Exhibit D-7–266; Bernard Strassburg, "Case Study of Policy-Making by Federal Communications Commission re Competition in Intercity Common Carrier Communications," draft, January 14, 1977.

however, the FCC still formulated its policy in the light of specific public needs and benefits. It did not relinquish its traditional regulatory standards to champion competition.

The arguments by the applicants were roughly the same as those originally presented by MCI. They would provide a wider range of services than AT&T. They would open up new markets with new low-cost technology, thereby meeting the criterion of public good. This argument, of course, raised the question of why AT&T was not serving these new markets. It was not that AT&T had not thought of offering certain kinds of services; the applicants were proposing services that were essentially the same as AT&T's. Rather, it was that AT&T was not lowering its prices enough to expand its private line customer base because that would affect its existing revenue base. To some extent it was burdened by historical costs, and to some extent it was acting like any monopolist faced with a technological change.[51] But even had AT&T wanted to, it was quite clear from the *TELPAK* investigations that the FCC would not have allowed it to lower all private line rates. Reducing rates on some routes would have raised all of the problems of discrimination that the FCC had been unable to resolve in its *TELPAK* investigations. The *Specialized Common Carriers* decision appears to have been a way for the FCC to allow lower prices for the use of the new microwave technology without allowing AT&T to discriminate between different users. To the Bell System presidents, gathered outside Chicago in the fall of 1971, it appeared that competition would be allowed but that AT&T would not be allowed to compete. Hardly a cheering prospect.

The FCC's procedure, designed to avoid a particular regulatory pothole, brought a rush of new carriers into the market and into the political arena. *Specialized Common Carriers* fundamentally changed the way in which telecommunications services were to be supplied, a radical change that seems not to have been intended by most of the FCC commissioners. Intended or not, the decision decisively increased competition in the industry. Insensitive to this larger implication, the agency noted that licensing these other carriers would virtually compel their interconnection with the Bell System; the new carriers clearly needed local distribution facilities that they could not supply. The FCC thus implicitly announced that the next assault on AT&T's position would be against its monopoly in the provision of service at the local level.[52]

The FCC refused to recognize any danger to AT&T from such intercon-

[51]See Kenneth J. Arrow, "Economic Welfare and the Allocation of Resources for Invention," in National Bureau of Economic Research, *The Rate and Direction of Inventive Activity* (Princeton: Princeton University Press, 1962), pp. 609–25.
[52]FCC, *Further Notice of Inquiry and Proposed Rulemaking*, FCC Docket 18920, June 21, 1971, 30 FCC 2d 288.

nection. It predicted that the total effect of competition would be slight and that Bell revenues would not be endangered. Echoing numbers used in *Above 890*, the Commission's staff claimed that only AT&T's private line business, three percent of its revenue, would be at risk. Competition from specialized common carriers, the staff asserted, "can be expected to have some beneficial results without adverse impact on service by established carriers."[53] There would be no danger of cream skimming and no threat to the existing rate structure.

While the Commission had been gradually working out these new policies, a presidential task force appointed by Lyndon Johnson had provided support for the idea of encouraging competition in this industry. The task force, which was chaired by Eugene Rostow, Under Secretary of State for Political Affairs, went far beyond the FCC to assert that competition should replace regulation as the norm in telecommunications. It agreed with the Commission that the Bell System's monopoly in ordinary long distance service should be maintained, while improvements in service were encouraged through competition. Even though the task force thought that AT&T should be able to respond to competitive firms, it too failed to see any threat to the integrated national telephone network in the growth of competition in ancillary services.[54]

AT&T argued to the contrary: The emerging competitive environment would require a restructuring of rates to eliminate nationwide averaging and reliance on average as opposed to marginal costs. In fact, the telephone company contended in the *Specialized Common Carriers* case that the change would dictate the adoption of competitive pricing. In the earlier *TELPAK* case, it had claimed that marginal costs were the appro-

[53]FCC, *First Report and Order*, FCC Docket 18920, June 3, 1971, 29 FCC 2d 870 at 878–85.

[54]President's Task Force on Communications Policy, *Final Report*, December 7, 1968; *Message from the President of the United States Transmitting Recommendations Relative to World Communications*, August 14, 1967, Appendix to *Final Report*.

Little followed directly from the task force's report except the establishment in the administration of the Office of Telecommunications Policy (OTP). This advisory group was headed by Clay Whitehead, who was in contact with Strassburg at the FCC and employed economist Bruce Owen (later of the Justice Department and an expert witness in the trial of the government's antitrust suit against AT&T in 1981). Both men supported policies that would increase competition. Starting their work by considering the treatment of satellites, they could make no sense of the decision in 1962 to bar AT&T from space. It seemed to warp the use of this new technology and restrict competition in a way that promoted inefficiency. The OTP quickly became a force pushing to open telecommunications to competitive activity. Paradoxically, Owen muddied the theoretical waters by supervising Richard Gabel in the Commerce Department as he wrote studies of separations that concluded that local service was subsidizing long distance activities. This curious position would surface during the *US* v. *AT&T* antitrust trial in Melody's and Owen's testimony. See Richard Gabel, *Development of Separations Principles in the Telephone Industry* (East Lansing: Michigan State University Press, 1967); *US* v. *AT&T*, CA No. 74–1698 (D.D.C.), Bruce M. Owen, testimony, June 13, 1981, Tr. 10975–6; Bruce M. Owen, interview, June 13, 1984; Strassburg, interview, March 27, 1985.

priate ones to use as a matter of theory. Here AT&T argued that the practice emerging in the marketplace would force their use willy-nilly. The FCC replied: "Where services may be in direct competition, departure from uniform nationwide pricing may be in order and in such circumstances will not be opposed by the Commission." But given the absence of agreement on cost calculations – a situation at the heart of the continuing furor over TELPAK – it is not clear what the Commission's statement meant.[55]

Indeed, a year earlier, in a cruel irony, the FCC had actually pushed the Bell System in the opposite direction. At the same time that it allowed entry into interstate private line service, the Commission had agreed to a revision of the separations formula that increased the disparity between prices and board-to-board costs in interstate telephone service. The Ozark plan, instituted in 1971, allocated an even greater part of the costs of local plant to interstate service. As Figure 3 shows, the Ozark plan would also allow the proportion to rise over time without negotiating further changes in the formula. The adoption of this plan accentuated the price distortion that was inviting entry into long distance telephone service.[56]

By 1971, Romnes and his management team felt themselves battered by the FCC's decisions. *Carterfone, MCI,* and *Specialized Common Carriers* had left the Bell System's leaders uncertain about its future and uneasy about what the next turn in public policy might be. Moreover, their problems in dealing with these new developments were complicated and even temporarily overshadowed by the service crisis mentioned in the Introduction. Caught in a cost-price squeeze that was exacerbated by the high interest rates of those years, the Bell System had found it hard to raise capital. Rate increases were becoming more difficult to get as utility customers were welcomed into the regulatory process in the late 1960s to argue against the telephone companies. The increases granted were frequently less than the operating companies requested; they were based as well on historical costs, which understate current and future costs during inflation. Bell Operating Companies, together with other utilities, found themselves in a profit squeeze as their costs rose faster than their rates.[57] Operating costs also were under pressure because AT&T was trying to increase its minority employment. Training costs rose as the System hired

[55]FCC, *Final Report and Order,* FCC Docket 18920, June 3, 1971, 29 FCC 2d 870 at 915.
[56]The Ozark plan introduced the concept of the subscriber plant factor (SPF), which was computed from SLU but which – as Figure 3 shows – was far higher. FCC, *Report and Order,* FCC Docket 18866, "Separations Procedures," October 28, 1970, 26 FCC 2d 247.
[57]The problems were compounded by a traditional Bell reluctance to seek higher rates; it was seen as a violation of the service ethic. Rate increases approved by state regulatory commissions rose from an average of two a year in the first eight years of the 1960s to four in 1968, 8 in 1969, and a peak of 33 in 1972. *AT&T State Rate Case Reference Manual,* June 30, 1983, p. A 100; Andrew S. Carron and Paul W. MacAvoy, *The Decline of Service in the Regulated Industries* (Washington, D.C.: American Enterprise Institute, 1981), pp. 37–8.

people with fewer qualifications and as turnover rose dramatically.[58] AT&T's investment could not keep up with the growth of demand. Service suffered.

The shortcomings had appeared first and most sharply in the telephone service of eastern cities. Demand for communications capacity had risen sharply in the late 1960s, and the Bell System's switching capacity had not kept pace. Volume on the New York Stock Exchange shot up, increasing the demand for business service in New York City, and a ruling that welfare recipients should have telephones had provided an unexpected, one-time jump in the demand for residential service. The New York Telephone Company could not cope. Delays in obtaining dial tones were reported in the financial district of New York City in May 1969. Then the Plaza 8 exchange failed entirely when a new electronic switch became overloaded. The problems had become so severe by July that Benton and Bowles, the advertising agency, took out a full-page ad in *The New York Times* listing the names of 800 people over the caption "These are the people you haven't been able to reach at PLaza 8–6200." New York Telephone replied the next day by admitting that it had left Benton and Bowles's name and number out of half of the new Manhattan telephone directories.[59]

The president of New York Telephone acknowledged that service was poor and announced that an emergency team of 1,500 men would be brought into the city. He warned the public, however, not to expect immediate relief. The poor service resulted from reliance on a 1967 forecast that had predicted an economic slowdown and a consequent decline in the rate of growth of demand for communications. At a public hearing of the state Public Service Commission, William Sharwell, the operating vice president of the company, reiterated that the poor service resulted from New York Telephone's failure to anticipate the recent surge in demand. He did not stress the fact that the company was receptive to the pessimistic forecast as a result of its difficulty in raising capital in the face of declining real telephone rates and high interest rates. The FCC got into the act by requesting a meeting with the nation's telephone companies to discuss the complaints about service in New York, Florida, and elsewhere. At the Commission's request, AT&T began to furnish it with a monthly report on its service quality, measuring it on a scale with well

---

[58]Robert D. Lilley, interview, September 23, 1985, pp. 1–14; "Gilmer: Urban Crisis Demands Action 'Now'," *195 Management Report*, No. 12 (March 13, 1968); "Force Loss Reports Show Nonmanagement Turnover Continuing Upswing; 'Under 6 Months' Top Category," *195 Management Report*, No. 37 (August 7, 1969).

[59]"Dial Tone Delays Reported in City," *The New York Times*, April 10, 1969, p. 34; "These are the people you haven't been able to reach at PLaza 8–6200," *The New York Times*, July 14, 1969, p. 51 (ad); "Benton & Bowles Left Out of Half of Phone Books," *The New York Times*, July 16, 1969, p. 51.

Indiana Bell Telephone Company crew working in mid-Manhattan in 1969 during the telephone service problems in New York City.

over a dozen dimensions and indicating "weak spots" in any dimension in any region of the country.[60] This poor performance in the Bell System's traditional business complicated the choices facing AT&T's leaders in 1971. They were still trying to catch up with service needs and improve earnings. How could they advance into new areas if they could not even fulfill their long-standing mandate? Would they have to reorganize the entire System – abandoning the structure Vail had created – in order to be more responsive to their normal demands and to respond to the new emerging markets? The service crisis made a mockery of the Bell System's claim that it could satisfy all of the nation's new demands for telecommunications. The System's problems were not perceived as a temporary result of the Vietnam War and of the interaction of inflation and regulation. Internally and externally, the service failures of the late 1960s were seen as fundamental challenges to the Bell System's position in the industry. *Fortune* magazine announced that the decline of service heralded an "age of anxiety" for the Bell System. Overcoming the System's "internal liabilities," the writer concluded, "is the biggest struggle AT&T's executives face."[61]

AT&T under fire

These difficulties had not crept up on AT&T's leadership unnoticed. Indeed, one powerful element in the Bell culture was the tradition of conducting elaborate, sometimes multiple, staff studies on every situation facing the System. All of the problems that were discussed at the 1971 Presidents' Conference had been studied at length. But studying problems and solving them are very different activities, as the experience at the 1971 conference had shown. AT&T was structured to solve technological problems in the national network, but the company's very success in this regard made it difficult for it to solve its own internal organizational problems. The weight of tradition in this firm was heavy. In the more than half-century since Vail had imposed his 1909 organization on the Bell System, it had not experienced a major, top-down reorganization. In the late 1960s, some operating companies had begun to restructure their operations in response to the changing market, but these organizational innovations were scattered and partial. There had as yet been no pressure for change from the center of the Bell System at 195 Broadway.

The Bell System was a marvelously intricate hierarchical bureaucracy.

---

[60]"1500 Phone Men Being Sent Here," *The New York Times*, July 28, 1969, p. 1; "FCC Seeks Data on Phone Service," *The New York Times*, August 16, 1969, p. 1; "City Aide Would Cut Bill If a Plan Fails," *The New York Times*, August 19, 1969, p. 1; "Phone Users Cite Service Decline," *The New York Times*, September 22, 1969, p. 1; Bernard Strassburg to Thomas Scandlyn, January 20, 1970; "Quality of Service Reports," 1968–78.
[61]Allen T. Demaree, "The Age of Anxiety at A.T.&T.," *Fortune*, May 1970, p. 156.

Position within this vast organization was carefully layered so that people from disparate parts of the System would know how to relate to each other. Higher levels indicated higher authority. The fourth level was the highest level with the title of manager. A director was fifth level, and an assistant vice president was sixth level. The seventh level, vice presidents, and above constituted AT&T's senior management. Officers of the operating companies with similar titles were one level below their counterparts at 195 Broadway. Formal communications like the firm's numerous staff studies went up and down this ladder along approved pathways; the hierarchy acted like a filter, ensuring that the CEO would have only the information he needed to oversee the whole System.[62]

As in any large organization dealing with a relatively stable environment, internal barriers to change had grown up. Each unit of the Bell System functioned autonomously in pursuit of the System's familiar goals: universal service and steadily increasing service quality. Operating company presidents never received direct orders from 195 Broadway. Western Electric manufactured products developed at Bell Labs; the engineers at both institutions were imbued with the mystique of an integrated, smoothly functioning network, and generally they were left alone to exploit the technology. It would have been almost impossible to run a business as large as the Bell System, with its numerous regulatory jurisdictions and hundreds of thousands of employees, had it not been highly decentralized. The lack of central direction was nowhere more evident than in the budgetary process. AT&T's headquarters sent all of the operating companies substantial amounts of statistical data on a regular basis. But in setting the budgets, the most important figures flowed from the operating companies to 195 Broadway. Each of the companies forecast its construction needs and sent them to AT&T headquarters. There they were added up, tailored somewhat to fit System expectations of available capital, and thus transformed into the Bell System's annual budget.[63]

Promotion within this vast, decentralized setup was related to social as well as intellectual skills. Managers who had internalized the corporate culture were said to have "Bell-shaped heads"; they tended to be nice people who provided good service to their customers and communities. You could go anywhere in the System and find congenial colleagues, but one of the costs of this good fellowship was the fact that the System virtually ran itself. Headquarters actually had very little information about the business beyond the aggregate figures required for its regulators. In fact, the leaders of the Bell System often acted as if the regulators were their customers – as if they got revenue from regulators, not customers.

[62]AT&T directory of "Directors, Officers amd Principal Organization Heads of the Bell System," August 1, 1974.
[63]Charles L. Brown, interview, September 5, 1985, pp. 12–14; deButts, interview, October 25, 1984, p. 47; Archibald J. McGill, interview, June 20, 1985, pp. 8, 15.

They issued announcements that the FCC had given them so many millions of dollars when it approved a rate increase. Despite these unusual quirks, the Bell System had over the years been remarkably resilient; its members saw themselves as engaged in a holy mission of service. The Bell culture was as deeply rooted and as well integrated with the corporation as any such belief system in the history of this nation's business.[64]

The System endured, of course, because it worked. Even with an occasional lapse like the 1969 service crisis, the Bell System gave service unparalleled in the world, at least to its residential customers upon whom state regulators focused their and consequently the Bell System's attention.[65] Bell Labs was the premier private research organization in the world. The Labs and Western Electric worked together smoothly to keep the network efficient, innovative, and technologically integrated; these two organizations had, after all, been the source of systems engineering as it had developed in this country. It was thus hardly surprising when a management consultant found in the mid-1960s that Western was performing magnificently as a supplier to the Bell System, selling products for half of the price at which they could be obtained elsewhere.[66]

One measure of the System's long-term success was the fact that telephone prices fell in real terms even as the quality of telephone service improved. We are all able to dial directly to increasingly distant and obscure places, obtaining rapid and often clear connections undreamed of a generation ago. We get detailed bills showing toll calls individually that are only dreamed of in other countries. The cost of monthly residential telephone service relative to other consumer prices is shown in Figure 5. It fell by more than half in the years after 1940, and the cost of long distance calls declined even further. The impact of the separations process was clear. In 1947, when separations began, real monthly rates for residential customers fell sharply. As more of the costs of the local plant were allocated to interstate rates in 1955, local rates held steady. Then successive increases in this allocation, most notably in the Ozark Plan, channeled the improved efficiency of the Bell System into lower local residential rates.

For all its merits, however, the Bell System was poorly adapted to promoting internal organizational change. It was designed to bring the fruits of the new technology discovered at Bell Labs to consumers efficiently, not to cope with competition. The System consequently dealt with the service crises in New York and elsewhere much better than it did with the FCC's new policies. Installers and repairmen were rushed

---

[64]Gradle, interview, November 16, 1984, p. 15; Frederick W. Gluck, interview, September 23, 1985, p. 61; McGill, interview, June 20, 1985, pp. 6–9; William G. Sharwell, interview, July 10, 1985, pp. 97–8, 102.

[65]McGill, interview, June 20, 1985, p. 16; Kenneth J. Whalen, interview, July 18, 1985, pp. 32–3.

[66]McKinsey & Company, Inc., "A Study of Western Electric's Performance," March 1969; Gluck, interview, September 23, 1985, p. 5.

Figure 5. The real cost of monthly residential telephone service, 1940–1983. (Source: CPI component of the monthly charge for individual residence telephone service divided by the CPI; 1967 = 100.)

to New York, and – despite a crippling strike in the midst of the reconstruction – service was restored to normal within a few months.[67] The service crisis had marshaled the corporation's cultural and technological resources – its traditional strengths. By contrast, the implications of *Carterfone* for the internal organization of the Bell System received very little attention within the organization. For example, Robert Lilley, president of New Jersey Bell, heard from McKinsey and Company that the uniform approach to all customers of the regulated firm would have to be replaced by a focus on different market segments, particularly on large business customers. But Romnes tapped Lilley to come to 195 Broadway as an executive vice president to revamp AT&T's employee compensation

---

[67] A few service problems persisted for some time in isolated situations. See, for example, American Telephone and Telegraph Company, *1970 Annual Report*, *1972 Annual Report*, and *1974 Annual Report*.

plans before Lilley could act on this advice, and his successor in New Jersey did not pursue the consultant's suggestions.[68]

As was evident at the 1971 Presidents' Conference, the Bell System's problems would not be solved by ignoring them. At first AT&T had – as we have seen – behaved like most large bureaucracies, public or private, and had dealt with its extraordinary circumstances by creating ad hoc committees. The Broadband Planning Group and the Tariff Review Committee were only two of the temporary bodies formed during the 1960s. By 1970, however, it was evident that the corporation needed a more permanent and powerful group to chart an appropriate strategy for coping with its rapidly changing environment. It was symptomatic of the Bell System's nature that no such planning group existed at corporate headquarters; although AT&T had an enormous staff, it served operations, not planning. There was a "cabinet," composed of AT&T's top officers and the presidents of Western Electric and Bell Labs, which met on alternate Mondays. But although these meetings kept open a communication channel within the firm, the gatherings were too formal for serious discussion. More promising was the so-called Odd Monday Group, which met on alternate weeks and included the chairman and the officers reporting directly to him. Romnes decided to dignify that group with a better name – the Executive Policy Committee (EPC) – and to make it over into a body capable of providing long-range strategic planning and continuing oversight of company policy. It would be staffed by the Management Sciences Division, which was transferred to the EPC at the start of 1971. The division was headed by Henry Boettinger, who had played a leading part in the Broadband Planning Group a decade earlier, and it quickly began to generate ideas for the EPC to consider.[69]

As one might imagine, Boettinger's division was more open to radical departures in firm strategy than was the EPC. Initially the EPC included only Romnes, Moulton, Lilley, and John deButts (vice-chairman of the board). Alvin von Auw (assistant to the chairman) served as the committee's secretary, and his agendas and minutes helped to transform the amorphous Odd Monday Group into a strong planning organization. The EPC's membership was limited to AT&T's most senior executives and was characterized by their long experience in the Bell System, typically about thirty years. It thus embodied the myths and traditions of the network and the technological imperative that was at the heart of the Bell System.[70]

[68]Gluck, interview, September 23, 1985, pp. 4–8; Lilley, interview, September 23, 1985, pp. 33–4.
[69]Alvin von Auw, *Heritage & Destiny*, p. 310; H.I. Romnes, "Organization Notice," December 17, 1970. See also Management Sciences Division (MSD), "Report of Activities, 1971–72," February 14, 1972.
[70]H.I. Romnes's Opening Remarks at the Presidents' Meeting, Cleveland, Ohio, September 22, 1970.

The committee frequently stumbled over those traditions as it guided AT&T's policy responses to a rapidly changing environment.

At first, the EPC's effectiveness was also limited by Romnes's action, or rather inaction, when the president of AT&T retired in 1970. At that crucial time, Romnes was beginning to experience the illness that would increasingly debilitate him and cause his death only three years later. Nevertheless, he did not replace the Bell System's retiring chief operating officer. He assumed the president's job himself, in addition to the chairmanship. As a result, more of his time had to be devoted to operations and less to policy formation at a time when his energy level was falling. This crucial decision undercut his attempts to provide AT&T with the strong leadership the business clearly needed in the early 1970s.

Romnes was able to guide the firm through the first step in the process of corporate adaptations, that of articulating new goals. Further growth, Romnes told the Bell company presidents, was not an appropriate goal. AT&T was already the largest company in the world, and universal service had been achieved. Over 90 percent of American households had telephones by 1970.[71] Instead, Romnes said, the Bell System's goal would be "the continuous enhancement of the service we provide to the users of our switched network." Private lines were a useful source of revenue, but the switched network should be the primary focus of AT&T's activities. The firm's natural monopoly, its leader was willing to admit by 1970, did not extend to private lines. AT&T would compete in these peripheral markets, but they would remain at the edge both of the telephone network and of the Bell System's attention.[72]

Romnes was articulating a complex position. The company's natural monopoly, the switched network, had reached its mature extent in his view. Outside the network – in private lines and terminal equipment – no natural monopoly existed, and there AT&T would compete with everyone else. In effect, Romnes was drawing the mantle of natural monopoly closer while simultaneously reaching out to compete, and that combination of strategic objectives posed several hard questions for AT&T's leadership. How intensely should the company compete with the terminal equipment suppliers and the MCIs? How was it to manage the dual task of competing in these markets and enhancing its service in its monopoly switched network? The conflict was clear. The traditions of the network were framed in terms appropriate to the monopoly alone; it was not obvious how the competitive element would mesh with those traditions. Von Auw asked AT&T's top management in mid-1970 why, if AT&T agreed that competition was appropriate in private lines and elsewhere,

---

[71]*Bell System Statistical Manual 1950–1981*, p. 504.
[72]H.I. Romnes, "Closing Remarks," EPC/Presidents' Meeting, Washington, D.C., March 16, 1972; Alvin von Auw, "Statement of Position for the EPC," September 18, 1970.

"do our representations to regulatory authorities convey an impression of reluctance on our part that is too often interpreted as a desire to preserve our monopoly position?"[73]

A report of a panel of economic advisors to AT&T that same year echoed the discussion in 1970 between Baxter and Trienens. With Baxter, the economists – William Baumol of Princeton, Otto Eckstein of Harvard, and Alfred Kahn of Cornell – insisted that "Inherent in the concept of full competition and its benefits is the freedom to fail." Like Trienens, they deplored that mixture of competition and regulation in which a regulator protects the competitors, dividing the market among them. "Society," they asserted, "should certainly be unwilling to accept . . . the introduction of competitors along with the prevention of competition." But having stated the danger, the company's economic advisors failed to tell AT&T how to avoid it. Would competition be viable in a market containing the largest company in the world and a scattering of small entrants? Who would make the political decision that this situation would be acceptable? The economists ignored both the economic and political problems of instituting competition in telecommunications. They seconded Baxter's appeal for competitive experiments dependent on the "freedom to fail," but they had nothing to say about the political pressures that such failures would generate – pressures that would set the stage for Trienens's scenario. AT&T's economic guides spotted the minotaur, but they offered no suggestions as to how the firm's managers might escape from his maze.[74]

These discussions were academic and hypothetical, but they struck at the heart of the issues that Romnes and the EPC were grappling with at the time. Customer-owned terminal equipment was providing one of those problems. Despite Romnes's assurances, PCAs turned out to be neither cheap nor freely available. The owners of independent terminal equipment protested to the FCC that Western Electric's PCAs were too expensive and too often unavailable, and the Commission turned to the National Academy of Sciences for advice.[75] Earlier, Strassburg had relied on the parties involved to obtain information about microwave radio systems, but he was no longer willing to use that adjudicatory procedure. His decision to seek disinterested advice (and the Commission's contemporaneous institution of Bell System service quality indexes) revealed Bell's

---

[73]Alvin von Auw, "EPC Discussion Items for Follow-up," July 31, 1970.

[74]William J. Baumol, Otto Eckstein, and Alfred E. Kahn, "Competition and Monopoly in Telecommunications Services," November 23, 1970, reprinted in Hearings before the Subcommittee on Antitrust and Monopoly, Committee on the Judiciary, 93rd Congress, 1st Session, Senate, S. 1167, "The Industrial Reorganization Act," July 30-August 2, 1973, pp. 1333–49. See also the review of the Baumol et al. report by F.M. Scherer, *Antitrust Bulletin*, Vol. 16 (Winter 1971), pp. 963–9.

[75]*US v. AT&T*, CA No. 74–1698 (D.D.C.), Lowell E. Hoxie, testimony, March 10, 1981, Tr. 885–6, 914; Charles F. Rice, president, Rice International Corp., to Stuart W. Patton, Esq., September 13, 1971.

fall from grace at the FCC. No longer was the Bell System automatically judged to be the primary reliable source of information about the network. By the early 1970s, in fact, the network was beginning to acquire an abstract identity apart from the Bell System, and AT&T was becoming only one of many contending parties in its disposition.[76]

As these changes were taking place, the FCC pushed slowly ahead toward a decision on how non-Bell equipment should be attached to the network. The National Academy's panel of experts looked into the question of terminal connection and reported to the FCC in mid-1970. The report was so qualified that everyone found support for his views. The FCC emphasized the report's affirmation that more access could be provided as support for a less restrictive program than existed. AT&T emphasized the panel's insistence that care be taken when enlarging access and saw the report as a vindication of its own caution.[77] That, of course, prompted yet another study, this one by Dittberner Associates, which substantially agreed with the National Academy report. The FCC then formed a joint federal-state committee to consider terminal interconnection. Based on the results of all of these studies, the Commission announced in 1972 its intention to institute a program of registration, that is, permission for people to connect terminal equipment to the telephone network at will, subject only to the requirement that they register their equipment with the FCC. The FCC convened a joint federal-state committee to work out the details of its plan and resolve any jurisdictional questions that might arise.[78]

Even before the FCC made its decision, Boettinger's planning group had urged the EPC to preempt the Commission and accept registration. In words that echoed von Auw's, the staff planners urged "that we act on our own initiative rather than give the appearance of a belated and reluctant response that would inevitably be interpreted – indeed has been interpreted, as stemming from a desire to retain a protected market."[79] The specific suggestion was to "unbundle" tariffs, that is, to charge separately for equipment and access to the network, in order to prepare for competition in equipment. A Presidents' Meeting in September 1972 endorsed

---

[76]Bernard Strassburg, "The Development of the Telephone Network and Regulation of 'Foreign Attachments' Prior to Carterfone," unpublished, undated paper.

[77]National Academy of Sciences, "A Technical Analysis of the Common Carrier/User Interconnections Area," Report to the FCC Common Carrier Bureau, June 1970.

[78]FCC, *Notice of Inquiry, Proposed Rulemaking, and Creation of Federal-State Joint Board*, FCC Docket 19528, "Interstate and Foreign MTS and WATS," June 16, 1972, 35 FCC 2d 539, *aff'd sub nom. North Carolina Utils. Comm'n v. FCC*, 552 F.2d 1036 (4th Cir. 1976), *cert. denied*, 434 U.S. 874, 1977.

[79]AT&T, Management Sciences Division, "Certification of Customer-Provided Telephone Equipment: An Overview," May 10, 1971, p. 13.

this unbundled tariff, known internally as "network access pricing," but it approved only its development, not its implementation.[80]

The EPC, meanwhile, was considering its options relating to MCI. One possibility was to file a special tariff for the newly competitive Chicago–St. Louis route. Alternatively, national tariffs could be revised to lower rates on all heavily utilized routes, to move away from regulatory toward competitive prices in a more decisive way. Boettinger's group asked the EPC to decide just how competitive it wanted to be – overwhelming, permissive, or weak – and whether it proposed to meet all challengers.[81] But the committee was still hesitant to frame in such all-encompassing terms the precise manner in which it would break with Bell's traditional mode of operations. It did nevertheless decide that a special tariff in MCI's market looked more attractive in 1971 than a revision of national rates. A tariff for this single route was drafted and sent around for comments. Accompanying material to be submitted with the tariff quoted the FCC's statement in *Specialized Common Carriers* that departures from uniform nationwide pricing practices may be in order where services are in direct competition.[82]

Among others, the special tariff was sent to the three economists serving as AT&T's economic advisory board. Baumol reported that he was "more than a little uncomfortable." He proposed several sharp questions for the EPC. Like Howard Trienens, Baumol wanted to know what the company proposed to do if MCI went out of business. The economic advisors had said in their memorandum on competition that suspected predators should be required to maintain competitive prices even after the competition had left. Baumol said that failure to maintain a low price on the St. Louis–Chicago route would appear to be "deliberately destructive competition." He continued: What did the company propose to do about other routes? Was it going to rely on the MCI example to scare off other potential entrants? He suggested that the FCC staff was just waiting for such a proposal to ban all similar AT&T responses to competition.[83]

The EPC wavered and then, hesitantly, decided not to act. At first, it discussed the problem with Baumol and decided to proceed with the special tariff nonetheless.[84] But the committee considered the tariff again

[80]Alvin von Auw, "Summary," EPC/Presidents' Meeting, September 22, 1971.
[81]AT&T, Management Sciences Division, "Competing in the Intercity Private Line Market," October 15, 1971.
[82]Minutes of the EPC meeting, December 6, 1971; AT&T draft revision of Tariff 260, November 16, 1971; FCC, *First Report and Order*, FCC Docket 18920, May 25, 1971, 29 FCC 2d 870 at ¶ 89.
[83]William J. Baumol to Richard B. Holt, November 12, 1971; Otto Eckstein to Richard B. Holt, November 17, 1971; Alfred E. Kahn to Richard B. Holt, November 17, 1971.
[84]Alvin von Auw to EPC members, November 23, 1971; Alvin von Auw to John D. deButts, Robert D. Lilley, et al., December 3, 1971.

in February 1972, when it observed that MCI had only 14 customers using 18 circuits and that the Bell System had received only three disconnect orders. A special tariff would provide a clear declaration of AT&T's competitive intent, testing the FCC's new rules and discouraging potential competitors. Would it, however, be overkill, since MCI was still tiny and operating at a loss? There were, after all, other and larger examples of cream skimming, and the tariff likely would provoke either a regulatory or an antitrust response. The Tariff Review Committee recommended that the St. Louis–Chicago tariff not be filed and that a nationwide plan–the Hi-Lo tariff–should be prepared instead for filing later in the year. The EPC reluctantly agreed.[85]

At this point, the EPC felt itself besieged. Romnes had stated that he welcomed competition, at least outside the switched network. But now applicants were washing away the edges of the network, and the committee was having trouble developing a convincing corporate strategy. It had debated overreactions and underreactions; it had searched in vain for a balanced response to its rapidly changing environment. The new corporate goal articulated by Romnes–enhancing the network's capabilities– was not generating the specific guidelines management needed to cope with the sudden transformation that had occurred in the company's economic and political environments.

One result of AT&T's indecision was, quite naturally, internal ferment in the Bell System. Romnes had earlier recognized what was happening and had convened a Presidents' Meeting in Detroit on June 17, 1971, with only one item on the agenda: organization. He opened the discussion by referring to "the alarming growth in some places of service complaints to top management and regulatory authorities." He surmised that the Bell System's "failings apparently have been not so much technological failings as human failings, organizational failings." He turned the group's attention to a variety of ad hoc organizations that had been set up in the operating companies to correct or ameliorate these failings.

Just as ad hoc committees at 195 Broadway had evolved into the EPC, some of the special organizations already in existence might form the models for a more general reorganization. Kenneth Whalen, president of Michigan Bell, told of that company's Special Action Team. Charles Brown, president of Illinois Bell, described his Urban Customer Service Units, structured to respond rapidly and personally to complaints from alienated customers in large cities like Chicago; he also mentioned a

---

[85]Tariff Review Committee materials prepared for the EPC meeting, February 8, 1972. See also Baumol testimony in *US* v. *AT&T*, where he claimed parentage of the Hi-Lo tariff on behalf of AT&T's Council of Economic Advisors. *US* v. *AT&T*, CA No. 74–1698 (D.D.C.), William J. Baumol, testimony, December 7, 1981, Tr. 23210–12.

special group designed to compete vigorously in the business terminal market. Thomas Bolger, president of the Chesapeake and Potomac Bell Companies, described his attempt to deal with the same problem in northern Virginia. Romnes brought these experiments to the attention of the assembled presidents, suggesting that they formed a pattern. Each special group might appear to be a unique response to a particular situation. But the growing number of these groups suggested strongly that AT&T as a whole was going to have to respond to changes in the markets in which it operated.

But as yet – and ominously so – none of these experiments in organizational adaptation had taken place at the active behest of 195 Broadway. Indeed, such experiments had been explicitly enjoined. At the Detroit meeting, Romnes had remarked on the ambiguous relationship between the operating companies and AT&T headquarters at 195 Broadway. "Some of you," he said to the assembled presidents, "would like to know the answer to a simple question: 'Who's my boss?' On the other hand, there are some of you, I suspect, who would just as soon not know." But having remarked on the breakdown of the central organization, Romnes did not attempt to clarify the lines of authority; instead he assigned each member of the EPC to be the "representative" of a group of operating companies in order to facilitate communication. Consensus, not command, would be the recourse. The broader questions of organization facing AT&T would be left unresolved.[86]

AT&T had surely lost its way. A study by an outside consultant found that managers in the firm's General Departments felt themselves underutilized. They did not see 195 Broadway as "a purposeful unified entity with a significant, broadly understood mission." They were "disturbed by what they perceive[d] as uncertainties with respect to the goals of the business and the resolution of problems confronting it."[87] Romnes, ill and about to retire, told a Presidents' Meeting in March 1972, "It is a matter of personal regret that my retirement comes at a time when the Bell System does not stand as high in public repute as it has in the past."[88] He had tried to turn the Bell System toward competition but had failed. He had tried to reorient the System's massive bureaucracy and had, by 1972, only created confusion and dismay.

The choice of his successor was therefore all important. There were two leading candidates for the job. One was John deButts, vice chairman of

[86]H.I. Romnes, "Organization," prepared for the Presidents' Conference, Detroit, Michigan, June 17, 1971.
[87]Minutes of the EPC meeting, March 22, 1972; FCC Docket 19129, "AT&T, Charges for Interstate Services," FCC Staff Exhibit 6, "Study of AT&T Headquarters Personnel," by Stanley Peterfreund Associates, November 1, 1971.
[88]H.I. Romnes, "Closing Remarks," EPC/Presidents' Meeting, Washington, D.C., March 16, 1972.

the board. The other was Robert Lilley, executive vice president of AT&T. Both men were at the top of the Bell System hierarchy; they were the only operating officers in the original EPC. Both also had begun to initiate badly needed reforms. Lilley was attempting to solve the System's morale problems, and deButts had begun to centralize AT&T's budgetary process, introducing a new commitment budget in which operating companies forecast their earnings and linked their planned construction to those estimates.[89] But there the similarity ended. Lilley was a man in Romnes's mold. Like the current chairman, he had come up through Western Electric (although not Bell Labs); he had far less experience in the operating companies than deButts. Like Romnes, he was a highly intelligent, introspective man. He worked well with people and was interested in personnel matters, but he was not a commanding presence like deButts. Lilley favored compromise over confrontation; he represented continuity. DeButts signified forceful management, change, and potential confrontation.[90]

Romnes hesitated in the face of this difficult choice. He had not favored one man over the other by making him president of AT&T; he had kept this option open. At almost the last moment, Romnes finally selected John deButts as his successor and the board of directors ratified his choice. Romnes told his friend Lilley that the company needed a leader steeped in the telephone side of the business. That was John deButts, who became chairman of the board. As president of AT&T, Lilley would handle the administrative side of the business.[91]

Many turning points in this history were made by the narrowest of margins. The vote on the FCC's fateful *MCI* decision was only four to three. The election of deButts as chairman of AT&T's board was a similarly close choice. Once made, these decisions would force events to move in new directions. John deButts would uproot most of the innovative policies that Romnes had cultivated but had been unable to bring to fruition. DeButts would institute at AT&T a new regime that would marshal all of the Bell System's traditional strengths, but would force the company into a deadly confrontation with federal authority.

[89]Brown, interview, September 5, 1985, pp. 12–14.
[90]Lilley, interview, September 23, 1985, pp. 11–15, 32–5; Alvin von Auw, interview, February 10, 1984, p. 27.
[91]Lilley, interview, September 23, 1985, pp. 21–2; deButts, interview, October 25, 1984, pp. 52–3, 59; H.I. Romnes, Address to assistant vice presidents' staff luncheon, February 14, 1972.

H. I. Romnes, chairman of the board and chief executive officer of AT&T from 1967 to 1972.

John D. deButts, chairman of the board and chief executive officer of AT&T from 1972 to 1979.

III

Action and reaction

John deButts and "the decision to decide"

AT&T's board of directors had opted for charismatic leadership; John deButts would impose his authority on the sprawling Bell System and give it purpose. He would do so by drawing on the traditional conception of the Bell System rather than by articulating a new one. He would lead the company out of its early 1970s doldrums by energizing its management, by reasserting the role of 195 Broadway in the Bell System's decision-making process, and by inspiring the System's many employees to believe again that the corporation's familiar goals – the objectives Vail had given it – were laudable and achievable. On the other hand, deButts would try to launch the complex process of adapting the Bell System to the changing conditions it faced. He would introduce elements that in time would alter the Bell System's fundamental strategy. But the main thrust of his approach to both company strategy and public policy was conservative. As he reaffirmed the traditional culture and made the existing System run more efficiently, he would actually be making it more difficult for his innovations within the firm to take hold. In that sense, he would be trapped by his own finest achievements.[1]

On April 1, 1972, deButts took charge of a Bell System in deep trouble. The service crises in New York and other cities had shaken the Bell System's self-image as a flawless service organization and tarnished its reputation. Earnings had stopped growing. The regulatory decisions of the previous half-decade had opened up parts of the network – as yet, still small parts – to competition. The discussion of telecommunications, both within AT&T and in various governmental forums, increasingly emphasized the legitimacy of competition in this industry.

AT&T's new chairman had two basic and potentially conflicting problems to solve. He needed to get Bell back up to its normal standard of

---

[1]Selznick has written that aggressive leadership is most often conspicuous by its absence in crises. Typical sins are those of omission, not – as in deButts's case – of commission. See Philip Selznick, *Leadership in Administration: A Sociological Interpretation* (Evanston, Ill.: Row, Peterson, 1957).

performance and profitability in its traditional activities: furnishing plain old telephone service. But equally, he needed to develop a coherent policy toward the emerging competition in private lines and in terminal equipment. Romnes had welcomed competition in terminal equipment and supported the beleaguered troops in New York, but he had failed to provide a compelling and consistent policy that would focus the System's efforts. As a result, in 1972 the Bell System clearly lacked the overall policy it needed to function effectively in its changing environment.

DeButts quickly began to provide the System with the leadership it lacked. He was a gregarious, articulate, aggressive manager who delighted in vigorous discussion and decisive action. Unlike Romnes, who was an engineer at heart, a quiet, contemplative man, deButts was outspoken, challenging, and imperious. Although less than a year of Romnes's career had been with an operating company, deButts had spent twenty-five years with one or another member of the Bell System. Romnes had advanced through Bell Labs, AT&T headquarters, and Western Electric. DeButts had worked for the Chesapeake and Potomac Telephone Company, New York Telephone, and Illinois Bell. In the 1950s he had spent one year in Washington, D.C., as part of AT&T's staff on government relations, but most of his experience was in operations, running the telephone business. He had joined AT&T headquarters at 195 Broadway in 1966 and became vice chairman the following year. In 1972 deButts thus came to the chairman's job with a very different perception of the company than Romnes. Technology and the design of the network were not at the center of deButts's mission. Relations between AT&T and the operating companies were. DeButts would never ask, even rhetorically, whether he was the boss of the operating companies' presidents; he would not tolerate that degree of ambiguity.

Forceful as he was, deButts recognized that he needed to develop a managerial consensus if he was going to improve morale and achieve his goals within the business. He would keep the iron hand in a velvet glove. Careful discussion and reiteration of his policies would characterize his leadership. As wags in the Bell System said, an exchange of views with deButts involved walking into his office with your ideas and walking out with his.

AT&T's new CEO recognized that his first task was to clarify and affirm the Bell System's goals. Morale was dangerously low. The operating company presidents were perturbed by the lack of direction from AT&T's corporate headquarters. They had begun to experiment with new policies and operating procedures on their own, but it was clear that systemwide responses were needed to the major problems Bell was facing. DeButts's primary mission would be to convince the managers and employees to pursue the goals he had selected. There were a million employees in the Bell System and tens of thousands of managers; deButts had to get his message to this mass of people if he was going to make the Bell System a vital business again. He entered the chairmanship on the run, determined to develop and quickly implement the coherent policy that AT&T needed.[2]

The outlines of the deButts strategy emerged very quickly. Romnes had proclaimed that he welcomed competition; deButts stated unequivocally that he did not. AT&T would compete and compete well, he said, if the FCC continued to encourage entry into the telecommunications markets. But if he had a choice – if AT&T had a choice – the national telephone network would be run as a regulated monopoly. As deButts explained: "We need to ask ourselves whether the benefits classically attributed to competition – a quickened pace of innovation, a broader range of customer options and lower prices – would in fact flow from the introduction of competition in an industry universally recognized as unrivaled in technological innovation, an industry that has generated an explosive diversification of its services in recent years, an industry that has done a better job than any other that I know of in keeping prices down." With a paean for Vail's ideal of universal service, deButts answered his own question with an emphatic No![3]

At the same time that he emphasized the importance of the Vail tradition, deButts moved to refurbish the Bell System, to bring it into line with its changing environment. Echoing Gifford, he stressed service as the organization's main task: "Service . . . is our only product, our only reason for being. If we don't meet the public's expectations, the public will make other arrangements." But, he continued, " 'other arrangements' will have to be made in any event if we don't remain a viable business – that is, a profitable one."[4] In what would become a trademark of his speeches within the Bell System, deButts linked the need to furnish high-quality telephone service and the need for satisfactory earnings.

The price of AT&T's stock had sagged badly in the late 1960s and early 1970s, threatening the firm's ability to fund adequate capital expenditures in the years ahead. If stock could not be sold on favorable terms, the company would have to sell more bonds – raising its already high debt/equity ratio – or put off the construction of new and improved facilities. Low earnings and high interest rates in the 1960s had translated into a slowdown in the construction of new plant, a bird that had come home to

[2]For another view of this transition that emphasizes continuity rather than change, see Alvin von Auw, *Heritage & Destiny: Reflections on the Bell System in Transition* (New York: Praeger Publishers, 1983), p. 160.
[3]John D. deButts, speech at a New York Telephone Company management meeting, April 28, 1972, p. 12.
[4]John D. deButts, "Closing Remarks," Presidents' Conference, Key Largo, Florida, May 12, 1972, p. 3.

roost in 1969. The Bell System's new leader was determined to forestall another service crisis. He wanted to eliminate "weak spots" in the network, and to achieve that goal, earnings had to be improved: "Over a period of years, then," deButts reiterated, "service and earnings *must* track."[5]

When the presidents of the Bell Operating Companies gathered for their regular spring conference in Key Largo, Florida, in May 1972, they had ample opportunity to discuss the System's poor earnings. DeButts noted just before the conference that more than half of AT&T's shareholders had paid more for their shares than they could sell them for and that earnings had been "essentially flat" for two years.[6] Vice President Alvin von Auw followed deButts's opening remarks at the conference by noting that the number one priority of the assembled company presidents – as shown by their suggestions for the conference agenda – was the System's lack of profitability. "Our earnings problems continue to be so critical," one president had insisted, that "it is difficult to put a top priority on anything else." Better management of capital expenditures and rate relief were needed. Systemwide coordinated action was necessary if Bell was to avoid providing "substandard service in these days of vocally effective and irritable consumers."[7] Chairman deButts admonished the presidents to control expenses, sharpen depreciation practices, and handle inventories more efficiently. We are not, he said, "managing as well as we know how."[8]

To run the Bell System more effectively, as deButts well realized, AT&T had to make decisions promptly on the major issues that had arisen in the early 1970s. He had already asked the presidents what they felt were the central problems. Eschewing "formal presentations by the learned gentlemen of 195 Broadway," the corporate headquarters, he threw the conference open to the discussion that he hoped would provide AT&T's top officers with "the context of experience and opinion" that would enable them to set a firm course for the Bell System. By long tradition, no decisions were to be made at the conference, but they would follow soon after the Key Largo meeting. "Let me assure you, gentlemen, we are going to make those decisions. Not all of them will be right. Some will change as conditions change. But we are going to decide – and you are going to know in language just as clear as we can make it what we have decided." The

[5]Ibid., emphasis in the original.
[6]John D. deButts, speech at a New York Telephone Company management meeting, April 28, 1972, p. 5.
[7]Alvin von Auw, "Priorities," Presidents' Conference, Key Largo, Florida, May 8, 1972, p. 1.
[8]John D. deButts, "Closing Remarks," Presidents' Conference, Key Largo, Florida, May 12, 1972, p. 2.

chairman had announced what came to be known in the Bell System as "the decision to decide."[9]

Although deButts left no doubt about who would make the decisions and when they would be made, he wanted managers throughout the Bell System to have the opportunity to voice their concerns. He wanted to inspire, not force, change. He was dealing with an organization that had a deeply ingrained culture and a structure of authority that had remained virtually unchanged since Theodore Vail had created it. It was as well an organization that could not afford any lapse in service while it retooled; the Bell System had to work 24 hours a day, 365 days a year. Given the company traditions of meticulous planning, decentralization, and slow but certain innovation, there was the danger that deButts might find himself separated from his troops. He worked very hard to avoid that fate.

The open discussion at the conference ranged over many topics, including the FCC's introduction of competition into the private line market. Several of the assembled presidents expressed hostility toward competition and – in the spirit of deButts's own approach – urged a vigorous response. Thomas Nurnberger, president of Northwestern Bell, declared: "I would meet 'em or beat 'em. You bastards are not going to take away my business." Charles Brown, president of Illinois Bell, appeared to concur: "[We] must take [into] account [the] prospect of intrastate competition. Large amount[s] of revenues [are] vulnerable which we can preserve if we choke [it or perhaps them?] off now. I think you have to hit the nails on the head." No decisions were taken at Key Largo on this or any other matter, but MCI and the Justice Department later attacked AT&T for Nurnberger's and Brown's expressions of opinion. Some critics even labeled the conference a secret meeting, an odd description for a regularly scheduled semiannual conference of Bell Operating Company presidents – a conference largely devoted to internal management problems.[10]

[9]In one example of the open discussion, Mark Garlinghouse, soon to become AT&T's general counsel, proposed that capital spending in each state be limited to the increase in net revenues from that state. This suggestion was aimed at the California regulatory commission, which was refusing to approve rate increases for Pacific Telephone in the (accurate) belief that AT&T would continue to invest in unprofitable states. Although not adopted, it expressed the fears that Trienens would echo later of raids by state regulators on AT&T's resources.

Minutes of the EPC Meeting, July 5, 1972; F. Mark Garlinghouse to Alvin von Auw, April 10, 1972; John D. deButts, "Opening Remarks," p. 3, and "Closing Remarks," p. 3, Presidents' Conference, Key Largo, Florida, May 8–12, 1972; John D. deButts, speech to assistant vice presidents' staff luncheon, New York, June 19, 1972, p. 3.

[10]Alvin von Auw, handwritten notes of the Presidents' Conference, Key Largo, Florida, May 10, 1972, pp. 12, 13. Brown's words are unclear due to the cryptic nature of von Auw's notes. Brown did not remember them well enough to elucidate their meaning when he was asked about them in the MCI trial eight years later. *MCI* v. *AT&T*, No. 74 C 633, U.S. Dist. Ct., Northern Dist. of Illinois, Eastern Division, Charles L. Brown, testimony, May 20, 1980, Tr. 9233–5, 9266. For the most recent misinterpretation of the Key Largo conference, see Steve Coll, *The Deal of the Century* (New York: Atheneum, 1986), chap. 1.

As the Key Largo gathering closed, deButts outlined his responses to the questions raised and the solutions posed. The financial crisis could be eased to some extent, he said, by better management and cost cutting. But the Bell System needed a new approach to budgeting and planning for capital expenditures. It needed many other changes as well – some major, some minor – if it was going to maintain the quality of its service. DeButts consequently asked von Auw to make a list of all of the commitments he had made when he returned to New York. DeButts had announced a decision to decide, and he wanted a mechanism to ensure that he did. Von Auw listed twenty-three "direct and implied" commitments that had been made, and he continued to track the manner in which each of these policies was implemented during the rest of the year. John deButts had launched his chairmanship in a dramatic style. He continued to keep the pressure on during the months that followed.[11]

Decisive as he was about internal company policy, deButts remained hesitant about the Bell System's stance toward terminal equipment. AT&T, despite its initial rush under Romnes to open up the network to customer-owned equipment, was unenthusiastic about the FCC's proposed certification or registration program. The company's technical managers had been overwhelmed at the time of *Carterfone* by the prospect of sharing responsibility for electrical connections with a group of amateurs. Their fears had declined over time as the anticipated horrors failed to materialize. The engineers were ready by 1972 to advance beyond Romnes's position, but their fears had proven contagious within the Bell System. Nontechnical managers were now obsessed with the possibility of harm to the network. This concern had become a lightning rod for all internal opposition – commercial, ideological, technical – to the use of independent terminal equipment. Afraid in the regulatory climate of 1972 to reject certification flatly, deButts instead remarked to the presidents of the Bell Operating Companies that the System still lacked a consistent position on this issue.[12]

It still lacked a clear policy in August 1972, when Boettinger came to the

[11]Alvin von Auw to John D. deButts, May 16, 1972; John D. deButts, speech to assistant vice presidents' staff luncheon, New York, June 19, 1972; Alvin von Auw, "Status of EPC Action on Presidents' Conference Commitments," October 6, 1972; von Auw to deButts, Progress Report on "Decision to Decide," March 1, 1973.
[12]John D. deButts, "Closing Remarks," Presidents' Conference, Key Largo, Florida, May 12, 1972, p. 5. DeButts also closed a discussion of recent FCC actions at AT&T's first annual meeting under his chairmanship by asserting that the company was cooperating in studies of certification. But he added, "We will continue to have grave reservations about this development unless and until it can be demonstrated that suitable standards and enforcement procedures can be developed to assure that the equipment is made right, that it is installed right and that it is maintained properly. The quality of service is our first concern." John D. deButts, "Remarks of the Chairman," Annual Meeting, Denver, Colorado, April 19, 1972, p. 9.

EPC with a new and radical proposal. He suggested that AT&T's leaders consider abandoning their efforts to predict and forestall in advance what harms would come from interconnection. These efforts were unconvincing to the outside world – the harms were largely hypothetical – and they had lost their force among AT&T's technical staff. Boettinger proposed that AT&T consider using a tort regulatory system. Anyone would be allowed to connect devices to the network, with the Bell System reserving the right to take appropriate action if damage occurred. But this call for a sharp break with AT&T's traditional policy fell on deaf ears. The EPC formally decided to oppose certification in March 1973. Unlike Romnes, deButts would not relinquish the Bell System's end-to-end responsibility, at least not without a fight.[13]

AT&T also settled with difficulty on a policy for dealing with MCI. The EPC kept track of this still small, albeit noisy, firm's commercial progress in deButts's first year as CEO, noting prominently the contrast between its small current size and its grandiose plans for expansion.[14] William McGowan went to see John deButts at 195 Broadway in the summer of 1972. Both men remembered this meeting as cordial. But McGowan also recalled that deButts explained that he could not respond to *MCI* with the welcoming stance Romnes had taken after *Carterfone*. He could not welcome competition and look for mutual benefit because the stock market was so bearish on AT&T. Investors thought that MCI would reduce the Bell System's profits, and deButts had to heed their concerns. If indeed he expressed this position – and we have only McGowan's recollection to go on – then deButts's new strategy was partially driven by the financial worries that had been so prominent at the Presidents' Conferences outside Chicago in 1971 and at Key Largo in 1972.[15]

That motivation seems consistent with the action the EPC subsequently took on pricing in response to competition. The committee had considered, accepted, and then finally rejected the idea of an exception tariff for the St. Louis–Chicago route. What was needed, the committee decided, was a systemwide response, and it debated the precise nature of that policy throughout deButts's first year. It adopted as a starting point the Tariff Revenue Committee's Hi-Lo tariff. The proposed tariff divided private line services into high-density, low-density, and short-haul (less than 25 miles) categories and set different rates for each. The tariff charged rates for high-density lines – such as those linking St. Louis and

[13]Henry M. Boettinger, Memorandum: "An Idea for Indirect Approach to Two Major Problems," August 28, 1972, p. 6. The need for an appeal process after the fact was recognized from the start. Minutes of the EPC meeting, March 19, 1973, p. 2.
[14]William W. Betteridge, Vu-Graphs used for talk "Hi/Lo with Telpak," EPC meeting, November 9, 1972.
[15]Ralph Nader and William Taylor, *The Big Boys* (New York: Pantheon Books, 1986), pp. 399–401.

Chicago – that were one-third of the rates on low-density routes.[16] Repeating its TELPAK strategy, AT&T did not seek to set prices below its costs – to the extent that the EPC knew what private line costs were – but only near incremental or board-to-board costs.

Businesses choosing between the Bell System and MCI, then, would find themselves facing roughly similar prices. AT&T would provide competitive pricing under the threat of competition. But how long would potential competitors continue to challenge AT&T and induce it to introduce competitive prices? Surely firms would get discouraged as they watched Motorola and then MCI win the regulatory battle, only to find that the expected pot of gold was largely illusory. They would then search for more lucrative markets.

The issues at stake were far more important than the revenue involved on even a major route like the one between St. Louis and Chicago. The EPC hinted as much in its final discussion before filing the Hi-Lo tariff with the FCC. The committee contended that the new tariff was not simply a response to competition. Competition of the sort posed by MCI provided only an occasion for a change that was already due. Nationwide averaging had achieved Vail's goal of universal service; now it was time for private line charges to reflect their costs.[17] The EPC clearly was making a virtue out of necessity, but the decision on Hi-Lo was doing far more than that. The new tariff violated one of the central tenets of nationwide rate averaging: the idea that high-density, long distance service would subsidize the Bell System's less lucrative business. The concession was limited – it was specified for the private line business alone – but it was nonetheless a large step away from the traditional Bell System policy of regulatory pricing. TELPAK had broken with the tradition of historical costs; Hi-Lo abandoned national rate averaging in private lines. It is easy to understand why the company's managers needed to reassure themselves that their apostasy from Vail's dogma was occasioned by forces more respectable than McGowan's aggressive attacks.

Under FCC rules that forced the telephone company to get permission before it could file new rates, AT&T submitted the Hi-Lo tariff to the agency in February 1973. (Later in the year, the Court of Appeals would find these rules unlawful.) The company filed the tariff in November, and after further regulatory delays it became effective on June 13, 1974, a year and a half after AT&T had proposed it. The next day, MCI filed lowered rates for its customers, launching a new round of competition between the David and Goliath of private line telecommunications.[18]

[16]The lower rates were for channel capacity; the terminal charges were the same. AT&T Application No. 930, February 26, 1973.
[17]Minutes of the EPC meeting, January 9, 1973.
[18]AT&T Application No. 930, February 26, 1973; *AT&T* v. *FCC*, 487 F.2d 865 (2d Cir. 1973); AT&T Transmittal No. 11891, November 15, 1973; James R. Billingsley to Richard

Shortly after AT&T filed the Hi-Lo tariff, McGowan once again came to see deButts. This meeting was as different from their initial meeting as night and day. Civilized communication was no longer possible. According to deButts, McGowan said that he could not compete with AT&T's new rates. He threatened to sue AT&T for the treble damages obtainable from an antitrust judgment. McGowan had come out of his corner fighting, and although deButts did not abandon his gentlemanly demeanor, he was not about to yield to threats.[19]

Like MCI's boss, the FCC responded negatively to Hi-Lo. On the one hand, the Commission wanted to lower prices to large industrial users of telecommunications services. On the other hand, it wanted to encourage competition while preserving nationwide rate averaging and low prices for local telephone service. The Commission had therefore encouraged MCI to become a low-priced supplier of private line services, but it tried at the same time to prevent AT&T from rearranging its price structure to match what MCI was charging. The agency had conflicting goals, and the problem with its strategy was that the revenue to support local service would be taken away just as surely by AT&T's loss of business to MCI as it would be by lower Bell System prices.

As with the FCC's rejection of TELPAK, Strassburg wanted to encourage the growth of competitive firms like MCI, both as an end in itself and as a means of keeping AT&T on the straight and narrow. His assertions, first that the *MCI* decision was an experiment and later that *Specialized Common Carriers* threatened only a minor part of AT&T's business, suggest strongly that he never intended to attack the Bell System's dominance of American telecommunications. He wanted competition, but not too much. He had, however, grabbed a tiger by the tail, and he found it hard to let go.

John deButts was threatened by that tiger, and he quickly concluded that the Bell System would have to change its internal structure if it was going to deal effectively with competition. He pursued the question of the Bell System's internal organization at the same time he dealt with terminal interconnection and the Hi-Lo tariff. Focusing on terminal equipment, he started by commissioning two studies of the company's current procedures. For one of these studies, he went outside AT&T, to McKinsey & Company. Frederick Gluck had led the McKinsey team advising Lilley at New Jersey Bell, and he had written a "think piece" for New York Telephone along the

E. Wiley, June 13, 1974; "Hi-Lo Goes Into Effect as AT&T Turns Down FCC Request for Further Extension; FCC Sees Ruling by Mid-October," *Telecommunications Reports*, Vol. 40, No. 24 (June 17, 1974), pp. 1–3; "MCI Files Competitive Response to Hi-Lo," *Telecommunications Reports*, Vol. 40, No. 24 (June 17, 1974), p. 18.
[19]*MCI* v. *AT&T*, No. 74 C 633 (N.D. Ill.), John D. deButts, testimony, April 7–8, 1980, Tr. 4015–21, 4082–91.

lines laid out in the New Jersey study. The consulting firm therefore
already had a well-defined attitude toward the Bell System when deButts
arranged with one of its partners – with whom he had served on the Council on Economic Education – to have lunch with him, Lilley, Gluck, and a
few others. Gluck explained his views; McKinsey & Company was retained to examine AT&T's effectiveness in selling terminal equipment.[20]
DeButts also directed one branch of the Corporate Planning Organization
(the successor to the Management Sciences Division) under Boettinger to
evaluate AT&T's research and development programs and another under
Brooke Tunstall, Director of Corporate Planning Studies, to examine
AT&T's entire organizational structure.[21]

When Gluck's team at McKinsey reported back to the EPC at the end of
1972, the news was gloomy. AT&T's existing sales organization, McKinsey
said, had nearly fatal problems. Lost customers cited AT&T's poor sales
efforts as factors in their decision to buy non-Bell terminal equipment.
Small wonder, according to McKinsey. AT&T's salesmen were spending
most of their time servicing existing customers' demands instead of selling
new products, had an "overwhelming administrative and coordination burden," and lacked guidelines with which to rank potential customers and
allocate their efforts among them. Without clear objectives or performance
measures, compensation and promotion did not mirror performance. Motivation was poor. Dissatisfaction and turnover were high. There was little
reason for a good salesman to remain in the Bell System.

Gluck argued that these problems derived from the absence of a "clear,
agreed-to definition of the role of the sales force in the new competitive
environment." Sales and marketing functions were divided between different departments, reducing their "organizational clout," and overall planning was "basically a budgeting exercise" related to capital expenditures.
Field experience had little impact on product development. Differences
between the organizational structures of the various operating companies
made coordination of marketing efforts difficult. AT&T's top management
had reiterated its intention to compete in terminal equipment markets
without translating this desire into an effective corporate strategy.

AT&T's structure derived from Vail's 1909 reorganization; it did not
embody the concept of markets or "profit center segmentation." The consultant's report provided organization charts and descriptions of General
Electric and IBM, arguing that both firms had reorganized themselves
along these lines in the 1950s. The recommendation was that business
terminal equipment – and other competitive activities by implication – be
organized as a separate business activity. All of the fragmented sales and

[20]Minutes of the EPC Meeting (A.M.), July 17, 1972; Frederick W. Gluck, interview,
   September 23, 1985, pp. 11–12, 32, 35, 41.
[21]Minutes of EPC Meeting, August 9, 1972, p. 2.

marketing operations for the terminal equipment market, those at 195
Broadway and in the operating companies, should be gathered under a
single senior marketing executive, separate from network and residentia
services.[22]

This was strong medicine. Organization by markets would supplant the
three-column functional organization that had served the Bell System wel
for over half a century. Operations, not marketing, had long been the
dominant function in the telephone company. Technological imperative,
not the lure of sales, drove the System. As a regulated monopoly, the Bel
enterprise had not had to worry about sales. It had concentrated or
improving its service through technological progress. The values associated with this tradition were deeply planted, and most of the company
officers making the crucial decisions about the McKinsey report had them
selves built their careers in operations. This included John deButts, who
had initiated the inquiry into Bell's marketing capabilities, and ever
though he was promoting change in the Bell System, deButts had a clear
allegiance to Vail's concepts and the traditional company culture.

McKinsey, by contrast, was presenting to AT&T a very different view o
its structure. The consulting company was generalizing from the organization of manufacturing companies like GE and IBM to a public utility
True, it had been asked to analyze that corner of the Bell System's activi
ties that most closely resembled these competitive firms. But it had as
sumed that the leaders of the Bell System wanted to expand this aspect o
their business. Although Gluck realized that his message was corrosive o
Bell System values, he did not moderate his report. IBM, one of his
examples of exemplary organization, was famous for its willingness to
transfer managers within the firm in response to their performances – both
good and bad. The number of times that a Bell System manager had been
dismissed from an important post for nonperformance was so small tha
the known cases were legendary. It would require more than a change o
form to make AT&T's marketing operations into another IBM. It would
require a revolution in thought and behavior.[23]

Gluck did not stop to think whether it was in AT&T's best interest to
start down this road. Given that the Bell System wanted to compete in the
terminal equipment market, this kind of reorganization was indicated
But should AT&T want to compete in this market? The counterargumen
was political, not economic. Perhaps AT&T could have improved its dete
riorating political position by withdrawing from this market. Given the

[22]McKinsey & Company, Inc., "Improving Selling Effectiveness in the Terminal Equipmen
Business," discussion draft, December 14, 1972; progress review, January 23, 1973, an
"Managing Business Terminal Equipment as a Competitive Enterprise," June 8, 1973.
[23]Gluck, interview, September 23, 1985, pp. 24–5, 40–2; William G. Sharwell, interview
July 10, 1985, pp. 28–9.

defects in its sales efforts, maybe the telephone company should have
compromised with the forces of competition, abandoning its terminal
equipment market to save its intercity service market.

It is exceedingly unlikely that the EPC, which could not even accept
the use of tort liability for independent terminal equipment, would have
been responsive to this advice. Telephones, after all, were the initial
product of the Bell System. And deButts was a fighter who did not smile
at the thought of compromise. McKinsey's advice was couched in terms
that its client wanted to hear, despite the call for reorganization.

It was hard for the EPC to heed even this call. Tradition won out over
innovation when the EPC first discussed the McKinsey report in January
1973. Although the committee agreed that something should be done,
"concern was expressed as to whether a separate marketing strategy for
the terminal equipment business could be developed and implemented
without jeopardy to the System's end-to-end responsibility for customer
service."[24] A change that threatened to reduce service performance was
suspect. A recommendation that put sales ahead of service was heretical.

The issue was sent down to the Corporate Planning Organization for
additional analysis, and Tunstall reported in March 1973 that many of the
operating companies had already abandoned the Vail structure. Only nine
operating companies had retained it in its original form. Almost half of the
companies had created some sort of network or switching department,
and five had formed customer service departments. Five had also split the
traffic function in two, setting up stand-alone departments of operator
services. These operating companies had been adjusting to the new conditions in the industry while AT&T had stood pat; several had developed
integrated marketing programs that were coordinated in entirely new
ways.[25]

The changes in the operating companies reinforced the message that
organizational reform was needed. The EPC directed Tunstall to analyze
the existing changes more thoroughly and to develop specific proposals
that the committee could evaluate, not merely for terminal production
and distribution, but for the Bell System as a whole. The committee asked
for these proposals in time for the fall Presidents' Conference.

In the meantime, Boettinger presented to the EPC his group's report
on research and development (R&D) in the Bell System. Although it dealt
with an entirely different subject than McKinsey had considered, the
Corporate Planning Organization came to many of the same conclusions as
the consulting firm. The nature of the demand facing the Bell System had
changed. No longer was the enterprise's central mandate to supply plain

[24]Alvin von Auw, Minutes of the EPC meeting, January 23, 1973.
[25]Minutes of EPC Meeting, March 28, 1973; Cornelius W. Owens, "The Organization Issue
in the Bell System," Presidents' Conference, Sea Island, Georgia, November 1, 1973.

old telephone service, and to pursue the goal of universal service. The need was to supply more varied demands than before, to differentiate products for particular customers: The number of types of apparatus (codes) available from Western Electric, for example, had increased by more than half in the last decade.

The Bell System's R&D program had been highly successful in the past, but now it was not as responsive to market pressures as it should be. R&D was being managed by a committee, a form of "consensus management." But in all of the various committees overseeing R&D, "there [was] no one who assume[d] the role of representing the owners of the business." Committee members–even members of the Tri-Company Councils–represented the operating companies, provided technical expertise, and furthered the programs of particular departments; but they did not consider the Bell System as a whole. As a result, marketing was neglected. R&D was guided by cost-and service-oriented representatives of the traditional Bell System groups. In the existing structure there was simply no way to integrate marketing and research. Consequently, "the overwhelming factors in determining new product characteristics have been technical and technological considerations."[26]

The emergence of competitive problems at Western Electric supported the corporate planning team's analysis. The Bell System's manufacturing arm had served the network well with its unrivaled ability to mass produce reliable electromechanical equipment at low cost. But in the early 1970s, Western was facing rising competition for almost all its products. Other manufacturers had filled gaps in Western's lines. As telecommunications equipment changed from electromechanical to electronic, Western was losing the edge it had maintained for over seventy-five years. Approximately one-fourth of its products were close to those of the competition in price and quality, and close to one-half were approaching parity by 1973. Western's position as the low-cost provider was being steadily eroded. In

[26]AT&T Corporate Planning Organization, "Research and Development Policy in the Bell System," June 1973. Boettinger emphasized that the market had not evolved independently of AT&T's past actions. The Bell System had realized Vail's vision of universal service in the half-century before John deButts took over as CEO. It was partly because AT&T had satisfied the demand for basic service that the demand for new customized services and products had arisen. In addition, the economy was growing and electronic technology was developing rapidly, again partly because of the work of Bell Labs. The sum of these changes was a new demand environment for Bell's R&D.

Conditions of supply had also been transformed. The FCC was favoring the entry of other firms into the telecommunications market, and these companies increasingly possessed technical sophistication that enabled them to compete effectively with the Bell System. As a result, the increasingly complex demands were being served by increasingly complex combinations of suppliers.

For an earlier view along the same lines, see *US* v. *AT&T*, CA 74–1698, U.S. Dist. Ct., Dist. of Columbia, Plaintiff's Exhibit 2524; J.W. Schaefer, "Introduction to the Panel on Corporate Interfaces," Skytop, September 30, 1970.

addition, a McKinsey report to Western added, "the key factor for cost leadership is shifting from manufacturing excellence to having the most cost-effective design at any particular time," that is, from Western's strength to its greatest weakness.[27]

Given the Bell System's long tradition of providing excellent service to its customers and Bell Labs's undoubted distinction as an industrial laboratory, Boettinger asked why they had not provided R&D tailored to the customers' needs. The answer was that this kind of response had to be managed. People who understood the problems had to have the authority to implement their ideas. Organizations had to be structured to respond to their managers and to generate feedback for future management decisions. This was not happening properly in the Bell System.

There was an alternative. Competition provides a substitute for this management function. In a world of small firms, managerial bureaucracies are not needed to alter the direction of large organizations. Small organizations, often run by individual entrepreneurs, see profit opportunities and rush to exploit them. They are managed, of course, but their problems are very different from those of large firms; the individual looms large and the organization as such is seldom imposing. This was apparent in telecommunications. Small firms were providing the specialized services that the Bell System was not, and the FCC seemed determined to allow even more small firms to enter the business. But the culture of the Bell System strongly supported the proposition that a large, integrated organization would do a better job in all branches of telecommunications – once it solved its management problems – than a collection of small firms. There was no doubt in the EPC or the Corporate Planning Organization that AT&T could be the most efficient supplier of all the goods and services it offered and that Bell Labs was the source of the most important inventions in the telecommunications industry. There was no doubt, either, that AT&T's mission was to enter vigorously into all of these markets.

The AT&T executives consequently did not draw the lesson that AT&T's highly integrated structure might no longer be needed in all of Bell's traditional markets from their finding that it was not working well in the early 1970s. It was, as they saw it, in the public interest, as well as in the interests of AT&T's owners, for the Bell System to pull its act together and preserve its position as the preeminent supplier of telecommunications services and products to the nation. Other people – located in the federal government's Office of Telecommunications Policy and the Department of Justice – saw

[27]Donald E. Procknow, interview, December 19, 1985, pp. 7–11; McKinsey & Company, Inc., "Meeting the Challenge of Competition for the Bell System Telecommunications Equipment Market," November 13, 1973, p. 4. Note that the price comparison is even less favorable to Western Electric than the report showed, since Western Electric's prices did not have to include marketing expenses.

the problem differently. Taking competition and free entry as the norm, their analyses went along very different lines than that of AT&T. They would cite AT&T's management difficulties as evidence that the firm was just too large. They would conclude from the successful reception by the markets of the new entrants that what was needed was a new industry structure, not a return to the old one. They would see a conflict between AT&T's competitive posture in some markets and its regulated monopoly position in others. They would stress the role of entrepreneurship in determining the industry's future and would largely ignore the areas in which system efficiency favored an integrated national network. They would call for a removal of regulatory barriers to entry.

The planners' analysis pinpointed the problem: Competitors were "out-innovating" and "out-marketing" the Bell System, "usually in areas where, traditionally, the Bell System has chosen not to exploit small, secondary markets for basic telephone service." There had always been rural areas served by independent telephone companies, and there were some surviving urban independents as well. Western Union still provided some long distance services under the protection of a government policy dating as far back as the Kingsbury Commitment of 1913. But with these important exceptions, the Bell System had been able to define the market it wanted to supply. Other firms satisfied demands, as the report noted, that the Bell System chose not to fulfill.[28]

The threads of these various reports were pulled together by a committee of operating company presidents that had been investigating related matters for the past three years. Romnes had appointed the Presidents' License Contract Committee in 1970 to deal with AT&T's chronic and growing deficit under the License Contract (which governed relations between the operating companies and the parent firm). After an exhaustive review of the General Departments and the interaction between the various elements of the Bell System, the committee reported to the EPC in the fall of 1973 that "stronger AT&T leadership, direction and control [are] required." Most important, the presidents said, was more control by AT&T over Bell Labs's R&D "to keep it relevant to the current state of communications technology. Researchers at Bell Labs need a better knowledge of the System, its priorities and objectives." Communication between the Labs and the operating companies was badly in need of improvement.[29]

The report of the Presidents' License Committee had a profound impact on the EPC. It had not been prepared by an outside consultant or by

[28]AT&T Corporate Planning Organization, "Research and Development Policy in the Bell System," June 1973.
[29]AT&T, "Final Report and Recommendations of the Presidents' License Contract Committee," October 1973.

the planning office; it had emerged from years of work by operating
company presidents. It was a cry from the center of the Bell System's
operations. AT&T would have to respond.

As these several incidents revealed, competition was invading the Bell
System's turf, and the choice as to which markets AT&T would serve was
being taken out of the firm's hands. Motorola had mounted a direct challenge, which had led to the FCC's *Above 890* decision. MCI had
knocked – loudly – on the door and been admitted. The initiative on certification was also drifting out of AT&T's grip, increasing the pressure on the
Bell System. With the waters of competition lapping at the foundations of
the regulatory castle, the Bell System had to coordinate better its various
technical efforts. Research had to be managed in a new way, with one eye
on the market. And – just a speck on the horizon – maybe the very nature
of AT&T would have to change too.

The Bell System responds

After a year as chairman, John deButts had made fundamental policy
decisions in the two areas in which the Bell System was facing competition: terminal equipment and private lines. He had sponsored two separate studies that had told him that his organization was falling down in the
first of these areas. He had heard clearly from the operating company
presidents. Something needed to be done. DeButts had no intention of
abandoning the organization's traditional focus on service and its role as a
public utility, but he clearly recognized that he had to add a more effective marketing dimension to the System.

As soon became apparent, it was one thing to reduce prices in response
to competitive service offerings but quite another to enhance the marketing capability of the Bell System. Stronger marketing was in basic conflict
with the System's utility tradition. Efficiency in the System had always
been defined in technological terms. The operation of the integrated
network was the firm's overriding concern; changing Bell from a quasi-
governmental steward of the national telephone network, from a monopoly public utility, to a private telecommunications firm would be a
slow, painful process. Any organization with a million people changes
direction slowly. But in the case of the Bell System, reorientation would
be especially difficult because of the manner in which the organization's
values and structure were intertwined. The combination had been highly
successful for so many decades that change was anathema to many of Bell's
most loyal employees and managers.

The concept of a new market-oriented Bell System was not one that
even deButts willingly embraced. Far from it; deButts wrapped himself in

Vail's mantle and set out to preserve the Bell System's hallowed role. In his many speeches and informal talks, he looked to the past far more than he looked to the future. As he had done already within the System, he announced to the world at the end of 1973 his opposition to the changes taking place as a result of the FCC's actions. Ironically, his focus on preserving Bell's public utility status would make it difficult for some of his fellow managers to implement wholeheartedly the reforms deButts himself was setting in motion.

The role of competition was an issue at the 1973 spring Presidents' Conference, where a discouraging picture emerged. The theme of the conference was "1980," that is, the prospects for AT&T in that year. Richard Hough, head of Long Lines, extrapolated a dismal view of the next decade from the social climate at the start of President Richard Nixon's second term. The growing distrust of the federal government at the end of the Vietnam War and the growing unease over the conduct of Nixon's reelection campaign had spilled over into a general distrust of bigness. It was not a good season for the world's largest corporation. Hough even envisaged a possible breakup of the Bell System, accompanied by difficult operating relationships, higher costs, poorer service, and lower earnings. There could as well, he added, be increasing government intervention in the management of the business, either as an alternative to a breakup or in addition to that decisive action. He was off by only a few years.[30]

Charles Brown, still president of Illinois Bell, noted the trend toward – in a curiously inverted turn of phrase – "competition as a regulatory tool." He observed, with as much foresight as Hough, that AT&T would continue to be regulated as long as it was subject to the charge that it was subsidizing competitive business with monopoly revenues – regardless of the 1956 Consent Decree. The TELPAK controversy had left its mark. Brown went on to note that regulators become protective of their clients and reluctant to let them go out of business (echoing the remarks his friend Howard Trienens had made at the 1970 panel discussion with William Baxter). Given the apparent inevitability of increased competition, Brown argued that the Bell System needed to have a competitive policy and that AT&T should press for full freedom to compete.

Brown also said that pressure for shorter-lived products would come with competition. The eternally durable telephone would be retired in favor of products with novelty and built-in obsolescence. Even though this change ran counter to Bell System traditions, it would be the inevitable result of increasing competition. The competitive market would offer

---

[30]Richard R. Hough, "Institutional Factors," presentation to the Presidents' Conference, Hot Springs, Virginia, April 30, 1973.

consumers a choice between more durable and less durable products. The resulting demand, freed of the regulators' bias toward slow depreciation and durability, would be for shorter-lived products than before. It was not a vision to cheer members of the Bell System; given AT&T's commitment to compete hard in the terminal business, it was one that cried out for preparation and even protest.[31]

Preparation was the job of the EPC's planning organization. Brooke Tunstall distilled from the company's various studies three alternative approaches to reorganizing the Bell System. The first option was to keep its traditional functional structure, as shown in Figure 6. The original Plant, Traffic, and Commercial departments of the Vail years had been joined over time by Engineering and Sales. But those additions had not altered the basic concept of the structure: All of the departments were organized along skill lines, grouping members of similar crafts together.

Taking its cue from the innovations already made by many of the operating companies, the second alternative was to reorganize around work flows rather than craft lines. Restructuring would keep the work on any job within a single department, thus easing the flow of information and commands relevant to the Bell System's traditional activities: responding to customer complaints, servicing and planning for the network, and expanding facilities. The Corporate Planning Organization thought that three departments would be needed to implement this idea, as shown in Figure 7.

Customer Services would contain all the activities relating to terminal equipment and the local loop between a telephone subscriber and a central office. Construction and engineering functions, formerly in separate departments, would be combined so that the customer services manager would control both the provision of plant and its day-to-day operation. Although this department would be in a position to respond quickly to any complaints coming from the local loop, it would not particularly emphasize marketing or give it a new role relative to operations.

Nor would marketing be highlighted in Network Services, which would include activities involving the network between central offices, that is, from board to board. This department would include network design, engineering, construction, and operation. These functions clearly ranked highest in the Bell System's hierarchy of values. The network mystique was a powerful force, and the network was at this time particularly important to Bell managers in view of the service failures of the late 1960s in New York and elsewhere. Integrating all network planning and operations, it was hoped, would enable the Bell System to avoid such failures

---

[31]Notes of discussion at the Presidents' Conference, Hot Springs, Virginia, April 30–May 4, 1973.

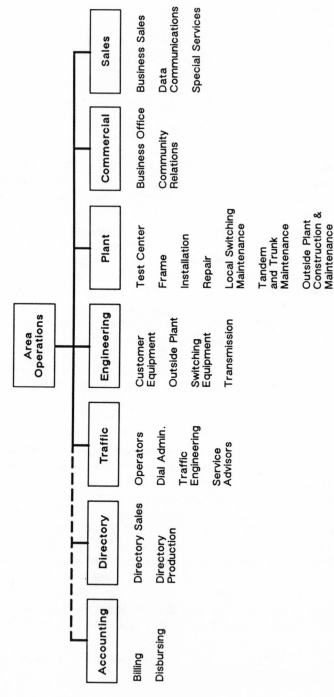

Figure 6. AT&T's organization structure—traditional alternative. (Source: AT&T Corporate Planning, "The Organization Issue in the Bell System," October 30, 1973.)

88

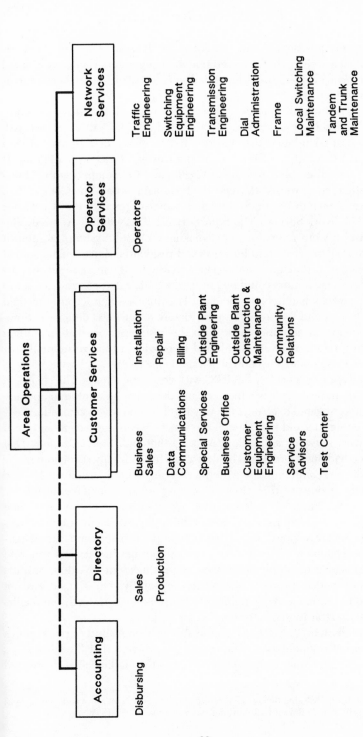

Figure 7. AT&T's organization structure – Customer/Network/Operator services alternative. (Source: AT&T Corporate Planning, "The Organization Issue in the Bell System," October 30, 1973.)

89

by accurately forecasting and providing for demand. Operator Services included all activities that involved telephone operators. They could stand on their own because they depended very little on either customer or network services.

Tunstall's third alternative followed the lines of McKinsey's recommended market segmentation. Relabeled the "Competitive Structure," this proposal abandoned the skill orientation of the first alternative and the process orientation of the second in favor of a focus on marketing. It would, Tunstall emphasized, help AT&T meet the competition for business customers, as well as those in the terminal market. The Competitive Structure (shown in Figure 8) shared certain features with the "Customer Services/Network Services/Operator Services (CS/NS/OS)" proposal (Figure 7). But it went much further. Breaking with Bell System tradition, it split customer services into business and residential departments so that all of the sales, installation, and repair activities for the increasingly important business customers could be grouped together and coordinated more closely than they had been in the past. The Business Service group would be able to respond swiftly and appropriately to business demands. Similarly, the several activities related to the residential market – including community relations – were combined to provide a total residential customer response under the control of a single manager.

In reality, this report left the EPC with very little choice. The chairman had already indicated clearly by word and deed that he wanted to upgrade Bell's marketing and to change the way this function was organized. AT&T was not going to stand pat. The choice was between the second and third alternatives, between a middle way and a thorough reorganization. That choice too had been foreclosed by deButts. He was highly suspicious of the most radical recommendation, the market-segmented structure. He had asked in the spring of 1973: "How . . . can we organize ourselves by market segments – the kinds of businesses we are in – without at the same time adopting the motivations of our competitors, thereby facilitating the fragmentation of our responsibilities that our competitors seek and thus jeopardizing the System integrity that has made our business great?"[32] No one had stepped forward to supply an answer. As this incident revealed, deButts was determined to promote change in the Bell System, but he was not prepared to renounce Bell's public utility orientation. Indeed, the reaffirmation of that tradition was the heart of his program.

In the fall of 1973, the EPC predictably echoed deButts's reservations about market segmentation. The committee worried that the advantages of segmentation would be more than offset by the inefficiencies that would

---

[32]John D. deButts, "Closing Remarks," Presidents' Conference, Hot Springs, Virginia, April 30-May 4, 1973, p. 3; Robert D. Lilley, interview, September 23, 1985, p. 59.

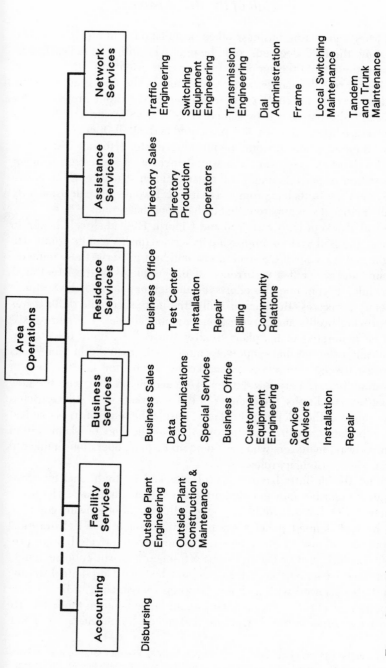

Figure 8. AT&T's organization structure—competitive alternative. (Source: AT&T Corporate Planning, "The Organization Issue in the Bell System," October 30, 1973.)

91

result from segregating business office, installation, and repair activities. Marketing, the EPC decided, could be improved without a radical departure, and the committee supported the process-oriented CS/NS/OS concept. The three alternatives were presented to the operating company presidents at their fall conference, where the EPC's strong preference for the second alternative was explained. The "CS/NS/OS organization," as this structure became known, was presented to the Bell Operating Companies for their adoption. It would be introduced after elaborate discussions at all levels of the company and would involve, if successful, a major reorientation of personnel and the organizational structure of the entire Bell System. DeButts had promised that AT&T would make decisions. By the fall of 1973, it was apparent that he had kept that promise.[33]

He had also kept faith with Vail and Gifford. He had already begun to revitalize the Bell System, improving its service quality and its profits. He thought that the CS/NS/OS structure would best preserve those immediate gains and prevent a recurrence of the problems of the late 1960s. Meanwhile, he continued his efforts to gain tighter control of the System's budgetary processes. But paradoxically, the more successful deButts was in improving profits and service along traditional lines, the more resistance he generated to his plans to alter the Bell System's orientation. Technically oriented managers were more inclined to dig in their heels and resist the new emphasis on marketing when they saw the System performing better. Very few of them were actually dealing with the new competitive conditions; the changes in Bell's markets were still restricted to the fringes of the telephone business. Losing the sense of crisis that had been so pervasive in 1971 and hearing the Vail ideology proclaimed from 195 Broadway, managers who had come up through operations hunkered down in their customary roles.

Behind the deButts banner, AT&T attacked its traditional functions with great vigor but moved only tentatively in new directions. The firm's dynamic CEO did not, could not, ignore the threat of growing competition; he had defined policies toward certification of non-Bell terminal equipment and toward the independent suppliers of private lines (represented by MCI). But he had drawn back from enthusiastic endorsement of the messages coming from McKinsey and his own Corporate Planning Organization. Faced with a choice between reorganizing to be a better competitor or a better service organization, he had chosen the latter. He opted for an organizational structure that defied simple characterization;

[33]Minutes of the EPC meeting, October 30, 1973; Corporate Planning Organization, presentation to the EPC, "The Organization Issue in the Bell System," October 30, 1973; Cornelius W. Owens, "The Organization Issue in the Bell System," Presidents' Conference, Sea Island, Georgia, November 1, 1973; Donald E. Guinn, interview, December 12, 1985, pp. 6–13.

neither traditional nor competitive, it was CS/NS/OS. Thus, although he planted the seeds of profound change, he actually devoted most of his considerable energy to cultivating the Bell System's customary functions. While expanding its marketing efforts, he kept them outside the main lines of corporate authority and denied them extensive budgetary control or influence.

DeButts was, nevertheless, determined to get the nascent marketing program moving, and he knew that his initial personnel choices would be crucial to that effort. Gluck had recommended that he go outside the Bell System for a man to spearhead the plan. AT&T's CEO knew, however, that an outsider could have little impact in that large organization without strong internal support. Gluck's own relations with AT&T were very formal and a bit distant; AT&T heard his ideas and then retired to work out their implications internally. DeButts had done exactly this when he had Tunstall present organizational alternatives to the EPC. A new marketing executive would need help from top management. Thus, in July 1973, deButts asked Kenneth Whalen, president of Michigan Bell, to come to 195 Broadway and be vice president for marketing. Whalen did not know the first thing about marketing – he was an operating executive – but he was large, fit, and aggressive: a good guardian angel for an outside innovator. His position as a former operating company president and a seventh-level executive in AT&T would enable him to approach anyone in the operating companies as an equal – or more. McKinsey staged a couple of all-day briefings to explain the concepts of marketing to Whalen, who concurred with the recommendation to hire an outsider to serve directly under him.[34]

AT&T's search turned up Archibald McGill, 42 years old – almost a decade younger than Whalen – an independent consultant who at the age of 33 had been the youngest vice president at IBM. He was hired as director of market management, a sixth-level position. As Whalen explained to the operating company presidents at their semiannual conference in the fall of 1973, McGill was one of four leaders of the marketing effort; he had responsibility for identifying and defining relevant markets and marketing opportunities for AT&T. His efforts would be supported by Edward Goldstein – a longtime Bell System employee – who was in charge of product management for the markets identified by McGill. As Whalen expressed his hopes: "In the past, the development of new customer products generally began at Bell Labs as new technology evolved. . . . Customer product develop-

---

[34]Shortly before Whalen assumed his new post, McKinsey & Company reported again to AT&T on what he and the Bell System should be doing. McKinsey & Company, Inc., "Managing Business Terminal Equipment as a Competitive Enterprise," June 8, 1973; Gluck, interview, September 23, 1985, pp. 27, 38–9; Kenneth J. Whalen, interview, July 18, 1985, pp. 4–5.

ment now begins at the marketplace as customer needs are identified."
Another executive was placed in charge of the sales effort itself, and a
fourth was given responsibility for marketing data.[35]

McGill, however, soon became first among equals, at least insofar as
the other Bell System managers were concerned. He attracted attention.
He was a hard-hitting, tough-talking, aggressive executive. He was the
antithesis of a man with a Bell-shaped head. Many in the organization
thought he was just what they needed to shake up the System; he was a
breath – or even a gale – of fresh air.[36]

McGill stepped into an organizational void at AT&T. The marketing
operation was alien to Vail's functional concept of the Bell System. McGill
had to construct a separate new organization to compete with the existing
ones, and he started by exercising the power he had been given to hire
more outsiders. This authorization – extraordinary for the Bell System –
helped McGill build a marketing team composed of both insiders and
outsiders, but it inhibited its integration with the rest of AT&T.

But McGill was not easily deterred. Never one to think small, he did
not stop charging forward when he had staffed his new group. McGill
decided that his most important task would be to change the strategic
direction of the corporation. He would have to spearhead the transformation from a technologically oriented company focused on its subscribers to
a financially driven, market-oriented one. Technological evaluations of
personnel and programs needed to be replaced by financial measures;
uniform service to all telephone users, by identification of and appeal to
discrete groups of customers. McGill agreed with Gluck that IBM – vastly
different in organization and attitude from AT&T – was the marketing and
sales model to emulate.[37]

It was a tall order. The Bell System was a massive organization that had
long been successful in its public utilities mode; its managers would not
change their orientation overnight; some would never change. The System's leaders had all grown up within it; they were not going to lead the
charge. Marketing was still considered to be essentially a terminal equipment problem. It did not affect the core of AT&T's business, the switched
telephone network. Marketing, like most of the other parts of the Bell
System, was an autonomous unit, off to the side, subordinate in importance to the network and operations. Goldstein described its place in the
System by recalling that when he had been in charge of marketing for

[35]Kenneth J. Whalen, presentation, Presidents' Conference, Sea Island, Georgia, November 5–9, 1973; Edward H. Spencer, "New Muscle in Marketing," *Bell Telephone Magazine*, Vol. 53, No. 3, 1974, p. 13.
[36]Edward M. Goldstein, interview, April 25, 1985, p. 40; Whalen, interview, July 18, 1985,
pp. 9–10.
[37]Archibald J. McGill, interview, June 20, 1985, pp. 21–2, 62–4.

New York Telephone, the president of the company would introduce him with the remark: "We don't have anything to sell, so I don't know what he does."[38]

Whalen himself was greeted with hostility when he, like Brown, suggested that products might have to be designed for obsolescence. The Bell System was still service oriented and focused on technological excellence. Bell Labs was supreme within the System; it was above attack. In effect, McGill would take his job to be the reshaping of the internal value system of AT&T, changing the measure of performance from technological performance to market returns, and altering the balance of power within the entire System.[39]

A hopeful straw in the wind was the formation of AT&T's Bell System Purchased Products Division shortly after Whalen and McGill arrived. This division was created in response to an ongoing FCC investigation into AT&T's vertical integration, a probe dating from the turbulent events of 1971. The FCC had raised once again the specter of cross-subsidies going from the Bell Operating Companies to Western Electric. AT&T responded by setting up the new division as an advisory body to help the operating companies evaluate the equipment available in the marketplace. The new group would echo and amplify the message from Whalen's marketing organization: Western's products had to meet the market test. But even if they did, of course, neither the FCC nor the Department of Justice might be satisfied that Western Electric should remain an integral part of the Bell System, tied closely to its major customers, the Bell Operating Companies. This question – ostensibly settled in 1956 – was revived by the emergence of competition, and it posed a threat to AT&T's already tense relationships with federal authority.[40]

The firm's political relations became even more strained when deButts decided to provoke a public discourse over the changes taking place in federal telecommunications policy. Public policy was changing with increasing speed as the FCC's decisions to allow competition in various parts of Bell's markets cumulated. DeButts decided to expose this trend to public view, extending his support of the Bell System's traditional values to the political arena. He would make certain that neither state commissioners nor the FCC would be able to ignore the implications of their actions.

[38]The story dates from the New York service crisis, when the state regulatory commission had forbade New York Telephone from marketing new PBXs. Goldstein, interview, April 25, 1985, p. 17, 73.
[39]McGill, interview, June 20, 1985, pp. 10–11; Whalen, interview July 18, 1985, pp. 7–8.
[40]FCC, *Memorandum Opinion and Order*, FCC Docket 19129, "AT&T, Charges for Interstate Telephone Service," Phase II, January 21, 1971, 27 FCC 2d 151; *US* v. *AT&T*, CA No. 74–1698 (D.D.C.), Defendants' Exhibit D-57C-154, Bell System Purchased Products Division Organization Announcement.

DeButts drew on work that Edward Crosland, his vice president for federal relations, had been doing for several years and upon ideas developed by Howard Trienens at Sidley and Austin. Concerned ever since the (U.S.) President's Task Force on Telecommunications Policy under Eugene Rostow had championed the idea of competition, Crosland had convened an advisory group to consider the implications of competitive telecommunications for consumers. The group, with members drawn both from within AT&T and from the broader political community, had concluded that competition in this industry would be bad for the public. In particular, the advisors insisted, if the contribution made by revenue from long distance services to local service through separations was eliminated, local rates would have to rise substantially. Howard Trienens was moving down a similar path. He maintained that the history of common carrier regulation revealed an implicit bargain between the government and the carrier. The carrier accepted the obligation to serve all customers (whether the service was profitable or not) and accepted without discrimination limits on its earnings in return for franchise protection from cream-skimming competition.

All of these ideas went into a speech deButts was scheduled to deliver in September 1973, at the Seattle meeting of the National Association of Regulatory Utility Commissioners (NARUC). This would be an important policy statement because of the audience and the timing. Alvin von Auw, who drafted the speech, wanted to bring these ideas together with views deButts had expressed in other talks. He circulated the text of deButts's NARUC speech to most of the company's top officers and advisors for comments. Extensive comments came back, notably from Crosland and Trienens, but little actual revision took place.[41] The resulting talk, entitled "An Unusual Obligation," was designed to arouse Bell System employees, members of NARUC, and the voting public to defend the public switched network against competition. In deButts's words, it was "to take to the public the case for the common carrier principle and thereby by implication to oppose competition, espouse monopoly."[42]

This dramatic reaffirmation of Vail's ideals was not made lightly. During the long process of writing and rewriting, deButts had shown drafts of his speech to many officers of AT&T and found widespread support. Opposition to his stand on terminal equipment came from engineers like Goldstein, who cautioned that the anticipated harms from terminal intercon-

[41]Alvin von Auw, interview, February 10, 1984, pp. 23–5, and August 12, 1985, pp. 1–5; John G. Fox, interview, November 6, 1985, pp. 27–9; Edward B. Crosland, interview, January 8, 1986, pp. 5–6; James Rowe to Edward B. Crosland, August 30, 1973 (circulated by Crosland to the members of the EPC); Howard J. Trienens to Edward B. Crosland, October 13, 1973.
[42]John D. deButts, "An Unusual Obligation," speech at the Annual NARUC Convention, September 20, 1973.

nection had failed to materialize. The firm's Washington, D.C., office also suggested that the government might react adversely to the speech. But the overwhelming response within the Bell System was positive – even enthusiastic. Most of the firm's executives offered suggestions in keeping with the main thrust of the speech.[43]

DeButts nevertheless had last-minute doubts about his position. He took those doubts to the man who might have been standing in his shoes, Robert Lilley. Could he depart so radically from the welcoming stance Romnes had taken toward competition? Lilley had reservations about what deButts proposed to say. They did not agree on the public stance that AT&T should take; Lilley did not even think that breaking up the Bell System – the term "divestiture" was not yet in use – would materially hurt the stockholders. But Lilley did not press his views. He countered deButts's doubts about reversing direction with the observation that the threat of competition had grown enormously since the time of Romnes's statement. Lilley also reiterated the obvious fact that deButts was now in charge. With a reminder to deButts that he could never be a retiring intellectual like Romnes, Lilley sent his CEO out to do battle. "Go ahead," he said, "I think it's worth the fight."[44]

This fateful interaction between deButts and the president of AT&T reveals yet again how tenuous was the Bell System's historic confrontation with public authority. DeButts's proclamation of the System's opposition to competition would affect the terms of debate both inside and outside AT&T for years to come. The echoes of the NARUC speech are still reverberating in the United States today. Would Lilley, if their roles had been reversed, have made a different choice by continuing more closely along the path Romnes had marked? Lilley argued later that deButts's gamble might have paid off, in which case our retrospective judgments might be quite different.[45]

Reassured, deButts charged ahead, with no hint of self-doubt. He began his Seattle speech with a reference to the 1927 NARUC address in which Walter Gifford had said that the Bell System had "an unusual obligation to see to it that the service shall at all times be adequate, dependable and satisfactory." Today, deButts said, AT&T also had an obligation – the unusual obligation of the speech's title – to oppose competition and favor regulation. This obligation stemmed both from the Bell System's experience with regulation and from its experience with compe-

[43]John D. deButts, interview, October 25, 1984, p. 26; Edward M. Goldstein to Alvin von Auw, providing feedback on the draft of deButts's NARUC talk, September 11, 1973; Thomas G. Cross to Alvin von Auw, on the accuracy and sources of terminal equipment data, September 11, 1973; Goldstein, interview, April 25, 1985, pp. 11–13; Alvin von Auw binder of comments on deButts's draft NARUC speech.
[44]Lilley, interview, September 23, 1985, pp. 22–3.
[45]Ibid.

tition. The latter was turning out to be "*contrived* competition" with "government-sponsored market allocation" (the alternative that AT&T's economic advisors had said was to be avoided at all costs).

DeButts cited data purporting to show that the use of non-Bell terminal equipment was causing degradation of the network. He asserted that "we cannot live with the deterioration of network performance that would be the inevitable consequence of 'certification' and the proliferation of customer-provided terminals that would ensue from it." He warned his audience that the financial burden resulting from the loss of Bell System terminal business would fall squarely on the local ratepayer as a result of the separations process.

Competition was beginning in the private line field as well. But to call the condition under which MCI supplied private line services between Chicago and St. Louis competition, deButts said, would be "to adopt a definition of that word that does not accord with that in any dictionary I have consulted." It was not competition because the Bell System was not able to respond. AT&T had applied for permission to file its Hi-Lo private line rates in February, but had not yet—in September—been able to do so. This was not competition; it was *contrived* competition. If competition was to be the order of the day, AT&T would compete—and compete vigorously—but to do so, it had to be free to move in the competitive environment.

DeButts concluded: "The time has come, then, for a moratorium on further experiments in economics—a moratorium sufficient to permit a systematic evaluation" of the feasibility and desirability of competition in telecommunications. The systematic evaluation should be done in a public forum, presumably Congress, while state and federal regulators—NARUC and the FCC—waited for its conclusion. There were, deButts acknowledged, risks in taking this question to the public. To the argument that he had done it to protect AT&T's profits, deButts repeated Gifford's 1927 assertion that the goal of the Bell System was service, subject only to the requirement that it earn a reasonable profit. To the argument that he was simply looking backward to the good old days, deButts replied that the lessons of the past could be ignored only at one's peril and that the Bell System's organization was a model for the future.

The NARUC speech climaxed the drive John deButts had mounted to revitalize the Bell System. Everyone in the System knew that their chairman had spoken. He had appealed to the old Bell values, reassuring those who felt threatened by the new competition. True, he had also tinkered with Bell's organizational framework, but his NARUC speech showed that these changes and the new marketing activities were undertaken in pursuit of traditional goals. They were designed to avoid the disasters of the late 1960s and to meet existing competition. But they could not—in light of the NARUC speech – be considered the first step in a process of transformation that would take AT&T out of its public utility status. Only the appointment of McGill pointed to a new role for AT&T, and he was still a voluble outsider in 1973. DeButts had wrapped himself in the flag of public service.

It was hard to ignore deButts in any circumstances, and the aggressive NARUC speech could not have been better designed to attract the attention of public officials. The regulators sat up and noticed. DeButts could see Strassburg in the audience at the NARUC convention, shaking his head and frowning as deButts spoke. The many constituencies of the Bell System – friend and foe – heard his statement as it was reported and distributed. DeButts looked forward with enthusiasm to a great public debate between the advocates of regulation and the devotees of competition. Convinced that the Bell System had given the United States the best telephone service in the world, he had reason to believe that his views would prevail.[46]

Antitrust crossfire

John deButts had spoken clearly and forcefully on behalf of the world's largest corporation. He had spoken about a matter of vital concern to the U.S. economy. He had reaffirmed the traditional company values in a manner that resonated throughout the Bell System, improving morale and reinforcing his campaign to improve the organization's performance. But outside the System, the NARUC speech either whistled into the wind or provoked a hostile reaction. Although deButts had hoped to arouse debate, he got instead the kind of negative scrutiny that a business living near the edge of antitrust law certainly should not have sought. In Washington, D.C., his ringing speech sounded more like a challenge to a duel than an invitation to talk. Eschewing the theme of compromise, deButts

[46]DeButts did not emphasize the effect of competition in long distance service on local rates because his NARUC audience was well aware of it. The convention passed a resolution supporting legislation transforming separations payments into a federal surcharge on interstate services that the Treasury would pay to the regulated providers of local telephone service. The FCC was not sufficiently mindful of the link between interstate competition and local telephone rates for the state commissioners. They wanted to take the separations process out of the Commission's hands. "Resolution to Seek Justice in the Pricing of Telephone Service," adopted by the 85th NARUC Annual Convention, Seattle, September 20, 1973; deButts, interview, October 25, 1984, p. 27.

Two weeks after deButts's speech, AT&T petitioned the FCC for the moratorium he had described. The FCC denied the petition. AT&T, *Petition*, "Regulatory and Policy Problems Presented by the Licensing of a Proliferation of Competing Common Carriers," October 4, 1973; FCC, *Memorandum Opinion and Order*, FCC Docket 18920, "Specialized Common Carriers," December 13, 1973, 44 FCC 2d 467.

had stated a position that seemed so extreme that there was no room for talk.

Nor was compromise likely to be his keynote if deButts turned for advice to his new general counsel. The patrician Horace Moulton had retired at the end of 1972, after serving in that capacity for over seventeen years. DeButts had selected Mark Garlinghouse for that critical post. Garlinghouse had had a long and distinguished career in the Bell System's legal departments; most recently, he had spent three years as AT&T's vice president for state regulatory affairs. A successful and aggressive debater, he had leaped at the chance to assume operating responsibilities and had been rewarded by a string of successes in regulatory forums. This experience, coupled with Garlinghouse's natural entrepreneurial sense, made him more responsive than most lawyers to AT&T's commercial opportunities. It also, however, made him less sensitive to the legal, that is, antitrust constraints under which the Bell System had long operated.

Garlinghouse also suffered in his role as general counsel from an aspect of his aggressive personality. He was seen by his colleagues as an open-minded man who was eager to hear all sides of a question. But he expressed this desire in a perverse way: He would open a discussion by stating an extreme position and wait for his listener to counter with opposing arguments. He never seemed to understand that his initial statement frightened most people into silence. As a result, he received little feedback and gradually came to believe his own opening gambits. DeButts, a forceful, imposing executive himself, liked the Garlinghouse style and worked closely with him. DeButts's NARUC speech was in the confrontational style of his new general counsel, and it was received similarly.[47]

That Garlinghouse's advice might soon be needed was made all the more likely by events in Washington in the aftermath of the speech. DeButts's belligerent address had stirred up a hornet's nest. Immediately after the speech, Strassburg met with representatives from various government bodies concerned with telecommunications, including the FCC, the Defense Department, the Senate Judiciary Committee, and the Justice Department. They decided that deButts had thrown down his gauntlet, challenging the federal government. He was going to use the vast political power of the Bell System to reverse the course of public policy. They resolved to watch the giant firm closely in order to make sure that it did not break any laws in this titanic match, that it fought fairly. The first response to the NARUC speech, then, was increased vigilance toward AT&T, not an opposing argument.[48]

The seed of suspicion fell on fertile ground in the Department of Justice.

[47]Alfred C. Partoll, interview, May 17, 1985, p. 26.
[48]Fox, interview, November 6, 1985, pp. 29–30.

The department had never completely abandoned its efforts to dismember the Bell System. A number of lawyers had left the department in 1956 in protest over the Consent Decree; others had stayed and continued to crusade against the country's largest monopoly. Internal memos and draft complaints had circulated within the Justice Department throughout the 1960s. Staff members had followed the controversy over TELPAK and reflected on its antitrust implications. They recorded complaints from equipment manufacturers and concluded, in one instance: "They cannot compete effectively with Western Electric because AT&T systematically uses its control of telephone service companies to promote the sale of Western Electric equipment and to discourage the purchase of other equipment." The Assistant Attorney General even recommended to his superior in 1970 that a new suit be filed. But instead of following this advice, the Nixon administration terminated the ongoing investigation of AT&T the following year.[49]

What the administration could not terminate, however, was the Justice Department's deep-seated concern about AT&T. In November 1973, that concern turned abruptly into action that was profoundly threatening to the Bell System. The department issued a Civil Investigative Demand to AT&T, asking it to produce documents about its relations with the specialized common carriers. The FCC's *Specialized Common Carriers* decision had posed several difficult questions for the telephone company, and the Justice Department had watched as it developed its answers. Now McGowan's lobbying activities began to take hold. The department's long-standing concern about Western Electric was revived as well, but in a separate internal inquiry.[50]

The first question AT&T had faced after the *Specialized Common Carriers* decision, whether to alter the Bell System's private line rates, had been answered in the affirmative in early 1973, although the Hi-Lo tariff did not take effect until mid-1974. A second question, how to interface Bell System lines with MCI's and Datran's facilities, had been more difficult to answer. AT&T had said in 1970 that it was willing to provide private line local loops for new carriers, but it tried nevertheless to maintain control over the way interconnection was implemented. Indeed,

[49]John S. James, Memorandum to George D. Reycraft, "Western Electric," March 22, 1961; Robert L. Wright, Memorandum to the Hon. Lee Loevinger, "AT&T Complaint," May 28, 1963; Samuel Z. Gordon, Memorandum to Baddia J. Rashid, "Recommendation to Close Investigation of AT&T-Western Electric Alleged Monopolization of Manufacture and Sale of Telephone Equipment," May 21, 1970; Robert B. Hummel, Memorandum to Charles L. Whittinghill, "AT&T/Western Electric Alleged Monopolization of Manufacture and Sale of Telephone Equipment," December 3, 1971.
[50]U.S. Department of Justice, Antitrust Division, Civil Investigative Demand No. 1570, November 26, 1973, ordering AT&T to provide certain documents relating to interstate private line services as part of its investigation of the possibility of antitrust violation; Phillip L. Verveer, interview, July 29, 1985, pp. 6–7.

AT&T opposed requests by MCI and Datran to use part of the radio spectrum to provide their own local loops, emphasizing its concerns about congestion of the radio spectrum in urban areas and stressing the greater efficiency of its high-capacity trunks compared to the facilities of the entering carrier.[51]

AT&T sought to limit MCI's interconnection to a single exchange area (and not to provide Bell interexchange facilities to complete MCI calls). After all, from the Bell System's perspective, MCI was a parasite, living off the spread between nationwide average rates and the costs on MCI's routes. There was fear within the company that if it allowed MCI to "piece out" its network, it would "sign away the right to review what they [MCI] do with our plant."[52] AT&T also decided to base its rates on the costs applicable to each location where interconnection was made–as opposed to using a nationwide average, as it did with Western Union. For this purpose, AT&T's management developed in 1972 the so-called Capital Contribution Plan, under which connecting carriers would pay a lump-sum contribution to the cost of building new plants instead of ongoing rental payments. In this way, AT&T would not be underwriting the costs and risks of its competitors' ventures. The EPC noted explicitly that the specialized common carriers were competitors, not partners like the independent telephone companies.[53]

But what was the relationship between AT&T and MCI? Were MCI and the other specialized common carriers entering the industry as competitors of AT&T? Or were they part of a single common carrier network? Under the Capital Contribution Plan, the specialized carriers clearly were treated as competitors. They would, moreover, have paid as if they were purchasing rather than leasing facilities over which they would have no control and in which they would have no equity rights. AT&T wanted to charge for the facilities as if it were selling them, but retain control as if it was leasing them. It was not about to be a benign parent to its fledgling competitors.

MCI widened the gap between the specialized carriers and AT&T even further. Although McGowan's firm already had the advantage of operating under the umbrella of AT&T's national average prices (albeit with the

[51]FCC, *First Report and Order*, FCC Docket 18920, "Specialized Common Carriers," June 3, 1971, 29 FCC 2d 870, at 962; FCC, *Further Notice of Proposed Rulemaking*, FCC Docket 18920, November 29, 1972, 38 FCC 2d 385.

[52]James S. Groves to Richard T. Dugan, memo transmitting "MCI Contract Revisions, Basic Issues," June 23, 1971.

[53]Minutes of the EPC meeting, September 18, 1972; Charles W. Jackson, "Approaches to Charging Other Carriers for Local Plant Leases," June 23, 1972; F.L. Wiley, "Capital Contribution to the Bell System by Non-Telephone Common Carriers," November 10, 1972. See also *US* v. *AT&T*, CA No. 74–1698 (D.D.C.), *Defendants' Third Statement of Contentions and Proof*, March 10, 1980, pp. 626–32.

prospect of Hi-Lo before it), MCI requested interconnection on the more favorable basis of the existing tariff governing Bell's relations with Western Union. The telegraph company had made a fateful decision in 1879 to abandon the telephone business to AT&T; in the decades that followed, it had gradually lost its position as the nation's leading telecommunications firm. Since that time, the Justice Department had been looking out for Western Union (as it had in the Kingsbury Commitment of 1913). The most recent example of Justice's concern was a 1970 agreement in which AT&T had provided the telegraph company with interconnection to the Bell System network at particularly favorable rates for five years. MCI was now claiming equal treatment under the nondiscrimination clause of the Communications Act. The same rules that applied to an infirm elderly citizen, it said, should apply as well to aspiring infants.

AT&T denied MCI's claim and gave notice to Western Union that it wanted to revise its rates. AT&T asserted that interconnection was a local matter, subject to state jurisdiction, and it filed its new interconnection tariffs before state commissions, not the FCC. It hoped thereby to maintain its position that MCI was a local – not a national – company and to increase MCI's costs of opposing its tariffs. Meanwhile, MCI was following every lead, trying to squeeze through every gap in the Bell System's walls. AT&T continued to beat back these individual attacks while cleaning up its act so as to present a smooth, impregnable surface to its pesky competitor.[54]

MCI's McGowan was hardly a passive recipient of Bell policies. He steadily increased his demands. AT&T had offered to provide local private line interconnection to specialized common carriers. After seeming to accept this offer initially, MCI insisted that it be allowed to provide intercity "foreign exchange" service as well. With this service – an intercity private line connected to a so-called foreign exchange – an AT&T subscriber in one location could behave as if it were in another. McGowan wanted to sell this service to his customers. To do so, he needed to connect MCI's lines to Bell switches. AT&T argued against connecting MCI to its switches on the grounds that MCI had authority only to provide dedicated point-to-point private lines with no switching. AT&T did not want MCI to compete by reselling Bell's own services. The FCC had denied lower rates for small

[54]John D. Goeken, MCI, to Richard T. Dugan, AT&T, January 5, 1971; James S. Groves to W.E. Albert et al., July 26, 1971; "Background Information, Other Common Carrier's State Tariff Filings" (typescript), September 20, 1973; J. Hugh Roff, Jr., AT&T, general attorney, to all general counsel, September 7, 1973; Thomas W. Scandlyn, AT&T, to Kelley E. Griffith, FCC, March 30, 1973; Thomas W. Scandlyn to Bernard Strassburg, September 5, 1973; Thomas W. Scandlyn to Bernard Strassburg, September 28, 1973; Daniel E. Emerson, AT&T, to Dean Burch, chairman, FCC, October 19, 1973. See also Paul Meunch, "Interconnection Policy," talk presented to the IEEE Communications Society, Washington, D.C., September 16, 1975.

users of the Bell System's private lines (TELPAK). McGowan was now proposing to offer the same facilities to customers at these lower prices. AT&T objected strenuously. The issue was so hotly contested that one observer commented: "If you say 'interconnect' three times in the middle of the Gobi Desert, you'll draw a crowd and start an argument."[55]

As the debate over interconnection heated up, MCI found itself overextended. Without a sharp improvement in its financial situation, MCI might well be bankrupt and McGowan would be out of the telecommunications business. MCI's boss responded by sharply curtailing his firm's ambitious construction plans to avoid disaster.[56] His inability to finance construction of an alternate communications network made it all the more imperative that his company gain access on favorable terms to the Bell System's network. If MCI could not grow by using Bell's foreign exchange service, it might not be able to stay the course.

McGowan consequently intensified the pressure on AT&T. He met with Strassburg and explained that MCI's very survival was involved in the question of its access to AT&T's intercity services. The problem was that the FCC had authorized only local interconnection with the Bell System. Strassburg thought that the chance that the FCC would approve MCI's claim to increased interconnection was no better than 50–50. Then, in an October meeting between McGowan, Kenneth Cox – an officer of MCI since he had left the FCC in 1970 – and Strassburg, a plan was formulated. Strassburg would embed the substantive issue – whether MCI could obtain foreign exchange service from AT&T – in a procedural one – whether interconnection tariffs were under state or federal jurisdiction. The Commission would, it was decided, be more likely to favor MCI on procedural rather than substantive grounds. Strassburg, who had seemed to approve AT&T's interconnection filings in front of the state commissions, went before the FCC the next day with a letter disapproving AT&T's appeal to the states. The chairman signed it on behalf of the Commission, giving his attention to the question of state versus federal

[55]MCI also claimed that it was entitled to interconnections for common control switching arrangement (CCSA) services – an arrangement for a restricted switched network within the general switched network – whereby private line circuits are furnished for the exclusive use of the CCSA customer, using switching machines that are shared with other customers. FCC, *Decision*, FCC Docket 19896, "Bell System Tariff Offerings," April 23, 1974, 46 FCC 2d 413, 48 FCC 2d 676, 1974, *aff'd sub nom. Bell Tel. Co. of Pa.* v. *FCC*, 503 F.2d 1250 (3d Cir. 1974), *cert. denied*, 422 U.S. 1026, 1975; "Users Uncertain and Concerned About Interconnection, Told By State and Federal Regulatory Spokesmen that Future Is Not as Muddled as It Would Appear; NAM Group Hears Spokesman for Major Parties in Dispute," *Telecommunications Reports*, Vol. 39, No. 45 (November 12, 1973), p. 3.
[56]McGowan later blamed the cancellation on AT&T's intransigence, but he made no mention of the phone company when he explained his decision to his associates at that time. *US* v. *AT&T*, CA No. 74–1698 (D.D.C.), William G. McGowan, testimony, April 9 and 13, 1981, Tr. 3685–9, 4007–20, and particularly Tr. 4038–43. See also Larry Kahaner, *On the Line* (New York: Warner Books, 1986).

jurisdiction – not to the question of which Bell services were at issue. Then Strassburg assured MCI in a separate letter later that month that AT&T's foreign exchange service was indeed covered by the chairman's letter.[57]

MCI followed up the letter from the FCC with a complaint in the federal district court, asking that AT&T be required to furnish MCI with intercity foreign exchange service. A witness from Strassburg's staff testified – apparently without FCC approval – on MCI's behalf. Hough of AT&T's Long Lines submitted an affidavit to the court and to the FCC, saying that MCI's use of Long Lines' intercity services would result in "sub-optimization of the network planning function" and "an immediate threat to all service." But just as the technical hazards from terminal interconnection that AT&T had talked about for the previous five years had failed to materialize, so the technical argument here was unconvincing. The court ordered AT&T to furnish the intercity connections to MCI.[58]

The legal contest then took a new turn, and AT&T, temporarily in a stronger position, badly overplayed its hand. The Bell System started to fulfill MCI's request for intercity foreign exchange service in January 1974, but it also appealed the district court's order. The appeals court overturned the order in April on the grounds that the FCC was still dealing with the question of which Bell facilities MCI was entitled to use. AT&T responded by immediately pulling the plug on all of the new foreign exchange connections that it had made for MCI. This was surely a foolish reaction for a company of AT&T's size and power. Since Vail's days, the Bell System had for the most part avoided serious conflicts with public authority by behaving with unusual circumspection. In this instance, its behavior was appropriate for an inconspicuous firm, not for the largest company in the world. The circuit court had ruled on procedural grounds only, and – as the court had emphasized – the FCC's decision was still to come. Garlinghouse later defended the decision as consistent with AT&T's appeal. If AT&T had not wanted to deny MCI the foreign exchange connections, why had it appealed the lower court's order? The FCC too might fail to take AT&T's opposition to MCI's expansionist claims seriously if the company had not acted. In any case, Garlinghouse

[57]*US* v. *AT&T*, CA No. 74–1698 (D.D.C.), Bernard Strassburg, testimony, December 8, 1981, Tr. 23375–82; *Defendants' Third Statement of Contentions and Proof*, pp. 687–8; Defendants' Exhibit D-24A-117A, Kenneth Cox, "10/3/73 Notes of Mtg w So Pac"; Dean Burch to Daniel E. Emerson, October 4, 1973; Laurence E. Harris, MCI, to Bernard Strassburg, October 15, 1973; Strassburg to Harris, October 19, 1973.
[58]*MCI* v. *AT&T*, 369 F. Supp. 1004 (E.D. Pa. 1973); Kelley E. Griffith, FCC, to Judge Clarence C. Newcomer (E.D. Pa.), December 13, 1973; *SPCC* v. *AT&T*, CA No. 78–0545, U.S. Dist. Ct., Dist. of Columbia, Defendants' Exhibit S-T-1, Richard R. Hough, written testimony, June 3, 1982, p. 91; *MCI* v. *AT&T*, CA No. 73–2499 (E.D. Pa.), Affidavit of Richard R. Hough, November 14, 1973.

said, MCI had only 10 to 15 foreign exchange customers, and a day's notice was sufficient for them to make alternate arrangements.[59] But Garlinghouse's argument notwithstanding, AT&T had clearly put itself at greater risk by abruptly pulling the plug on its tiny competitor.

Then, the FCC let the other shoe drop only one week later. It agreed with the district court that AT&T was obligated to supply foreign exchange service to MCI. And, in very harsh language, it condemned AT&T's opposition. Walter Hinchman, who had just replaced Strassburg as chief of the Common Carrier Bureau, set a new tone for the FCC's decisions. "We find and conclude," the Commission stated, ". . . that Bell is unlawfully applying and proposes to continue to apply the tariff schedules . . . filed with state regulatory commissions . . . and that Bell has discriminated against MCI and other specialized carriers. . . . We further conclude that the aforementioned conduct and practices are in violation of the [Communications] Act, and the declared policy of the Commission."[60]

This may all sound like a tempest in a teapot, but McGowan would argue later that AT&T's disconnection had had a decisive impact on MCI's growth. AT&T had acted so fast that MCI did not have time to discuss other arrangements with its customers; the customers simply found that their lines had been disconnected. Many of them did not return to MCI when the connections were restored. According to McGowan, "They had had it. They had enough trouble . . . and embarrassment."[61] Whether or not AT&T's action actually had these effects, the Bell System's action would later be cited – along with TELPAK and the cost of PCAs – as evidence of AT&T's anticompetitive intent.[62]

The issues, as always, were not as clear-cut as they seemed to the participants. There were puzzling internal contradictions in the positions taken by both AT&T and MCI. In many of its regulatory and legal pleadings, AT&T described MCI as a small facility, similar to an independent telephone company, offering point-to-point private line service only on specific routes. But AT&T also claimed that MCI was an alternate carrier, providing end-to-end service in competition with the Bell network. For its part, MCI was trying to provide service equivalent to that of the Bell System without constructing equivalent facilities. It was able to

[59]*MCI* v. *AT&T*, 496 F.2d 214 (3d Cir. 1974); *US* v. *AT&T*, CA 74–1698 (D.D.C.), F. Mark Garlinghouse, testimony, December 11, 1981, Tr. 24006–11, 24073–9, and William G. McGowan, testimony, April 9, 1981, Tr. 3696–8.

[60]FCC, *Decision*, FCC Docket 19896, "Bell System Tariff Offerings," April 23, 1974, 46 FCC 2d 413, at 435–6.

[61]*US* v. *AT&T*, CA 74–1698 (D.D.C.), William G. McGowan, testimony, April 9, 1981, Tr. 3699; deButts, interview, October 25, 1984, p. 22.

[62]*MCI* v. *AT&T*, No. 74 C 633 (N.D. Ill.), Closing Argument of C. Kamin for MCI, June 10, 1980, Tr. 11347–9; *US* v. *AT&T*, CA No. 74–1698 (D.D.C.), *Plaintiff's Memorandum in Opposition to Defendants' Motion for Involuntary Dismissal Under Rule 41(b)*, August 16, 1981, pp. 96–8.

charge low board-to-board prices for services AT&T was forced to sell at higher station-to-station prices, that is, it was outside the separations process. And McGowan claimed the right to use Bell's facilities to compete with AT&T – at best, a difficult position to maintain. Nevertheless, MCI was able to plead its case more effectively than AT&T by appealing to common carrier law and the doctrine of fairness, that is, by portraying itself in this instance as a customer, not a competitor, of AT&T.[63]

By adopting the view of MCI as a customer, the FCC could avoid conceptualizing the issue as one of extending competition to a significant degree. It mandated interconnection on the terms MCI requested, on the grounds of traditional regulatory principle. It held that the specialized common carriers were entitled to the Bell services they wanted on the basis of fairness and the need for a nondiscriminatory tariff. Rather than extending competition, the Commission insisted it was merely protecting the special, limited competition it had allowed in its earlier decision.[64]

Strassburg, as we have seen, had done more than this, and his independent actions had compounded the confusion. Leaving aside the question of whether his strategy sessions with MCI were proper behavior for a public official, there was still the matter of the official FCC statements that reiterated the claim made in *Above 890* and *Specialized Common Carriers* that only a small corner of AT&T's business was affected. Three percent was the number given. If one accepted this figure, AT&T surely was overreacting to such a minor request. But clearly, more than this was at stake. Only AT&T – and probably McGowan – seemed to realize that MCI's demands for intercity services represented the small nose of a very large camel.

McGowan revealed part of this large animal even before the FCC ordered AT&T to comply with MCI's request to use Bell's intercity services. While the appeals court was considering the issues raised by AT&T's and MCI's legal maneuvers, MCI filed a private antitrust suit against AT&T. MCI had been arguing before the FCC for three years that AT&T had been discriminating against it both in its tariffs and in its day-to-day administration of the tariffs. Despite the Commission's increasing tendency to accept MCI's construction of events, McGowan elected to

---

[63]Prophetically, MCI also included in its comparison the relationship of the operating companies to Long Lines and demanded that it be treated precisely like Long Lines. AT&T claimed that there was no discrimination, stating that the operating companies provided service to Long Lines in a cooperative venture. They cooperated through shared engineering and design – the systems approach – the management of joint costs, and the integrated nationwide rate structure that had been designed over the years in cooperation with the FCC. Thomas W. Scandlyn to Bernard Strassburg, September 5, 1973; see also Meunch, "Interconnection Policy."

[64]FCC, *Decision*, FCC Docket 19896, "Bell System Tariff Offerings," April 23, 1974, 46 FCC 2d 413.

extend his conflict with the Bell System to the antitrust arena. He had threatened as much to deButts in their stormy meeting, and he was not a man to make idle threats. If he could not make money by taking business away from the Bell System, he would force a more direct transfer of revenue.[65]

MCI, joined in this effort by Datran, also complained to the Department of Justice, which had been watching the debates and legal maneuvers with growing interest. By this time, the firm executive hand that had curbed the Justice Department just two years earlier was gone. The scandals of 1972 and 1973 had driven first Vice President Agnew and then Richard Nixon from office and made Gerald Ford President of the United States. Executive authority went into retreat; departmental and agency power increased. Even a strong President would have been hard pressed to keep control of the many power centers in the federal government in these circumstances. Gerald Ford was not the man for that job. MCI's and Datran's complaints fanned the Justice Department's embers of hostility toward Bell into flame.

Even a small government bureaucracy has several layers. Below the level of political appointees who receive most of the media's attention, the Justice Department is composed largely of younger lawyers. They joined with young economists who were just beginning to make their influence felt on other government policies to construct a theory for an antitrust suit against AT&T.[66] This theory was based on the concept of "a bottleneck monopoly." As the name suggests, this is a monopoly over a necessary part of a larger economic process. Market power in the bottleneck can be extended to other markets by charging high prices for access to the bottleneck, by setting severe conditions, or by refusing access entirely to outsiders.

According to this theory, the intercity network had been the bottleneck in the days of the Kingsbury Commitment, but now, in the 1970s, the local telephone networks were occupying that crucial position in the industry. AT&T, according to this argument, was now using the Bell Operating Companies' local monopolies – protected under state regulation – to prevent entry into the manufacture of equipment and the provision of interexchange services, that is, to shield Western Electric and Long Lines. The argument brought together the Justice Department's long-standing concern over AT&T's vertical integration and MCI's current complaints about its horizontal integration. The Bell System, they argued,

[65]*MCI* v. *AT&T*, No. 74 C 633 (N.D. Ill.), *Complaint*, March 6, 1974; deButts, interview, October 25, 1984, pp. 18–19.
[66]The economists were Robert Reynolds and Daniel Kelly in the department and Roger Noll and Bruce Owen as consultants. Phillip Verveer, "Regulation and the Access Problem: What's Happened and Where We are Now," in Alan Baughcum and Gerald R. Faulhaber (eds.), *Telecommunication Access and Public Policy* (Norwood, N.J.: Ablex, 1984), p. 86.

was illegally extending its legitimate, regulated monopoly of local service to all parts of the telecommunications industry. They cited AT&T's pricing policies in TELPAK and Hi-Lo; its interconnection policies, as shown by its insistence on PCAs for terminal equipment; and its less than generous treatment of MCI. They did not say that AT&T's position as a monopoly regulated by the FCC was illegal, but rather that AT&T was using this monopoly illegally in its response to the new competition introduced by the FCC.[67]

As AT&T was scissored between two differing public policy concepts of what its role should be, the risk to the giant firm mounted. The FCC regarded MCI as a *customer* of AT&T and was applying regulatory doctrines of nondiscrimination to the Bell System's responses. The Justice Department regarded MCI as a *competitor* and was applying antitrust standards to these same actions. Both of them, moreover, regarded AT&T's reactions to the new demands on the network as too aggressive and ungenerous. What appeared to the Bell System to be protective of the network appeared to the Justice Department to be protective instead of AT&T's monopoly.[68]

The balance of public policy was shifting from supporting Bell System's efficiency to promoting competition in telecommunications, and AT&T prepared to defend itself. Garlinghouse and the company's vice president for legislative affairs, John Fox, were negotiating with Thomas Kauper, the Assistant Attorney General for Antitrust, continuously after April 1974. These negotiations came about in a curious manner. The government of Puerto Rico had asked the telephone company to manage its new phone system (supplied by ITT) and to teach the Puerto Ricans how to operate it. Garlinghouse and Fox went to Kauper to make sure that this contract would not be in violation of the 1956 Consent Decree. Kauper offered to give them a "business letter" to that effect, but he carefully specified that this letter would not affect the Justice Department's current investigation of AT&T. The AT&T officers were horrified to encounter the ongoing investigation. Despite the Civil Investigative Demand of the previous November, they had heard nothing more from the Justice Department. This in itself was unusual, since the two parties typically were in contact whenever an investigation was underway. It may well be that Justice only became serious about the matter at that time. MCI had filed

---

[67]The Supreme Court had just confirmed a lower court finding that the Otter Tail Power Company had "used its monopoly power in the towns in its service area to foreclose competition" in other towns. Although the parallel was not exact, the economists drew on *Otter Tail* to make their case. *Otter Tail Power Co.* v. *US*, 410 U.S. 366, 1973, at 377.

[68]*US* v. *AT&T*, CA No. 74–1698 (D.D.C.), *Plaintiff's Third Statement of Contentions and Proof*, pp. 85–9.

its suit in March and AT&T had disconnected MCI's lines in April, events that probably intensified the Justice Department's investigation.

But once Kauper had dropped his bombshell, the two parties began a dialogue that lasted throughout the summer and into the fall. AT&T answered questions and even filed a brief in September 1974. Yet there were always more questions. Fox went to see William Saxbe, the Attorney General, whom he knew, to get assurances that no suit would be brought against AT&T without prior discussion with the company. The assurances were freely given.

It was in this context that Fox and Garlinghouse received a message from Saxbe on November 19, 1974, insisting that they meet with him the next day. Garlinghouse and several AT&T lawyers flew to Washington. Delayed by the weather, they arrived late in the morning to meet with Saxbe, Kauper, and members of the Justice Department's antitrust staff. Saxbe opened the meeting by announcing that he was going to file a lawsuit against AT&T that same day. Everyone – whether they were from AT&T or the Justice Department – was surprised. But although Kauper was caught off guard by Saxbe's decision, he had, after all, helped to formulate the theory behind it, and he was not reluctant to pursue the case.

Saxbe assured Garlinghouse and his colleagues that he had the backing of the President and the cabinet. But after the fact, President Ford did not recall having spoken to Saxbe about it. William Simon, the Secretary of the Treasury, was violently opposed to the suit, and he insisted that it had never been discussed at a cabinet meeting. Saxbe apparently was acting on his own. The AT&T lawyers argued against the suit, raising points ranging from the lack of public interest to the lack of a legal basis for the action. But Saxbe left abruptly to keep an appointment on Capitol Hill.

Garlinghouse and Fox immediately tried to prevent the filing of the suit. They attempted to reach President Ford, but he was out of the country. Simon, who was contacted by his friend deButts, tried repeatedly to talk to Saxbe, but he could not get through before Saxbe himself left town. The die was cast and AT&T suddenly discovered itself fighting a three-front war against the FCC, MCI, and the Department of Justice. Earnest as he was about provoking debate, deButts had certainly not sought this kind of struggle when he delivered his NARUC speech.[69]

What precipitated the suit during a Republican administration, which is normally friendly to big business? Clearly, the Justice Department's ongoing interest in the Bell System had been intensified by deButts's address the previous fall. The various abortive attempts to revive the suit against

[69]DeButts, interview, October 25, 1984, pp. 30–1; Jim G. Kilpatric, interview, May 9, 1984, pp. 18–20; Fox, interview, November 6, 1985, pp. 13–23.

Western Electric had kept the issue alive, and it was again active in 1974. The squabbles with MCI in the spring had provided a separate impetus for a suit, and the twin concerns with the Bell System's vertical and horizontal integration reinforced each other. Moreover, the looseness of the Ford administration—demonstrated graphically to AT&T at the last moment—allowed Saxbe almost unlimited discretion, and he decided to support forcefully those pressing for a suit.

The government's complaint, filed on November 20, 1974, alleged that AT&T had monopolized and conspired to monopolize various telecommunications markets. The complaint was quite general—as they usually are in major antitrust cases—and it provided a wide base to accommodate the more specific allegations that would be generated by subsequent investigations. The relief requested was also sweeping. The government sought to have Western Electric divested from AT&T and divided into separate companies, and to have some or all of the Bell Operating Companies split away from AT&T's Long Lines. The question of Bell Labs was postponed for a later decision.[70]

Confronted by these surprising and formidable challengers, deButts (advised by Garlinghouse) responded in characteristically uncompromising fashion. The company's general counsel had been meeting with MCI lawyers during the summer to discuss their private suit against AT&T. MCI's demands were in the neighborhood of $50 million; Garlinghouse advised deButts that the suit was not worth more than $1 or $2 million— close to the amount of the lawyers' fees at that time. DeButts declined to settle. When the Justice Department filed its suit, he took the same line. He held a news conference at which he declared AT&T's innocence. Protesting the justness of AT&T's position, he said that he would never approach the government to settle the case. AT&T would prove its case in a court of law. "I cannot understand," he said, "why the Justice Department would want to get rid of something that is working efficiently. . . . We have done well by our customers; we have done well by our employees; we have done well by our share owners. We are proud of that record."[71]

Indeed, deButts and the entire Bell System had much to be proud of, but AT&T's management had failed in the early 1970s to chart correctly the shifting political tides in the United States. They had improved the efficiency of the Bell System by reaffirming its traditional values and

[70]*US* v. *AT&T*, CA No. 74–1698 (D.D.C.), *Complaint*, November 20, 1974.

[71]John D. deButts, "Opening Statement," news conference, November 21, 1974; "Company Replies," *The New York Times*, November 21, 1974, p. 1; "No Consent Decree Will Be Sought, Its Chairman Says," *The New York Times*, November 22, 1974, p. 55; "AT&T Will Fight Antitrust Action, Says Ability to Raise Capital May Be Affected," *The Wall Street Journal*, November 22, 1974, p. 8; Fox, interview, November 6, 1985, p. 24.

providing it with forceful leadership. But those same values drew AT&T into deeper conflict with public authority. DeButts had belligerently proclaimed that the government, as well as the Bell System, should adhere to the established traditions of the regulated monopoly. With great verve and determination he had steered AT&T close to the rocks of public conflict. In 1974 the telephone company ran aground.

IV

The conflict broadens

The Consumer Communications Reform Act of 1976

John deButts was incensed by the government's antitrust suit. The charges were, he thought, baseless. AT&T – a company that was above all a good corporate citizen – had surely not broken the law. The telephone company had tried to accommodate the FCC's new policies toward terminal equipment, subject only to the need to protect the telephone network. It had given MCI everything that it was entitled to at any time, albeit not an inch more or a moment early. The problems that had arisen were, in deButts's view, the result of excess zeal in carrying out the Bell System's mission or of the repeated shifts in direction that the FCC had made – shifts that made planning a precarious enterprise. This was certainly not the stuff of a major antitrust suit. As for breaking up the Bell System: "If it ain't broke, don't fix it."

The courtroom seemed a poor place to frame national telecommunications policy, and deButts sought to shift to personal negotiations with members of the President's cabinet, or their lawyers. He was in constant touch with members of Ford's cabinet about other matters. Negotiations had ended the previous suit, and negotiations had produced the agreement on separations that had solved the problem of wartime telephone pricing.

But relations between AT&T and the federal government – in particular the FCC – had soured in recent years. The TELPAK controversy had been handled in a confrontational manner, and during the mid-1960s the agency had taken a step toward a more formal adversarial relationship when it instituted its first major investigation of the Bell System's rate base and rate of return. Differences of opinion had increasingly been expressed in more formal and impersonal ways. Strassburg and deButts were about as compatible as Luther and the Pope. Hinchman, Strassburg's successor at the FCC, was openly hostile to AT&T. Any negotiations would have to overrule the FCC, as – deButts thought – would any sensible public policy. The Bell System's CEO had offered the government a choice in his NARUC speech. But a year later, it did not look as if this choice was to be made by calm deliberation. Confrontation rather than negotiation was emerging as the norm in framing telecommunications policy.[1]

DeButts consequently adopted a two-part strategy to deal with the attacks on the company. His lawyers tried to get the government's suit thrown out, and he tried to circumvent his opponents by an appeal to Congress. The legislative strategy, however, opened a whole new front for controversy. It did not inhibit the courts, which remained unsympathetic to AT&T's arguments. And all the while, the growth of competition was generating a sense of unease among the company's top managers in the mid-1970s that was reminiscent of the ferment at the start of the decade.

Even though the earlier distress in part reflected a lack of direction from 195 Broadway, the later discomfort was sometimes eased, sometimes increased, and always affected by deButts's ceaseless effort to improve AT&T's operations. John deButts had started many organizational hares in his first two years as CEO, and he spent much of his time running them down. A massive organization cannot be redirected simply by announcing changes. Change has to be managed. Hundreds of thousands of employees had to be motivated to accomplish their traditional tasks with greater enthusiasm. Thousands of managers had to be convinced that deButts's goals could be accomplished and that, where necessary, they should change their customary patterns of behavior to adjust successfully to a new environment. All of this had to be done if morale, earnings, and service were to be improved. DeButts harnessed his great energy to this job, and these internal tasks occupied the bulk of his time.

He and Garlinghouse, his combative general counsel, did not, however, neglect the government's suit. They began by arguing that this new suit was illegal under *res judicata;* it was precluded by the existence of the 1956 Consent Decree. They also argued that the court lacked jurisdiction because the relevant questions were before the FCC.[2]

Judge Joseph Waddy rejected their first argument and asked the FCC to comment on the second. On the last day of 1975, the FCC filed an *amicus curiae* brief on this issue. The Commission did not follow the lead of the court that had referred the Carterfone complaint to the FCC under the doctrine of primary jurisdiction. Instead, the agency reviewed the difference between its statutory framework in the Communications Act and the antitrust standards of the court. It reminded the court that "the Communications Act does not explicitly authorize the Commission to

[1]William R. Stump, interview, November 30, 1984, pp. 22–4; Bernard Strassburg, interview, March 27, 1985.
[2]*US* v. *AT&T,* CA No. 74–1698, U.S. Dist. Ct., Dist. of Columbia, AT&T, *Answer,* February 4, 1975.

alter AT&T's corporate structure." The Commission went on to say that in areas in which the FCC had made no ruling, it saw "no general reason why antitrust policy should be deemed inapplicable as a matter of law." Speaking of both interconnection and tariffs, the FCC washed its hands of antitrust matters: "These carrier-initiated tariffs which have not been approved by the Commission do not in our opinion immunize the carrier against claims that the tariffs are anticompetitive."[3]

The battle between the government advocates of regulating monopoly and of antitrust prosecution was apparently going to be decided without a shot being fired. On November 24, 1976, Waddy issued an opinion that the court did indeed have jurisdiction over the matters raised by the Justice Department complaint. But AT&T–the world's largest regulated monopoly–would not leave the field so easily. It appealed Judge Waddy's decision, contending that regulation immunized Bell from antitrust liability, even though the FCC did not support that position. As the appeal moved toward its unsuccessful conclusion, the case slipped into a procedural limbo. Judge Waddy was seriously ill, and little other activity was taking place.[4]

AT&T had nevertheless started to gear up for a trial, and in particular for the beginning of "discovery," the process whereby each party obtains access to the records of the other. The logistics of this suit–the number of people and papers involved–were unbelievably complex, and AT&T had to organize a special department, Administration D, just to provide support for its lawyers. Antitrust trial work would be handled primarily by outside counsel: Dewey, Ballantine in New York and the giant Chicago law firm of Sidley and Austin. But a great deal of the preparation would be

---

[3]Despite these limitations on the FCC's power, the Commission did not want to abdicate its authority to the court. It argued that the expert regulatory commission should have primary jurisdiction in cases of overlap, and it closed its argument with a plea to the court to consult the FCC if it planned to do anything radical: "The court, we suggest, may not require entry into the communications market, may not frustrate FCC orders to interconnect telephone systems, and may not base any antitrust relief upon tariff provisions that have been approved or prescribed by the Commission. These matters are impliedly delegated to the Commission's exclusive jurisdiction. . . . We urge the Court to take no action that will substantially alter the industry structure without initial consideration by the FCC of how such action will comport with the 'public interest,' as perceived by the Commission in the light of its mandate under the Communications Act." *US* v. *AT&T*, CA No. 74–1698 (D.D.C.), *Memorandum of Federal Communications Commission as Amicus Curiae*, December 30, 1975, pp. 15, 20, 22, 29.

[4]Judge Joseph C. Waddy, *Memorandum Opinion and Order on Jurisdictional Issues*, November 24, 1976, *US* v. *AT&T*, CA No. 74–1698, 427 F. Supp. 57 (D.D.C., 1976); *AT&T* v. *US*, AT&T, *Petition for Writ of Certiorari to the United States District Court for the District of Columbia*, January 6, 1977. Although Judge Waddy's opinion was appealed to the Court of Appeals and to the Supreme Court, both courts declined to hear the appeal and the decision stood, *cert. denied*, 429 U.S. 1071, 97 S. Ct. 824, 50 L. Ed. 2d 799, 1977; *cert. denied*, No. 77–1009 (D.C. Cir., May 27, 1977), *cert. denied*, 434 U.S. 966, 98 S. Ct. 507, 54 L. Ed. 2d 452, 1977.

done by in-house attorneys–in contrast to IBM's practice in its long-running antitrust suit–because, as the AT&T lawyer in charge said, "antitrust and regulation are, for us, two sides of the same coin." Even though the FCC had in effect bowed out of the case on the grounds that its actions did not preclude the antitrust proceeding, the telephone company would base its defense in the government suit and the many private antitrust suits it was facing on the pervasiveness of regulation.[5]

Under attack as he was from so many quarters, AT&T's chairman had good cause to reconsider the course he had charted. Was the uncompromising stance he had taken in his NARUC speech and was taking in the government's suit the best one? DeButts received conflicting advice from his associates. Garlinghouse started from the position that his chairman's moratorium idea was dead. The public had acquiesced in the growth of competition, even if it had not made any clear statement in this regard. Should not AT&T then reverse field, he asked, abandoning its role as a public utility? It could take its cue from the Sherman Antitrust Act rather than the Communications Act and behave as a competitive firm. It would need as well to abandon its commitment to universal service, to work for the elimination of the contribution Long Lines made to local service rates through separations in order to make its long distance services competitive. AT&T, in short, should work with the Justice Department to create competitive conditions in an industry that would then be reorganized along board-to-board lines.[6]

Different advice came from Edward Crosland, who was senior vice president in charge of relations between the Bell System and the federal government. He stood at the same level in the AT&T hierarchy as Garlinghouse, with whom he disagreed. The message of the NARUC speech was still valid, Crosland asserted. DeButts should continue publicly to champion the same traditional values that he was so successfully advocating within the Bell System. With the proper approach, the System's public utility role would be reaffirmed by Congress. Garlinghouse wanted to accept the FCC's initiative and work with the Justice Department, but Crosland wanted to make an end run around the Commission and, presumably, the Justice Department as well. To bolster his position, he reconvened and expanded the panel of outside advisors he had earlier consulted.

The advisors concluded that properly drafted legislation would solve many of the Bell System's policy problems. A favorable bill could be

[5]Harold S. Levy, AT&T General Solicitor, "Notes for Presidents' Conference, Week of November 8, 1976."
[6]Alvin von Auw, *Heritage & Destiny: Reflections on the Bell System in Transition* (New York: Praeger Publishers, 1983), pp. 91–2; Alvin von Auw to Robert G. Lewis, June 27, 1986.

passed, they said, because of two important assets of the Bell System: the System's positive public image, which derived from the excellence of the American telephone system, and the separations policy. The System's interstate rates were, as a result of separations, subsidizing local operations, while the aspiring interstate competitors were free of the obligations to provide universal service and to subsidize local rates. But as deButts well knew, when the Bell System tried to meet the competition with lower interstate rates, the competitors and the government objected strenuously. "Confusion and contradiction," said Newton Minow, former chairman of the FCC, "thus imperil the nation's communications service." A solution will come only "when national policy makers make a choice between contradictory objectives." The place for them to do so was in Congress, which had passed both the Sherman Antitrust Act and the Federal Communications Act. Eugene Rostow, who had served as chairman of President Johnson's Task Force on Telecommunications, concurred.

Minow recommended a two-part strategy. AT&T should first try for congressional reaffirmation of the need for a unitary telephone network. Failing that, it should push for legislation that would at least put all of the competitors on an equal footing, that is, legislation that would deregulate most of the Bell System's operations. Despite AT&T's strong preference for the first option, the choice would be up to Congress. AT&T would come out ahead if the legislature could be persuaded to make a choice and avoid "the worst of both possible worlds: a combination of rigid regulation and unfair competition."[7]

DeButts, normally receptive to the views of his general counsel, found Crosland's approach more congenial. He did not, however, see the need to choose between the two strategies. He would pursue both. Direct negotiations with the Justice Department would be avoided because deButts expected AT&T to be fully exonerated in court or to face more sympathetic opponents after the administration changed in Washington. But he would make the case for pricing flexibility–for competitive pricing–wherever he could. At the same time, AT&T would present its case to Congress. AT&T's leaders, like their political advisors, thought that a century of public service would get its just returns on Capitol Hill.

They did not pay much attention to the problems that the largest corporation in the world would be likely to have garnering congressional sup-

[7]Edward B. Crosland, report presented at the EPC meeting, July 7, 1975: "Competition in Telecommunications – A Congressional Solution," June 23, 1975, see especially Tab C, "Comments of Advisory Board Members," comments of board member Newton Minow, pp. 1–3. See also the sympathetic report by some economic advisors in FCC Docket 20003, "Economic Implications of Customer Interconnection, Jurisdictional Separations and Rate Structures," Bell Exhibit 22, Herman G. Roseman and Irwin M. Stelzer, National Economic Research Associates, Inc. (NERA), "Economic Problems of Regulated Competition," April 1975.

port or to the opposition that its political activity might arouse. Power in Washington had become more diffuse in the years since World War II as the government grew in size and complexity. This process had accelerated in the "Watergate Congress," elected in 1974 in the wake of the Nixon impeachment hearings. The chairmen of the congressional committees had been forced to surrender some of their power to control committee operations; the various subcommittees, most relevantly the House Sub-committee on Communications, had acquired their own staffs and had become primary loci of power.[8] These changes took place against the background of a nation experiencing a profound crisis of confidence. The legitimacy of all large organizations was being undermined by inflation, the conduct of the Vietnam War, and Watergate. The decline in presidential authority, the dispersion of congressional power, and public distrust of large institutions were bound to complicate any legislative campaign AT&T might mount. But in 1975 Crosland's expert advisors did not stress these political storm clouds; their forecast was for clear skies and a difficult but successful voyage. DeButts (whose Washington experience dated from the congenial 1950s) agreed. He reported to the Bell System Presidents' Conference in November 1975, that the decision to seek specific legislation had been made. The campaign for this bill, deButts said, "may well be *the most* important public affairs effort we have ever undertaken." This was, he exhorted, "no time to sound retreat but to press every advantage that we have with all the force we can muster. Nineteen seventy-six may well prove the year of decision for our business."[9]

The proposal in question actually had been born in conversations with NARUC and the organization of independent telephone companies, USITA. The independent companies worked on it with AT&T. Crosland cleared it with the Bell System's two big unions, the Communications Workers of America and the International Brotherhood of Electrical Workers. Everyone climbed on board as Crosland walked the bill around the industry, but despite Crosland's best efforts, it still was known instantly and universally as the "Bell bill."[10]

Its full name was the "Consumer Communications Reform Act (CCRA)"

---

[8]The Communications and Power Subcommittee of the House Commerce Committee was split in two. Communications went to Torbert MacDonald of Massachusetts, who built a staff led by Harry (Chip) Shooshan. Shooshan's staff was taken over by Lionel Van Deerlin when MacDonald died in 1976, and Van Deerlin became subcommittee chairman. Roger H. Davidson and Walter J. Oleszek, *Congress Against Itself* (Bloomington: Indiana University Press, 1977); Harry M. Shooshan III and Charles L. Jackson, interview, March 27, 1985, pp. 3–4.
[9]John D. deButts, "Closing Remarks," Presidents' Conference, Sea Island, Georgia, November 14, 1975, pp. 1, 6–7, emphasis in the original.
[10]Edward B. Crosland, interview, January 8, 1986, pp. 36–9.

of 1976. Like deButts's NARUC speech, the CCRA was designed to provoke discussion, and like the speech, the bill staked out an extreme
position. It did not seem to be designed for compromise. It promised
instead to harden the opposing positions. Seeking always to initiate a
debate, deButts looked again as if he had tried to end one. He challenged
Congress with a stance so unyielding that there was little apparent room
to negotiate, to accommodate opposing interests. The CCRA made it
appear in Washington that deButts was digging in, preparing to fight for
the principles of the NARUC speech.[11]

The bill was cast as an amendment to the Communications Act of 1934.
It reaffirmed the nation's commitment to universal service and went beyond existing law to state that a unified telephone network had been and
continued to be essential for the achievement of that goal. The bill bluntly
asserted that the existing rate structure, by which it meant primarily
separations, had promoted universal service. Competition in interstate
services was doubly dysfunctional: The competing carriers duplicated resources and imperiled the existing rate structure. The bill would avoid
these dangers by setting much stiffer standards for the authorization of
new carriers and by approving the use of incremental, or marginal, cost
pricing. Thus, the CCRA repudiated the FCC's policy of increasing competition in interstate communications. Only under exceptional conditions
would the agency be empowered to authorize additional entry. AT&T, in
contrast, would have the freedom to set prices at a level competitive with
those offered by the existing entrants. TELPAK and Hi-Lo would be
lawful. The FCC's long-standing debate over the use of incremental or
average costs would be resolved decisively in favor of the former. Board-
to-board entry would be discouraged, competitive pricing encouraged.[12]

The Bell bill would write into law both parts of the contradictory position AT&T had taken before the FCC in the rate cases. Although AT&T
would be the monopoly supplier of telecommunication services, it would
be allowed to price competitively to maintain its monopoly. Consumers
would get the benefits of competitive pricing, but competitors would not
be encouraged to try to crack the monopoly. Of course, if AT&T's defense
of its position was not to imperil the subsidy of local operations obtained
from interstate service, marginal cost pricing would have to be introduced
selectively. The Bell System would have to discriminate in favor of those
customers facing competitive suppliers. It would, in short, have to use

[11]Edward M. Block, interview, December 3, 1985, pp. 48–50, 81–6.
[12]This would preempt the opposing decision that the Commission would issue in October
1976. 94th Congress, 2nd Session, House, H.R. 12323, "Consumer Communication Reform Act of 1976," introduced March 4, 1976; FCC, *Memorandum Opinion and Order*,
FCC Docket 18128, "Revisions of Tariff FCC No. 260 Private Line Services, Series 5000
(Telpak)," adopted September 23, 1976, released October 1, 1976, 61 FCC 2d 587.

TELPAK as a model. The CCRA would enhance one goal of the 1934 act – universal service – at the expense of another – nondiscriminatory pricing. Rather surprisingly, the bill also endorsed the Bell position on terminal equipment. AT&T had argued unsuccessfully before the FCC that the regulation of customer-provided terminal equipment should be left to the state regulatory commissions. One might reasonably claim that the 1934 act had already left that power with the states, but this contention had been rejected by the FCC (which received the blessing of the courts). The CCRA would draw a firm jurisdictional line around federal authority, thwarting the FCC and, most likely, leaving the Bell System in control of end-to-end service in most jurisdictions. This was a vulnerable position to try to hold in 1976, and a bill designed to foster compromise surely would have yielded more ground on this point. Goldstein and others suggested as much to Crosland, but he rejoined that the terminal provisions were needed to get union support of the bill. In this way, the Bell System's vertical integration controlled its legislative strategy; no compromise on terminal equipment was offered. In fact, neither the workers whose jobs were at stake nor the executives loyal to Vail's ideals had much use for this suggestion. But the Bell bill, whatever deButts's initial motives, clearly had been drafted to defend the NARUC principles, not to achieve conciliation.[13]

Ill-conceived as a bargaining platform, the CCRA also started its legislative passage under less than auspicious conditions. The measure was introduced late in the 94th Congress, and it would have been truly remarkable if it had passed at that time. Legislation of this magnitude seldom can be passed in a single session of Congress. A comparable bill was introduced in the Senate, and both would have had to pass before Congress adjourned in October.[14] AT&T apparently anticipated the delay. Its strategy was to gather widespread support for the bills, creating a sense of momentum before pressing for committee hearings, debate, and passage. At first it appeared that this maneuver might work. The House bill collected 175

[13]Edward M. Goldstein to Robert G. Lewis, October 25, 1986, attachment; Shooshan and Jackson, interview, March 27, 1985, pp. 30–6.
[14]The CCRA was introduced in Congress by Teno Roncalio, Wyoming's sole representative. One informal story about these events suggests that his sponsorship was an accident. Congressman Roncalio did not get many bills from his constituents in Wyoming, and he was always on the lookout for good causes. He was talking to someone at a Washington cocktail party in the spring of 1976 and asked if this person had a bill. It was no secret by then that AT&T was interested in a legislative solution to its regulatory dilemmas, and Roncalio's respondent turned out to have a draft bill, which he gave to the congressman. Roncalio, in turn, submitted it to Congress the next day, and AT&T's legislative staff read about it in the newspapers. R.L. McGuire and Michael Baudhuin, interview, November 16, 1984.
    John deButts said that Roncalio was requested to introduce the bill by some independent telephone companies. 94th Congress, 2nd Session, House, Committee on Interstate and Foreign Commerce, Subcommittee on Communications, Hearing on H.R. 12323, John D. deButts, testimony, September 28, 1976, p. 67.

sponsors and the Senate bill 17 by the time of adjournment. Meanwhile AT&T had launched a formidable public relations campaign to increase the grass-roots pressure on Congress. Because the Bell System operated in every state, community, and indeed most homes throughout the country, AT&T could generate a considerable amount of political energy. It could reach local political leaders through the Bell Operating Companies, each of which had public relations and public affairs departments that could provide staff support for a broad-based effort of this sort. This network was activated at deButts's personal behest. Bell officials reached out to intellectual and political elites. Literature was distributed describing the threat that competition posed to the subsidy local rates received from long distance. But the campaign quickly lost momentum; there was no sense of crisis about the telephone system among the elites—and the general population as well. After all, deButts had the Bell System running better than ever, and it was difficult for even a sophisticated opinion leader to perceive how the FCC's halting steps toward competition were endangering the public interest. The great debate fizzled out.[15]

This was unfortunate for AT&T, which needed all the support it could get in Washington. It had angered a vital subcommittee in its rush to obtain sponsors for the CCRA, and it would pay dearly for that choice of tactics. Lionel Van Deerlin, chairman of the House Subcommittee on Communications, and his staff were irritated when a bill in their field of authority was introduced without consulting them. In the normal course of passage, any such bill would have to go through their subcommittee before it could be enacted, but they were not about to hold hearings on a measure that had not even been discussed with them before it was introduced. Regardless of how many congressmen had put their names on the measure, the subcommittee was determined to defend its turf. The company's political advisors had not paid sufficient attention to the nitty-gritty of congressional politics. AT&T had clearly blundered by not greasing the tracks at the subcommittee level before it tried to move the bill through Congress.[16]

Van Deerlin was sufficiently annoyed to enter the legislative contest on the other side, using the numerous weapons that a subcommittee chairman had in his arsenal. He announced hearings in 1976 on the general subject of competition in telecommunications, in effect sidetracking the Bell System's drive for the CCRA. It would be virtually impossible to get the rule-conscious House to do anything specific while a respected subcommittee

[15]"A New Direction in Telecommunications Policy—Is It in the Public Interest?" and "Why Federal Regulatory Policies May Drive Up Home Telephone Rates," prepared by the Bell System for distribution to community relations groups, 1976; Kenneth J. Whalen, interview, July 18, 1985, pp. 40–2; Block, interview, December 3, 1985, p. 49.
[16]Shooshan and Jackson, interview, March 27, 1985, pp. 23–9.

had the general matter under consideration. Van Deerlin clearly had the tactical advantage in his struggle with the telephone company.

Two important witnesses at the subcommittee hearings were Richard Wiley, chairman of the FCC, and William McGowan, chairman of MCI. Just as pharaoh had hardened his heart against the Israelites, the FCC had by this time rethought and solidified its commitment to competition. Wiley succeeded in rousing the subcommittee's protective feelings toward the regulatory agency. Even though Congress spent much of its time browbeating the Commission chairmen, the legislature also provided the Commission's mandates and budgets. After Wiley's testimony, the subcommittee staff and the FCC staff began to work together, and this informal network relentlessly drew the subcommittee closer to the agency's position.[17]

McGowan too was an effective witness. He understood the tactics of arguing before government bodies. He made the arguments that were most appealing to the group he was addressing, and – not unnaturally – he was usually received well by that group. To Congress, he presented himself as the little guy being squeezed out by a giant monopoly. He skillfully played on the sympathy Americans have always had for the audacious challenger. McGowan accused AT&T of bringing its enormous corporate weight to bear on Congress, a charge that resonated on the Hill, where the Bell System's public affairs campaign had so recently been focused. He claimed that he wanted to use new technologies and serve new markets, but Bell looked only to the past. He said that he wanted only to take care of customers who were not well served by the Bell System. He disparaged the clear signs that MCI was trying to enter precisely the market served by the Bell System. McGowan shot from the hip and kept moving.[18]

The Bell System's witnesses, Hough from Long Lines and deButts himself, did not make a dent in the subcommittee's resistance. It was intrinsically hard to argue the case for monopoly. In an interchange noted prominently by the subcommittee staff, Congressman Louis Frey, the ranking Republican, tried to elicit from deButts a vision of the Bell System's role in telecommunications during the next generation. It took five tries before he could get an appropriate response. DeButts finally said, "Our business in this industry is to provide people with communications of all forms. We think down the road we should continue to provide all people with all forms of communications using whatever technology is

[17]Shooshan and Jackson, interview, March 27, 1985, pp. 29–35, 37–8.
[18]94th Congress, 2nd Session, House, Committee on Interstate and Foreign Commerce, Subcommittee on Communications, Hearing, "H.R. 12323 and Related Bills, Competition in the Domestic Communications Common Carrier Industry," Statement of William G. McGowan, September 29, 1976, pp. 34–7A.

available at that particular time, and doing everything we can to develop new technology as time goes on in order to keep the service good and as inexpensive as possible." It was the kind of speech that found a sympathetic audience inside the Bell System, but not outside, and especially not in Congress. There was considerable concern on the Hill about the size and power of the Bell System, and deButts's repetition of "all" and "everything" seemed to speak to that issue, leaving no room for others to share with Bell. Neither Van Deerlin nor his staff found deButts's vision appealing.[19]

Congressman Timothy Wirth followed Frey. He recalled to deButts an occasion a few months earlier when Crosland had testified before a rather large audience. Wirth had asked all of those who worked for the Bell System to stand up. Nearly the entire audience rose. Wirth noted with approval that deButts had come this time without an entourage, but he hounded the Bell CEO about the amount AT&T had paid its employees to come and hear their representative testify on that earlier occasion. He pressed, too, about the amount of money the Bell System had spent on its other lobbying efforts. Wirth echoed McGowan's argument that AT&T was making illegitimate use of its regulated revenues to maintain its regulated monopoly.[20]

By the close of the 94th Congress, Van Deerlin had stopped the Bell steamroller. The CCRA had bogged down because of the tactics used to introduce it, the bill's unyielding stance toward competition, and the effective opposition from the FCC and Bell's competitors. The provisions on terminal equipment were particularly disabling. They would have turned back the clock by about five years. The many small equipment vendors swarmed around Congress, decrying Bell's heavy hand. A bill without the terminal equipment provisions, one that dealt only with the nascent intercity competition, might have had a fair chance of passage. But although such a compromise would have appealed to Congress, there was no support for it within the telephone company's top leadership.[21] AT&T's officers were handling the situation as if all things should be equal between the company and its opponents. But with a corporation of the size and power of the Bell System, with a company whose relations with federal authority had become tense and troubled, the subcommittee arena was not a friendly debating society. Instead of the law it wanted, the Bell System got a slow roasting.

[19]94th Congress, 2nd Session, House, Hearing on H.R. 12323, John D. deButts, testimony, September 28, 1976, p. 61; Shooshan and Jackson, interview, March 27, 1985, pp. 39–40.
[20]94th Congress, 2nd Session, House, Hearing on H.R. 12323, John D. deButts, testimony, September 28, 1976, pp. 62–9.
[21]Such a bill would have joined AT&T and the FCC in opposition to MCI's Execunet service. Support from the FCC would have done much to bring the subcommittee around. Shooshan and Jackson, interview, March 27, 1985, pp. 23, 28–9, 36, 74; Block, interview, December 3, 1985, p. 81.

Rather than push for a specific bill, Van Deerlin and Frey issued a statement calling for a "basement to attic" revision of the 1934 Communications Act. It looked as if Congress would not reaffirm its commitment to regulated monopoly, but there was some chance that it would legislate full competition.[22] Even this prospect was, at best, cloudy. The CCRA had generated a fragile coalition of opposing interests that might – it was as yet unclear – hang together long enough to promote an alternative measure. Given the number and variety of the concerned parties, and given the complexity of the issues, the only result that seemed guaranteed was a very slow journey through the legislature.

As the process slowed, it expanded. The effort to resolve common carrier questions had been transformed into a complete rewrite of the Communications Act. Issues of pricing – whether marginal or average costs should be used – were thus mixed with issues of competition in broadcasting, freedom of speech, and children's television. Opposition came from large companies like IBM and newly formed consortia of smaller companies such as the Ad-Hoc Committee for Competitive Telecommunications (ACCT) formed by MCI and other aspiring competitors. The Bell bill became a tar baby that accumulated issues and interests as time passed. The increasing complexity of the political process reduced the power of any interest group, including the massive Bell System, to push through specific legislation it favored. A stalemate became more likely, and AT&T could not afford a tied ball game.[23]

Although the CCRA was introduced again at the start of the new Congress, that was only a formality. The bill was dead. Congressman Van Deerlin was determined to make a fresh start, and he directed his subcommittee's staff to prepare "option papers" on nine areas of telecommunications involving broadcasting and common carrier activities. The Senate also initiated activity, passing over the Bell bill and opting for subcommittee hearings. When Senator Ernest F. Hollings convened the hearings in

[22]"House Communications Subcommittee Leadership Plans 'Basement to Attic' Revamping of Communications Act; Baker Renews Call for Committee Study," *Telecommunications Reports*, Vol. 42, No. 41 (October 12, 1976), p. 11.
[23]In the summer of 1977, IBM went so far as to commission a large-scale study of competition in the telecommunications industry by a Boston consulting firm. John Meyer, professor of economics at Harvard University and a leader in the movement to deregulate and restructure transportation, directed the study. Not surprisingly, the project concluded that there was no natural monopoly in telecommunications, that regulation was inefficient, and that the trend toward competition was sound. More interestingly, Meyer argued that competition need not raise local rates. Instead, he proposed an extensive restructuring of local rates to a more usage-sensitive basis that, he argued, would raise more revenue without endangering universal service. This study appears to have had little direct impact on the policy discussion, but it illustrated the manner in which varied interest groups were being attracted to the telecommunications question and were complicating the legislative process. John R. Meyer, Robert W. Wilson, M. Alan Baughcum, Ellen Burton, and Louis Caouette, *The Economics of Competition in the Telecommunications Industry* (Cambridge, Mass.: Oelgeschlager, Gunn & Hain, 1980).

March 1977, deButts reiterated the views he had expressed to the
NARUC convention over three years before. The trend toward competition, he said, was a threat to the telephone network and to efficient, low-
cost telephone service. Congress should stop the FCC from pushing telecommunications policy in this direction.[24]

Although deButts was unyielding, the FCC was by this time also overreacting, showing its hostility to the Bell System as it resolved the complex
issues of cost accounting raised in the TELPAK investigations. Only the
results of the FCC actions were apparent at the time, but the full story
came out later in one of AT&T's antitrust suits. The Bell System had been
advocating the use of incremental costs in setting rates in competitive
markets. Rates based on these costs, called by the mid-1970s "long-run
incremental costs," would let the Bell System compete on a comparable
basis with entering firms. The FCC had argued for the use of "fully
distributed costs," as average costs were called. This extension of public
utility accounting in the face of emerging competition would maintain
traditional regulatory pricing and the all-important support long distance
was providing for cheap local telephone service.

Beneath the surface at the agency, however, a new position had started
to take shape. At the time Strassburg had retired in 1973, he had on his
desk a draft opinion from the last *TELPAK* investigation (the extensive
private line rate-making proceeding). This draft report accepted AT&T's
argument for competitive pricing. It followed that long-run incremental
cost studies were "suitable for a choice among rate alternatives." The
various parts of Baumol's expert testimony for AT&T–both on long-run
incremental costs and on the need to use other costs for some services to
earn a satisfactory return for the Bell System as a whole–fitted together
into a coherent whole.[25] Strassburg and his staff were apparently ready to
agree that long-run incremental costs were to be the basis of future rate
making. They were not prepared to abandon fully distributed costs completely; the group decided that rates had to be *near* a fully distributed cost
standard as well. In other words, the use of marginal costs would be
constrained so as not to deviate too far from average costs, but the former
would be the primary standard.[26]

[24]94th Congress, 2nd Session, House, Committee on Interstate and Foreign Commerce,
Subcommittee on Communications, staff-prepared "Options Papers," April 21, 1977; 94th
Congress, 2nd Session, Senate, Committee on Commerce, Science and Transportation,
Subcommittee on Communications, "Oversight Hearings on Domestic Telecommunications Common Carrier Policies," John D. deButts, statement, March 21, 1977.
[25]*SPCC* v. *AT&T*, CA 78–0545, U.S. Dist. Ct., Dist. of Columbia, Defendants' Exhibit S-
2825C, "Second Draft of Working Group in Docket 18128."
[26]Rates also had to pass a burden test devised by Baumol. To pass this test, new rates had to
contribute as much surplus to the system as existing rates, that is, they had to avoid
imposing a burden on customers who were paying other rates. See also Chapter 2, note 16.
SPCC v. *AT&T*, CA 78–0545 (D.D.C.), Defendants' Exhibit S-2676, H.L. Baker, memorandum to Bernard Strassburg, "Meeting of 7–20–73 on Docket 18128."

But when Strassburg retired, Walter Hinchman took over the investigation and this promising development in FCC policy making was abruptly
reversed. Hinchman did not share his predecessor's views, and he produced his own draft by early 1976. The Commission based its final decision later in the year on this opinion. It approved the use of fully distributed costs for rate setting and took Baumol to task for inconsistency when
he advocated the use of long-run incremental costs to price competitive
services while proposing higher rates for monopoly services.[27] Even
though the decision was by then largely symbolic, the FCC's position on
costs forcefully and finally undercut the assurances the agency had given
in the *Specialized Common Carriers* decision that the Bell System would
be able to reprice its services in response to competition.

Nor did the Commission stop there. It muddied the waters of congressional debate by revising its definition of cross-subsidies. Using the fully
distributed cost calculations it had just approved, the agency stated that
the presence of different rates of return indicated cross-subsidies that
were (in words that seemed to delight Hinchman and the Commission)
"unjust and unreasonable, and therefore, unlawful."[28] The fully distributed costs of interstate services, of course, included costs for that part of
the local telephone plant assigned to interstate service under the latest
revision of the *Separations Manual*, the Ozark plan. Interstate rates that
did not cross-subsidize other services therefore had to be high enough to
cover the costs of part of the local plant. They would necessarily be above
the rates charged by competitors not burdened with local plants. They
would be regulatory prices characterized by the use of historical costs,
nationwide averaging, and separations.

This definition was markedly different from the FCC's 1950 definition,
because the separations process had changed in the meantime. As illustrated in Figure 4, SLU had been replaced by a series of modifications
that had shifted more and more of the local plant to interstate jurisdiction.
The FCC had defined deviations from SLU as cross-subsidies in 1950. It
defined deviations from the Ozark plan as cross-subsidies in 1976. An
interstate tariff that showed no cross-subsidy under the 1950 definition
would therefore involve a subsidy under the 1976 definition. In the face of
growing competition in interstate services, the Commission was, in effect,
insisting that AT&T charge higher rates. Good for the competition; bad
for AT&T.

This decision had two important effects. It made it hard, if not impossible, for the Bell System to use competitive pricing, and it made a mockery

[27]FCC, *Memorandum Opinion and Order*, FCC Docket 18128, 61 FCC 2d 587, particularly
at 617ff., 64 FCC 2d 971, 1977, *aff'd sub nom. Aeronautical Radio, Inc.* v. *FCC*, No. 77–
1333, 642F.2d 1221 (D.C. Cir., June 24, 1980).
[28]Ibid., 652.

of the congressional and later the legal definition of cross-subsidies. As of 1976, there were at least three definitions that could be used, all of which gave significantly different results. At one extreme was the FCC's definition, indicating that interstate services like the now infamous TELPAK were being subsidized. At the other was the board-to-board definition used by the Bell System before the Second World War. Under that definition, all of the local plant was considered intrastate, and interstate services were subsidizing local rates through the separations process. In the middle was the FCC's 1950 definition, which also showed a subsidy in 1976 flowing from interstate services. Who could make sense of all this?

AT&T's leaders wanted to use competitive prices in competitive markets. They believed that board-to-board thinking and cost allocations based on SLU were correct. They knew in their hearts that interstate long distance services were subsidizing local telephone rates. The FCC, however, had preempted the term, and AT&T did not contest the Commission's usage. It instead adopted a euphemism for "cross-subsidy," maintaining that interstate services made a "contribution" to local service – a contribution that was in jeopardy as interstate competition increased. The company clearly was right, but it was just as clearly ignored by the FCC.[29]

Although taking a definitive stand on rates, the Commission remained unsure of its attitude toward the Bell System's vertical structure. It terminated its extensive five-year investigation of the System's structure with an inconclusive report in 1977. The staff had recommended divestiture of Western Electric, but the administrative law judge had termed this recommendation "unwise and . . . even . . . catastrophic." The Commission dealt with the disagreement by avoiding the question of divestiture. It did not find that the Bell System had paid excessive prices for any Western products, but it still ordered the System to make its Purchased Products Division more independent.[30]

Issues that had been muddled by the FCC became hopelessly tangled during the ongoing congressional debates. The Ad-Hoc Committee for Competitive Telecommunications opened a new line of attack, proposing to the Senate that AT&T be divided into competitive and monopoly parts with "separate facilities, books of account, and employees and officers." The Committee hired Arthur D. Little, Inc., to study this proposal, but the consulting firm concluded quickly that divestiture would be far more effective in encouraging competition than a requirement that AT&T establish separate subsidiaries for competitive activities. Articulating arguments be-

---

[29]See, for example, FCC Docket 20003, *Response of the Bell System Companies*, April 21, 1975, and Bell Exhibit 45, "The Impact of Competition for Intercity Services and Terminal Equipment on Separations Assignments and Procedures," April 21, 1975.

[30]FCC, *Phase II Final Decision and Order*, FCC Docket 19129, "AT&T, Charges for Interstate Telephone Service," March 1, 1977, 64 FCC 2d 1.

ing made by the FCC staff and by the Justice Department, the study concluded, "The incentive for anticompetitive cross-subsidies within the AT&T system would not be significantly decreased with a wholly-owned subsidiary structure." But with independent firms spun off from the Bell System, the report said, "any opportunity or incentive to cross-subsidize . . . from monopoly services would be eliminated." As usual in these discussions, no definition of "cross-subsidy" was given and the existence of subsidies was simply assumed.[31]

Paul Henson, Chairman of the Board of United Telecommunications, Inc., an independent telephone company, proposed that Congress divide the telecommunications industry along entirely different lines. He suggested a two-tier structure (reminiscent of COMSAT Corporation) in which the Bell System would be a "carriers' carrier." It would still be a monopoly, supplying the facilities to be used by the competitive firms in telecommunications services. The Bell System, in other words, would no longer sell services to the public; it would sell only to carriers who would compete with each other. MCI's argument that competing carriers should be allowed to use the Bell System's facilities would then be carried to its ultimate conclusion. Like the Federal Reserve System, Bell would be obligated to supply all of its facilities without stint and would be precluded from competing with the alternate carriers. The network facilities would extend to one telephone set – a so-called primary instrument – per subscriber, but any additional terminal equipment would be supplied competitively.[32]

The primary instrument concept enjoyed a brief vogue. John deButts, called upon to respond to this proposal, agreed that the idea was a good one. It would preserve at least a vestige of end-to-end service by the Bell System, particularly in the residential market that was so critical to the telephone company and to state regulators. DeButts even agreed that the telecommunications industry could be divided into competitive and monopoly spheres. But he could not go along with the concept of a carriers' carrier – a strong conclusion that he stated with a promise of further study.[33] By this time, however, the pace of change in telecommunications was

[31] 94th Congress, 2nd Session, Senate, Committee on Commerce, Science and Transportation, Subcommittee on Communications, "Oversight Hearings on Domestic Telecommunications Common Carrier Policies," Statement of Herbert N. Jasper, Ad Hoc Committee for Competitive Telecommunications (ACCT), March 28, 1977, p. 15; Arthur D. Little, Inc., "Analysis of Telecommunications Industry Restructuring," prepared for the Committee, C-80949, September 1977, p. xvii.

[32] 94th Congress, 2nd Session, Senate, Committee on Commerce, Science and Transportation, Subcommittee on Communications, "Oversight Hearings on Domestic Telecommunications Common Carrier Policies," Statement of Paul Henson, March 28, 1977.

[33] John D. deButts, Replies to questions of Senator Schmitt of the Senate Subcommittee on Communications, May 9, 1977, and Senator Hollings of the Senate Subcommittee on Communications, June 10, 1977. See also Henry M. Boettinger, interview, January 18, 1986, p. 34.

accelerating, and the primary instrument concept–like the terminal equipment provisions of the Bell bill–was too far behind the frontier to have any significant chance of adoption. The FCC investigated the question for almost a year before firmly rejecting it in 1978.[34]

It was not at all clear, however, what other measures might be acceptable, and AT&T kept scrambling to bolster its weakened position. The government's antitrust suit was ever in the background, like a vulture on a fence, and the firm could not afford to relax. The company participated in (or perhaps orchestrated) a telephone industry task force that submitted recommendations to both the House and Senate subcommittees in December 1977. The task force recommended a return to the regulatory instant between the FCC's *Carterfone* decision in 1968 and its *MCI* decision the following year. But unhappily for deButts and the Bell System, the opposition was by then an effective political force. The newer firms had mounted their own lobbying efforts, combined into consortia, and attracted support on some issues from established powers like IBM, which had sponsored the massive study of competitive telecommunications. The political atmosphere was also changing as President Jimmy Carter began to take up the cause of competition. The idea of "deregulation" was taking hold in Washington, D.C., and this created an intellectual climate that the new telecommunications firms were able to use to their advantage.[35]

Half a year later, in June 1978, Lionel Van Deerlin introduced his own bill, rewriting the entire 1934 Communications Act. Van Deerlin wanted to use competition as the primary means of organizing both broadcasting and telecommunications. The FCC would actually be abolished, replaced by a new agency with a much narrower mandate. Antitrust would be substituted for regulation wherever possible. Instead of opposing the government's antitrust suit against AT&T, Van Deerlin was in effect supporting it.[36]

The tradeoffs in the bill were interesting. On the one hand, it removed from the Bell System the restraints of the 1956 Consent Decree. But on the other, it required any "monopoly carrier"–that is, AT&T–to divest itself of equipment manufacturing capability–that is, Western Electric. Another provision in the bill set up a fund to subsidize local telephone rates. But it mandated compulsory interconnection between common carriers, an order that would have eroded the revenues needed to fill the

[34]FCC, *Report and Order*, FCC CC Docket 78–36, "Implications of the Telephone Industry's Primary Instrument Concept," August 2, 1978, 68 FCC 2d 1157; Shooshan and Jackson, interview, April 3, 1985, pp. 14–16; Stump, interview, November 30, 1984, p. 62.
[35]Telecommunications Industry Task Force, "The Dilemma of Telecommunications Policy," September 1977, and Recommendations, December 1, 1977; Martha Derthick and Paul J. Quirk, *The Politics of Deregulation* (Washington, D.C.: Brookings Institution, 1985), chap. 2.
[36]95th Congress, 1st Session, House, H.R. 13015, "Communications Act of 1978," June 7, 1978.

fund. What Van Deerlin gave to the Bell System with one hand, he took away with the other. Nor was it an even trade. Where the Bell System sought more freedom to act competitively, the bill supported it. But where AT&T tried to maintain its monopoly or even hegemony, the bill mandated otherwise. The trades were thus perceived quite accurately as blows at the established structure. The contrast between Van Deerlin's bill and the Bell bill could not have been more complete. Van Deerlin had resolved all of the contradictions in the company's proposal in favor of increasing competition and decreasing the Bell System's reach.

Van Deerlin's bill was an ambitious measure that was not really de-signed to pass Congress and become a law. In addition to arousing opposi-tion from broadcasters, any bill requiring the divestiture of Western Elec-tric was assured of implacable hostility from AT&T, which on this issue could muster considerable congressional support. In the long and com-plex legislative history of telecommunications in the 1970s, divestiture was seldom even considered as a reasonable policy option. In fact, the Van Deerlin bill was really a statement of principles and an agenda for discus-sion. It suggested – to use a word that seems excessively mild in the context – a new "direction" for federal communications policy and offered proposals on how this policy could be implemented.

In the view of the subcommittee staff, the specifics were all negotiable, but the Van Deerlin bill was as extreme in its way as was the CCRA.[37] Neither measure, as it turned out, was successful as a tactical ploy. Van Deerlin took his bill on the road in the fall of 1978. He held 33 days of hearings in various cities and heard almost 500 witnesses. Several Bell System witnesses spoke on behalf of deButts's NARUC principles, but they were less than a dozen arrayed against the hundreds who testified to the contrary. Witnesses frequently started by praising the general thrust of Van Deerlin's bill and then – as the staff had anticipated – objected to the particular part of the bill that pertained to them. Van Deerlin had cast his net widely and pulled in a lot of fish. So large, in fact, was the number of interests seeking to protect existing or anticipated market positions that their suggestions quickly stalled the bill. There was no core set of issues around which support could be built; the bargaining process anticipated by the staff did not take place.[38]

Van Deerlin's bill therefore ended up in roughly the same position that the Bell bill had in the previous Congress. It had some support but also a full measure of intense opposition. An important bill needs a few strong champions or a dramatic event to generate pressure for passage. These bills had neither. The industry, despite the ferment in technical and

[37]Shooshan and Jackson, interview, March 27, 1985, pp. 56–7.
[38]95th Congress, 1st Session, House, Interstate and Foreign Commerce Communications Subcommittee, Hearing on H.R. 13015.

regulatory circles, was not in a publicly perceived crisis. There were as yet no committed champions of telecommunications legislation in Congress or the White House.[39] Even though the Van Deerlin bill went nowhere, it had blocked the path to a congressional resolution acceptable to AT&T. DeButts's congressional strategy was in tatters by the end of 1978. The Bell bill had not been passed. Worse, it had induced a reaction that had placed AT&T on the defensive. The firm's effort to get out ahead of the pack–to lead rather than react–had failed. MCI's antitrust suit was churning on and the government's suit was intact–lurking ominously at the edge of the field. AT&T's leaders had misjudged the political setting of the 1970s just as surely as they had correctly diagnosed the Bell System's internal need for decisive action. John deButts had tried to deal with both problems by an appeal to the values and goals of Vail and Gifford. Although his policies had reinvigorated the world's largest corporation, they had carried the company into a deep swamp of political and legal problems. The path of compromise, ardently followed, might have led the Bell System out of that morass–as it had during the Vail years–but the firm's management was still trying in the late 1970s to get the regulated monopoly telecommunications policy it wanted and to dam the rising waters of competition.

Competition in message toll service

Just as the momentum for congressional action started fading, a critical court decision legitimized competition at the very heart of AT&T's business. A federal court allowed competitive entry into the long distance part of the Bell System switched network, into what AT&T called "message toll service" (since a toll was collected for each message). The dam that had been constructed to protect AT&T's regulated monopoly in ordinary long distance service was suddenly swept away.

In a way, the process started with AT&T's Hi-Lo tariff, which took effect, after all of the regulatory delays, in June 1974. MCI filed revisions to its tariff, lowering its rates the very next day. From the start, MCI had been making a market in shared communications services. These were initially shared private lines; they were shared according to blocks of time, and they were restricted–as are all private lines–in their destinations. MCI filed another tariff revision in September, adding its Metered Use Service: Execunet. It was different from MCI's earlier service in two respects. First, the bulk of the charges for the service were based on

---

[39] For parallels, see Peter Temin, *Taking Your Medicine: Drug Regulation in the United States* (Cambridge, Mass.: Harvard University Press, 1980).

usage. The charges were very much like those for the Bell System's message toll service; you paid according to the time and distance of your call. Second, the Execunet service did not have to go to a specified location, only to specified cities. AT&T objected that this was, in fact, message toll service; MCI was proposing to use the switched network for ordinary telephone service, and it was exceeding the authorization given in the *Specialized Common Carriers* decision to offer private line services. MCI responded that Execunet was simply a variant on the service it had already been allowed to provide.[40]

MCI reiterated its commitment to offer only private line services, a position it had articulated strongly only a few months before. In April 1974, Kenneth Cox – the commissioner who had left the FCC in 1970 to become an officer of MCI – reminded a court dealing with one of MCI's complaints that his firm had informed the FCC that it would not offer "switched voice telephone service." A month later, MCI took the same position in a separate court proceeding. MCI's claim to offer Execunet service appeared to be based on its classification as an authorized private line service.[41]

But MCI did not stop there. Following its long-term strategy, it assumed that it had achieved its objective and then blamed AT&T for its inability to offer a service. It contended as well that it should be able to offer Execunet even if it was a switched service. McGowan and his lawyers said that AT&T's monopoly of message toll service was in violation of the antitrust laws, and they challenged the FCC to make a broad study of the role of competition in switched long distance service. In this line of argument, MCI assumed that it had the right to offer message toll service and then argued that AT&T was excluding it from that market in violation of the antitrust laws. In fact, of course, MCI at that point had been authorized only to provide private line service, and it was petitioning to enter the market for switched long distance service. It had not yet acquired that right.[42]

This was a critical turning point for MCI, for the Bell System, and for national telecommunications policy. Through a gradual disclosure of its features by MCI, Execunet emerged as message toll service. Anyone with a push-button telephone in certain cities could call anyone in other speci-

---

[40]James R. Billingsley, AT&T, to Richard E. Wiley, chairman, FCC, May 19, 1975, and Bert C. Roberts, MCI, to Walter Hinchman, FCC, June 5, 1975, in FCC, *Decision*, Appendix B, FCC Docket 20640, "MCI/Lawfulness of Execunet Service Tariffs," June 30, 1976, 60 FCC 2d 25 at 64–8.

[41]Kenneth A. Cox to the Hon. Thomas F. Quinn, U.S. Ct. of Appeals, Third Circuit, Re *MCI* v. *AT&T*, No. 74–1104, April 8, 1974; *Washington UTC and NARUC* v. *FCC*, Nos. 71–2919, 72–1198, U.S. Ct. of Appeals, Ninth Circuit, MCI *Motion*, May 15, 1974.

[42]FCC, *Decision*, FCC Docket 20640, June 30, 1976, 60 FCC 2d 25, ¶23–4, 28, 41–3, 50–1, and Appendix B, pp. 78–9, 83.

fied cities. There were no lines dedicated to one customer's use; the bulk
of the charges were for the calls themselves, not for access to the system.
All of this became apparent in 1975 as MCI began to promote its new
service. AT&T's vice president for federal regulation made the point to an
obtuse FCC by placing a call over MCI's lines to a recorded weather
service in Chicago from the Commission's own offices in Washington,
D.C.![43]

The FCC brushed the sand out of its eyes and tried to deal with the
issue by distinguishing between message toll service and the types of
services authorized by its *Specialized Common Carriers* decision. Its earlier decision, it said, was not a general mandate for competition, merely
an authorization of competition in those special circumstances in which it
was in the public interest. Competition in the provision of telephone
services had been allowed solely in one type of service, private line, that
involved only about 3 percent of AT&T's business.

Having stated that it was possible to distinguish between private line and
switched services, the FCC then had to decide where Execunet lay. Unfortunately, the Commission had already expanded the private line category
so that it included many switched elements, and there was no longer an
obvious way to determine exactly where the boundary should be placed.[44]
The FCC nevertheless ruled that MCI's Execunet had stepped over the
boundary between private lines and the public switched network; it was not
authorized by the *Specialized Common Carriers* decision. Private line
service, the agency said, originated or terminated "at a specific location
designated by the customer via a communication channel dedicated to his
private use and not used or usable for public communications services and
accessing only destinations also specifically designated by the customer."
Making some allowances for "bureaucratese," the language of public officials, this is what most intelligent observers would have decided that private line service actually was. The Commission went on to document in
excruciating detail the differences between Execunet and private line ser-

[43]See MCI's ads: "Now, Talk Is Cheaper," *The Wall Street Journal*, September 11, 1975, p.
9; "Tell us which cities your company calls every day and we'll show you how to save 15%-
60% on long distance," *The New York Times*, September 14, 1975; "End Obscene Phone
Bills," *The New York Times*, September 18, 1975, p. 36; AT&T, *Opposition*, Attachment A,
"Affidavit of Thomas W. Scandlyn," FCC Docket 20640, December 29, 1975.
[44]This decision had to be made in light of the prior FCC decision regarding foreign exchange
and CCSA services.
    MCI argued that Execunet was similar to those services already classified implicitly as
private line in terms of the *Specialized Common Carriers* decision, and AT&T argued that it
was different. AT&T's problem arose in explaining how the Execunet service differed – a
difficult argument to make. It did not in fact differ much from foreign exchange in its
electronics, although it had two "open" ends instead of one. The FCC had set up the
Execunet service in its earlier foreign exchange decision. At that point, MCI was not asking
to be allowed to offer a metered service, but only stating that, as a competitor of AT&T, it was
entitled to the same private line facilities (including switched foreign exchange connections).

vice and rejected MCI's Execunet tariff.[45] For the first time in many years, AT&T and its federal regulatory agency were in basic agreement, allied against a further expansion of competition in the industry.

All too quickly, however, McGowan dealt these new allies a devastating blow. MCI appealed the FCC's decision in the courts, where the case fell to a three-judge panel led by Judge Skelly Wright. This was an ominous circumstance for the agency and the phone company. In a liberal court, Wright had distinguished himself by his outspoken criticism of regulatory agencies, declaring in 1970, for example, that the Civil Aeronautics Board was "unduly oriented toward the interests of the industry it is designed to regulate, rather than the public interest it is designed to protect."[46] In a similar vein, Judge Wright reversed the FCC's decision on Execunet in mid-1977 and allowed MCI to offer the service, at least temporarily. He did not try to contest the FCC's decision on whether Execunet was a private line service, accepting the FCC's finding that it was not. Instead, Wright stood the issue on its head by considering whether the FCC had lawfully restricted MCI to offering only private line services. The Commission had attempted to deal with the issue narrowly, but Wright expanded the problem and removed it from the FCC's control. This decision challenged in a fundamental way AT&T's position as a regulated monopoly and the FCC's role as the dominant force in determining telecommunications policy.

Judge Wright followed his unusual logical path to its dramatic conclusion. It was clear from the FCC's opinions and representations that the Commission thought that the *Specialized Common Carriers* decision had given MCI and others only the right to offer private line services. It was equally clear from MCI's official statements in 1974 that it understood the decision in that restricted way. Judge Wright did not dispute that interpretation of what the Commission had done. He insisted, in fact, that the Commission had restricted its attention completely to private lines and thus had made no finding about the right of MCI to offer ordinary long distance service. This in itself does not seem to be a startling point; there were many things that the FCC had not done. But Wright went on to say that the Commission's failure to consider the larger question gave MCI a legal right to offer Execunet service. Noting that the FCC had not previously restricted MCI's service offerings, the judge insisted that "novelty has led to error."[47]

Wright's argument hinged on a distinction between facilities and services. MCI had relied on this distinction in its arguments, and the judge

[45]FCC, *Decision*, FCC Docket 20640, June 30, 1976, 60 FCC 2d 25 at 42–3.
[46]*Moss* v. *Civil Aeronautics Board*, 430 F.2d 891 at 893 (D.C. Cir. 1970).
[47]Judge Skelly Wright, *Decision*, July 28, 1977, *MCI* v. *FCC*, No. 75–1635, 561 F. 2d 365 at 374, (D.C. Cir.), *cert. denied* 434 U.S. 1040, 1978.

followed the company's lead. He argued that the applicable section of the law was designed to prevent unnecessary duplication of facilities, not services. Another subsection gave the Commission authority to restrict services, but–in Judge Wright's words–the FCC "cannot impose any such restriction unless it has affirmatively determined that 'the public convenience and necessity [so] require'."[48] Thus the Commission's failure to make an affirmative determination that Execunet service was not in the public interest created a presumption that MCI had the right to offer it. The FCC had acted improperly when it rejected MCI's tariff. Its intent in doing so could be put aside. The law required that the *Specialized Common Carriers* decision be interpreted more broadly than the Commission intended or wanted. The FCC should undertake the formal determination of whether competition served the public convenience and necessity, but MCI could offer Execunet while the investigation was in process.

The court overruled the FCC and set itself up as a better interpreter of FCC policy than the FCC itself. Admittedly, Strassburg had neglected to dot all the *i*'s and cross all the *t*'s in the *Specialized Common Carriers* decision, but neither he nor anyone else at the FCC had meant to give MCI blanket permission to offer any service it chose. The court took the opposite position, in part because of the difference between courts and commissions. The FCC dealt prospectively with facilities and services. It made a decision on whether the public's necessity and convenience would be served if a facility were built, a service offered, or a rate changed. The court, by contrast, dealt with existing facilities, services, or rates and asked whether they should be disallowed by virtue of being in conflict with the law. The court, like the Commission, was biased toward the status quo, but the Commission's reference point was the status quo ante. The court dealt with the situation after the change had been made. MCI's argument that it should be allowed to file rates subject only to the FCC's suspension or rejection thus appealed to the court. By maintaining that it was a common carrier like the Bell System, MCI successfully argued that there was a presumption in favor of its ability to offer new services. It could not convince the FCC on this point, at least in the mid-1970s, but it did convince Judge Skelly Wright.

The outcome of this case also reflected the personal differences between Strassburg and Wright. Strassburg wanted to promote competition, and his influence on the FCC in the *MCI* and *Specialized Common Carriers* decisions had been considerable. But Strassburg wanted to introduce competition in a carefully controlled manner within the existing industry and regulatory structure. He never expressed a desire to realign the rate structure or to reorganize AT&T. Wright, by contrast, bought

[48]Ibid., 375–7, referring to Sec. 214(a) and (c) of the law.

MCI's argument that it should be admitted as a full competitor to AT&T because the existing structure of telecommunications was outmoded. Instead of seeking to preserve the existing major institutions, Wright acted as a radical reformer.

Of course, the opening through which Wright drove the industry had been created originally by the FCC. Just as its *Above 890* decision had generated pressures that led to *MCI*, the *MCI* decision generated pressures that led to *Specialized Common Carriers*. That decision, in turn, gave rise to the pressures that led inexorably to *Execunet*. The Commission had made its decisions as if each was an isolated choice, as if each had no implications for future Commission decisions. Strassburg had been quite explicit about this in *MCI*. He regarded that decision as an experiment; he thought that he had preserved the freedom to evaluate subsequent experience and to make future decisions as a free agent. He had forgotten to factor William McGowan – the archetypal entrepreneur rushing to exploit a profit opportunity – into his calculations. Strassburg and the commissioners had, in this regard, been myopic. Only a year before *Execunet*, the FCC had concluded in a major investigation, "We find that there is no apparent basis for the telephone industry's claims that private line and terminal equipment competition either have had, or are soon likely to have any significant adverse impact on telephone service revenues or on the rates for basic telephone services."[49] The Commission seemed oblivious to the economic and political pressures it was unleashing. But not everyone was; certainly McGowan was not, nor for that matter was AT&T.

Richard Wiley, chairman of the FCC, and Walter Hinchman, Strassburg's successor as head of the Common Carrier Bureau, were indignant at Judge Wright's action. They called Henry Geller, former FCC general counsel and head of the newly formed National Telecommunications and Information Agency (NTIA) in the Commerce Department, and asked him to support an appeal. Even Hinchman – who had shown his opposition to AT&T in the *TELPAK* decision and elsewhere – thought that Wright had overstepped his bounds and had "destroyed the Commission's carefully phased introduction of competition into this market."[50] But Geller insisted, throughout a series of stormy meetings, that the cat was out of the bag and there was no way to stuff it back in. Given the way the *Specialized Common Carriers* decision had been written, there was no legal basis for an appeal. The FCC tried, but the Supreme Court refused to hear the case.[51]

[49]FCC, *First Report*, FCC Docket 20003, September 27, 1976, 61 FCC 2d 766 at 776.

[50]Walter R. Hinchman, "Remarks before the International Communications Association," Las Vegas, Nevada, May 15, 1978.

[51]The NTIA was established in April 1978 by a merger of the Office of Telecommunications Policy, which was formed in response to President Johnson's 1968 Presidential Task Force on Telecommunications Policy and the Commerce Department's Office of Telecommunications.

Henry Geller, interview, June 20, 1984, pp. 6–9. On Hinchman's views, see the ac-

Having lost the battle to disallow Execunet service as such, the FCC and AT&T tried to redraw their battle lines on the issue of interconnection. Execunet service clearly required connection with local Bell System facilities, and MCI argued that this was mandated because the court had authorized the service. This was the position that the FCC had taken in *Specialized Common Carriers*, but the FCC now reversed itself and denied MCI's argument. The Commission contended that *Specialized Common Carriers* had only authorized interconnection of private line service. Further action could be taken only after a public hearing. AT&T, of course, seconded the Commission's position and argued for a strict reading of the federal Communications Act. The act addressed interconnection as a means of providing joint service between two noncompeting carriers, not as a competitive issue. There was no requirement for interconnection in a competitive setting, AT&T said, and the FCC should ignore demands to order it. MCI, of course, appealed this blatant attempt to circumvent Judge Wright's decision, and in the spring of 1978 the court mandated interconnection for Execunet.[52]

All that had to be decided, then, was what rates the Bell System could charge for the use of its facilities. If MCI was allowed to subscribe to local telephone service at ordinary business rates, it would be doubly favored in its competition with Long Lines. It would receive the local service for rates subsidized in part by Long Lines' message toll service charges through the separations process. In addition, it would not be obligated to earn a return on part of the local plant, as Long Lines was required to do. Even had MCI had the same long distance facilities as the Bell System, its capital costs would have been over one-third less. That surely would be adding insult to injury.[53]

The third difference between regulatory and competitive prices had finally come into play. After the *Above 890* decision, owners of private microwave radio systems had tried to take advantage of the spread between historical and current cost accounting. After *MCI* and *Specialized Common Carriers*, MCI had tried to take advantage of the spread between nationwide average prices and marginal costs on specific, heavily traveled routes. Now, after *Execunet*, MCI planned to profit from the gap opened up by the separations process, that is, from the ever-increasing spread between station-to-station and board-to-board prices.[54]

count of FCC Docket 18128 in the testimony of Walter Hinchman, *SPCC* v. *AT&T*, CA 78–0545 (D.D.C.), Tr. 4958–5006.

[52] *MCI* v. *FCC*, No. 75–1635, *Motion for an Order Directing Compliance with Mandate*, April 14, 1978, 580 F.2d 590 (D.C. Cir.), *cert denied*, 439 U.S. 980, 1978.

[53] For separations data, see *US* v. *AT&T*, CA No. 74–1698 (D.D.C.), Defendants' Exhibits D-24B-1006 and D-24B-1007.

[54] Separations were also a factor in TELPAK, as noted in Chapter 2, since private line rates had been set before the *Above 890* decision in light of the user's choice between private lines and message toll service.

AT&T had responded vigorously after each of these regulatory decisions. TELPAK had slashed prices to large private line users by seven-eighths. Hi-Lo set private line rates for high-density routes that were one-third of the rates for low-density routes. A similar response surely was indicated here.

AT&T argued that it was highly inappropriate for MCI to subscribe to local service as if it were an ordinary business customer. If MCI was offering services comparable to Long Lines' message toll service, it should share the costs of the local distribution network. Shortly after the court ordered AT&T to interconnect with MCI, therefore, the Bell System filed the Exchange Network Facilities for Interstate Access (ENFIA) tariff with the FCC. This tariff, filed in May 1978, to take effect 90 days later, imposed charges on the specialized common carriers equal to the charges for local interconnection assigned to AT&T's Long Lines by the separations process.

The proposed ENFIA tariff therefore was nondiscriminatory; it charged all long distance carriers – Bell and non-Bell alike – the same amount for local interconnection. It assured the Bell Operating Companies of continued support for local service even if the new entrants took business away from Long Lines. And, as AT&T knew well, it increased MCI's and the other carriers' costs by about 40 percent (if their costs were near Long Lines'). The new carriers saw the huge profit opportunity opened to them by *Execunet* vanishing with a stroke of AT&T's pen. They protested strongly to the FCC, arguing that the proposed tariff prejudged issues the Commission had not yet resolved. The investigation of competition in message toll service called for in the *Execunet* decision was still in its preliminary stages; it could not be completed for at least two or three years. It could easily take longer. Yet AT&T was already proposing to treat specialized common carriers and Long Lines on the same footing.[55]

The controversy over the proposed tariff threatened to create growing problems as the FCC's investigation into the merits of competition in message toll service progressed. If AT&T's ENFIA tariff took effect, the new entrants might be paying far more than would be deemed appropriate at the conclusion of the Commission's investigation several years later. On the other hand, if the Commission found some way to reject the tariff immediately – as being clearly unsupported by cost studies or in violation of some regulation – the specialized carriers might be charged far less than

[55]*Petitions* of MCI Telecommunications Corp. et al., to reject tariff, FCC CC Docket 78–371, "ENFIA," June 20, 1978; *Reply* and *Opposition* of Bell System Operating Companies to petitions to suspend and investigate tariff, FCC CC Docket 78–371, July 6, 1978; FCC, *Notice of Inquiry and Proposed Rulemaking*, FCC CC Docket 78–72, "MTS/WATS Market Structure," February 23, 1978, 67 FCC 2d 757.

was appropriate during the long investigation. Moreover, the price charged for local interconnection during the investigation would affect the conditions of competition that would prevail at its end. Was there any way to determine a price that was not capricious?

Henry Geller of the NTIA thought there was. He wrote to the FCC in September, outlining these uncomfortable possibilities and suggesting that the FCC encourage AT&T and the specialized common carriers to negotiate a temporary tariff "to ensure some degree of fairness to all parties while fundamental policy issues are being resolved in the longer term."[56]

The FCC and AT&T both accepted Geller's initiative. Negotiations between AT&T and the specialized common carriers began almost immediately, with the FCC, NTIA, Congress, and myriad interested parties sitting in. Both parties wanted to look reasonable in this prominent fishbowl, but their positions were far apart. AT&T admitted that a small discount might be appropriate for the new carriers in view of the extra digits a customer needed to dial to get onto Execunet or Southern Pacific's Sprint rather than Long Lines. The new carriers admitted, in turn, that they might make a token contribution to the operating companies in view of their new status. But if the difference was not between paying nothing and paying 100 percent of Long Lines' charges, it was between paying 10 and 90 percent.[57]

The impasse was broken by an AT&T suggestion that the specialized common carriers increase their contribution to local costs as they grew. They would pay 35 percent of Long Lines' charges in the first year, 45 percent the next, rising by 10 percentage points a year to 75 percent in the five years during which the temporary tariff would be in effect. MCI accepted the principle of a graduated charge but said that it would not be able to raise capital with the 75 percent figure in the agreement. Even though the growing company was no longer in the dire financial straits of five years earlier, it could not afford to agitate the financial waters. AT&T, in a move that both showed its weakened position in 1978 and set the stage for renewed conflict later on, yielded. The parties spelled out only the first three years of the progression, leaving the eventual move from 55 to 75 percent to be decided on and publicized three years down the road. The agreement stated that the specialized common carriers would pay 35 percent of the charge paid by Long Lines for local interconnection of message toll service until their combined revenues exceeded $110 million, 45 percent until the revenues reached $250 million, and 55 percent

[56]Henry Geller to Charles D. Ferris, FCC, September 6, 1978.
[57]Charles D. Ferris to James R. Billingsley, September 11, 1978; Billingsley to Ferris, September 15, 1978.

thereafter. The sales volumes represented predictions of the new competitors' sales in successive years.[58]

AT&T, faced with the adverse decision in *Execunet* and the apparent intention of the FCC and NTIA to ensure the specialized common carriers at least a start in the message toll service business, could do no better. The temporary ENFIA tariff would provide discount local interconnection for the new competitors, but the discount would be temporary. Even though the full process could not be spelled out in 1978, it would be confirmed – AT&T's negotiators thought – in late 1981. Half a loaf is not as good as a whole, but it is far better than none: interconnection at ordinary business rates under preexisting tariffs.[59]

The agreement reveals the folly of Baxter's 1970 prediction that common carriers could "cut prices to meet [entrants] and chase them back out." There would not be a test of Long Lines' natural monopoly. There would be no way to know which firm had the lower costs. The specialized common carriers had become the "innocent investors" Trienens had described. They were protected by the political process. They would be even stronger and able to command more political support when the ENFIA agreement came up for extension in 1981.

MCI, Southern Pacific, and the other specialized carriers, to be sure, faced some problems of their own – albeit in the uncertain future. The price umbrella held over them by the ENFIA agreement was due to be folded up in five years. Even if AT&T's anticipation of a smooth increase in their charges for local interconnection did not materialize, the discounts were unstable. As the specialized common carriers continued to compete with AT&T, their charges eventually would be brought in line with Long Lines'. When that happened, MCI and the others would be faced with Baxter's scenario. This test might come too late to affect the political and judiciary processes underway in 1978, but it could well affect the commercial future of the entrants in the 1980s.

The negotiated ENFIA tariff went into effect in April 1979, providing a comfortable price umbrella for MCI, Southern Pacific, and the other companies that would join them. Separations costs had risen to almost two-fifths of the Bell System's interstate revenues. Since MCI and the other specialized common carriers had to pay only half of these charges, their rates could be almost 20 percent lower even if their costs were exactly the same as the Bell System's.

[58]The ENFIA tariff had several elements, some of which differed from carrier to carrier on the basis of the nature of their connections to the Bell System. But the charge for the non-traffic-sensitive local loop costs was the largest part of the tariff. By its nature, its justification was the same for all carriers. FCC, *Memorandum Opinion and Order*, FCC CC Docket No. 78–371, April 12, 1979, 71 FCC 2d 440 at 446.
[59]Alfred C. Partoll, interview, May 17, 1985, pp. 34–6.

This situation had several important implications. The arrangement necessarily attracted other common carriers to use AT&T's local facilities to provide competing message toll service. The number of these services and the volume of their business grew rapidly after 1978. The agreement also measured how far the FCC had swung toward the policy of actively promoting competition in the industry; the Commission was subsidizing the existing specialized common carriers and new entrants that would now use the Bell System to cut into AT&T's markets. The competition was constrained or, to use deButts's expression, "contrived" to produce a new industry configuration. The existence of this subsidy meant that the growth of alternative carriers could not provide a test of the comparative costs of AT&T and the competing firms. There was no way to discover who was the low-cost supplier of message toll services. The invitation to enter, provided by the ENFIA rates, would be compelling even for a firm with significantly higher costs than those of the Bell System.

The issue of comparative costs was critical. AT&T had long argued that its large size and integrated structure enabled it to be the low-cost supplier of many telecommunications services – specifically, those services offered by the national switched network.[60] If the Bell System was indeed the low-cost supplier of ordinary long distance service, the entry of competing services represented an inefficient use of resources through the substitution of new high-cost suppliers for the existing low-cost firm. In the terms that AT&T had used since the debate had started, MCI and the other carriers could "piece out" the network, supplying those facilities that they could furnish cheaply and exploiting the Bell System for the remainder. Under the ENFIA tariff, AT&T gave the competitors a large enough margin to ensure that even a relatively inefficient supplier could survive – and prosper.

AT&T's opponents, both its critics and its competitors, maintained that the growth of the other common carriers showed that the Bell System was inefficient and that competition was desirable. This, of course, was not the case. These firms were growing under the price umbrella held over them by the ENFIA compromise – an agreement reached under the FCC's gun. Competition may or may not have been desirable, but the growth of these competitors was not evidence one way or the other. Despite the contentions of William Melody, the economist first for the FCC and then for the Justice Department, and others who tried to argue from the growth of competition to the conclusion that competition was socially useful, the increased competition in telecommunications resulted from policy decisions made in the FCC and the federal courts. It was not a result of

[60]FCC Docket 20003, Bell Exhibit 57, "Multiple Supplier Network Study – The Cost of Multiple Intercity Networks Compared to a Single Integrated Network."

inefficient performance by a high-cost monopoly. There is simply no way to reason from the existence of MCI's Execunet or Southern Pacific's (later GTE's) Sprint service to a conclusion as to whether this policy was good or bad for consumers or for the national economy.[61]

Without hesitation, however, one can conclude that the ENFIA policy was not good from the Bell System's perspective. From AT&T's vantage point, the situation was parlous by the late 1970s. The stance deButts had adopted in his NARUC speech had yielded a steady return of political defeats. The congressional initiative was stalled. The firm was beset by private and public antitrust suits. AT&T was devoting more and more resources to its defense, but to no avail. The FCC seemed even more determined than before to substitute contrived competition for regulated monopoly. The courts – in particular Judge Skelly Wright – had dealt AT&T a severe blow by opening the switched network to competitors who could now piece out the system. The great public discourse that deButts had hoped for had not materialized. As the firm's political and legal position deteriorated, competition had moved from the edges of the Bell network to its very center by 1978.

AT&T's internal ferment

Public apathy toward the future of telecommunications stood in sharp contrast to the enthusiasm John deButts had aroused within the Bell System. His NARUC speech, with its appeal to the ideals of Vail and Gifford, had fallen on fertile ground, and in the months that followed, a new sense of purpose had flowered within AT&T. The organizational initiatives pursued by deButts had reinforced the message of his NARUC speech. AT&T appeared from within to be on the offensive; it was no longer dominated by forces beyond its control. Realizing how hard it was to move even slightly away from the functional organization first imposed on the Bell System by Vail, deButts toured the country, spreading his message far and wide within the System. He was a powerful and effective spokesman for his new policies. He brought middle-level managers to a series of innovative seminars in New Jersey, where they gave their reactions in return. DeButts had learned from Romnes's experience; he was not about to make policy statements from the top of the organization and hope that they would find their own way, willy-nilly, to implementation.

DeButts's reorganization program had two parts. AT&T was replacing Vail's functional organization with the CS/NS/OS organization and at-

[61]See, for example, *US* v. *AT&T*, CA No. 74–1698 (D.D.C.), William H. Melody, testimony, June 8, 1981, Tr. 9314–15.

tempting to graft the marketing division onto the new structure. Placing the marketing function in a subordinate position in the new organization was a conservative move, dictated by deButts's reluctance to compromise the Bell System's traditional orientation to operations and to the technical aspects of providing service. It was also typical of the way that large organizations normally introduce change: outside and a little to the side of the regular structure of authority.[62]

Both innovations met resistance. Nearly everyone in the Bell System – with the prominent exception of McGill – had grown up in Vail's functional style of organization. Everyone knew where he stood – whether a plant man, a commercial person, or a traffic person – and what his status was. If he were, say, in traffic and needed something from commercial, he knew how to approach that department to get results. It was traumatic to give up those relationships and to establish a new set of identities in the System.[63]

The marketing department was especially threatening to the old Bell hands. Its position outside the normal organization was both its strength and its weakness: its strength because it did not directly challenge the authority of the operating departments – it coexisted with them; its weakness because it lacked the organizational position to command resources from other departments. This structural peculiarity, of course, was exaggerated by the conflict between the Bell System's traditional role of service – emphasized strongly by deButts throughout his time as CEO – and the marketing department's new role. As service organizations, the operating companies had been used to asking customers what their service needs were and then specifying a system to satisfy them. There was no question of offering options; the Bell System knew best. If marketing reported that a customer was unhappy, they were told to go back and explain to the customer why he should be happy. There was hardly any feedback from customers to design. There was certainly no tradition that the customer was always right.[64]

It is important to understand that these attitudes were firmly grounded in success, not failure. Over the decades since Vail had given the Bell System its primary orientation, the national telephone network had become a marvel of advanced engineering and of modern managerial techniques. Systems engineering was a Bell innovation, as was statistical quality control. The managers who ran the network in the 1970s had every reason to be proud of what they were doing. When you picked up the telephone, you got a dial tone. When you placed a call, you got an answer.

[62]Anthony Downs, *Inside Bureaucracy* (Boston: Little, Brown, 1967).
[63]William G. Sharwell, interview, July 10, 1985, pp. 2–3; Morris Tanenbaum, interview, May 23, 1985, pp. 2–3.
[64]Whalen, interview, July 18, 1985, pp. 3–4; Tanenbaum, interview, May 23, 1985, 67–9.

The people who made that possible firmly believed that the best logic for the Bell System and for the public it served was a technical logic that emphasized the integrity of the network and the necessity to preserve its smooth operation. DeButts also believed that the switched network was the essence of the Bell System. He was an operations man. He repeatedly stressed the need to improve service to the public, and as he succeeded, paradoxically, he seems to have actually stiffened the resistance to change within the System by reaffirming the traditional network culture.

Whalen and McGill understood the need to overcome this resistance. They recommended and deButts accepted the decision that the marketing vice presidents in the operating companies should begin to report directly to the company presidents. No longer would they report to the chief operating officer, the operating vice president. This innovation was a direct challenge to the power of operations in the companies, and the operating vice presidents responded to the seeming demotion just as one might expect. They fought this latest effort to alter the System.[65]

DeButts stood at a crucial fork in the road and decided that he would not order the operating companies to implement the recommendation. He set out to persuade and cajole the operating companies into adopting it. He traveled around the country, visiting company presidents and sitting down with their officers, selling both his CS/NS/OS organization and the need for a strong marketing department. The companies were unenthusiastic. They still wanted the marketing vice president to report to the head operating officer and not be at the same level of authority. DeButts patiently argued for the new style of organization. He was an unusually effective business leader – the sort of man who commanded respect and personal allegiance. But the cards were stacked heavily against him in this case. The Bell System had long been technically centralized and managerially decentralized. The company presidents and operating vice presidents were accustomed to making their own decisions in matters such as this. Straight-lining of authority was not the Bell way to do things. The well-entrenched Bell culture was on their side, as was their knowledge that deButts was as committed as they were to the service ethic. They sometimes could not believe that he meant what he said about marketing.[66]

Had they looked more closely at the entire deButts strategy, the operat-

[65]John D. deButts, interview, October 25, 1984, p. 13; Whalen, interview, July 18, 1985, pp. 11–12; Thomas E. Bolger, interview, September 27, 1985, p. 3; William L. Weiss, interview, November 20, 1985, pp. 3–8; John L. Clendenin, interview, November 22, 1985, pp. 7–8.

[66]DeButts, interview, October 25, 1984, p. 13; Robert D. Lilley, interview, September 23, 1985, pp. 63–4; Whalen, interview, July 18, 1985, pp. 11–12; Bolger, interview, September 27, 1985, p. 3; Weiss, interview, November 20, 1985, p. 8; Donald E. Guinn, interview, December 12, 1985, pp. 15–16, 23; Clendenin, interview, November 22, 1985, pp. 7–8.

ing company executives might have concluded that their CEO was indeed determined to change the Bell System. His concern for service was linked to his attention to profits. He increasingly forced the operating companies to justify their construction plans by reference to their earning power. DeButts brought in Charles Brown from Illinois Bell to be his chief financial officer and extended the budgetary reforms he had already begun under Romnes. Under what was described as a "commitment budget process," operating company presidents were required to forecast their expenses and earnings. They were held to these targets by AT&T's financial officers, who were reluctant to allocate capital for investment to companies that could not fulfill their commitment. Although the needs of the System as a whole were not forgotten, Bell construction plans began to be linked loosely to company earnings performance. AT&T's network planners and their counterparts in the field began to formulate construction plans along these new lines for one year at a time, then four years, then six.[67]

The budgetary reforms provided AT&T with much more accurate financial information than it had had before 1972. Corporate headquarters began to exert more pressure on operating company managements that were falling behind the performance records of the better companies. Teams from 195 Broadway visited the laggards and pressed hard for improvements. The new information revealed once again, for example, that AT&T had a painfully difficult problem with Pacific Telephone. The California regulators had taken an antagonistic stance toward the telephone company for at least a decade. They had anticipated the FCC's *Carterfone* edict with their own decisions in the mid-1960s allowing foreign attachments to the telephone network. They had resolutely refused to allow rates to keep pace with inflation in the following years. The state commission acted in the belief that AT&T would not let service in California deteriorate, and they were right. But the budgetary reforms implemented by deButts and Brown in the mid-1970s made it increasingly difficult to ignore the subsidy California was receiving from the rest of the Bell System. AT&T's unhappiness about that subsidy increased. How long, Brown asked deButts, would AT&T continue to encourage the California commission to bleed the rest of the system? The chairman had no answer. Engaged as he was in a campaign to eliminate weak spots in the nationwide System, he was not willing to allow California's service to deteriorate in order to make a point about rates.[68]

[67]William M. Ellinghaus, interview, June 13, 1985, p. 44; Sharwell, interview, June 11, 1985, pp. 15–20; W. Brooke Tunstall, interview, May 30, 1984, p. 11.
[68]Charles L. Brown, interview, September 5, 1985, pp. 16–17. See, for example, CPUC Case No. 9625, "Investigation of Interconnection Standards," and California Rate Case, Docket No. 58223, 1978.

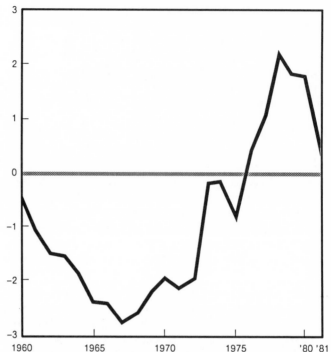

Figure 9. Ratio of the Bell System's return to average common
stock equity to the average return of Moody's twenty-four utilities, 1960–1981. (Source: AT&T Treasury Department, General
Reference Binder, February 1983, p. B302.)

The budgetary reforms, the deButts strategy, and the marked improvements in morale throughout the Bell System were followed by higher
earnings. Circumstances favored deButts. AT&T calculated its financial
returns on its book value, which reflected historical costs. These figures
were adjusted in the inflationary 1970s as historical costs became increasingly irrelevant to current earnings, but it was not easy to conclude exactly what the Bell System's true earnings were. Earnings per share rose
to all-time highs on a current dollar basis even as service was being
improved. Discounting for inflation reduces the calculated rate of return,
but AT&T still looked good. Its return to common stock equity, which had
been below the return to other public utilities throughout the 1960s and
early 1970s, moved ahead of them in 1976. As shown in Figure 9, the Bell
System celebrated the centenary of Bell's original patent in good financial
shape. The stock market agreed with deButts's evaluation of what had
been accomplished, and AT&T's stock – whose decline in the late 1960s

had so depressed Romnes – began once again to rise. The market-to-book ratio rose above 1.0.[69]

As the price of the stock rose, it became cheaper once again to finance capital expansion by stock issues rather than by debt. The firm's debt-equity ratio, which had risen as the Bell System invested to improve its performance in the face of poor earnings in the early 1970s, began to fall. DeButts noted the improving balance sheet with pride: "We have done what we set out to do and that is deliver earnings that would produce a market price sufficiently above book to permit the marketing of equity and thereby to strengthen the financial structure of the business. Our debt ratio is coming down, our interest coverage is going up and we have been able to refinance some high interest rate debentures to lower our debt cost."[70]

DeButts had recognized that it was not enough to bring the top management of the operating companies along with him; he also had to bring the troops. He instituted a set of week-long meetings in Princeton, New Jersey, for middle-level – fifth- and sixth-level – managers of the sprawling Bell System. These seminars, known as the "Corporate Policy Seminars (CPS)," were designed to be a two-way street. AT&T's management told the managers where they thought the company was going, and they received feedback from the seminar participants on these policies and on the problems they were experiencing at their level of the firm. Seminar participants even expressed their attitudes toward the Bell System's management. The opinions expressed in the meetings were carefully catalogued, summarized, and transmitted to AT&T's top managers. The reports enabled them to recognize and deal more effectively with tensions developing in the middle and lower levels of the System. To many of the participating managers, the seminars were their first chance to hear their CEO and his team of top corporate officers explain what they were trying to accomplish.

There were forty-one sessions of the first Corporate Policy Seminar, involving 250 vice presidents and over 1,000 department heads. They provided an unusual opportunity in the hierarchical Bell System for managers to air their ideas in a relatively unstructured setting. They were regarded as so successful that CPS I was followed by CPS II (on the financial needs of the Bell System in inflation), CPS III (on systemwide

[69]John D. deButts's speech before the Washington Society of Investment Analysts, Washington, D.C., March 22, 1977; American Telephone and Telegraph Company, *Annual Report*, 1972–9; William S. Cashel, interview, March 26, 1986, p. 4; *Bell System Statistical Manual, 1950–1981*, AT&T Comptrollers-Accounting Division, June 1982, pp. 412–13.

[70]John D. deButts, "Closing Remarks," Presidents' Conference, Hot Springs, Virginia, November 4, 1977, p. 5; "Four Associated Companies Offer to Purchase Their Outstanding High-Interest Debentures," *AT&T Management Report*, No. 4 (January 27, 1977). "$800 Million of 30-Year Debentures Redeemed; Debt-to-Equity Ratio Reduced," *AT&T Management Report*, No. 48 (December 16, 1977).

planning), and CPS IV (on changes in the Bell System's structure). The seminars had become almost an annual activity by 1980, promoting communication and also conceptual integration within the Bell System. The results were a renewed sense of purpose in the giant organization, a sharp improvement in morale, and a widespread conviction that 195 Broadway was now providing the kind of effective leadership the System had so clearly lacked earlier in the decade.[71]

The seminars, improved earnings, and solid performance records demonstrated that the Bell System had made tremendous progress in the years since the service crises of the late 1960s and the doleful Presidents' Conference in 1971. Investment had been poured into the problem areas, and the renewed sense of Bell System identity and purpose that deButts generated encouraged care in the operation of the improved facilities. As deButts asserted in 1975: "We knew what our troubles were and we knew how to fix them." He cited the reduction in weak spots from 240 in 1972 to 80 in 1974. He set a new goal: "zero weakspots by Day One of telephony's second century" in March 1976. Under his leadership, the goal was achieved in good time.[72]

The beginning of telephony's second century was also a time for taking stock more generally. At that time, Frederick Gluck of McKinsey & Company suggested that his consulting firm do a "10,000-mile" check on the reorganizations it had helped to stimulate. Only the year before, he had compiled a disturbing report on Western Electric. A decade earlier, Western had been performing splendidly as supplier for the Bell System. Now, as telecommunications equipment changed from electromechanical to electronic, Western was losing ground relative to other producers. Western had produced well over half of all telecommunications equipment made in the United States through the mid-1950s. It produced less than one-quarter of the total in 1975 and, of course, a much smaller percentage of total electronic equipment. To a considerable extent this was inevitable, given the growth of consumer electronics, radio, and TV, but Western's strategy of trying to command leadership across the board was not working. An increasing number of its products were at parity with those of its competitors—that is, close enough in price and quality for a reasonable purchaser to go either way. McKinsey raised a red flag about Western's future.[73] The shift to electronic equipment had created a new environment in which Western's expertise was less valuable, and its economies of

[71]Alvin von Auw, *Heritage & Destiny*, pp. 303–7.
[72]For an early review of AT&T's progress in resolving its service problems, see American Telephone and Telegraph Company, *1974 Annual Report*. John D. deButts, Remarks at the AT&T Annual Meeting, April 16, 1975; "Lindholm: Diligence Achieves Zero Weakspots," *AT&T Management Report*, No. 11 (March 12, 1976).
[73]McKinsey & Company, Inc., "Meeting the Challenge of Competition for the Bell System Telecommunications Equipment Markets," November 13, 1973; Frederick W. Gluck, interview, September 23, 1985, pp. 14–17.

scale in production could be matched by others. These trends could hardly be ignored by managers who wanted to gear up for a competitive industry. The recession of 1975 came in the midst of these developments, and it seemed to define a turning point in Western's fortunes. Employment went down by one-quarter during the recession and did not recover with the economy.[74]

Worry about Western Electric was growing as McKinsey & Company was authorized to launch a general study of structural change. In March 1976, as the centennial of Alexander Graham Bell's invention of the telephone was celebrated, Gluck sent his report to Executive Vice President Thomas Bolger (who had advanced to AT&T from the Chesapeake and Potomac Telephone Company in 1974). Gluck asserted that AT&T's existing structure and management processes were becoming increasingly inadequate for dealing with the challenges arising from the company's environment. In particular, the structure was designed to deal with a unitary market and precluded aggressive approaches to individual customers or portions of the market. The overall organization under the CS/NS/OS configuration was based on geographic and functional considerations. It preserved too much of the traditional geographic basis of the Bell System's activities and emphasized the hallowed functions of responding to consumer complaints and dealing with network problems. Gluck noted that AT&T's organization enabled the Bell System to perform its customary functions very well at the cost of making it difficult to introduce new functions. In addition, the planning and information systems of the Bell System were heavily oriented to operational budgets. Not surprisingly, the budgeting process was attuned to the needs of the overall organization. There was no way for extraordinary stimuli to make their way to the top of the bureaucracy in a timely fashion.

Finally – and to Gluck this was the most telling critique – "no one below the Office of the Chairman [that is, the EPC] can be identified as responsible for the definition and execution of strategies for individual segments of the business." The marketing department could identify problems or opportunities in particular market segments, but it lacked the authority or the resources to deal with these situations by itself. It had to negotiate with other parts of the Bell System, which were still organized essentially along traditional lines, for resources and commitments to particular projects. As the consulting company observed, the need for change had not come from a deterioration in AT&T's performance of its traditional activities. The market had changed. As long as AT&T had been in a simple monopoly environment, a functional organization had performed very well; but in the rapidly changing context of the mid-1970s, the old Bell way of doing business was inadequate.

[74]Donald E. Procknow, interview, December 19, 1985, pp. 15–17; *Bell System Statistical Manual, 1950–1981*, p. 702.

The report closed with a stern warning: "we believe that you must move strongly and decisively to come to grips with this major and fundamental management challenge. Continued dependence on marginal change and refinement of your existing management approach when you are dealing with a fundamentally different set of management problems simply cannot work and, more insidiously, may give the appearance of progress when none has been made."[75] In brief, the 1973 reorganization had not turned the Bell System around. Marketing had challenged the engineers, and the logic of the network had won. DeButts had tried to solve a reasonably specific problem using consensus management and a small part of the System's enormous resources. In the opinion of the firm's management consultants, that strategy had failed.

AT&T's experience with its Dimension private branch exchange (PBX) illustrates the balance of forces that persisted within the firm in the first half of the decade. This particular device, a switch for installation in customer offices, was the Bell System's primary offering to a market opened to competition by the FCC's *Carterfone* decision. The problem that AT&T encountered with it was due to the fact that Dimension was a traditional analogue switch. It was perfectly adequate for most customers, and indeed AT&T made a great deal of money selling the Dimension. But because it was an analogue switch, those who used it had to use modems to connect their computers to the network or install separate digital wiring for them. The Bell System was developing its digital network at this time, but Bell Labs's strategy was to start with the national network and then extend digitalization progressively to smaller and smaller parts of the network. This orderly progression made good sense to managers concerned with the network's long-run capabilities. It did not make sense to customers who wanted a digital switch at once. They wanted to avoid the costs of extra modems or extra wiring – as well as the cost of later shifting to digital transmission – in their private exchanges. Many just wanted the newest technology, whether it would save them money or not.[76]

The Bell engineers were not interested in what the salesmen reported that customers wanted, in spite of Whalen's ambitious 1973 plans. They were not going to let the peddlers tell them what to make. They were the custodians of the network, and they knew what was best. As the Bell System engineers saw it, the huge sunk cost of the local exchanges mandated a deliberate, careful evolution from analogue to digital. In addition, they argued, analogue switching provided high quality and low cost for voice traffic – which is mostly what the network carried. So what was the point of a digital PBX and digital terminals if the local exchange plant was

[75]Frederick W. Gluck to Thomas E. Bolger, March 15, 1976: "Perspective on a Major Management Challenge Facing American Telephone and Telegraph Company."
[76]Charles E. Hugel, interview, March 18, 1986, pp. 27–8.

all analogue? In short, the engineers were optimizing the network and the salesmen were trying to respond to customers' preferences and needs. The two groups were in two different worlds, speaking two different languages. They couldn't (or wouldn't) hear each other.

The engineers explained that the Dimension PBX would do everything that was needed. The customers should be happy with their machine and Bell's explanations. But alas for the engineers, times had changed and the customers had a choice. Some of them did not want a machine that represented the end of the old technology, even if it was capable; they wanted the beginning of the next generation of switches, and they turned to other suppliers for their equipment.[77] As William Cashel (who took over from Brown as chief financial officer in 1977) expressed it, the Bell System continued to stress "long-term debt and long-term telephones." But as the industry changed and as customers developed shorter time horizons, that position became more and more difficult to maintain.[78]

The engineers persisted, and they drove Goldstein and McGill of AT&T's marketing department up the wall. Both men tried, with virtually no success, to make the case that the company's marketing needs dictated a new approach to managing change. They met with managers from Bell Labs and Western Electric in various Bell System committees. They did what they could through traditional channels such as the Tri-Company Councils. But they could not make headway with either Bell Labs or AT&T's upper management, and they lacked the authority to commandeer resources themselves. Dimension sold well – it was not another Picturephone – but it did not establish AT&T as a leader in the PBX field. GTE, ITT, Northern Telecom, Rolm, General Dynamics, and other firms began to penetrate the market for switches in customer offices. At best, Dimension left the Bell System at parity with the competition. Meanwhile, the controversy that swirled around inside the company hardened the lines between the marketing department and the engineers.[79]

McGill, who had been brought into AT&T to promote change, acted like a lightning rod for all of the emotions – mostly negative – aroused by these controversies. His strident manner of expression and his relentless disparagement of traditional Bell System procedures stirred up conflict (and probably activated a number of ulcers). McGill was aggressive, brash, insistent. Style in this case had something to do with function. Had McGill been mild-mannered and pleasant, had he possessed a Bell-shaped head, he would not have been hired. Nor would he have been able to do his job, that is, promote change in the massive Bell System. It was

[77]Archibald J. McGill, interview, June 20, 1985, p. 17.
[78]Cashel, interview, March 26, 1986, p. 22.
[79]Edward M. Goldstein, interview, April 25, 1985, pp. 42–4, 65–6; McGill, interview, June 20, 1985, pp. 20–1.

common in the late 1970s for Bell managers to say that McGill was his own worst enemy. But he was not. He, like them, was doing his job by being the man they loved to hate.

McGill used every forum he could find to market the idea of marketing. He thundered against the Dimension PBX in meetings with representatives of Bell Labs and Western Electric. He used the Corporate Policy Seminars to express his vision of a renewed Bell System. He spoke to Brown, now the president of AT&T and its chief operating officer, whenever he could. But he made only slow progress outside of his own marketing division.[80]

Within marketing, it was a different story. McGill had brought some of his personnel from other firms, and on his own turf he had Whalen's support. He began to segregate the programs in his division according to AT&T's different markets. He instituted a set of procedures for targeting and selling business customers (the "Business Marketing System") in 1976. Marketing staffs in the operating companies were drawn to McGill's policies because he was the only one within the Bell System who maintained an exclusive focus on the business markets they were losing and had new ways of dealing with them. Encouraged by McGill, they began to develop direct ties to 195 Broadway, cutting across the traditional lines of authority.[81]

Despite a few such gains, McGill, Whalen, and Goldstein had been unable to jar the Bell System out of its customary grooves by the time deButts reshaped his team of top corporate managers in 1976. At that time deButts moved in William Ellinghaus, who had brought New York Telephone back to proper Bell System standards, to join Brown as a vice chairman of the board. With Ellinghaus came William Sharwell (his operating vice president in New York), who was placed in charge of Administration D, the antitrust research organization. From their new vantage point in corporate headquarters, Ellinghaus and Sharwell saw a curiously mixed business setting. Profits and service quality were up; the company appeared to be doing very well, and the stock market, particularly institutional investors, seemed pleased with the deButts regime. But the management consultants were warning of troubles to come, McGill was a thorn in everyone's side, the FCC was on a firm course away from the Bell

[80]Brown, interview, September 5, 1985, pp. 47–8; deButts, interview, October 25, 1984, pp. 40–2; Goldstein, interview, April 25, 1985, p. 54; McGill, interview, June 20, 1985, pp. 12–14, 34–5, 39–40, 57–8; Sharwell, interview, July 10, 1985, pp. 100–6; Whalen, interview, July 18, 1985, pp. 10, 25–6.

[81]McGill, interview, June 20, 1985, p. 46; Archibald J. McGill to business segment heads, business marketing heads: "Strong Recommendation Letter" transmits organization guidelines for AT&T and OTC Business Marketing, June 16, 1979, SL:SR 79–06–282; "Organizing to Create a Marketing Orientation," May 1979; AT&T Corporate Planning Division, *Bell System Market-Segmented Reorganization*, March 1979.

System goals, competitors were increasing in strength and numbers, and – of course – the antitrust suit was bubbling away in the background. Spirits among the managers were high, but the atmosphere was somewhat reminiscent of Weimar Germany.[82]

Sharwell responded to this sense of impending crisis by asking Elling-haus for authority to form a small group of AT&T senior managers (sixth- and seventh-level) who could discuss the current pressures on the com-pany and formulate some new approaches. It would not be an operating body. It would not have the power to implement its suggestions. But it also would not have the distractions of dealing with detailed operational questions on a day-to-day basis. Ellinghaus approved, and Sharwell's Fri-day Committee began to meet regularly during 1976.[83]

The Sharwell committee turned out to contain a flock of doves. In their view, the hard-liners in the Bell System seemed to be charging off a cliff. The committee members, by contrast, wanted to find a way to avoid confrontation with the various governmental bodies – the FCC, Congress, the courts – that were hounding the Bell System. They met and talked, focusing on the need to make choices, to give up something of AT&T's historical position. Like the political advisors in 1975, the group dealt primarily with process. They considered substance – What specifically should Bell give up? – but that question raised too many problems to be pursued in any depth.

The discussions of process were codified by Alfred Partoll, a member of AT&T's legal staff, who wrote a series of cogent memos that circulated beyond the confines of the Friday Committee. Partoll was in charge of the lawyers dealing with matters of interexchange petitions before the FCC, and he was eating a steady diet of lost cases. He thought that AT&T's continued resistance to the registration program for customer terminal equipment was weakening its efforts to oppose competition in interexchange communications. There were no legal or market links between the two areas of policy, but they were argued before the same commission (just as they had been argued before the same Congress in the Bell bill). AT&T's unyielding opposition to registration was, Partoll thought, discrediting its sounder arguments against interexchange com-petition; the Bell System was making itself appear to be a blind oppo-nent that lashed out against competition of any sort and eschewed com-promise. That invited disrespect and weakened its credibility.

Partoll had organized a set of informal meetings with the lawyers head-

[82]The antitrust lawyers cautioned the operating company presidents to minimize their anti-trust exposure by keeping their tariff filings clean and their "skirts immaculate." Harold S. Levy, "Notes for President's Conference, Week of November 8, 1976."
[83]Sharwell, interview, June 11, 1985, pp. 6–7, 12–15, and July 10, 1985, pp. 44–5; Partoll, interview, May 17, 1985, pp. 8–9, 22.

ing the various sections of AT&T's legal staff. They met with Garlinghouse in an attempt to develop a coherent AT&T legal strategy. But Garlinghouse was not the man to nurture these dissident tendencies. His aggressive style demanded instant answers to hard questions. He intimidated the younger lawyers who were just beginning to look for a new strategy, and despite his willingness to contemplate other approaches, he was not a collegial thinker. The meetings petered out.[84]

When Partoll brought his concerns to the more open atmosphere of the Friday Committee, he argued for the creation of an organization or the appointment of a single executive who would be designated to take an overview of all of AT&T's problems. This would include its difficulties in the regulatory forum, the government's antitrust suit (then winding its way through a variety of procedural issues), the legislative arena, and–of course–the marketplace. The central problem for this person or group would be that the public policy process was increasingly dominated by fears of AT&T's ability to cross-subsidize its competitive activities with revenues from its monopoly services. This fear was "at the core of the dismal line of decisions of the FCC." It was part of the bottleneck monopoly theory that underpinned the Justice Department's suit. It was beginning to emerge as a focus of activity in Congress, where various structural changes in AT&T were being proposed to prevent cross-subsidies.

As Partoll noted, AT&T denied vigorously that it cross-subsidized any of its competitive products or services. It maintained, on the contrary, that the separations formula instead provided a contribution that flowed from the increasingly competitive long distance services to the Bell System's monopoly local services. In the ongoing FCC discussions of cost accounting, AT&T tried to show that proper accounting would reveal that its prices were cost based. But the telephone company was not persuasive. The Justice Department, Congress, and the Commission all contested AT&T's views and continued to worry about subsidies flowing in the opposite direction.

It was time, Partoll said, for AT&T to consider the general implications of this debate. Various structural alternatives were going to be proposed, and the company should define its position in regard to each of them. In addition, the competition in intercity service allowed by the *Execunet* decision was bound to expand. What were the implications for market segmentation, for separations, for the Bell System's prices? Partoll thought that the company needed an officer with no operating responsibilities to ponder and develop answers to these difficult questions.[85]

Sharwell, who was in sympathy with Partoll's concerns, seized on the

[84]Partoll, interview, May 17, 1985, pp. 5–9.
[85]Alfred C. Partoll, "Legal Memorandum," October 26, 1977.

immediate opportunity posed by the court decisions in *Execunet*. Although threatening to AT&T, they seemed to Sharwell to have opened a window through which reconciliation with the FCC would be possible. The agency was badly shaken by Judge Wright's actions in *Execunet*. It seemed in fact to need help from AT&T in formulating its new policies. In the hope that the FCC would be a better bet than either Congress or the courts, Sharwell proposed that AT&T offer the Commission a truce in the field of terminal equipment in order to negotiate some limitation of competition in interexchange communications. By abandoning the lost cause in terminal equipment, AT&T would position itself better in the intercity market and nurture with the FCC a more general spirit of cooperation, the likes of which had not been seen for almost two decades.[86]

Partoll even drafted a letter of reconciliation to the FCC, to be signed—presumably—by John deButts. It began, "Dear Chairman Ferris, I am writing to you to convey my earnest desire to explore in whatever way you deem appropriate, mutual efforts to establish for the future a more constructive relationship between the Commission and the Bell System." The draft went on to announce the System's acceptance of competition in the terminal equipment market and in intercity services. This "new spirit of accommodation" was to be offered, Partoll proposed, in an effort to promote a return to the more informal procedures that had characterized relations between AT&T and the FCC before TELPAK. The draft, which mentioned the various areas in which renewed cooperation might lead to reconciliation was never sent to the FCC.[87]

As the "window" closed, Sharwell's committee returned to its main preoccupation: legislation. Like the political advisors of an earlier day, Sharwell's group now saw Congress as the most promising path out of AT&T's maze of public problems. It was not so much that Congress seemed to be moving swiftly toward a resolution. Quite the contrary. Congress was grinding along more and more slowly as the Bell bill became mired in controversy and then was replaced by Van Deerlin's equally moribund proposal. But the alternatives to the legislative process looked worse. The FCC, despite the fantasy of a rapprochement, remained hostile. The Department of Justice was relentlessly advancing its antitrust suit, and the number of private suits was increasing rapidly. Sharwell and his group concluded that if it was possible to get a decision from Congress, this was likely to be the most favorable public policy that AT&T would be able to realize.

The group was unable to offer anything more precise than that vague promise. Sharwell's committee, individually and collectively, declined to

[86]*US* v. *AT&T*, CA No. 74–1698 (D.D.C.), Plaintiff's Exhibit 7840, William Sharwell, Memorandum, August 8, 1977.
[87]Draft letter, Alfred C. Partoll to Charles D. Ferris, February 24, 1978.

say what that favorable outcome might be. They talked endlessly about process and about specific problems, but they were unable to define an integrated set of goals for AT&T's strategy. They were unable to crystallize a specific vision of AT&T's future in part because they were an informal staff organization in a corporation whose CEO had proclaimed and implemented the forceful strategy that they were trying, in effect, to change. DeButts had drawn a line in the sand in his NARUC speech. The outcome of that policy in the public realm was a series of intolerable problems, and the Sharwell group studied those problems individually at almost excruciating length. But all of the problems were interrelated and every solution involved tradeoffs. The decisions about those tradeoffs ultimately had to be made by the line officers. At AT&T that was where the new vision, if there was to be one, had to come from. So long as deButts was the chairman of the board, that could not happen, and dissident messages from the staff were filtered out before they got to the top of the company. It was not that deButts or anyone else rejected advice; rather, the advice was muted and lost in the hierarchy.[88]

The mild message coming from the Sharwell committee did not travel very far. Sharwell briefed Ellinghaus on the committee's deliberations and conclusions, but that was only one of many briefings that the vice chairman of the board received, and it was not one that was memorable by the need for an explicit response. Brown knew about the committee. He regarded it as a useful forum for the development of new ideas. But he also did not consider it to be the sort of strategic planning group that could produce specific recommendations for the line officers. Only McGill, official dissident and outsider, articulated and promulgated a new vision of AT&T's future, a vision at odds with deButts's appeal to the ideals of the past.[89] Sharwell's committee did nevertheless produce a substantive proposal in one area for a major change in corporate strategy. A committee study explored ways in which Western Electric might be broken up and partially spun off–divested–from AT&T. The plans went down to the factory level, detailing how AT&T could retain capacity in basic technologies like electronic chips while relinquishing to other firms less fundamental areas such as terminal equipment. Some manufacturing capability was needed to retain technological leadership and ties to Bell Labs. But the study concluded that the Bell System did not need all of Western Electric, as it then stood, for that purpose.[90]

If you asked someone from Western Electric how to divide its activities,

[88]Sharwell, interview, June 11, 1985, pp. 24–32; Partoll, interview, May 17, 1985, pp. 8–10, 16–19, 22; Goldstein, interview, April 25, 1985, pp. 32–3.
[89]Brown, interview, September 5, 1985, pp. 24–5; Ellinghaus, interview, June 13, 1985, pp. 5–6; Partoll, interview, May 17, 1985, pp. 47–8; McGill, interview, June 20, 1985, p. 41.
[90]AT&T, "Transitional Phases for Western Electric," June 1, 1979.

the answer was that it could not be done. This view had been enshrined in the 1956 Consent Decree, and it remained an essential ingredient of Bell System ideology and corporate strategy. The effort to keep Western competitive in the markets that the Sharwell committee was willing to abandon had prompted advice from McKinsey and agitation from McGill. It underpinned the effort to change AT&T from a public utility to a competitor. Sharwell's alternative scenario would have turned this process on its head, reorienting the Bell System toward its network operations, not its product sales. Like the CS/NS/OS organization and the formation of the marketing department, Sharwell's proposal would have been only a small step in the operations of the company. It nevertheless would have signaled an abrupt change in direction. It was, not surprisingly, ignored.[91]

Despite the absence of recommendations that appealed to AT&T's line officers, Sharwell's committee appeared useful enough to his superiors to be formalized. The EPC had outlived its usefulness as a planning group. Any such attempt to maintain distance and thus perspective in a large bureaucracy needs to be regularly renewed; an effective planning committee becomes increasingly enmeshed in the operation of the bureaucracy; it loses perspective as it gains control. So it was with the EPC. Managers down the line decided that every subject had to be considered by the committee to be well resolved. The EPC bogged down in detail as it tried to implement the policies it had proposed. The committee found it impossible to sustain involvement with more than one or two topics, and it began to meet less and less frequently. A new planning organization was needed.

Six months after the *Execunet* decision, in December 1977, deButts asked Ellinghaus to chair a new Planning Council for which Sharwell would be the secretary. The council's members included Garlinghouse, Bolger, Whalen, James Olson (Brown's successor as president of Illinois Bell and then an executive vice president of AT&T), and Alvin von Auw (assistant to the chairman of the board and secretary of the EPC). The council's charge was to oversee and coordinate the company's responses to regulatory and legal proceedings. The council was to assign responsibility for the analysis of specific issues and to review business plans for AT&T.[92]

The council closely resembled the policymaking organization that Partoll had described; it seemed to symbolize a commitment to the formulation of an integrated view of AT&T's position in the marketplace and in its various legal confrontations. But the Planning Council suffered from the same problems that the Sharwell committee had encountered. The type

[91]Sharwell, interview, July 10, 1985, pp. 16–24; McGill, interview, June 20, 1985, pp. 51–3; Tanenbaum, interview, May 23, 1985, pp. 15–17.
[92]John D. deButts, Organizational Notice, December 20, 1977; Alvin von Auw to Charles L. Brown, Memorandum, November 1, 1977.

of integrative planning that involved elaborate, decisive tradeoffs, the kind of planning that was needed, had to come from the top of the line at AT&T. The formation of the Planning Council indicated that AT&T's officers recognized the need for those decisions to be made and made soon. But at that time, there was still no way that they could be made or implemented by the company.

One line officer, Charles Brown, recognized that the Bell System was sliding toward a major crisis, and he sent a blunt memo to the chairman and the two vice chairmen of the company, Cashel and Ellinghaus. Brown (then president of AT&T) suggested that the company was facing its biggest challenge since the days of Theodore Vail. Even though the FCC had made the terminal equipment market into a new, competitive world, Brown noted that the Bell System's strategies had not changed. "We are," he said, "operating on the basis of trying to win all the business we can, trying to serve every historical market and trying to keep our universal service goals intact." But the old policies could not work in the new world. As Garlinghouse would write to the EPC a few months later: "in a competitive environment Bell cannot be all things to all people in all markets."[93] Even more important, Brown continued, the Justice Department had succeeded in advancing its antitrust case to the point where even the most hopeful prospect facing AT&T was long and costly litigation. Here too, Brown decried the company's extreme stand: "Our strategy remains one of massive resistance until and if DOJ [the Justice Department] indicates a mood to negotiate. Even if we 'win it all', the delay, uncertainty, restriction of action and private antitrust suits may leave us badly handicapped at the finish." Brown identified AT&T's many antitrust suits as one of the company's most pressing problems; he wanted to give one person the sole job of considering them and other related questions.[94]

Partoll too continued to pound away at the firm's policy of across-the-board resistance. He described to Garlinghouse how he would begin the Planning Council's work. He reiterated his plea for a nontraditional response to new regulatory rules, in particular the anticipated FCC proposal of a separate subsidiary to prevent cross-subsidies. The company's traditional response would be to challenge the FCC's power to force AT&T to create such a subsidiary. It would then argue that even if the FCC had such power, it should not be exercised because the public interest would be adversely affected by any requirement to create a separate organization; the company would urge that the problems of cross-subsidization could be solved by new accounting methods, eliminating

[93]Charles L. Brown to John D. deButts, William S. Cashel, and William M. Ellinghaus, December 14, 1977; F. Mark Garlinghouse to the EPC, April 11, 1978.
[94]Charles L. Brown to John D. deButts, William S. Cashel, and William M. Ellinghaus, December 14, 1977.

the need for a separate subsidiary. Partoll urged that this obstructionist approach be replaced by an attempt to formulate a policy on separate subsidiaries that might be proposed to the FCC and to the Department of Justice. Could they be encouraged to talk to each other? What could AT&T live with? What were the probable consequences of fighting the FCC tooth and nail? Partoll urged the Planning Council to consider a nonconfrontational stance on the issue of separate subsidiaries.[95]

But compromise along those lines was not Garlinghouse's style, nor was it consistent with deButts's strategy of confrontation. The new year, 1978, began with the hawks at AT&T firmly in charge. They had pulled the company out of its doldrums under deButts's inspirational leadership, but they had not been able to devise a vision of the future that would sell outside the Bell System. John deButts had been cheered inside the System for his NARUC speech and his revitalization of AT&T. But the Department of Justice, MCI, and the other private parties had replied by filing antitrust suits that were proceeding inexorably toward trial. No settlement negotiations were in progress. Congress had killed the Bell bill. The FCC had weakened AT&T's position in the terminal markets. A federal court had opened up the intercity market for ordinary telephone service to competition. Although none of these events were in any precise sense caused by deButts's famous speech, the contrast between the internal and external responses to his invocation of the Vail tradition could not have been sharper.

[95]Alfred C. Partoll to F. Mark Garlinghouse, December 28, 1977.

V

Fighting on all fronts

The new realism

The tension between AT&T's corporate strategy and its political and economic environments was fast becoming unbearable. John deButts, like Canute, had tried to stem the tide of change, but the waters of competition had risen ever higher. With the court decision allowing MCI's Execunet service to continue, competition reached the heart of Bell's operations, the national switched network. It no longer made sense to decry competition; AT&T was already in competition in many of its most important markets. It was under attack in public and private antitrust suits for its responses to competition. Only in local operations was the firm's position secure and unchanged, but there were indications that competition might emerge even there in the future.

No one saw this situation more clearly than Charles Brown. AT&T's president watched the vitality of the company being drained away by its uniform opposition to change and by the slowness of AT&T's internal reforms. He had expressed his deep concern to deButts, Ellinghaus, and Cashel in December 1977: "We need at this time some careful work on the overall strategies of where this business should be directed. We are entering major cross currents, the forces and directions of which we deal with mainly when action points are reached." Reviewing the problems before the nascent Planning Council, Brown had concluded: "It is a time which demands orderly, yet uninhibited, thinking about what our goals should be, how we want future markets to develop, what we are willing to trade off if it becomes necessary or desirable. . . . But who is asking the right overall questions? What is missing in our corporate setup at this time is a clear responsibility for pulling together all the identifiable skeins in this complex situation. What is required is that top management understand as fully as possible the interrelationship of forces and of events."[1]

Brown proposed the appointment of a corporate officer to solve this problem and to provide AT&T with "an understanding of the whole and

---

[1]Charles L. Brown to John D. deButts, William S. Cashel, and William M. Ellinghaus, December 14, 1977.

160

vision of the future." No search was needed to fill this job. Brown had
already identified himself as the man most likely to give AT&T a new
corporate strategy to replace the Vail tradition. Brown was by instinct a
competitor, by training a network engineer, by experience an operations
man like deButts. There the resemblance ended. DeButts was gregarious, persuasive, at ease speaking before large groups, and, as we have
seen, a single-minded advocate of the Bell tradition. Brown was reflective, most at ease in one-on-one encounters, inclined to listen to the
opinions of others, and determined to drive AT&T and the Bell System in
new directions.

He did not, in 1978, challenge deButts's public policy strategy, given
the uncompromising tenor of the NARUC speech and the personality of
the chairman of the board. But he began the process of reorienting AT&T
toward the new competition. He was aware of the growing demands on
the Bell System for data transmission and specialized business services.
Late in 1978 Brown described the recent growth in the size and complexity of the Bell System, noting, for example, that 70 percent of the interstate telephone network had been built in the last decade. How apt a
label, Brown asked his audience, do "you think 'Ma Bell' is for the kind of
business I've been describing – a high technology business applying advanced marketing strategies to the satisfaction of highly sophisticated customer requirements?" It is, Brown said, a symbol of the past. "I would
appreciate your passing the word that Mother doesn't live here any-
more."[2] The new Bell System, Brown thought, needed a new corporate
structure. He was convinced that the CS/NS/OS organization, for all of its
virtues in improving service quality, did not position the company to
compete effectively in the coming "information age" – particularly in the
contested markets for business communications. He pressed ahead with a
new and more radical reorganization at a time when the great mass of
AT&T managers surely thought that the previous changes in corporate
structure would be as permanent as Vail's long-lived functional organization had been.[3]

Brown asked Gluck from McKinsey to take another look at AT&T's
efforts to reorganize. Gluck's "think piece" could not have surprised
AT&T's president. The report said exactly what Gluck had said in 1973

[2]Charles L. Brown, "Meeting Change with Change," speech to the Commercial Club,
Chicago, November 21, 1978.
[3]*SPCC* v. *AT&T*, CA No. 78–0545, U.S. Dist. Ct., Dist. of Columbia, Charles L. Brown,
Testimony, July 2, 1982, Tr. 5334–5; Charles L. Brown, interview, May 29, 1984, p. 14;
Brown, interview, September 5, 1985, pp. 40–1; William M. Ellinghaus, interview, June
13, 1985, pp. 11–12; Archibald J. McGill, interview, June 20, 1985, pp. 36–7; Alfred C.
Partoll, interview, May 17, 1985, pp. 48–9; William G. Sharwell, interview, July 10, 1985,
p. 4.

and again in 1976; it only stated the case more forcefully. With the scope of competition widening rapidly and AT&T changing slowly, Gluck saw a fateful gap opening: "the strengths that have led to your traditional position of superiority are becoming less relevant" as "competition is being encouraged, and new and powerful competitors are entering the business." The time for strong action had come.[4] As Gluck and Brown both knew, the 1973 reorganization had been traumatic for many Bell System managers, but it had left most of the basic company structure intact and the traditional value system deeply rooted. The internal emphasis was still on administration, as befits a good public utility, and not on the market-centered decision making needed by a competitive firm. Although a marketing department had been added, it had been grafted onto a basically unchanged structure. There was no single executive with responsibility for specific sets of customers. The firm was not getting good, timely information on conditions in particular market segments. Marketing had only one of many "votes" on the allocation of internal resources.

AT&T needed to shift its focus from functions (Vail) or service tasks (deButts) to major customer groups. Reiterating the message that he and McGill had been trumpeting for five years, Gluck emphasized the need to organize all of the Bell System's activities by markets. He recommended that AT&T reorganize along the lines of the 1973 "competitive structure." His proposal is shown in Figure 10, where three important differences from Figure 8 may be seen. First, the division was a little finer than had been proposed in 1973; directory services and public communications were now singled out as separate customer groups. Second, network services were identified clearly as support services, not as a market group. The chart makes it very clear that the network was to become part of the overhead, not an independent profit center. Third, the customer groups were to include manufacturing and product development. Gluck stated directly: "this organizational concept would require a complete dismantling and reassembling of the operating companies, Bell Laboratories and Western Electric, as well as AT&T headquarters and Long Lines."[5]

What was implicit in 1973 had become explicit five years later. To exist in a competitive world, McKinsey advised, AT&T had to shed its public utility structure and adopt the form and function of a competitive firm. Since Western Electric and Bell Labs had resisted change in 1973, they were not likely to welcome this new message. In Gluck's view, these organizations

---

[4]McKinsey & Company, Inc., Memorandum to Charles L. Brown, "Structuring the Bell System for the Future," January 11, 1978, p. 4; Frederick W. Gluck, interview, September 23, 1985, pp. 50–2.

[5]McKinsey & Company, Inc., Memorandum to Charles L. Brown, "Structuring the Bell System for the Future," January 11, 1978, p. 11. Figure 10 is Exhibit III from this report.

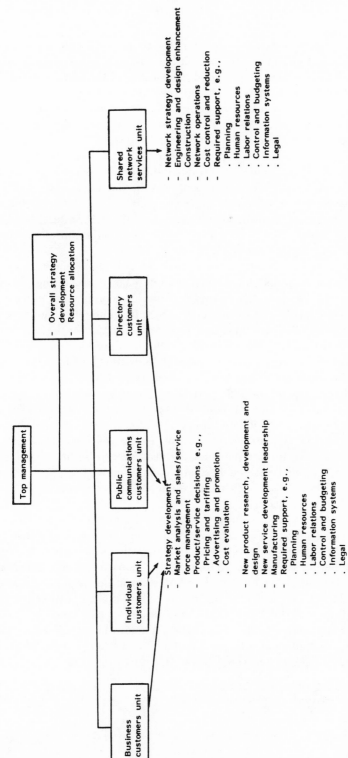

Figure 10. Key responsibilities of new organizational units. (Source: McKinsey & Company, Inc., "Structuring the Bell System for the Future," January 11, 1978.)

were being overtaken by the exploding telecommunications market; they could no longer dominate this vast market across the board. But this was clearly not a conclusion they wanted to hear. Could Brown get through to them? Would deButts allow him to make changes this drastic?

Even given a free hand, Brown was unlikely to accept all of McKinsey's advice. The report treated AT&T as if it were an industrial firm. But even in 1978 the company was still a closely regulated service organization that sold and leased products to support its services. The AT&T network was not a support organization for the rest of the Bell System; it was the center of AT&T's activities. It, not equipment, was the "money machine." Gluck did not seem to see this critical distinction between AT&T and McKinsey's other clients. Brown, keenly aware of the Bell System's unique qualities and position, nevertheless was attracted to the consultant's emphasis on individual markets.

Brown moved for quick action in the aftermath of *Execunet*. DeButts accepted Brown's proposal to launch another major restructuring – an unusual decision for the CEO of a major American corporation, especially one that was steadily improving its earnings, providing its basic services with improved efficiency, and receiving good marks from the securities markets. In a similar situation in 1920, DuPont's president had rejected the recommendation that his firm abandon its existing functional organization for a decentralized structure based on product lines. Only after the severe financial panic of 1921 and large monetary losses did DuPont change course and adopt the multidivisional structure.[6] DeButts had no such immediate crisis to justify a proposal for major organizational change coming from AT&T's president. He saw all too well that this decision marked a decisive turning point for the giant enterprise he headed. Although he himself remained hesitant, committed to the public utility concept, he decided to loosen the reins and let Brown take the Bell System along a new path.

In February 1978, Brown appointed a task force led by Bolger and Whalen to recommend "an organizational structure which will orient the existing Operations and Marketing organization toward particular segments of the market as opposed to traditional department objectives." Its proposal was targeted for a Presidents' Meeting at the beginning of May. A basic blueprint for restructuring was to be sent to the operating companies for review during the summer, and the final guidelines were to be issued on September 1. The operating companies were scheduled to submit their plans for reorganization to AT&T's corporate planning office in the fall; implementation would begin on January 1, 1979. From initial

[6]Alfred D. Chandler, Jr., *Strategy and Structure* (Cambridge, Mass.: MIT Press, 1962), pp. 96–113.

inception to implementation, the entire reorganization was scheduled to take less than a year.[7]

Brown was determined to ram the necessary changes through, breaking down the sort of resistance that had arisen in 1973. Bolger and Whalen's task force moved rapidly into high gear. A large staff, collected overnight, began to generate specific plans for reorganization. As the task force gathered steam, Gluck withdrew, his job as a catalytic agent completed. McGill moved in to support the overall thrust of the reorganization plan and to provide sympathetic staff for the planning organization. Brown pressed the proposal on the operating companies in a manner that altered significantly the Bell style of decentralization.

Even though no overt connections were drawn between the solution of AT&T's internal problems and its changing legal environment, reports of the two processes – internal and external – came hard on the heels of each other. Symbolically at least, the two issues that Brown had raised in his December memo were being drawn closer together. The corporate planning organization presented the task force's plans to a meeting of AT&T's top management in April 1978. AT&T's legal department presented its current analysis of the 1956 Consent Decree and the relief that might be expected in the government's antitrust suit to the EPC at almost the same time.[8] As the legal department noted, the Consent Decree was thought to have immunized the Bell System's structure from antitrust attack. Twenty years after the decree, this effect – if ever present – had totally disappeared. Judge Waddy had rejected AT&T's claims that the earlier decree precluded a new antitrust suit. Thus the decree's major benefit had disappeared, and its costs were still all too obvious. The decree limited AT&T to "common carrier communications services," whose identifying characteristic was that they were regulated by states and the FCC. AT&T had tried to enlarge the scope of FCC control over the market, but the makers of computer and communications equipment had fought back and successfully thwarted this effort. A new round in this struggle was taking place at that moment in the FCC's Second Computer Inquiry. But as AT&T's lawyers noted sadly, the burden of the Consent Decree would grow more onerous over time, and there was no way that the Bell System could unilaterally reduce it.[9]

[7]AT&T Corporate Planning Division, *Bell System Market-Segmented Reorganization*, March 1979; April 14, 1978, proposed agenda for May 1–5, 1978, Presidents' Conference; John D. deButts to Company Presidents, "OTC Organizational Guidelines," System Planning Letter SP-78–09–204, September 1, 1978.
[8]AT&T unsigned memorandum, "Summary of the Presentation to the Cabinet on 4/24/78"; F. Mark Garlinghouse to members of the EPC, April 11, 1978, with attached legal memoranda; minutes of the EPC meeting, January 19, 1978, March 13, 1978, May 18, 1978, and June 22, 1978.
[9]Legal memo, "Preliminary Evaluation of the 1956 Consent Decree," March 31, 1978, transmitted by F. Mark Garlinghouse to members of the EPC, April 11, 1978.

Turning to the relief likely to be sought by the Department of Justice in the current antitrust suit, AT&T's lawyers took seriously the possibility that the government might prevail. The argument was straightforward. As a matter of politics, the Department of Justice was, AT&T's lawyers said, interested in "hurting" the Bell System. The Justice Department had little interest in establishing injunctive forms of relief; it inherently distrusted the government's ability to police injunctions. To hurt Bell without imposing injunctions, the Department of Justice would request divestiture of identifiable parts of the Bell System. Since the department viewed the System as a collection of separate activities that could be operated just as well independently as together, divestiture would, in its view, involve few costs.[10]

AT&T's lawyers concluded their survey of the antitrust picture with the assertion that AT&T's traditional corporate goals – universal service and network optimization – could not be pursued in a fragmented, competitive market. The Bell System's role as a universal public utility would be precluded if the Department of Justice's prevailed. AT&T would have to choose among its current services and markets. The lawyers argued that AT&T's management "should *first* determine where it wants to/should go in view of technology and market forces." This determination should be made independently of the existing Consent Decree and regulatory constraints, since they might well be swept away in a resolution of the antitrust suit. Only after this strategic choice was made could the company decide on tactics. Without reference to Brown's reorganization plans, the lawyers raised again the issues Partoll had discussed the previous fall, reiterating Partoll's call for new studies of the choices the firm was facing. Although AT&T's president had not yet answered the stark question posed by the lawyers, he had initiated a reorganization that would in fact generate a decisive answer within a few years.

Brown was determined to drive that restructuring .through at once, without waiting on the sorts of studies recommended by the lawyers. In fact, it appears that those studies were never undertaken. The reorganization plan was presented to AT&T's management only two weeks after Garlinghouse gave his legal memos to the EPC. In supporting reorganization, the corporate planning group argued that a mismatch between internal conditions and external challenges threatened the long-run viability of the corporation. To remove this threat, the corporate planners looked to the literature of business strategy. They made particular reference to Alfred Chandler, and his argument that vertical integration and a divisional structure organized by product rather than by function had been

[10]Legal memo, "Preliminary Evaluation of the Relief that the Department of Justice May Seek," March 31, 1978, transmitted by F. Mark Garlinghouse to members of the EPC, April 11, 1978.

the keys to success in some of the nation's largest, most important companies. By citing Chandler's research on private industrial firms—DuPont and others—the planners blended McKinsey's implicit statement that AT&T should abandon its public utility orientation with the legal department's explicit claim that the firm was being forced to abandon its traditional posture.[11]

The plan itself sharply accelerated the process of shifting AT&T's focus from service to sales and its structure from that of a unitary functional to that of a multifaceted, market-focused organization. Two new entities were to be added: business services and residence/public services. The proposal divided the customer service organization into two distinct market-focused units along the lines of the competitive alternative originally discussed in 1973 (see Figure 8). These two new structures incorporated market planning, product design, and development (which had been relegated to the marketing department under the earlier organization). The basic changes, therefore, were twofold. First, the very different needs of business and residence customers were to be met by two different organizations. Second, the marketing department started in 1973 as a separate appendage to AT&T's main structure was now to become a major element in these two separate organizations, each of which would be vertically integrated and thus capable of dealing with all of its customers' needs.

The plan did not propose to restructure AT&T's corporate entities along product lines, but rather to impose product-line authority on the existing organizations. Instead of reconfiguring Bell Labs and Western Electric along business and residence service lines, the proposal vested the management of each segment of the business with the financial tools needed to influence that part of Bell Labs and Western Electric relevant to the segment's markets. The managers of organizations dealing with market segments were empowered to make a claim on corporate resources by presenting business cases. The control over financial resources would be the key to transforming the System.

The plan therefore embodied a complicated budgetary process designed to make the Bell System responsive to demands from individual market segments. It was a dramatic change in the existing budgetary procedures. Under the Vail-deButts style of functional organization, financial plans were made largely on the basis of the network's technical needs, as interpreted by the engineers. Projections of demand and crises like those of the late 1960s provided the bases on which allocations were made. Specific funding could be obtained through the Tri-Company Coun-

[11]AT&T unsigned memorandum, "Summary of the Presentation to the Cabinet on 4/24/78"; Alfred D. Chandler, Jr., *Strategy and Structure*, pp. 96–113. Compare the chart of DuPont's proposed structure on pp. 108–9 with McKinsey's proposal in Figure 10.

cils or through appeals for particular projects, but overall, the budget was set up on functional lines.

With the 1978 reorganization, Brown was attempting to transform the budgetary process into an instrument for pursuing lines of business. Each of the market segment organizations would have to present a formal, detailed proposal for the development and delivery of a new product or service in order to get resources. The proposal would have to include an explicit statement of marketing objectives, expenses, revenues and earnings projections, key target dates, and more. It would be presented to a central management body for consideration in competition with other product proposals.[12]

Bolger had presented this plan to the Presidents' Conference in May. Here the full implications of Brown's initiative could be seen.[13] The 1978 reorganization was not just an addendum to the 1973 program; it was a decisive attempt to reorient the entire Bell System. The division between residential and business markets, for example, abandoned the stance appropriate for a public utility enjoined to treat all customers equally (nondiscriminatorily). Markets and customers, the plan recognized, differed. Under regulation, even small customers had exerted an important influence on telephone service through the regulatory system. Under competition, large customers would have the largest impact.

This shift was embodied in the creation of a major department to serve the growing business market – an expansion of McGill's business marketing system. Business demand was growing rapidly, and it posed serious challenges to the Bell System. The need to transmit data rapidly and without error, to provide for greater internal switching capacity, and to develop smaller communications networks within or attached to the national network – all of these needs posed technical problems that were leading AT&T in new directions. Despite the focus of regulatory and congressional attention on residential customers and Bell's traditional goal of universal service, AT&T was shifting its focus toward business. Romnes had looked for a corporate goal to replace Vail's concept of universal service; Brown was articulating one. AT&T would concentrate on the needs of business in the information age.

Bringing marketing into the mainstream of Bell activities was itself a major change. In 1973 there had not been enough marketing men in the

[12]A Presidents' Meeting, solely on the subject of reorganization, was held in New York on August 17, 1978. Presentations were made by, among others, William Cashel, "Financial Aspects of Restructuring;" Jere Cave, "Capital Budget Process;" Robert Flint, "Commitment Budget for 1979;" and Brooke Tunstall, "Guidelines for OTCs." See also "Presidents Examine Restructure Guidelines–Company Plans Expected by October 15," *AT&T Management Report*, No. 32, August 25, 1978.
[13]Agenda for May 1–5, 1978, Presidents' Conference; Thomas E. Bolger, "Report of the Operations/Marketing Task Force."

System to staff a functioning department; McGill had been imported and given authority to hire more outsiders to create such a department. Now marketing was being given a major role in the departmental structure, and power would shift accordingly. Whalen had said in 1973 that one function of the marketing department was to take the initiative for product development away from the engineers at Bell Labs. With it would now go the commanding position that the engineers had in the System. The internal power structure that had so frustrated McGill and Goldstein's efforts would have to change. "Marketeers," as they were disparagingly called by the conservatives, would supplant the engineers and the network mystique as the driving force behind company strategies.

The power structure within the operating companies would also have to change. Under deButts's system, as under Vail's, the presidents set policy and interacted with AT&T and the outside world; the operating vice presidents ran the business. The division of authority was similar to that between the chairman and the president of AT&T. Clearly, the operating vice president's job was a plum in the Bell System. That was where managers were tested, proved themselves, and set the stage for their advancement. But under Bolger's plan, this position would disappear. The operating vice presidents would be replaced by the heads of the business, residence, network, and operator service departments, who would report directly to the company presidents. Brown insisted that the business marketing department have the authority gained by reporting directly to the president. When asked what would happen if a company chose to continue using an operating vice president, he said that was fine. But when headquarters wanted to talk to someone about business marketing, it would call the head of that department directly, bypassing the operating vice president.[14]

Such calls would increase in frequency because the reorganization would significantly alter the relations between the operating companies and 195 Broadway. The heads of the departments would report not only to the presidents of their companies but also to their opposite numbers at AT&T headquarters. The vice president in charge of marketing services in say, Illinois, would owe loyalty not only to his president but to AT&T's vice president of marketing as well. This form of matrix organization was a severe break from the Bell System's traditional decentralized, geographic structure. It signaled the growth of a new kind of expertise within the System. No longer would knowledge of local conditions dominate the business; knowledge of specific national markets would become more important. The business market was growing, and increasing attention to the national arena in which these customers operated was needed. Infor-

[14]Edward M. Block, interview, December 3, 1985, p. 56.

mation had to travel both up within the operating companies and across within departments; authority would flow down and across the matrix.

AT&T was not exactly "straight-lining" the command structure of the Bell System, pulling all authority to headquarters, but clearly the change involved a marked centralization of power. AT&T had set overall policy before, and technical standards for the network had long been centrally controlled, but corporate headquarters had left the companies to manage most of their own affairs. The companies had been content to do so and leave the broad questions of policy to 195 Broadway. Now AT&T was encroaching on the operating companies' domain. The use of budgets as command tools, the demotion of the operating vice presidents, and the matrix organization all drew power to New York. The position of the operating company presidents would be eroded, along with that of their operating vice presidents. The semiannual Presidents' Conferences would contain less dialogue and more instruction.

Changes of this magnitude can seldom be effected without opposition, and Bolger's presentation of the reorganization plan was not greeted by universal applause. The Bell company presidents did not like it because their authority would be diminished and their operating responsibilities increased. Without operating vice presidents, they would be far more involved in the actual running of the business than they had been for years. The operating vice presidents themselves naturally were opposed to the abolition of their jobs. They were supposed to be going up in the organization, but as the reorganization was implemented, there would be no place for them to go but down. The need was for more departmental vice presidents, not higher executives.[15]

Brown, however, was determined to reorient the Bell System in the post-*Execunet* world—and to get the job done quickly. He overrode the objections from the operating companies and held to the crushing schedule he had set. Dissatisfaction came back to him through the give-and-take of CPS III. The Bell managers asked about the costs and benefits of the change, about the problems of transition, and about more fundamental problems as well: "The Bell System reorganization implies a change in mission while it is unclear whether a decision has been made regarding the kind of business the Bell System should be in [in] the future."[16]

Brown replied to questions like these with a summary of the Bell System's undoubted strengths. Technology stood first, as it traditionally had with the Bell engineers. Brown reminded the managers that Bell's service quality had "faltered" in the late 1960s, but the prophets of doom at that time, he said, had been wrong. The System had attained zero weak spots

[15]William L. Weiss, interview, November 20, 1985, pp. 4–6.
[16]Joseph D. Reed, director, Corporate Policy Seminar, to Charles L. Brown, memorandum, June 14, 1978.

under deButts's management, while making 1977 the best financial year ever. But, continued Brown, they could not rest on their laurels. The System was not sufficiently responsive to customers; it was beset by problems, from the ongoing antitrust suits-to the FCC's Second Computer Inquiry; the future was unclear. The corporate reorganization was not being undertaken blindly. It was only part – the part that affected the managers most directly – of a corporate redirection underway at 195 Broadway. Brown cited the EPC, the Planning Council, the Sharwell committee, and a pending new planning assignment for Partoll as factors in the decision-making process. He admitted, however, that the future direction of the business was still not entirely clear. Ambiguity and uncertainty had replaced the security of a regulated monopoly, but one thing was clear: The press of competition meant that the Bell System had to become more market oriented.[17]

The managers heard, but they were not all convinced. Many thought that the traditional Bell procedures and organization were too valuable to relinquish. Others felt their own positions and chances for advancement threatened by the changing corporate orientation. Throughout the discussion ran an undercurrent of hostility toward Brown and his team – Bolger, McGill, and others – who were leaning hard on the operating companies to fall into line.[18]

Although Brown was able to impose his authority on the operating companies, he was not so successful with Western Electric and Bell Labs. They were not prepared to reorganize their own activities along market lines, and they trotted out familiar arguments in favor of the status quo. Bell Labs invoked its own particular mystique, its productive congeniality, its undoubted past accomplishments. Western Electric, making light of the difficulties it was beginning to experience, insisted that it was one of the premier manufacturing operations in the world and that its system of product management was already organized along market lines. Both organizations questioned the wisdom of deviating from their tested formulas.

As it turned out, the basic changes in the Bell System went up to the borders of these two organizations, but they were left to function in their customary styles. The question is not why Bell Labs and Western Electric wanted this outcome, but why Brown let them get away with it. The answer is, in part, that he and deButts still had a telephone company to run, and while introducing structural changes, they needed the enthusiastic support of the management of Bell Labs and Western Electric in the

[17]Charles L. Brown, speech to CPS III, Buck Hill Falls, Pennsylvania, April 28, 1978.
[18]Brown, interview, September 5, 1985, pp. 42–3; Gluck, interview, September 23, 1985, pp. 56–7; McGill, interview, June 20, 1985, pp. 33–4; Sharwell, interview, July 10, 1985, pp. 26–7; Donald E. Guinn, interview, December 12, 1985, pp. 20–1; Charles E. Hugel, interview, March 18, 1986, pp. 12–13; Weiss, interview, November 20, 1985, pp. 8–9.

day-to-day operations of the System. They had confidence in the judgment of those managers and found it impossible to ride roughshod over
their objections. That had not been the way the Bell System managed
change, and Brown, like deButts, was a product of the Bell System. He
could not resist the appeal to Bell's past technological glory. He seems to
have discounted the decline in Western Electric's price advantage as
equipment shifted from electromechanical to electronic; he did not believe that, over the long haul, other laboratories would duplicate Bell
Labs's excellence. He reasoned that these two fine organizations would
themselves be able to allocate their internal resources effectively. They
would, of course, but along their traditional lines.[19]

DeButts supported the reorganization in the May Presidents' Conference, but he looked backward rather longingly and voiced his apprehension about the pending changes. He reiterated the Bell System's commitment to service as its primary goal and argued that the advocates of
market orientation needed to keep the service component clearly in
mind.[20] He opened a Presidents' Meeting in August with the admission
that AT&T's management had not been as prompt as it might have been in
recognizing the distinctive needs of data communications users and the
desires of other customers in the PBX field. To correct that situation, the
Bell System needed to move ahead rapidly with the reorganization. But
deButts also mentioned the reservations expressed throughout the System about the wisdom of the new course, reservations that had been
encouraged by the knowledge that they were shared by the chairman of
the board. DeButts said, "Certainly I have reservations. They are reservations, however, about some of the second and third order effects of our
restructuring—strengths of our business that we risk impairing if we proceed heedlessly." He could minimize but not still his apprehension that
AT&T would dissipate its corporate strength by trading a service for a
market orientation. He returned to reorganization at the close of the day,
talking this time about the balance between local initiative and central
control. He acknowledged that the new plan risked overcentralization,
but the danger could be avoided, he said, by remaining flexible. As was
evident by the end of the meeting, Brown had obtained his CEO's support for his reorganization, but not his enthusiasm.[21]

The problem of providing internal switching capacity for large business
customers illustrated the kinds of dangers deButts saw. The switching

---

[19]Brown, interview, September 5, 1985, pp. 44–5; McGill, interview, June 20, 1985, p. 24;
Donald E. Procknow, interview, December 19, 1985, pp. 30–2; Ian M. Ross, interview,
April 3, 1986, pp. 26–7.
[20]John D. deButts, "Closing Remarks," Presidents' Conference, May 5, 1978.
[21]John D. deButts, "Opening Remarks," and "Closing Remarks," Presidents' Meeting, New
York, August 17, 1978.

could be performed either by PBXs at the customers' premises or by the switches at the telephone company offices (Centrex). The technology made both alternatives feasible; the choice between them was complex. But under Brown's reorganization, PBXs were the responsibility of business services while Centrex fell to network services. Instead of ascertaining the customers' needs and designing the best arrangement for them, the two departments would vie with each other for business. To this extent, the ability of the Bell System to provide an exact fit for its customers would be degraded. This disadvantage would be offset by the hoped-for advantages of internal competition.[22]

The dangers that deButts spoke of were real. AT&T was driving forward rapidly through a major transition: A special kind of public utility was preparing to play a new role in the mainstream of American industrial companies. This was a difficult, painful transition – a major break with the strategy embodied in deButts's NARUC speech and in his efforts to stop the FCC from opening new corners of the industry to competition. A reorganized AT&T would be more like its competition, and deButts was fearful that the company would lose touch with some of the best aspects of the Vail tradition. That was why the author of this reorganization was Brown, who would replace deButts as chairman of the board the following year. In fact, it can be taken as a sign of deButts's misgivings about the reorganization and about the changing external environment described by his lawyers that he chose to announce his early retirement late in 1978. The six years he had been CEO had been trying and tension-filled. He had devoted great energy to the task of revitalizing the Bell System. He had every reason to announce his retirement when AT&T's earnings were at their historic peak. But surely the gloomy reports from the firm's legal battlefront and the Brown-led charge on reorganization made deButts's decision seem all the more reasonable.[23]

In September 1978, AT&T distributed detailed guidelines for the operating companies, signaling the end of planning and the beginning of implementation. The task was enormously complex. Extensive changes in the payroll system, redefinitions of job functions, personnel shifts, and revisions of department and corporate budgets all were needed, and all had to take place on a tight schedule. At a conference of operating vice presidents in early October, the AT&T planners pointed out that five of the companies had worked up plans under which the management of the

[22]Weiss, interview, November 20, 1985, pp. 10–13.
[23]AT&T news release, October 18, 1978; "AT&T Names Brown to Succeed deButts as Chairman and Chief Executive Feb. 1," *The Wall Street Journal*, October 19, 1978, p. 4; "In a surprise move, deButts to retire; it is time, he says, for other things," and "Charles L. Brown elected AT&T Chairman as deButts announces Feb. 1 retirement," *AT&T Management Report*, No. 39 (October 20, 1978); "Behind AT&T's Change at the Top," *Business Week*, November 6, 1978, p. 114.

business segment lacked responsibility for revenue, expenses, and capital investments. This clearly ran counter to Brown's aim to reorganize the business by market segments and to use financial accountability as a means of control. Five companies also had problems with their residence segments. Others had submitted plans aligning pricing and forecasting activities in ways not envisaged in the reorganization plan.[24] These discrepancies threatened to impede the development of matrix management, which required communication between the coordinating department at AT&T headquarters and the comparable units in the field. A fortiori they would impede the reorientation of the Bell System toward market segments.

The management of AT&T tried to convince the operating companies to fall into line through a series of system planning letters distributed in early 1979. These letters spelled out in great detail how the departments were to be organized and recommended changes in the operating companies' plans. McGill, promoted to vice president for business marketing in August 1978, and still at the forefront of change, distributed a letter recommending a structure for the business marketing organization of the operating companies. He proposed that marketing be organized by accounts. Particular account executives would be held responsible for the business generated in their product or service area and would have control over most of the activities related to that part of the market. The plan was based "on the establishment of customer trust through a problem solving Account Executive backed by an effective team of support and staff resources." McGill closed his letter by quoting Bolger's charge: "the orientation of this structure is one based solely on one major criterion, and that is a structure to meet customer needs."[25]

AT&T's traditional functional orientation was at last being swept away. Although each organization would not be vertically integrated, as Chandler's theory recommended, the links between the various market-segmented organizations would be attenuated. The reorganization strengthened the vertical connections between the different activities of AT&T at the expense of the horizontal connections. Brown had made his choice. Urged on by Gluck from outside and McGill inside, he had decided to provide AT&T with a new vision. Western Electric and Bell Labs were still not fully attuned to that vision, but there was reason to believe that they would see the light as Brown implemented his new policies. This was all the more likely after Brown rode the wave of

[24]Operating Vice Presidents' Review of Reorganization, October 5, 1978.
[25]Archibald J. McGill to business segment heads and business marketing heads, "Strong Recommendation Letter": organization guidelines for AT&T and OTC business marketing, June 16, 1979, SL:SR 79–06–282.

reorganization into office as chairman in 1979. In some regards, he had already been acting as CEO before moving into AT&T's top post. From 1978 on, it had been apparent that he would provide the signals the Bell System needed, signals from the top that would mark a new approach to public policy and to the firm's market challenges.

Congressional controversy: the House

Charles Brown took office as AT&T's CEO in February 1979, and he quickly proclaimed a new public stance, the counterpart of his internal reorganization. He told the National Telephone Cooperative Association: "I am a competitor – and I look forward with anticipation and confidence to the excitement of the marketplace." The *Execunet* decision had opened Bell's entire long distance network to competition, changing irrevocably the problems AT&T had to solve. Brown accepted those changes in the industry. "Competition is here and it's growing," he said. "It's a fact of life in our business and it has been for some time." With this proclamation of "A New Realism," Brown swept away deButts's attempts to obtain public approval of Vail's system. In the public realm, Brown identified three central problems. One of them was the familiar separations or subsidy dilemma; Brown said that cross-subsidies were important in the public debate, and he reiterated the AT&T view that the subsidies ran *from* Bell's competitive long distance services *to* its monopoly local services. Because the subsidy kept local rates low, a way would have to be found, he said, to balance the need for competition and the need for universal service. A second problem was that of reconciling competition with the need for an efficient national network. Brown quoted with approval *The Washington Post*: "The test, so far as the general public is concerned, is whether – when the dust settles – people will still be able to dial a set of numbers and be quite confident that the phone that rings will be in the right house." A third problem involved the basic character of the industry: Should it retain public utility aspects and responsibility or not? "Is ours a unique enterprise endowed with unique accountabilities to the public and therefore committed to service as our first responsibility? Or are we to be simply competitors among competitors, in motivation indistinguishable one from the other and free to enter – or free to leave – whatever markets profit might dictate?" DeButts had left no doubt in the way he answered that question in his 1973 NARUC speech. Just over five years later, Brown announced that AT&T was prepared to answer the question in a new way. His personal preference – that AT&T should still be somewhat different, somewhat better – was expressed in the modifier "simply." But

Charles L. Brown, chairman of the board and chief executive officer of AT&T from 1979 to mid-1986.

clearly he was prepared to go as far as Congress and the courts wanted him to go in the new direction.[26]

As he proclaimed his new policies, Brown moved in several ways to take control of AT&T and its environment. The EPC, started by Romnes a decade earlier to provide a forum for the analysis of critical issues, had bogged down (as noted in Chapter 4). The Planning Council was a useful body, but it lacked executive authority. One month after becoming CEO, Brown announced the formation of the Office of the Chairman. It would be a smaller body than the EPC and was intended to provide the forum the EPC no longer offered for the discussion of fundamental questions – like the ones Brown had posed in his speech. Decision-making authority was shifted to the Office of the Chairman, which was the kind of small group that Brown liked to work with and thought was most effective. The EPC was then merged with the Planning Council to take over its advisory functions. To clear ground for the consideration of major issues, Brown also tried to settle some of AT&T's private antitrust suits after Garlinghouse retired at the end of 1979. He succeeded with ITT and Datran; he was unable to do so with MCI and Litton.[27]

Brown tried as well to open lines of communication with the FCC. He went to Washington and opened discussions with the Commission. In an effort to extricate AT&T from its deepening morass, he ignored rank and talked directly with the agency's staff. He told Larry Darby, Hinchman's successor as chief of the Common Carrier Bureau, that AT&T wanted to file tariffs that the FCC would approve. It had not been able to do so for many years; the FCC had rejected tariff after tariff as unlawful. What, Brown asked, are the rules that the FCC wants us to follow? Give us the costing methodology you want us to use, and we will file tariffs in accord with it. Darby replied that Brown did not understand regulatory principles. The FCC could not tell AT&T in advance how to design its tariffs; it could only accept or reject as unlawful specific tariffs as they were proposed. Discovering an approved methodology, the bureaucracy seemed to say, was a variant on the old game of Twenty Questions.[28]

Brown, disheartened by his reception at the FCC, switched his attention to Congress. He took Partoll with him to visit members of Congress

[26]Charles L. Brown, "A New Realism," Address to the National Telephone Cooperative Association, February 23, 1979. See also Brown, "Competition and Monopoly in Telecommunications: The American Experience," speech before the Canadian Telecommunications Carriers Association, New Brunswick, Canada, June 17, 1979, and "Telecommunications in Transition: A Bell System Perspective," speech before the Federal Bar Association, Arlington, Virginia, March 24, 1980.
[27]Charles L. Brown, memo to all AT&T officers, March 8, 1979; Kenneth J. Whalen, interview, July 18, 1985, p. 39; Howard J. Trienens, interview, January 19, 1984, p. 55.
[28]*US* v. *AT&T*, CA No. 74–1698, U.S. Dist. Ct., Dist. of Columbia, Statement of George Saunders, January 16, 1981, Tr. 193.

and their staffs, as well as Henry Geller, head of the National Telecommunications and Information Administration (NTIA) in the Commerce Department. Partoll made a survey of legislation for the new EPC just before the markup of the 1979 House of Representatives bill. He identified five "essential" legislative objectives for AT&T: preservation of the unitary Bell telephone network; resolution of the antitrust suit; reduction of "burdensome" regulation; removal of the 1956 Consent Decree's restraints; and provision for an adequate transition period. Although superficially this does not seem very different from deButts's defiant posture, it was. It acknowledged that competition was a permanent feature of the terminal equipment and intercity telephone service markets. This was a completely new stance for AT&T. Instead of asking Congress to terminate competition, AT&T was now seeking to be set free of its many restraints so that it too could compete. As Partoll remarked, however: "there is an inconsistency between the desire to maintain regulation as a basis for the preservation of the core network and necessary antitrust protection and the desire to eliminate regulation as a burden which handicaps our ability to compete." Neither Partoll nor Brown would be able to resolve this fateful inconsistency, but AT&T's CEO nonetheless pushed ahead in his search for new legislation.[29] As the head of the largest corporation in the world, one that had ties to every congressional district in the country and was regulated by every state, in addition to the federal government, Brown never had any difficulty getting access to the legislature. But by the same token, he had to tread lightly in Washington, D.C. AT&T corporate policy forbade hiring FCC staff or commissioners. Kenneth Cox had gone from the FCC to MCI overnight; no one could hope to duplicate that transition to AT&T. Bell System policy also forbade contributions from corporate funds to political candidates or parties even when this was permitted under state law. The telephone company had to be very careful how it behaved in the political arena.[30]

Brown emphasized his dedication to realistic solutions by becoming personally involved in the legislative effort on a day-to-day basis. As he soon learned at the opening of the 96th Congress, the bills from the previous Congress were no longer in contention, but the forces that had given rise to them were still in evidence. Three new bills were introduced in the spring of 1979, and all of them took their cue from the bill that Van Deerlin had introduced late in the previous Congress. They had as their goal the promotion of competition in telecommunications, differing among themselves

[29]Minutes of the EPC meeting, June 27, 1979; package of materials prepared for the June 27, 1979, EPC meeting.
[30]Contributions to federal candidates were prohibited by federal law. Minutes of the EPC meeting, October 6, 1975; Harry M. Shooshan III and Charles L. Jackson, interview, April 3, 1985, pp. 70–5; Sharwell, interview, July 10, 1985, p. 49.

only in their precise definition of this goal and in the mechanisms that would be used to achieve it.[31]

Van Deerlin's new bill (like his previous one) dealt with broadcasting as well as common carrier services, but it was, from Brown's perspective, a relatively practical measure. Van Deerlin had begun to compromise. Most notably, the new bill no longer called for AT&T to divest itself of Western Electric. It was clear to Van Deerlin's staff that no bill forcing divestiture could get any cooperation from the telephone company. Instead of Justice's divestiture, the new bill would require AT&T to place certain operations in the hands of subsidiaries, which would be required to maintain separate accounts as a means of eliminating cross-subsidies.[32]

Despite the complexities of the various bills, the issues in the 96th Congress were clear. The bills' common goal was to allow competitors to enter and prosper in telecommunications without breaking up AT&T. The problem was that AT&T's competitors, supported by the FCC, claimed that the Bell System's integrated structure allowed it to subsidize its competitive activities and to compete unfairly in those markets. The goal of legislation was therefore to prevent cross-subsidization and thus to eliminate AT&T's ability to engage in predatory pricing. This goal was pursued indirectly (through structural reforms of AT&T) instead of directly because Congress was even less able than the FCC to maintain a consistent view of cross-subsidization.

As Partoll had warned years before, fear of cross-subsidization was becoming the mainspring behind the government's various actions, but the issue remained murky and ill-understood. The FCC had defined cross-subsidization in its 1976 decision on rate-making to be any devia-

[31]Senator Hollings, chairman of the Senate Subcommittee on Communications, introduced a bill that relied heavily on the establishment of fully separated subsidiaries ("Communications Act of 1979," S. 611). AT&T would have to place its services for the intraexchange market, the interexchange market for basic services, the interexchange market for competitive services, and the market for terminal equipment in separate subsidiaries. They could all be owned by AT&T, but the relationships between them would have to be the same as those between unaffiliated companies. Senator Barry Goldwater, ranking minority member of the Hollings committee, introduced a bill that stated that the goal of telecommunications policy was the promotion of competition and even declared that it was to be achieved in a six-year period. Instead of outlining how it would be achieved, however, Goldwater directed the FCC to implement the congressional will ("Telecommunications Competition and Deregulation Act of 1979," S. 622). Neither bill saw much activity, as the Senate sat back to see what the House would do.

[32]Van Deerlin's bill deregulated all intercity services except those of what it defined to be the "dominant carrier" ("Communications Act of 1979," H.R. 3333). The dominant carrier concept here echoed a distinction between category 1 and 2 common carriers in Hollings's bill: It was a device to distinguish AT&T from everyone else. The nondominant, or category 2 common carriers would be free from regulation, and the management of Long Lines would be given a choice in Van Deerlin's bill. It could offer competitive services through an integrated organization, subject to full regulation, or through affiliates that would not be subject to regulation. Relations with these affiliates would have to be at arm's length.

tion from prices based on fully distributed costs. But Strassburg himself had been ready to deviate from that standard. He had been prepared to adopt an incremental cost standard, and the Commission would eventually shift to that policy.[33] Even when the FCC was still using fully distributed costs, there was no clear rationale for the manner in which they were calculated; the standard was purely arbitrary. Most of the congressmen forced to cope with this issue did not not understand the technical complexities of the cost calculations. They were, nevertheless, forced to judge the appeals of AT&T's competitors, who trotted out the cross-subsidy slogan every time they called for additional restraints on the Bell System. In most of those appeals, the cross-subsidy issue seems to have been just a smoke screen to obscure the actual anticompetitive nature of the constraints being requested.

Admittedly, some of the issues were difficult to clarify, but certain salient points should have been easy to understand. The 1971 revision of the separations process had shifted an increasing share of the costs of the local plant to the interstate jurisdiction, raising dramatically the contribution from long distance to local service. This clearly was a subsidy in board-to-board accounting terms. (Because of the problem of cost determination discussed earlier, it might or might not have been in a station-to-station framework.) The specialized common carriers had entered telecommunications along board-to-board lines, and Judge Wright's *Execunet* decision had confirmed their right to use the Bell System's local plant to do so. On that basis, Long Lines was giving, not receiving, subsidies. AT&T spokesmen from Brown on down insisted that the emperor of cross-subsidies did not have any clothes, but their pronouncements had no perceptible impact on Congress or the FCC in the late 1970s.[34]

A more subtle and therefore more complex dispute centered on the Bell System's alleged cross-subsidies to its equipment makers and network designers. AT&T was accused of using revenues from the Bell System's regulated local services to support R&D of products and services used in competitive markets. This it clearly did, but what AT&T's critics saw as a fault of the integrated Bell System appeared to its participants as one of its most advantageous attributes. The synergy between operations and research was at the core of Bell's technological preeminence and its

[33]FCC, *Memorandum Opinion and Order*, FCC Docket 18128, "Revisions of Tariff FCC No. 260 Private Line Services, Series 5000 (TELPAK)," adopted September 23, 1976, released October 1, 1976, 61 FCC 2d 587 at 652; *SPCC* v. *AT&T*, CA No. 78–0545 (D.D.C.), Walter Hinchman, testimony, June 30, 1982, Tr. 4980–97; FCC, *Notice of Proposed Rulemaking*, FCC CC Docket 84–1235, "Guidelines for Dominant Carriers' MTS Rates and Rate Structure Plans," adopted November 21, 1984, released January 9, 1985, 100 FCC 2d 363.
[34]For example, see Telecommunications Policy Task Force, "The Dilemma of Telecommunications Policy: A Supplement," October 31, 1978.

corporate ideology. Critics pointed to the Bell System's internal communication as illegitimate, but AT&T's supporters proudly pointed to it as a valuable national resource. Any problems could be solved by a good accounting system.[35]

Neither Brown nor any of AT&T's other officers was able to convince the legislature (or, for that matter, the executive agencies or the Justice Department) that AT&T's claims were justified. So Congress hacked away in search of a solution for a largely imaginary problem. It settled in 1979 on the idea of using "fully separate subsidiaries" as a way of placing a moat between the Bell System's regulated and competitive activities. Because they would have separate books, managements, and employees, the competitive subsidiaries would not, it was hoped, benefit unfairly from their associations with the regulated parts of the Bell System. This idea stemmed from an earlier FCC inquiry, and it was being discussed in the course of the Commission's Second Computer Inquiry, which had started in 1976.[36] Separate subsidiaries would, from AT&T's perspective, obviously be preferable to divestiture, and it was clear to AT&T's leadership in the spring of 1979 that pressures for some sort of separation of the firm's activities were building rapidly. Ellinghaus initiated a study of this concept in March 1979, at the same time as the three bills were being introduced in Congress. He gave a task force under the direction of Robert Allen, vice president for business

[35]The issues could get quite arcane. Consider, for example, the Bell System's problems in dealing with its biggest long distance customers. It had started to manage these accounts on a national basis in the early 1960s and was handling over 150 of them nationally by 1979. As a result of changes in FCC-mandated accounting, AT&T proposed to handle these accounts through an agency of Long Lines that would bill the operating companies for the marketing expenses related to local services. Long Lines would be used because it was a national organization, not because it was a long distance carrier, and it would sell both local and long distance services on a national basis, exploiting the advantages and efficiencies of the Bell System's integrated structure. But since the marketing would be national, it would be difficult to assign costs to any single state jurisdiction. Was this evidence, as AT&T saw it, of the efficiency of an integrated organization, or was it an opportunity for anticompetitive cross-subsidization within this same system? The two views were held by different groups who seemed not to communicate.

See F. Mark Garlinghouse, memo to members of the EPC, with attachment, "Problems Associated with Long Lines Incidental Participation in the Provision of Intrastate-Tariffed Services to Large, Multi-State Customers," October 23, 1979.

[36]In its First Computer Inquiry, the FCC decided that the new data communications should not be subject to regulation. None of the computer manufacturers, from IBM on down, wanted regulation. The Commission assumed that AT&T was barred from offering these unregulated services by the 1956 Consent Decree; the question, then, was how other carriers like GTE could do so. The FCC decided that they could sell them through subsidiaries structured under a new doctrine called "maximum separation." The subsidiaries had to have separate books, separate management, and a separate sales force. They could not own or operate their own transmission facilities. They had to relate to the parent company from afar. FCC, *Final Decision and Order*, FCC Docket 16979, "Computer Inquiry," March 18, 1971, 28 FCC 2d 267 at 270; FCC, *Tentative Decision and Further Notice of Inquiry and Rulemaking*, FCC Docket 20828, "Second Computer Inquiry," July 2, 1979, 72 FCC 2d 358.

services, only 30 days to formulate a report on the feasibility of various alternative structures for the company.[37]

But events forced a decision on at least the principle of separation before the task force's report could be discussed. Goldstein, then AT&T's assistant financial officer, was to testify before the Senate Subcommittee on Communications early in May about the difficulties AT&T was having in redesigning its accounting systems to show the costs of individual services. He realized that AT&T's assertion that accounting separation would serve to detect and avoid cross-subsidies would sound silly in the context of his remarks. At virtually the last minute before he appeared before the subcommittee, he urged Brown to let him tell the senators that the telephone company was willing to discuss separate subsidiaries. Brown agreed to this sudden tactical retreat, and Goldstein had the personal pleasure of temporarily discomfiting Southern Pacific's Gus Grant, who had prepared testimony designed to show that AT&T already had so many subsidiaries that it could hardly object to a few more.[38]

Having yielded on the principle, the question, then, was how AT&T would establish a separate subsidiary.[39] Brown said AT&T's concerns were that it maintain "control of the management of the core network," preserve the Bell System's vertical and horizontal integration, and avoid unreasonable restrictions on its activities. In addition, Brown passionately wished Congress to find a "comprehensive solution" that would end the apparently endless chipping away at the Bell System's mandate. In his mind, this would involve relief from the 1956 Consent Decree and regulatory approval of pricing that did not invite entry by cream skimmers. What was AT&T willing to offer in return? Brown suggested one or more AT&T subsidiaries and the possibility of wholesaling its intercity facilities to competitors. The EPC agreed with Brown's goals and debated the price that might have to be paid for them. AT&T was, under Brown's guidance, becoming very specific about a public policy resolution that would enable the Bell System to live in the competitive context it now accepted.[40]

[37]Report of Robert E. Allen task force to the EPC, June 28, 1979.
[38]95th Congress, 2nd Session, Senate, Committee on Commerce, Science and Transportation, Subcommittee on Communications, Hearing on S. 611 and S. 622, Edward M. Goldstein, testimony, May 2, 1979; Edward M. Goldstein, interview, April 25, 1985, pp. 83–5.
[39]Partoll had previously argued that the Commission might well support the idea of using separate subsidiaries. The primary disadvantage of this device, Partoll said, was that it could lead to divestiture. This was, of course, a view from the "age of innocence," but Partoll reiterated his concern about eventual divestiture and raised new questions about the economic viability of any such separate organization. Alfred C. Partoll, memorandum to F. Mark Garlinghouse, Walter B. Kelley, and William G. Sharwell, October 13, 1977, attached to Partoll memo to Charles L. Brown and James E. Olson, May 4, 1979.
[40]Alfred C. Partoll, memo to Charles L. Brown and Alvin von Auw, "Integrated Approach," March 27, 1979; von Auw memo to Brown, May 10, 1979.

The Allen task force, reporting back to the EPC during this ongoing discussion, proposed that AT&T remain in the terminal equipment business. The Bell System's marketing data showed that customers wanted to purchase total systems, including both terminals and telecommunications services, from a single firm, and it had long been the system's corporate strategy to furnish precisely this kind of end-to-end service. The task force recommended that the Bell System continue this policy even if it meant setting up a separate subsidiary. The task force concluded, however, that it would be worthwhile to restructure in this fashion only if certain conditions were met. The subsidiary should, for instance, have no responsibility to serve as a supplier of last resort. If terminal equipment was not to be provided by the core AT&T organization, then the separate organization should not have the same obligations that participation in that core entailed. If an AT&T subsidiary was "simply" to be a competitor among competitors, it needed to be regarded as just one of the crowd.

The task force nevertheless hoped that there would be more communication with AT&T's projected subsidiary than with a firm selected at random. Even if arm's-length provisions were inevitable, Allen urged his colleagues to lobby for a limitation of these provisions to activities that Congress perceived as possible sources of cross-subsidization or of other abuses of AT&T's position as a regulated common carrier. Given congressional fears of AT&T's predatory intent, it is hard to know what other kinds of desirable communications existed; but the task force wanted to keep as many of the advantages of vertical integration as it could. Allen did not recommend that the subsidiary itself be vertically integrated; start-up costs would be too large for any research or manufacturing activity. Instead, he suggested that the new organization be able to use Bell Labs and Western Electric under suitable accounting safeguards.[41]

Ironically, as Brown and the EPC geared up in the early summer of 1979 to consider the bills pending in Congress, the legislative process ground to a halt. Van Deerlin attempted to bring his bill out of the subcommittee. He tried to amend the bill (to "mark it up," in congressional terminology) enough to get the votes needed for passage in the subcommittee. But an internal struggle developed between Van Deerlin and subcommittee member Timothy Wirth, who had his own ideas about what form telecommunications regulation should take. Defeated in his own subcommittee, Van Deerlin stopped the markup process and announced to the press that his attempt to rewrite the Communications Act appeared to be dead. He said that he would abandon his efforts to revise the entire 1934 act and focus only on common carrier issues.[42]

[41]Report of Robert E. Allen task force to the EPC, June 28, 1979.
[42]"Broadcast Elements Dropped: New Bill to Replace H.R. 3333 Being Prepared – Will Deal Exclusively With Common Carrier Items," *AT&T Management Report*, No. 27 (July 20,

Van Deerlin and Brown could agree about that general goal; AT&T's chairman was still pressing hard for a legislative resolution of his company's problems. The most serious of these was the government's antitrust suit, which was just then emerging from its long dormancy. Brown wanted to free the Bell System of the 1956 Consent Decree and, if possible, short-circuit the government's suit. He was willing to form fully separated subsidiaries to accomplish these goals, at least under the terms discussed by the EPC, and he traveled to Washington to talk specifics with Van Deerlin and his staff. Out of this meeting emerged a diagram of a restructured Bell System that Van Deerlin and the subcommittee staff circulated (along with a memo from the congressman).[43] A comparable draft measure, differing only in details, was circulated in the subcommittee by AT&T's Washington representatives.[44] Both proposals broadened the role of the separate subsidiary so that it could deal with all of Bell's competitive markets, not just terminal equipment.

These propositions generated rapid, but by no means unanimous, reac-

1979); "House Subcommittee Leaders Decide to Postpone Markup Sessions, Move into Closed Discussion Sessions, as Focus Shifts Directly to Common Carrier Issues," *Telecommunications Reports*, Vol. 45, No. 28 (July 16, 1979), p. 1a.

[43]Van Deerlin described a proposed Bell structure consisting of three parts. The first part, the Traditional Facilities Partnership (TFP), would consist of the Bell Operating Companies and Long Lines. It would provide universal service under regulation and under the 1956 Consent Decree. It would also supply message toll service and WATS long distance services. A separate organization, the Bell Competitive Subsidiary (BCS), would provide competitive services in unregulated markets. It would have entirely separate books and an entirely separate board. It would purchase services from the TFP at the same nondiscriminatory rates available to other firms. Western Electric, the third part, would be required to supply any competitive products through a separate subsidiary of its own. It could supply the network, the TFP, on the same basis as it had always done, but if it wanted to sell products to the BCS, it had to do so through a separate subsidiary of its own. This subsidiary might in fact be part of the BCS. Bell Labs would be left unaffected by the reorganization, except that it would have to develop an accounting mechanism to divide its work between the regulated and unregulated divisions of Western Electric and to perform services for the BCS, only on a contract basis. Accounting separation was thought to be sufficient to avoid cross-subsidies in Bell Labs. Lionel Van Deerlin to subcommittee members, Memorandum with attachment titled "AT&T Structure in Competitive Markets," July 10, 1979 (typescript).

[44]They employed a diagram similar to Van Deerlin's, in which AT&T's core network including the Bell Operating Companies, Long Lines, Western Electric, and Bell Labs was seen as one unit relating to a Bell-unregulated entity or entities on the same basis that it related to other competing carriers. The core network would sell exchange services and interexchange message toll services to end users under regulation. Even on the Bell proposal, it was stated that the core network's interexchange services would be subject to resale. There would be little opportunity for price discrimination under these conditions. TELPAK had been based on AT&T's ability to distinguish between large and small users. MCI's initial proposal for shared private line services had exploited a profit opportunity created by this market segmentation. MCI wanted to bring the two markets together, enabling all customers to enjoy the benefits of the lowest prices and, incidentally, making money from the arbitrage. With a guarantee that other firms would also be able to arbitrage out any remaining discriminatory prices, there would be little incentive for AT&T to repeat its experiment with TELPAK. "THE CONCEPT," a single-page diagram dated July 1979.

tions. IBM argued that competition should be relied on as much as possible, and stated that cross-subsidization could be avoided through the combination of a rigorous accounting system and a requirement that services be available on a nondiscriminatory basis. But the giant computer firm did not support the notion of fully separated subsidiaries, possibly because it feared that its participation in these markets might be subject to similar constraints. Although IBM thought that Van Deerlin had gone too far, the Ad Hoc Committee for Competitive Telecommunications thought that he had not gone far enough. In particular, the Committee thought it was an outrage that interexchange message toll service would be left in the regulated core, rather than in the unregulated sector. In a letter and memo to Van Deerlin, the Committee said that the proposal was "wholly unwarranted . . . highly undesirable . . . dangerous . . . and totally ineffectual." The Committee members saw themselves being excluded by a clever parliamentary maneuver from the long distance telephone service market.[45]

Despite these objections, Harry "Chip" Shooshan, Van Deerlin's chief of staff, enlisted the help of AT&T's congressional liaison to fashion a bill based on the results of the meeting between Brown and the California congressman. The resulting draft, naturally, was acceptable to the telephone company. Becoming fearful that he would be thought too closely allied with AT&T, Shooshan then released and disowned what AT&T thought was a confidential working draft. AT&T's congressional lobbyists reacted angrily. Shooshan replied in kind, creating a "fire storm of controversy." Brown's determined effort to get Congress moving again had failed; Van Deerlin and his staff were more hostile to AT&T than before, and there were no viable bills in the legislative process.[46]

The subcommittee temporized by setting up a series of briefings with Alfred Kahn, then chairman of the Council on Wage and Price Stability; Hinchman, who had left the FCC's Common Carrier Bureau; and Geller. Geller presented to the subcommittee a telecommunications primer written by the NTIA. It embodied the administration's position toward telecommunications—to the extent that the Carter administration had a policy—and favored competition and the use of separated subsidiaries to

[45]"IBM's Preliminary Views on House Subcommittee Proposal on Telecommunications Industry Structure," July 1979; Herbert N. Jasper to Lionel Van Deerlin, July 18, 1979, and attachment, "ACCT's Preliminary Comments on July 10 proposed 'compromise' on AT&T Structure."
[46]Shooshan and Jackson, interview, March 27, 1985, pp. 62–73, and April 3, 1985, pp. 4–7; John G. Fox, interview, November 25, 1985, pp. 3–6; "Heated Controversy Over Proposed AT&T Legislative Language to Change Staff Draft of Bill in House Raises Question Whether Project to Revise Basic Statute Is Dead; Version of Events Varies, but Some Believe Recess 'Cooling Off' Will Permit Revival," *Telecommunications Reports*, Vol. 45, No. 31 (August 6, 1979), p. 1.

solve the "AT&T problem." AT&T, the primer said, should be released from the 1956 Consent Decree as long as the FCC had the power to impose accounting and structural separation between the firm's regulated and unregulated activities. Any legislation along these lines should be neutral toward existing and future antitrust suits.[47]

In December, Van Deerlin began again; he introduced a new bill patterned after the NTIA primer and restricted to common carrier regulation. The bill extended FCC jurisdiction to cover all interexchange services at the same time as it deregulated terminal equipment. It replaced the separations process with a system of access charges paid by all interexchange carriers for connection to local telephone facilities. Part of the funds raised by these charges would be earmarked for a national telecommunications pool to support nationwide basic service at reasonable rates even in high-cost areas. This was the sort of compromise Brown had said would be necessary between the goals of maintaining universal service and promoting competition.[48]

The new bill required the FCC to classify carriers as dominant or nondominant, based on their market shares. Nondominant carriers were to be subject to significantly less regulation. They would have to pay access charges, make service available on a nondiscriminatory basis, and be subject to traditional public utility regulation to the extent that they provided basic telecommunications services. Dominant carriers, meaning AT&T and possibly GTE, would be subject to continuing regulation of products, services, and facilities not offered by a fully separated subsidiary using an acceptable system of cost accounting. The 1956 Consent Decree would be amended to allow AT&T to provide unregulated telecommunications services (although not mass media services, i.e., broadcasting, TV or electronic publications) through a fully separated subsidiary.[49]

Specific language in the bill – the "savings clause" – prohibited it from being construed as affecting the applicability of federal antitrust laws or expressing the sense of Congress with respect to any pending litigation, most notably the antitrust suit brought by the Justice Department against AT&T. This provision – and those like it in the other bills – promised more

[47]NTIA, "Comments and Recommendations on Communications Common Carrier Legislation," November 9, 1979.
[48]96th Congress, 1st Session, House, Committee on Interstate Commerce, Communications Subcommittee, "Telecommunications Act of 1979," H.R. 6121, introduced December 13, 1979.
[49]Fully separated subsidiaries would be allowed to have no more than one common director with their parent company; would have separate finances, employees, and facilities; and would obtain access to network facilities and services on the same terms and conditions as any other customer. Dominant carriers were to be prohibited from disclosing any valuable commercial information acquired through the provision of regulated services unless it was made available to all unregulated entities, including those that were unaffiliated, on the same terms and conditions.

than it could deliver. All of the parties involved, whether in or out of Congress, could not help but see that any law of this sort would exert an influence on the court. How could a federal judge, even a redoubtable one, ignore completely the will of the Congress in a matter of such broad import? Despite the disclaimer, the bill surely would, if passed, have an impact as AT&T intended on the government's antitrust case.

Van Deerlin and his staff negotiated a series of compromises with Wirth, who was concerned about the size and power of AT&T. He and his staff expert, David Aylward, were more determined than Van Deerlin and Shooshan to see that the giant company was carefully regulated under the new law. After the Wirth and Van Deerlin forces compromised their differences, a substitute measure easily glided through the subcommittee in early 1980. Not content with forcing AT&T to stop cross-subsidizing from its noncompetitive activities, Wirth had insisted on a provision prohibiting "reverse cross subsidies," that is, revenues that would flow from the nonregulated to the regulated sector! This prohibition accurately indexed the level of confusion that now existed on the Hill and elsewhere about the matter of cross subsidies. Unable to untangle the problem, the subcommittee was trying to write a law that would cover any possibility.[50]

Congress appeared to be making significant progress, but the truce between Wirth and Van Deerlin was still tenuous. Despite Wirth's participation in the January markup, he disagreed with Van Deerlin about the financing of R&D. Wirth argued that R&D financed by regulated services should be made public. Financed by all of the people, the fruits of the research belonged to all of the people. Van Deerlin and Shooshan supported AT&T's view that this was unfair to the Bell System, which had created its own research program and was entitled to use its products. Van Deerlin called on Kahn to mediate the dispute, but Congressman James Broyhill proposed an alternative that carried the subcommittee. He required AT&T, over a transition period, to move the research and manufacturing operations that supported its unregulated services into the unregulated subsidiary (a move that the Allen task force had advised AT&T to avoid). Broyhill solved Wirth's problem by forcing AT&T to divide its R&D activities between its regulated and unregulated halves. It was not a compromise that AT&T liked, but at least it moved the bill ahead through the legislative maze.[51]

Congress did not have unlimited time, if only because other parties could also shape telecommunications policy. The FCC was setting rules for the design of a limited separate subsidiary (in its Second Computer

[50]"Amendment in the Nature of a Substitute offered by Mr. Wirth," H.R. 6121, January 23, 1980.
[51]David K. Aylward, interview, September 26, 1985, pp. 38–40; "Proposal to Revise Sec. 219 of H.R. 6121," offered by Congressman Broyhill, May 15, 1980.

188 *The fall of the Bell System*

Inquiry) even as the committee members wrangled about their requirements. The private antitrust suit brought against AT&T by MCI was in
trial at this time. Despite the House's long attention to telecommunications, there was a growing risk that its efforts would be overtaken by
regulatory and antitrust developments. The congressional forum attracted
too many participants to the debate to permit an easy resolution.

As if to illustrate this point, Wirth offered an additional amendment to
the bill when the full Commerce Committee marked it up in July 1980.
The amendment was supported by the American Newspaper Publishers
Association – whose outside counsel was Richard Wiley, former chairman
of the FCC – and apparently prepared for Congress by the publisher of
The Washington Post. The amendment prohibited any Bell entity from
providing "periodicals, and any service or product like or similar to all or
part of the function of a newspaper or periodical or any portion of a
newspaper or periodical." Just as the specialized common carriers wanted
the bill written to protect their markets, so the newspaper publishers
wanted to be shielded from Bell's potential competition. The general
thrust of FCC and congressional activity was to allow competition to
determine how new technology would affect communications. Wirth's
amendment ran directly counter to that general thrust in order to protect
the newspaper publishers. The publishers maintained that they only
wanted to protect access to the news, and Van Deerlin as well as Wirth
accepted that line of reasoning. This First Amendment argument, however, was at best tenuous. It was clearly subordinate to the economic self-
interest of the politically powerful newspaper publishers.[52]

The full committee also had to struggle again with the question of how
the law and the antitrust case were related. Van Deerlin proposed an
amendment suggested by Congressman Peter Rodino, chairman of the
House Judiciary Committee, to emphasize that the bill would not prohibit
a judge from imposing structural remedies in any pending or future antitrust case. Although many private suits were pending, Rodino's foremost
concern was obviously the government's antitrust suit, fast approaching
trial in late 1980.

Van Deerlin expressed the hope that the amendment would satisfy
Rodino's concerns, but it did not. Rodino's staff wrote a comprehensive
memorandum to Van Deerlin on the antitrust implications of the bill.
Shooshan, excitable as always and eager to maintain his subcommittee's
independence, wrote a blistering reply, replete with unflattering remarks
about Rodino himself. The chairman of the Judiciary Committee was, if

[52]"Amendment to Committee Print of June 24, 1980 (Telecommunications Act of 1980),
Offered by Mr. Wirth," H.R. 6121, July 30, 1980; Shooshan and Jackson, interview, April
3, 1985, pp. 37–43.

anything, confirmed in his view by this outburst. As soon as the Commerce Committee reported the bill to the full House, Rodino formally requested the Speaker to refer the bill to the Judiciary Committee for examination of its antitrust implications. The delay would be fatal to the measure, but the Judiciary Committee had its way. Rodino's committee held hearings on the bill and reported it out "adversely, without prejudice" at the beginning of October, only a month before the 1980 election. Even if Rodino had not expressed the opinion that the bill was "seriously flawed" as far as the antitrust issue was concerned, a major rewrite of the Communications Act could never pass in the shadow of the election.[53]

There was also no Senate bill to complement the House's action at the tail end of the 96th Congress. A new Senate measure had been introduced in the summer by Senator Hollings, but the bill had not made it out of committee. Like Van Deerlin's earlier bills, it covered broadcasting as well as common carrier services and drew opposition from broadcasters, newspapers, and other groups. Senators Ernest Hollings and Howard Cannon notified the members of the Senate Commerce Committee on July 29 that comprehensive hearings would be needed. Citing scheduling difficulties, they argued that the decision to hold hearings would make passage of the bill "unlikely" during this Congress. Senator Robert Packwood, the committee's ranking minority member, argued against scuttling the bill, but he was unable to persuade his colleagues to act. The Senate bill languished in the course of the summer.[54]

The 96th Congress had spent a great deal of time discussing telecommunications without making much progress toward legislation. Congress had reaffirmed its commitment to the expansion of competition in telecommunications and it had refined the concept of fully separated subsidiaries. It also had expressed itself on one important matter: There was in 1980 no provision in any of the bills before Congress stating that the best way to fashion the telecommunications industry was to dismember AT&T and the Bell System. But Congress had not succeeded in writing legislation capable of passage. The House was slowed down by Wirth's continuous drive for more Bell System concessions to the specialized common carriers and then to the newspaper publishers. His efforts, combined with

---

[53]96th Congress, 2nd Session, House, Committee on the Judiciary, "Adverse Report together with Additional and Supplemental Views" (to accompany H.R. 6121), October 8, 1980; Joseph L. Nellis, interview, February 19, 1986, pp. 10–11; Warren Grimes, interview, March 7, 1986, pp. 6–20.

[54]96th Congress, 2nd Session, S. 2827, "Communications Act Amendments of 1980," introduced June 12, 1980; "In Landmark Action, House Committee Favorably Reports Amended Legislation to Revise Communications Act by 34–7 Margin; Prospects for Final Adoption This Year Seem Dim, as Senate Committee Leaders See no Possibility of Completed Consideration This Year," *Telecommunications Reports*, Vol. 46, No. 31 (August 4, 1980), p. 4.

Rodino's sudden interest in the bill in July, prevented the House bill from reaching a vote. The Senate did not even get as far as the House. It was about where the House had been in the last Congress, stating general principles and making grandiose plans for a revision of the entire 1934 Communications Act. Congress deliberated without being able to resolve its disagreements. As a result, the initiative in refashioning telecommunications policy passed, at least temporarily, to the FCC in the summer of 1980.

The congressional stalemate in telecommunications was remarkable in view of its achievements in other areas of public policy. The deregulation movement, which had gained strength during the latter half of the 1970s, resulted in several bills promoting competition in previously regulated sectors of the economy. The Securities Act Amendments of 1975, the Railroad Revitalization and Regulatory Reform Act of 1976, and the Airline Deregulation Act of 1978 all expressed views close to those embodied in the various telecommunications bills. But unlike Van Deerlin's bills, they were passed and signed into law. In 1980 alone, Congress passed a second railroad deregulation act, the Motor Carrier Act, and the Depository Institutions Deregulation and Monetary Control Act.[55]

Telecommunications policy, by contrast, bred a stalemate, not the legislation Van Deerlin and Brown both wanted. They were thwarted because, in this industry alone, a host of relatively small firms faced a near monopoly exercised by the world's largest corporation. The problem of Bell System size and power loomed over the debate in a manner that distinguished the dialogue from the ones taking place in regard to other regulated industries.[56] Moreover, the problems in telecommunications were uniquely complex and the situations distressingly ambiguous. In none of these other fields was service quality improving while the price of service was falling. No natural monopoly arguments provided respectability to the maintenance of the status quo; no conflict ran as deep as that between low-cost universal service and competitive long distance service. None of these issues could be revalued without significant tradeoffs, compromises that Congress was unable to work out in 1980.

[55]Martha Derthick and Paul J. Quirk, *The Politics of Deregulation* (Washington, D.C.: Brookings Institution, 1985), ride roughshod over this contrast in their book, obscuring the vastly different balance between congressional and regulatory action in telecommunications and these other fields.

[56]An internal AT&T report using these phrases continued: "Size and power are seen to lead to tendencies to cross-subsidize, influence government, use a variety of anticompetitive practices, or just enjoy the advantage of dominant positions in complementary markets. It is the underlying reason for desires for restrictive regulation, more competition, and fragmentation of the Bell System." "Contending Pressures," February 8, 1979, position paper prepared by the Strategic Planning Division for the Planning Council meeting.

The Second Computer Inquiry

The events that had threatened to bypass Congress in 1980 cumulated and transformed AT&T's legislative and judicial environments by the beginning of the following year. The first and seemingly the most important of these developments was the FCC's decision in its Second Computer Inquiry in April 1980 (known generally as *Computer II*). The Commission extended the decision it had reached in its First Computer Inquiry in two decisive ways. It refined its definition of regulated and unregulated services, and it permitted AT&T to offer unregulated services by means of a fully separated subsidiary. The second change brought AT&T into the discussion of the first point, and it brought the Justice Department in as well, arguing that whatever the FCC might do, the 1956 Consent Decree barred AT&T from selling unregulated products and services. The Justice Department had a different agenda for the Bell System.

In its earlier decision, the FCC had tried to distinguish between communications and data-processing services, allowing common carriers other than AT&T to offer the latter through separated subsidiaries. The distinction, never very clear, had become increasingly opaque as the 1970s progressed. The kind of communication in which all data processing was done at a central computer was less and less descriptive of reality as "smart terminals" increasingly incorporated processing functions. In fact, questions about AT&T's Dataspeed 40/4 terminal – the first of a family of interactive terminals that could enter, store, display, edit, and even print data, as well as transmit and receive them through the telephone network – had arisen almost as soon as the FCC issued its decision. The Commission recognized quickly that its distinctions between different kinds of services had not anticipated the problems posed by terminals like Dataspeed 40/4. This had prompted the agency to open its Second Computer Inquiry in 1976.[57]

The FCC issued a tentative decision and called for comments in July 1979, replacing the earlier division of telecommunications services by a new one and reiterating that "enhanced non-voice" service could be supplied by vertically integrated "dominant" common carriers only through separate subsidiaries. The subsidiaries were required to purchase the voice and basic nonvoice services they needed on a tariffed basis, like unrelated companies. The services of the subsidiaries would not be regulated, but AT&T would be permitted to offer them, the Commission argued, because they were "incidental" to regulated communications. The

[57]FCC, *Final Decision and Order*, FCC Docket 16979, "Computer Inquiry," March 18, 1971, 28 FCC 2d 267; FCC, *Order* (Decision on Remand), FCC Docket 16979, April 3, 1973, 40 FCC 2d 293; FCC, *Notice of Inquiry and Proposed Rulemaking*, FCC Docket 20828, "Second Computer Inquiry," August 9, 1976, 61 FCC 2d 103.

1956 Consent Decree could, of course, be interpreted to allow the FCC this much flexibility. But the agency was manifestly straining the spirit and pressing against the letter of the Decree in this regard.[58]

AT&T responded to the tentative decision by arguing for a subsidiary less separated from the parent company. AT&T proposed that accounting separation be used. The firm did not want any restrictions placed on equipment purchases by the subsidiary from its affiliated manufacturer or on the purchase of services from its underlying carrier "on an appropriate cost basis." Citing its long-standing arguments about the benefits of an integrated structure, the company argued that the inability to purchase goods and services would severely impede the resale organization. Appropriate cost accounting would take care of the cross-subsidy issue. In addition, AT&T asked that the subsidiary have access to Bell R&D activities and the right to fund research done by the Bell System without incurring the obligation to share information or products with its competitors.[59]

Brown asked one of his executive vice presidents, Charles Hugel, to study various ways in which a subsidiary could be set up. Hugel had chaired a presidents' study group on competition and AT&T's structure when he was president of Ohio Bell, and he had developed some ideas about possible ways of splitting the company. When he became an executive vice president of AT&T in 1978 he and a few colleagues, acting on their own and not communicating with deButts, had tried to estimate the cost of dividing the company into interstate and intrastate businesses. Hugel called it an "inter-intra" split; it was presciently close to the actual division in 1984. Hugel concluded that such a split would be far too expensive to be undertaken. Brown, however, knew that Hugel had been thinking along these lines and asked him to investigate less draconian changes in AT&T's structure.[60]

Meanwhile, Henry Geller of the NTIA reacted to *Computer II* by adopting a middle ground between AT&T and those competitors who called for more stringent rules of separation between the subsidiary and the parent company. NTIA agreed with the Commission that the exchange of customer and competitive information between the Bell System and its subsidiary should be prohibited unless such data also were made available to competitors. But Geller, unlike Congressman Wirth, saw no reason to restrict the exchange of what was described as "proprietary information" (information that was the sole property of the firm), as long as

[58]In an alternative argument, the FCC (and AT&T) stated that the subsidiary would still be subject to regulation even if no tariff had to be filed; the services and products in question would be "detariffed," not deregulated. FCC, *Tentative Decision and Further Notice of Inquiry and Rulemaking*, FCC Docket 20828, July 2, 1979, 72 FCC 2d 358.
[59]*Comments of American Telephone and Telegraph Company on Tentative Decision*, FCC Docket 20828, October 2, 1979.
[60]Hugel, interview, March 18, 1986, pp. 1–3, 16–21.

it was billed on a compensatory basis. NTIA argued that AT&T should be required to share its technical plans for the development of the network with its competitors to ensure that they would have the information they needed to design their own products. But the agency said that there was no reason not to allow the subsidiary and AT&T to engage in joint ventures as long as AT&T's facilities were made available on equal terms to competitors and the joint ownership of such facilities was prohibited.[61]

The Department of Justice, by contrast, was not interested in compromise. In response to the FCC's tentative decision, it argued that the 1956 Consent Decree restricted AT&T to regulated common carrier activities. Justice would regard any Commission decision permitting AT&T to extend its activities into the unregulated data processing field "as without determinative effect." The FCC might be able to upstage Congress, which could not get its act together to rewrite the Communications Act. Many congressmen may well have preferred FCC action to their own: Problems with an FCC-mandated subsidiary would not be laid at their door. But the Department of Justice was not about to let its antitrust suit against AT&T be hampered. It was looking for a judicial restructuring of the telephone company more radical than the FCC could effect under the Communications Act of 1934. The FCC's ruling would not necessarily have any impact on the antitrust suit in progress, but it would in effect give away one of the Justice Department's bargaining chips: AT&T's relief from one of the major constraints in the 1956 Consent Decree. Justice might well need that counter if it sat down to bargain with AT&T.[62]

The FCC rejected Justice's arguments and went ahead with its final *Computer II* decision in April 1980. Enhanced services were defined as those that acted on the format, content, or other elements of transmitted information, provided additional direct or restructured information, or involved interaction with stored information. They would not be regulated, and AT&T was allowed to provide them through a fully separated subsidiary to be established by March 1, 1982.[63] The Commission had flirted with the idea of placing ordinary telephones within the regulated island while leaving fancier PBXs, modems, and other terminals offshore. But this echo of the primary instrument concept had received only mixed reviews in the comments on the tentative decision and was abandoned in favor of putting all terminal equipment in the competitive sea. Since that was where complex terminals clearly should be, and since it was almost

[61]*Response of the National Telecommunications and Information Administration to the Tentative Decision and Further Notice of Inquiry and Rulemaking*, FCC Docket 20828, October 2, 1979, pp. 25–7.
[62]*Comments of the United States Department of Justice*, FCC Docket 20828, October 12, 1979.
[63]FCC, *Final Decision*, FCC Docket 20828, adopted April 7, 1980, released May 2, 1980, 77 FCC 2d 384, at 420–1.

impossible to distinguish in any reasonable way between one kind of terminal and another, all were lumped together. Embedded terminal equipment was to remain within the regulatory perimeter until transitional concerns with the detariffing process were resolved in a further proceeding.

Under the FCC's doctrine of maximum separation, the parent company and its subsidiary would have to have separate officers, directors, personnel, and books of account. Joint ventures and shared facilities were prohibited; all basic transmission services used or sold by the subsidiary would be acquired from the parent company under generally applicable tariffs; and the subsidiary would not be allowed to obtain from the parent company or its affiliated operating companies assistance in planning and marketing its own services. Virtually all transactions between the parent company and its subsidiary would have to be conducted on an arm's-length basis.

This division between basic and enhanced services forced the Bell System to unbundle its products and services at a time when Brown was guiding the firm toward information age markets that called for a total system solution to the communications demands of its customers. AT&T, with its tradition of end-to-end responsibility, hoped to continue providing such service even if some parts of it had to be purchased in competitive markets. It wanted the edge provided by the ability to market a complete, integrated communications system, much as IBM based its marketing strategy in the computer field on the concept of a computer system. *Computer II* thwarted the company's business strategy insofar as the subsidiary was unable to resell basic services, (only its own enhanced services and products), but Brown would have been happy to settle for this concept in lieu of divestiture.

Indeed, the subsidiary offered certain offsetting advantages for AT&T. Brown's market segmentation plan had been designed to organize AT&T into units that would act in different markets with considerable autonomy. The FCC's decision forced the firm to move even further in this direction. AT&T's subsidiary would be active in the market for business terminal equipment and at the interface between communications and data processing. It would be focused squarely on a specific market segment. Brown thought that, on balance, the *Computer II* decision was good because it gave AT&T—or at least its subsidiary—pricing flexibility. Ellinghaus disliked it for the inefficiencies it would produce. McGill applauded it. He was quite willing to give up the benefits of integration in favor of a sharper marketing focus. He thought the trade-offs were getting more and more onerous for AT&T; this opportunity might not come again.[64]

[64]Brown, interview, June 9, 1984, p. 39; Ellinghaus, interview, June 13, 1985, p. 62; McGill, interview, June 20, 1985, pp. 48–9; Sharwell, interview, July 10, 1985, pp. 39–41.

In the course of defending its decision, the FCC rejected AT&T's claim that it would incur a variety of administrative and operational costs in creating a separate subsidiary on the grounds that these calculated costs were inappropriate. AT&T had cited costs, the Commission argued, that would be needed to enter the enhanced market in any organizational form. The relevant costs for the Computer Inquiry decision were the marginal costs, the extra costs, of doing this by means of a separate subsidiary. "These marginal costs," said the Commission "are generally negligible."[65]

The FCC declared that even if AT&T was correct that there were economies from vertical integration that would be sacrificed in the move to prevent cross-subsidization, it was necessary to sacrifice some of those advantages in order to preserve competition. The defense of competition no longer rested on the absence of a natural monopoly. The agency's position now was that even if a monopoly firm could achieve lower costs, regulation should prevent it from realizing them. The Commission in 1980 took its stand firmly with AT&T's opponents. Any natural monopoly that the Bell System still enjoyed was counter to the public interest. Competition–justified in general by its allocative efficiency–was to be supported in terminal equipment and enhanced services even if it was inefficient, in fact, especially if it was inefficient (for only then would it need extensive support).

The FCC concluded that its fully separated subsidiary offered the necessary compromise between the efficiency of the Bell System's vertical integration and the needs of its competitors. Although it did not change the incentives of the firm, it did reduce the ability of AT&T to engage in predation without detection. In other words, the aim of the separate subsidiary requirement was not to reduce the incentives for cross-subsidi-

[65]FCC, *Final Decision*, FCC Docket 20828, May 2, 1980, 77 FCC 2d 384, ¶254.
The subsidiary was not permitted to construct or operate its own transmission facilities. Transmission facilities, particularly those that were local, were the source of the telephone company's bottleneck monopoly power–the power that gave rise to the cross-subsidization issue in the first place. To allow the subsidiaries to own transmission facilities would be to place them in the position of the parent company. This action clearly was self-defeating. The aim of the FCC was to differentiate clearly the functions of the separate units created out of AT&T. The subsidiary had to maintain its own books of accounts, of course, and had to employ its own personnel. It was precluded from sharing leased or owned space with other affiliated entities, compelled to use separate computer facilities, and obligated to develop its own software for enhanced services. The last of these provisions was based on the assumption that enhanced services were diverse and, consequently, that few benefits were to be gained by offering a full line. In addition, there was the suspicion that the fixed costs of software development would be borne by the consumers of regulated basic services. Finally, information gathered in the course of providing basic monopoly telephone services and used in marketing-enhanced services had to be made available to competitors on the same terms and conditions under which it was shared with the separate subsidiary. FCC, *Final Decision*, FCC Docket 20828, May 2, 1980, 77 FCC 2d 384, ¶229–245.

zation, but rather to reduce the opportunities. The Commission was going to great organizational lengths to require AT&T (and initially GTE) to expend a major effort in corporate reorganization to reduce the possibility of cross-subsidization.

In settling the specific issues of where the boundary between the parent company and the subsidiary should be, the FCC was, it said, pragmatic and provisional. It tried to balance the benefits of reducing cross-subsidization with the costs of foregoing economies of scale and scope. So, for example, the Commission decided that the sharing of operating personnel or facilities was too likely to promote cross-subsidization to be allowed, but the sharing of R&D could not be prohibited for fear of losing the benefits of vertical integration.

The Commission decided that the costs of forming a separate subsidiary would diminish as company size increased and that the benefits of separation would increase as a company's market power, measured by market share, increased. It concluded that there was no point in imposing the requirement for a separate subsidiary on carriers that "lack the potential to cross subsidize or to engage in anticompetitive conduct to any significant decree." Therefore, only AT&T and GTE were "dominant" carriers subject to these requirements.[66]

AT&T's EPC concluded that the firm had more to gain from approving the decision than opposing it, but the members of the committee disagreed strenuously with the Commission's treatment of existing terminal equipment. The proposed transfer of a $4 billion undepreciated investment account to the subsidiary posed a set of intricate problems, the most important of which was the impact this would have on the separations process. As AT&T had noted for many years, the costs of local equipment were spread between the interstate and intrastate rate bases. If a significant amount of terminal equipment was to be removed, so that both its costs and its revenues went to a separate subsidiary, the local operating companies would find their revenues reduced more than their costs.[67] The FCC showed its awareness of these problems by establishing a joint federal-state board to recommend changes in separations procedures to

[66]FCC, *Final Decision*, FCC Docket 20828, May 2, 1980, 77 FCC 2d 384, ¶198, 206–8, 213, 220, 223, 228.
[67]The local companies collected all of the revenues from the rental of terminal equipment, but part of the cost was allocated to interstate service through the separations process. If terminal equipment was owned by a separate subsidiary (or telephone users), the local companies would both avoid costs and lose revenues, but–due to separations–more of the latter than the former. Minutes of the EPC meeting, May 15, 1980; AT&T, *Petition for Reconsideration*, FCC Docket 20828, June 12, 1980, pp. 56–60; FCC Docket 20003, "Economic Implications Relating to Customer Interconnection, Jurisdictional Separations and Rate Structures," Bell Exhibit 45, "The Impact of Competition for Intercity Services and Terminal Equipment on Separations Assignments and Procedures," April 21, 1975.

deal with the results of terminal equipment deregulation – that is, to pre-serve the low local rates thought necessary for universal service.[68]

After some successful skirmishing over the transitional provisions in the decision, AT&T's senior managers decided that they were satisfied with the response they had gotten from the FCC. They pronounced themselves pleased with the Commission's decision in the fall of 1980, even though the agency had meanwhile decided that the new rules would be applied only to AT&T and not GTE. The latter firm, the Commission decided on reconsid-eration, lacked AT&T's opportunity for anticompetitive behavior.[69]

Still, AT&T was satisfied with *Computer II*. The FCC's action was limited to enhanced services and terminal equipment, and it could not bring to a halt either congressional pressure or the government's antitrust suit, which was fast approaching its trial date. The FCC had already declared that it lacked the authority to restructure AT&T's primary activi-ties. In fact, if the Justice Department prevailed in its interpretation of the 1956 decree, the FCC lacked even the power to do as much as its Computer Inquiry attempted. In the meantime, however, the Commis-sion had brought the concept of fully separated subsidiaries to a concrete realization and had begun the process of restructuring AT&T along these lines. It was, in effect, adding impetus to AT&T's ongoing efforts to reorga-nize itself along lines of business while creating pressure for other govern-ment bodies to follow its lead in making telecommunications policy. Even though Congress had so far been incapable of action, *Computer II* estab-lished firmly the idea that fully separated subsidiaries provided a reason-able way to isolate the competitive and regulatory parts of AT&T's busi-ness and to solve the nation's telecommunications quandary.

Within AT&T the planning process accelerated. Hugel reported the results of his studies in the form of two cases. Case A considered only the formation of a vertically integrated, fully separated terminal equipment

---

[68]FCC, *Notice of Proposed Rulemaking and Order Establishing a Joint Board,* FCC CC Docket 80–286, "Amendment of Part 67 of the Commission's Rules," June 12, 1980, 78 FCC 2d 837. This task was related to but distinct from the FCC's ongoing investigation of entry into the MTS/WATS market. This investigation, started in response to Judge Wright's *Execunet* decision, could no longer fulfill its primary mission of evaluating the desirability of competition. Together with the joint board, it would turn its attention to the implications of competition for telephone pricing. FCC, *Report and Third Supplemental Notice of Inquiry and Proposed Rulemaking,* FCC CC Docket 78–72, "MTS/WATS Mar-ket Structure," August 25, 1980, 81 FCC 2d 177.

[69]A separate proceeding was set to consider the pace at which embedded equipment would be detariffed. That proceeding would also consider key transitional issues such as capital recovery and the separations of revenue. See Chapter 7, pp. 324–25.

AT&T, *Petition for Reconsideration,* FCC Docket 20828, June 12, 1980; FCC, *Memo-randum Opinion and Order,* FCC Docket 20828, adopted October 28, 1980, released December 30, 1980, 84 FCC 2d 50; "Restrictions Relaxed, Changes Made By the FCC as It Reconsiders the Final Decision in Computer II," *AT&T Management Report,* No. 39 (October 31, 1980).

subsidiary. Although the design corresponded to Van Deerlin's bill, it also satisfied the requirements of *Computer II*. In addition, it provided the background for Case B, a hypothetical structuring of the regulated Bell System. Corporate headquarters in this plan would exercise only financial and planning control over relatively independent organizations within the company. In addition to Western Electric, Bell Labs, and a few other existing subsidiaries, there would be two new entities, an "interdistrict" company and an "intradistrict" company. The interdistrict company would include Long Lines and the interstate parts of the operating companies in a national organization. The intradistrict company would be a management staff for the support of six regional entities that, in turn, would coordinate the intrastate services of the operating companies. Hugel's inter-intra split was less complete in 1980 than it had been in his informal plan of two years earlier, but the newer proposal got much more visibility within the company's top management.[70]

Brown's organization of the new subsidiary and its place in the Bell System took elements from both of Hugel's cases without following either of them very closely. The first task was to design a management structure for an organization consisting of two separate parts. Although the subsidiary would be severed from the main body of AT&T, there was every intention to keep it firmly within the Bell System. To accomplish this, Brown set up a tripartite management structure for AT&T headquarters. A small corporate staff provided overall direction and integration for the Bell System as a whole. The General Departments, which in the past had been concerned primarily with operations, were divided into two groups. One group oversaw the Bell regulated entity; the other supervised the development of the fully separated subsidiary. Ellinghaus was in charge of the former, Olson of the latter. Morris Tanenbaum, president of New Jersey Bell, was brought to New York to set up the new, streamlined corporate staff.[71]

Two crucial decisions were quickly made. The EPC had already recommended against forming two subsidiaries – one for business and one for residential customers. In a similar vein, Brown determined that initially the fully separated subsidiary should not have its own manufacturing capability. It would be too traumatic, he decided, in the midst of both the market segmentation reorganization and the formation of a separated subsidiary, to split Western Electric between the parent organization and the subsidiary. Some personnel were exchanged between Western and the subsidiary, but the transfers were not well received and the coordination

---

[70]Charles E. Hugel, presentation and slides, Chicago, September 10, 1980.
[71]"General Departments Realignment Dramatically Signals a Massive Bell System Reorganization," *AT&T Management Report*, No. 30 (August 22, 1980); General Departments' Organizational Chart, September 1980.

was minimal. McGill's vision of a series of vertically integrated organizations dedicated to the exploitation of identified market segments was only partially realized.[72]

The new organization would have, however, "line accountability for the delivery of customer service." The managerial changes of the 1970s had introduced into the Bell System salesmen who were divorced from service responsibilities. They received credit for a sale even if it was canceled or created costs that rendered it a net loss. In that sense, line accountability was still less than complete. The new subsidiary would follow the IBM model, in which a single person was responsible for the whole process, from sales through installation and eventual customer satisfaction. But change was slow, and even as late as 1980, commissions were still paid on sales rather than installations.[73]

To facilitate the division of assets between the Bell regulated entity and the fully separated subsidiary, AT&T's board of directors approved plans to buy the outstanding stock of those few Bell Operating Companies that were not already wholly owned. The board consolidated the Bell System's pension plans for the same reason, and it combined all of the System's international operations under the umbrella of a new organization: AT&T International. With these actions, the way was cleared to launch the new unregulated subsidiary.[74]

The Justice Department, however, was not convinced that AT&T was able to take these actions under the 1956 Consent Decree. The FCC could set rules for Bell System participation in unregulated markets, but that did not bestow upon AT&T the right to operate in those markets. AT&T, seeking to clarify its legal boundaries, asked the federal court in New Jersey with authority over the 1956 Consent Decree for a declaratory judgment allowing it to enter unregulated markets through a fully separated subsidiary. The Justice Department opposed AT&T's motion. Judge Vincent Biunno of the New Jersey court heard the arguments, but he did not make a decision until well into 1981.[75] This stately pace rendered the Justice Department's opposition highly problematical. AT&T had to ini-

---

[72]Brown, interview, September 5, 1985, pp. 56–7; Sharwell, interview, July 10, 1985, pp. 42–3.

[73]Charles L. Brown, "Opening Remarks," Assistant Vice Presidents' Meeting, Basking Ridge, N.J., May 29, 1981; Randolph C. Lumb, interview, February 5, 1986, pp. 38–40.

[74]"In Other Board Action . . . ," *AT&T Management Report*, No. 30 (August 22, 1980).

[75]*US* v. *Western Electric Co.*, CA No. 17–49, U.S. Dist. Ct., Dist. of New Jersey: Defendants' "Notice of Motion and Motion for Construction of Final Judgment of January 24, 1956," filed March 4, 1981; "Memorandum of the United States in Opposition to Defendants' Motion for Construction of the Final Judgment," April 9, 1981; Transcript of Proceedings before the Honorable Vincent P. Biunno, U.S.D.J., on defendants' motion for an order construing the Final Judgment, April 13, 1981; Judge Biunno, *Opinion*, September 3, 1981, 531 F. Supp. 894; *Order Regarding Motion for Construction*, September 23, 1981.

tiate planning for its subsidiary immediately in order to meet the March 1, 1982, deadline for its formation. By the time Judge Biunno acted, events were beginning to move very rapidly in the antitrust arena–events that threatened to alter irrevocably the context in which both AT&T and the FCC operated. The concepts of *Computer II* nevertheless would still point the way toward a possible resolution of AT&T's dilemma.

Settlement negotiations: the Chinese menu

The government's antitrust suit, never far from the attention of AT&T's leaders or, for that matter, of Congress, had been gathering steam all this time. In the summer of 1978, President Carter had appointed Judge Harold H. Greene to the U.S. District Court for the District of Columbia. Cases were reassigned to equalize the load, as they always are when a new judge is appointed, and because of Judge Waddy's terminal illness, the AT&T case was reassigned to Judge Greene. In the four years since the complaint had been filed, there had been no settlement discussions between the Department of Justice and AT&T, the result both of deButts's intransigent stand and of the Carter administration's lack of attention to the case.[76] The lawyers in charge of the government's case did not feel

[76]There had been an abortive discussion in 1977 originated by a third party. David Shapiro, counsel for DATRAN, maintained in the spring of 1977 that AT&T could settle the Department of Justice suit by simply giving up Western Electric. He explained this position to Howard Trienens, then counsel for AT&T in this suit, who responded that it was a ridiculous suggestion and that it betrayed Shapiro's lack of understanding of the Bell System. Nonetheless, Shapiro arranged a luncheon in September 1977 for himself, Howard Trienens, and Ken Anderson and Jules Fried from the Department of Justice. Shapiro asked the assembled antagonists if they couldn't settle the government's antitrust suit. Trienens replied that he had no authority to settle the case and thought that the government should just drop it. Anderson and Fried insisted that there had to be some structural relief, that is, some divestiture by AT&T, but that they hadn't thought much about the subject. They were working on the liability part of the case, and they were not in a position to discuss relief in any detail.

After the men from the Department of Justice left, Shapiro gave Trienens a three-page document detailing his ideas for a settlement. The proposal envisaged a settlement that would "complement and enhance FCC policies fostering competition" and would not deal with areas that the FCC had ruled on since the filing of the suit. The main provisions of the proposed settlement were that the Bell System would create a separate subsidiary for marketing private line services in competition with specialized common carriers and that the part of Western Electric that made terminal equipment in competition with other vendors would be divested. Only that part of Western Electric would be divested, and no operating companies would be affected. The proposal would embody the FCC's 1974 position on AT&T's structure. It would arrest the evolution toward competition and even turn the clock back to before *Execunet*. It stated explicitly that "a decree should not seek to bring to the United States a European model of fragmented telephone entities."

When Anderson spoke to Harold Levy, AT&T's counsel in charge of the government's suit, about "AT&T's proposal for a settlement" in October, Levy denied that there was such a thing and that he had ever seen the document that Anderson was discussing. Anderson

Harold H. Greene, judge, United States District Court for the District of Columbia, was assigned responsibility for *US* v. *AT&T* in 1978. (Photo © Dennis Brack–Black Star.)

authorized to settle it, and Attorney General Griffin Bell was interested only in attaining the goal abandoned in 1956–divestiture of Western Electric. There was no interest in such a settlement at AT&T. Until Greene took over, the case itself had moved forward at a snail's pace.[77]

The difference between Greene and Waddy was immediately apparent. Greene clearly was an activist. An energetic and liberal man, he had drafted the 1964 Civil Rights Act and the 1965 Voting Rights Act when he was in the Justice Department. With ample experience as chief judge of the local District of Columbia court, he was a fine judicial administrator who would not be daunted by the complexity of the AT&T case. He was going to push the case to trial; he was going to move the trial along; and he appeared willing to order dramatic relief if he could be persuaded that it was appropriate to do so. Judge Greene was well aware of the IBM antitrust suit, already in its fourth year of trial with no end in sight, and he had no intention of duplicating that scene in his courtroom. He was exactly the kind of judge the Justice Department wanted. The government, after all, was the plaintiff; it was the party trying to alter the status quo. AT&T was content initially to let the case bob along as it tried to find a political solution to its troubles. Later, as Brown's desire for some kind of settlement and his frustration with Congress increased, the defendants shared the judge's wish for action–although, of course, not the kind of action he seemed likely to take.

On September 11, 1978, Judge Greene issued four pretrial orders designed to put the case on a fast track. He established schedules and pretrial hearings, and in a pretrial order released in June 1979, he set a trial date for September 1980. He held closely to that date, allowing it to slip only into the very beginning of 1981. Judge Greene also required the parties to submit a series of contentions and proof–statements as to what each side contended and what it hoped to prove–the first one being due from the government in November 1978. There were three series, of which only the first and third were substantial. The third set of contentions and proof summarized rather well the position of the parties in the case. Known (by the color of their covers) as the Green Book for the government and the Gold Book for AT&T, they showed (as they were

---

was furious. He had Shapiro's proposal, which he assumed had come from AT&T, and he could not understand how Levy could maintain either of these positions. In addition, he clearly considered the proposal to be unacceptable, since it fell far short of what the Justice Department was hoping to achieve. And he thought as well that he was being whipsawed by various AT&T lawyers.

Trienens went down to Washington early in October with Levy and George Saunders from Sidley and Austin, met with Anderson, and cleared up the misunderstanding. But this incident did not lead to any settlement. It only generated bad feelings between AT&T and the Department of Justice. Howard J. Trienens, memo to Harold S. Levy, March 28, 1978.
[77]Fox, interview, November 25, 1985, pp. 11–12; Griffin B. Bell, interview, November 21, 1985, pp. 6–7.

designed to show) much of what the parties intended to present in the trial.

Judge Greene instituted another procedure as well in January 1979, known as the "stipulations process." The lawyers from the opposing sides got together, placed their contentions side by side, and determined what they could decide on – thus leaving only the differences between them to be presented at trial. The notion was that they could agree on the facts of the case and litigate their respective interpretations.[78]

But, of course, facts do not exist independent of interpretations. The extent to which one could get agreement on an issue reflected the importance of that issue to each side, rather than its factual content. The lawyers fought over the wording and shading of statements of fact without finding large areas of agreement. The process inevitably was time-consuming and wearing. It was particularly irritating to the Sidley and Austin lawyers representing AT&T because the Justice Department staff, typically very young, was afraid to commit itself and the government to anything. The government lawyers were seen by their opponents as obstructionists, and the special masters overseeing the process for Judge Greene complained to the judge that the government was holding up the case.

When Brown formally took over the chairmanship of AT&T in February 1979, he tried to make a fresh start with the Department of Justice. He and Alfred Partoll talked with John Shenefield, the Assistant Attorney General for Antitrust, about the case in April. AT&T's chairman expressed his view that the government's proposed relief – separating the operating companies, Bell Labs, and Western Electric from AT&T and possibly dividing up Western as well – was out of line with AT&T's alleged wrongdoing. Brown asked Shenefield whether he would consider a compromise. Shenefield replied that he would think about it but that he had some "technical" problems to solve before the discussions could go forward. He never got back to Brown. Partoll's ongoing discussions with Geller's staff at the NTIA explored the links between the progress of telecommunications legislation and the government's pending antitrust suit, but the thoughts they generated had no audience in the Justice Department.[79]

Preparations for trial continued, therefore, during 1979. The start of 1980 saw new personnel enter the case, creating at least the possibility of more substantive discussions. With Mark Garlinghouse's retirement, Brown had the opportunity to name a general counsel more in line with his conciliatory approach to public policy. There were lawyers within the Bell System who might have been able to do the job, most notably

[78]*US* v. *AT&T*, CA No. 74–1698 (D.D.C.): *Pretrial Order Nos. 10, 11, 12, 13,* September 11, 1978; *Pretrial Order No. 14,* and *Memorandum Order,* January 22, 1979; *Pretrial Order No. 16,* June 22, 1979; *Plaintiff's Third Statement of Contentions and Proof,* January 10, 1980; *Defendants' Third Statement of Contentions and Proof,* March 10, 1980.
[79]Howard J. Trienens, "Chronology of Negotiations"; Brown, interview, May 29, 1984, pp. 4–5; Henry Geller, interview, June 20, 1984, pp. 49–52.

204   *The fall of the Bell System*

Alfred Partoll and James DeBois, AT&T associate general counsel and Garlinghouse's right-hand man. DeBois handled all of the company's inside legal work other than antitrust and regulatory matters. Nevertheless, even though DeBois and Partoll appeared to be strong candidates to succeed Garlinghouse, Brown had in mind another person for the general counsel's job.

Brown's man was Howard Trienens, who on January 1, 1980, became vice president and general counsel of AT&T. He was (and continued to be) a partner in AT&T's law firm, Sidley and Austin, and he had been involved in Bell System cases for many years. A decade earlier, he had expressed (as we have seen) well-developed views about the nature of competition in telecommunications – views that he had articulated both publicly (in his discussion with William Baxter) and internally (in his comments on John deButts's NARUC speech). Friendly with Brown when he was president of Illinois Bell, Trienens seemed in 1979 to have the combination that the Bell System's head man now wanted: a knowledge of the business and its involvement with the government and an outsider's perspective on AT&T. He was also a problem solver, a man who loved to cut through gordian knots. If anyone could free AT&T from all of its legal entanglements, Trienens could. Just as Brown's appointment signaled a readiness to deal with Congress, so Trienens's appointment was a sign that AT&T wanted to talk seriously with the Department of Justice.[80]

After March, when Sanford Litvack replaced Shenefield as Assistant Attorney General for Antitrust, Trienens had the opening he needed. Litvack had joined the Carter administration late in its term for a one-year stint, with the possibility of staying longer if Carter was reelected. Unlike Trienens, Litvack was a neophyte in telecommunications matters. But he was in the mold of Trienens – an impressive corporate lawyer, capable of sophisticated discussion and rapid decision.[81]

Henry Geller soon tried to get these two men together. Active in the effort to put Van Deerlin's subcommittee back on the legislative track during the previous fall and in touch with AT&T's Partoll, he tried to extend his reach into the antitrust area as well. He acted largely on his own. The Carter administration, which had adopted a policy of departmental autonomy in the wake of Watergate, did not want to take the initiative on telecommunications policy. Geller was unable to arouse the interest of the Secretary of Commerce in telecommunications policy. Al-

[80]Asked why he allowed Trienens to retain his Sidley & Austin partnership while at AT&T, Brown replied that he needed the best lawyer in the world – that is, Trienens – and he would get him any way he could. Brown, interview, September 5, 1985, pp. 61–2; Trienens, interview, January 19, 1984, pp. 11–12; Donald S. Perkins, interview, November 25, 1986, p. 8; Geller, interview, June 20, 1984, p. 52.
[81]Sanford Litvack, interview, June 21, 1984, pp. 6–8.

though he could have gone directly to Carter's chief domestic advisor, Stuart Eizenstat, he did not anticipate receiving any support from him either. The NTIA had no political presence relative to the Department of Justice. If Griffin Bell, the Attorney General, were to say that the NTIA should mind its own business, that would be the end of the process.[82]

Nevertheless Geller persisted. He formulated a tactical approach to settlement and took it to Kenneth Anderson, who was in charge of the Justice Department team handling the case. Anderson took the plan to his superiors, but he got no more response than Brown had in his earlier approach. Geller also sent his format to AT&T and spoke with them about a settlement. He was not negotiating – he did not have the authority to do so – but he saw an opportunity to be a catalyst in starting negotiations. Geller had known Trienens from the Northwestern University Law School, where they had ranked first and second in the class of 1949, and he understood why Brown had chosen Trienens for his general counsel. In Geller's view, Trienens was the kind of person who could both understand the conflicts in the government's antitrust suit against AT&T and see ways to resolve – or sidestep – them.

Geller called his proposal for ending the suit a "Chinese menu" because it contained a variety of provisions from which the parties could choose a settlement formula. The items were grouped into two categories: regulatory (Column A) and structural (Column B). The regulatory elements were injunctions that would, for example, require AT&T to provide equal access to the network, to purchase equipment from a variety of sources, or to behave in some other specific way. Structural changes were those in which AT&T would be required to divest itself of one or another part of the company or to separate legally one part of AT&T from another. AT&T, like a restaurant patron, would be allowed to choose whether it wanted mostly structural or regulatory relief. The more it took from Column A, the less it had to take from Column B. But the total, measured in some indefinable unit, had to satisfy the Justice Department.

Geller's menu looked like punishment without theory to AT&T. The element of choice seemed to indicate that the government did not really know what it wanted – except to punish the Bell System. Anderson had already told AT&T that it would have "to leave limbs on the table," and his chilling words tended to confirm this view of the Department of Justice.[83] To Geller, however, the concept was clear. His aims were consistent with the wave of economic deregulation during the 1970s and with the views expressed volubly at the FCC and in Congress. These aims were to introduce competition into telecommunications, to reduce the scope of regu-

[82]Geller, interview, June 20, 1984, pp. 53–6; Litvack, interview, June 21, 1984, pp. 6–7.
[83]Geller, interview, June 20, 1984, pp. 49–51; Jim G. Kilpatric, interview, May 9, 1984, p. 4; Litvack, interview, June 21, 1984, p. 4.

lated activity, and to broaden the private, competitive arena. They were to be accomplished by forcing AT&T to be hospitable to new entrants, which could be done in one of two ways. AT&T could be restructured so that it had no incentive to resist entry, or AT&T could be enjoined to not resist entry or even to encourage entry by competing suppliers of equipment and service. The choice in the menu was not about ends; it was only about means. Geller and Anderson thought that either would do, and they believed that giving AT&T a choice would enhance the possibility of agreement.

Geller, of course, had a preference, and if he had been allowed to choose from the menu, he would have selected three things. AT&T would have been required to spin off three operating companies: Pacific Telephone and the two companies in which Bell had only minority interests, Southern New England and Cincinnati. They would provide competitive yardsticks by which to evaluate Western Electric's prices to the remaining Bell Operating Companies. In addition, interconnection along the lines of *Execunet* would be imposed by decree. Finally, Western Electric would be divided into Western and what AT&T soon began to call "Eastern Electric," a separate, unaffiliated company of more or less comparable size. This third provision was to correct the failure of the 1956 Consent Decree to resolve the Western Electric problem. The first and third parts of the meal were both directed to this end. This combination would ensure that the cure worked. These basic concepts were to have an impact on events even after Geller left office.

Anderson and Trienens began to talk on the basis of Geller's menu in 1980, but Anderson's days on the case were numbered. His superior, Deputy Attorney General Donald Flexner, thought that Anderson was running his own case without being responsive to departmental control. In the competition for support from the newly arrived Assistant Attorney General, Anderson was hopelessly outclassed by Flexner, his superior and Litvack's old friend. He prepared to leave as Litvack arrived.

Litvack then had to decide what to do with the negotiations that Anderson had started. He convened a meeting of his staff to talk about that problem, and he posed the kinds of operational questions that a lawyer who is not a policy theorist can be expected to ask. The economists wanted divestiture of some of AT&T's operating companies. "How many," Litvack asked, "needed to be divested? If you could get all, that would be terrific. If you could get only one, would that be sufficient? If half of them were divested, would that be sufficient? How do you know? What is the theory that tells you how many is sufficient?" Bruce Owen, economist and head of the Antitrust Division's Economic Planning Office, argued for total divestiture without, however, articulating the theory Litvack had

requested. To the question of whether divestiture of two or three companies would be enough, Owen replied: "If I walk from here to the door,
that's a step in the direction of San Francisco, but it's not very far." The
vivid analogy impressed Litvack, but he saw that it was offered in the
absence of theory.

Litvack understood that his staff could not provide answers to his most
important questions. The department was still trying to solve the technical problems that Shenefield had mentioned a year and a half earlier.
Flexner had put together a relief task force to deal with these and related
problems, and Litvack was persuaded to wait for the results of this study.
Feeling very much the new boy on the block, Litvack believed it would
be presumptuous for him to settle a major suit without thoroughly understanding the issues and having the staff support to justify his position. He
told Trienens at the end of February 1980 that the Anderson position was
insufficient for the Department of Justice. Even if AT&T agreed with it,
he was not in a position to do so. Negotiations ceased.[84]

In the interim, MCI's private antitrust suit against AT&T, filed shortly
before the government's, came to trial, with evidence being presented
during the first half of 1980. At MCI's request, this was a jury trial.
AT&T's case was handled by the same team from Sidley and Austin (led
by George Saunders) that was in charge of the Bell System's defense
against the government's suit. The two cases were intertwined in a number of ways. For one thing, the Justice Department had won the right
(over AT&T's objections) to use information gathered by MCI in discovery.[85] The MCI case, therefore, was a sort of dress rehearsal for the fast-
approaching trial of the government's suit before Judge Greene. In the
private case, MCI's lawyers highlighted the FCC's finding that AT&T had
acted "unlawfully" in rejecting MCI's application for foreign exchange
(FX) service. The harsh legal language was displayed on a screen to the
jury and seems to have created a context for their deliberations. The jury
upheld MCI on 10 of the 15 allegations against AT&T. It awarded damages of $600 million, based on its finding that AT&T had "willfully main-
tained its monopoly" in the business and data markets. These damages

---

[84]Geller, interview, June 20, 1984, pp. 47–8; Litvack, interview, June 21, 1984, pp. 2–4, 9,
14–15, 17–18.
[85]*US* v. *AT&T*, CA No. 74–1698 (D.D.C.), *Pretrial Order No. 11*, September 11, 1978;
AT&T, *Memorandum of Points and Authorities in Support of Defendants' Motion for
Reconsideration*, September 29, 1978, pp. 163–76. This issue ultimately reached the
Supreme Court, which, on January 8, 1979, denied review of the lower court order,
thereby allowing the Justice Department to obtain AT&T documents in the *MCI* and
Litton cases. *US* v. *AT&T*, 461 F. Supp. 1314 (D.D.C. 1978), *mandamus denied* (U.S. App.
D.C., unreported 1978), *cert. denied, sub nom.* 439 U.S. 1090, 99 S.Ct. 873, 59L. Ed. 2d
57 (No. 78–761, 1979).

were automatically trebled under the antitrust statutes to an awesome $1.8 billion.[86]

AT&T had been unable to convince the jury that it was the victim – not the architect – of FCC policy and the controversies it spawned. The image of a benign giant being goaded by tiny MCI simply was not convincing. AT&T was so big and powerful that a group of ordinary citizens could hardly be expected to take its side. The company did not seem able to gain adherents for its views in the courtroom any more than in Congress, and in both arenas the size and power issue was the backdrop for the particular play being enacted.[87]

Hard on the heels of the unfavorable MCI decision, Brown's idea man, Trienens, asked him why AT&T was fighting divestiture of its local companies when two other Sidley and Austin clients in the Midwest were trying to spin off theirs. These other utilities were trying to make a decision at the state level that would affect every locality in which they operated. They thought that local regulators did not allow them adequate returns, figuring that local operations would be supported by the rest of the system. Divestiture would put each local outlet on its own financial base. Why wouldn't divestiture of the Bell Operating Companies do the same for AT&T?[88]

Although Trienens's suggestion was heresy to the Bell System's traditional ideology, Brown found it interesting enough to bring it up in an August 1980 meeting of AT&T's board of directors. He set forth for the directors the several alternatives AT&T was facing in the antitrust case. The firm seemed likely to lose something from either its vertical components (Bell Labs and Western Electric) or its horizontal elements, that is, the operating companies. Brown set forth the alternatives on an easel in the board room. The political attractiveness of Trienens's concept was clear: It would eliminate much of the heat on AT&T from Congress and the Department of Justice. It had economic advantages as well. Pacific

---

[86]AT&T was found to have illegally refused to provide MCI with interconnection to foreign exchange services, tied local service to AT&T long distance service, and interfered with MCI's customers by abruptly disconnecting their intercity foreign exchange services in 1974 after the court injunction to provide them had been reversed. The jury also concluded that AT&T had negotiated in bad faith for MCI's interconnection agreement, filed state tariffs in bad faith, and engaged in predatory pricing in its Hi-Lo tariff and in preannouncement of the Hi-Lo tariff to discourage customers from using MCI service. Finally, the jury decided that AT&T had acted illegally by providing inappropriate or inefficient interconnection equipment and procedures. The jury did *not* find AT&T guilty on several counts. Specifically, the company's aid to Western Union was not found to violate the Sherman Antitrust Act, MCI was not charged unreasonable prices for interconnection, and TELPAK was not predatory. *MCI* v. *AT&T*, No. 74 C 633, U.S. Dist. Ct., Northern Dist. of Illinois, Eastern Division, June 13, 1980, Tr. 11536–9 (Jury Decision).
[87]See Gerald W. Brock, *The Telecommunications Industry* (Cambridge, Mass.: Harvard University Press, 1981).
[88]Howard J. Trienens, interview, January 19, 1984, pp. 19–20.

Telephone's poor earnings were noted, as they often were, and the point was made that the rest of the System would not support the West Coast firm if there were no more System. By comparison, the loss of the vertical elements, Bell Labs and Western Electric, would cripple AT&T in the competitive struggle over information age markets for integrated telecommunications systems. Although Brown's presentation converted at least one board member, the intellectual seed he and Trienens had sown did not fall on fertile ground. Most of the board members, no less than AT&T's managers, were imbued with the spirit of the Bell System. They saw the gains to AT&T's finances from divestiture as meager beside the benefits of integrated operation to the national System. They did not need to be reminded of the way in which microwave radio, direct distance dialing, new telephone sets, Touchtone service, and other network improvements had been put into service. There had to be a bigger gain if they were going to decide to give up the structure that had made the modern Bell System possible.[89]

The board's discussion seemed at the time to be academic. But Trienens had succeeded in introducing a new concept into the company's dialogue over public policy, and in the months that followed, his idea— alien at first—would slowly emerge as a potential alternative. It was already a possibility to Brown, who set out at once to explore Trienens's idea further. He asked Hugel to study the feasibility of the proposal and report back to him.

Just as Brown and Trienens were launching their new explorations, two events, one in the fall of 1980 and the other in the winter of 1981, fostered negotiations between the company and the Department of Justice. The first event, of course, was the landslide victory of Ronald Reagan in the presidential election. The Justice Department was shortly to be under new leadership. Litvack and his superiors' tenure there was limited, and this created, as Brown saw it, a window through which a settlement might be reached. It would be a great coup for Litvack to settle such a major case. It would be one of the final significant moves that the outgoing Carter administration could make. It might even defuse any political impact of a settlement if the outgoing Democratic administration were to get the concurrence of the incoming Republican administration. This appealed to both AT&T and Litvack; he was as conscious of the window as were his counterparts at AT&T.[90]

The second event was the anticipated beginning of the trial, which had been delayed slightly until January 1981. The trial staff at the Department of Justice was a bit nervous, as might be expected before the start of such a

[89]Perkins, interview, November 25, 1986, pp. 10–17.
[90]Brown, interview, May 29, 1984, pp. 17–18; Robert D. McLean, interview, September 19, 1984, pp. 11–12; Litvack, interview, June 21, 1984, pp. 8, 24–5.

major trial. Butterflies in the stomach–or worse–are normal before a
battle of this sort. The sense of risk was accentuated in this case by Judge
Greene, who chewed out Litvack in court in December. The judge,
summoning the Assistant Attorney General to an unusual appearance in
court, expressed his annoyance at the slow pace of the stipulation process.
That attempt to stake out what the opposing lawyers could agree on had
manifestly bogged down. Judge Greene said that the government had
brought this case and that it now had the obligation to staff it properly and
move it along expeditiously. He vented a suspicion that the Justice Department was not really committed to the case. He wanted assurances that
Litvack would assign to the effort as many people as were needed. Litvack
quickly gave Greene that assurance and then confronted Gerald Connell,
who had replaced Anderson in charge of the government's case. Litvack
admitted that he could not predict the future: "An atomic bomb may hit
the capitol tomorrow. But I can tell you what's not going to happen; I'm
not going to go back into that courtroom and tell Judge Greene that I
didn't [put more people on the case]. If you have to enlist my family to do
this, you're going to have the people, Jerry. I don't care if nothing else
happens in the division."[91]

Greene's annoyance with the Department of Justice soon produced
some unanticipated results. The department already had about sixty lawyers on the case, so it can be doubted whether the judge's insistence led
to a much greater allocation of manpower. The stipulation process was
inherently slow; this problem was unavoidable. But Litvack's court appearance put additional pressure on him, and it indicated to AT&T that he was
under the gun. The press of the impending trial, augmented by Greene's
attention to pretrial stipulations, created a temporary environment conducive to a settlement that would obviate the trial.

Litvack called Trienens to reopen negotiations in November.[92] The
negotiations were conducted by Jim Kilpatric of AT&T, Robert McLean of
Sidley and Austin, and James Denvir from the Justice Department.
Oddly, they were closer in substance to the earlier dealings between
Anderson and AT&T than to the Justice Department's current relief proposal. On December 22, 1980, these talks suddenly became serious.
Denvir presented to Kilpatric and McLean the Department of Justice's
proposed framework for a settlement, a three-page document that contained both regulatory and divestiture provisions–Column A and Column
B–in some profusion. The proposal was actually divided into three parts:
equipment, services, and everything else. The equipment section speci-

[91]Litvack, interview, June 21, 1984, p. 44.
[92]Or perhaps Trienens first contacted Litvack. The participants' memories differ, but it
   seems more likely that Litvack made the first move. Litvack, interview, June 21, 1984, pp.
   23–4; Trienens, interview, January 19, 1984, pp. 58–9.

fied that roughly half of Western Electric was to be divested, the Bell Operating Companies were to be enjoined to purchase equipment on the open market, and the research done for the Bell Operating Companies by AT&T would have to be published and made available to people outside the Bell System. As part of the new arrangement, the contracts under which Western Electric supplied the Bell Operating Companies were to be terminated.

There was also a mixture of divestiture and regulation in the service section. Three firms were to be spun off: Pacific Telephone and the two minority-owned operating companies. In addition, all of the operating companies were to be reorganized so that their local and intercity businesses would be handled separately. The operating companies then would be required to make the local part of their activities accessible to all common carriers (i.e., to their own separate intercity operations, to AT&T's Long Lines, and to other common carriers such as MCI that might wish to use the facilities). The third section consisted of a miscellany of injunctive provisions designed to encourage competition in the industry. The operating companies were, for instance, obligated to notify their customers of the existence of competition in long distance services, to provide technical information to competitors of the Bell System, and to publish performance indices.[93]

This framework resembled Geller's Chinese menu more closely than the Justice Department's relief plan because the department thought that AT&T would never agree to the latter. In the department's view, the relief plan was a wish list, not a realistic proposal. But, despite the similarity, the new starting point was considerably harsher than it had been only a year earlier. Gone was AT&T's choice. Gone too was the clear separation between structural and regulatory relief. The Justice Department was now proposing much more divestiture, and it was following congressional sentiment and the FCC's lead in *Computer II* by imposing divisions within the firm. The 1956 Consent Decree had drawn a line around AT&T's public utility function and restricted the firm to that business. AT&T would be a monopoly within its protected domain. Other firms would compete outside of it. But the FCC had abandoned in *Computer II* the effort to keep AT&T separated from the private, competitive market. It had tried to draw a new line within AT&T by using the device of fully separated subsidiaries. The Justice Department was now proposing a similar separation.

The Justice Department's new proposal was the basis for a series of intense negotiations at the end of 1980. The two sides agreed readily on a

[93]Department of Justice proposal of December 22, 1980, as clarified and modified through December 30, 1980.

variety of modifications in the Justice Department's framework. They agreed, for example, that AT&T would be required to separate its intercity and local exchange operations only "to the maximum extent feasible." Within the rules outlined for the structural and accounting separation of exchange and interexchange services, AT&T retained substantial freedom – as shown by the use of words like "reasonable" and "feasible" – to provide "functionally equivalent" access in ways that allowed it to preserve the advantages of integration.[94]

The negotiations moved along rather smoothly in late 1980, in part because the lawyers, who had been dealing with each other over stipulations for almost a year, were now quite comfortable working with each other. By the end of December they had reached agreement on the outlines of a settlement that they could present to their superiors. Trienens called on December 31 to see if Litvack had lined up support for the agreement among his superiors but failed to reach him in his office. Litvack, driving to Vermont to see friends on New Year's Eve, stopped at a gas station to call Trienens. With cold hands, he had trouble punching in his credit card number. But eventually he reached the AT&T counsel, and they agreed that the amended framework was a solid basis for a settlement. They would work on the details and approach Judge Greene to seek a postponement of the trial. The two lawyers had not reached an actual settlement; they had agreed only on the principles underlying a settlement. But, having agreed on the framework, there was every prospect that they would be able to settle the details and work out an actual decree.[95]

Litvack, Connell, and Trienens appeared before Judge Greene on the evening of January 5 to request that the scheduled opening of the trial on January 15 be postponed. They explained that they had developed a framework for a settlement but that it would require, Litvack estimated, two to three months to convert it into an actual decree. He admitted under questioning that he did not know the attitude of the incoming administration toward such a settlement. In fact, he did not even know

[94]In other provisions, the parties agreed that Eastern Electric, the divested part of Western Electric, would be approximately half the size of postdivestiture Western Electric. The operating companies' contracts with Western would not be terminated if the members of the Bell System could not be assured of an adequate source of supply. The charges for access to the local exchange were to be standardized, tariffed with the FCC, and broken down into discrete rate elements. Access was to be supplied by "reasonable" nationwide access codes. The Department of Justice also agreed to take steps to modify the 1956 Consent Decree in order to ensure that it was consistent with the *Computer II* decision, to eliminate any restrictions on the ability of AT&T to provide equipment and services to its customers or to acquire assets outside the United States, and to bring the patent provisions of the old decree into consistency with the new one. Department of Justice proposal of December 22, 1980, as clarified and modified through December 30, 1980.
[95]Litvack, interview, June 21, 1984, p. 26.

who the relevant members of the new administration would be. He believed in the principles that had been agreed on and thought that the staff of the AT&T trial team did too; he expected that a new administration would also support the new decree. This, of course, was pure speculation.

AT&T wanted the trial postponed because Section 5 of the Clayton Act said that evidence offered in an antitrust suit brought by the Department of Justice could be used as evidence in private antitrust suits if a decree was issued. AT&T wanted to have the decree issued before any evidence was taken. The Department of Justice argued that it would be exceedingly difficult to negotiate a settlement while trying the case because the same technically qualified people would be needed to do both jobs. The lawyers spent close to an hour talking with the judge.[96]

Two days later, Greene denied their request. He concluded that the framework was too loose to justify postponing the trial, particularly in light of Litvack's estimate of the time required to turn the basic principles into a specific decree. By the time the decree was written, there would be a new administration, and neither Litvack nor Trienens could say whether the framework would be at all acceptable to the new team in the White House and the Department of Justice. Greene reviewed his actions: On June 22, 1979, he had set the trial date for September 1, 1980, and approved less than six months' postponements since then; he had set a firm date. He expressed skepticism about the Department of Justice's argument that it had too few qualified persons to perform both tasks, and observed that Section 5 of the Clayton Act was designed to encourage negotiations to go faster and not trials to go slower. The trial, he concluded, would commence on schedule.[97]

With the trial date hanging over their heads, the lawyers negotiated intensively in the days following January 5. They fleshed out some of the regulatory parts of the decree and solidified their interests in the original framework as modified in the last week of December. They returned to Judge Greene on the day before the trial was to begin to ask again for a

---

[96]*US* v. *AT&T*, CA No. 74–1698 (D.D.C.), Transcript of Proceedings, January 5, 1981. A meeting at the Department of Justice in the week between Christmas and New Year's foreshadowed the opinion of the incoming Assistant Attorney General for Antitrust, although no one could have known that at the time. Bruce Owen argued strongly against the settlement framework, even though, as far as he knew, the settlement was a fait accompli. He argued that a decree that left AT&T largely structurally intact left it substantially a monopolist. Injunctive relief would not work and would involve the Department of Justice and the court in the operation of the telecommunications industry and of AT&T in ways in which neither of them was qualified. The FCC was the proper agency; these other groups lacked both the resources and the expertise. Owen was, in effect, forecasting the roles that the Justice Department and the court would play in any settlement. But even though Owen thought that this involvement depended on the regulatory nature of the decree, events would show that it was implied by even the most structural decree. Bruce M. Owen, interview, June 13, 1984, pp. 34–6.

[97]*US* v. *AT&T*, CA No. 74–1698 (D.D.C.), Judge Greene, *Memorandum*, January 7, 1981.

postponement. This time they did not ask for more time to negotiate, but rather for time to discover if the new administration – which was taking office in a week – was interested in this sort of settlement. They would also need time for the relatively easy task of translating the detailed framework into decree language. Two weeks would suffice to ascertain the new administration's position, and Trienens and Litvack thought it would then take sixty to ninety days to write the decree – although Connell and Judge Greene felt the job could be done in less time. Trienens's closing plea was for the court to grant two weeks to save two years of work.[98]

Judge Greene granted this postponement in light of the further progress that had been made in the negotiations. Although the trial would open on schedule on January 15, it would be only for opening statements from the two sides. The trial would continue on February 2 unless the new Attorney General was able to state to the court that he supported the settlement framework as modified in subsequent negotiations, that he believed the framework could be transformed into a decree within 30 days, and that he would commit the resources necessary to do this. If he did so, the taking of evidence would be postponed an additional 30 days. But if a completed decree was not submitted to the court by March 4, 1981, testimony would begin on that day.[99]

Negotiations continued throughout January, and Deputy Attorney General Charles B. Renfrew, another holdover from the Carter administration, wrote to Judge Greene on January 29 in response to his order. Renfrew requested a further one-month delay, not because – as Judge Greene had anticipated – the new administration agreed with the proposed settlement, but because the Assistant Attorney General for Antitrust had not yet been designated and the new administration had no position at all. Renfrew said, however, that a new Assistant Attorney General would be appointed soon and that he would have a chance to express an opinion before March 4.[100]

Even though these were not the grounds on which Judge Greene had said he would delay the trial for another month, he did so.[101] Negotiations continued, becoming more and more detailed and generating a series of longer and longer decree drafts. To AT&T's lawyers, the path to agreement began to resemble a distressing quagmire. The areas of disagreement still outstanding between AT&T and the Department of Justice had become clear by the middle of February. The biggest single problem

[98]*US* v. *AT&T*, CA No. 74–1698 (D.D.C.), Transcript of Proceedings, January 14, 1981, p. 6.

[99]*US* v. *AT&T*, CA No. 74–1698 (D.D.C.), Judge Greene, *Memorandum Order*, January 16, 1981.

[100]Charles B. Renfrew to the Hon. Harold H. Greene, January 29, 1981.

[101]*US* v. *AT&T*, CA No. 74–1698 (D.D.C.), Judge Greene, *Memorandum*, January 30, 1981.

came from Justice's increasing demands for separation of the operating companies' local exchange operations from their other activities. The government's lawyers wanted to make certain that these boundaries would actually constrain the Bell System; AT&T was equally eager to preserve the integrity of its organization. It was unclear how the fully separated subsidiaries mandated in the decree drafts would be organized, and their relationship with Western Electric was still cloudy.[102]

As it turned out, of course, these problems were not resolved and AT&T was not spared a trial. Litvack informed Judge Greene on February 23 that it was unlikely that the incoming Assistant Attorney General, identified by then as William Baxter, would have an opportunity to review and agree to the proposal by the March 2 deadline. Baxter had expressed his displeasure with the regulatory nature of the draft decree. Litvack himself could no longer champion it. The proposal was dead.[103]

So ended the first serious attempt to resolve the issues outstanding in the lawsuit by what was essentially a regulatory solution. It followed the FCC's tradition of redefining the boundary between the public utility and private competition without dividing up AT&T. It was consistent with the thrust of the telecommunications bills debated in Congress. The telephone company would have been part regulated utility and part competitor—as it had been since *Above 890*—with all of the internal contradictions in incentives that this mixture implied. Structurally, AT&T would have remained substantially as it was. It would have had a few more competitors than it already did. Western Electric would have had to compete with Eastern Electric, in addition to Rolm, Northern Telecom, General Telephone, ITT, and others. Pacific, Southern New England, and Cincinnati would have been independent operating companies, in addition to General, Continental, United, and others. But AT&T still would have been the central firm in the national telephone network. It would have had to make internal management changes to comply with the concept of fully separated subsidiaries, but it was unclear what difference these changes would have made in the operation of the company or the network.

Litvack, despite his continuing efforts to reach a settlement, had become convinced that the complex regulatory provisions could not work. He had come around to Owen's conclusion, although by way of a different line of reasoning. Owen, arguing as an economist, asserted that incentives would always win out over injunctions. Litvack argued as a lawyer that the

[102]An innovative provision in the Justice Department's draft of January 20 included quotas on the purchase of new equipment from Western, a regulation that foreshadowed an amendment to Senator Packwood's bill some months later. AT&T unsigned "Memorandum," February 16, 1981.
[103]Sanford Litvack to Judge Harold H. Greene, February 23, 1981; transcript of press conference with William F. Baxter, April 9, 1981, pp. 23–4. Baxter denied ever discussing the case with Litvack, but Baxter nonetheless took credit for killing the negotiations.

216 The fall of the Bell System

regulatory aspects of the decree were just too complicated for a court to handle.[104]

In any case, the decision was not Litvack's. The incoming Assistant Attorney General was unwilling to go along with the framework that had come originally from Geller through Anderson to Litvack and had been worked on and modified in conjunction with AT&T. If he was going to settle, he would start over again on an entirely different basis. This was a harsh message to AT&T. Brown was not the sort of man who was inclined to kill the messenger, but he was deeply disappointed that the trial would have to begin. He had actually begun to prepare the company for a settlement. The board of directors had been informed and a public information program outlined. Suddenly that effort had to be abandoned. He and his colleagues had to prepare for another encounter in the courtroom, this time before the formidable Judge Harold Greene.

[104]Litvack, interview, June 21, 1984, pp. 35–7.

VI

Reaching agreement

Administration infighting

The new Reagan administration finally announced the appointment of William Baxter as Assistant Attorney General for Antitrust in February 1981. Baxter, an intense and extremely bright Stanford law professor, was a man of very decided views. His ideology blended two parts of neoclassical economics with one part of law, and he was committed to implementing that ideology as only a true believer can be. He was (and is today) absolutely convinced of the wisdom of his actions. He has never seen the need to look back.

Baxter's conservative outlook on regulation, which he distrusted, and competition, which he applauded, produced an easy fit with the new administration. But although he had frequently expressed his opinions on the telecommunications industry over the previous decade (starting with his appearance with Trienens in 1970), he and the Reagan appointment team apparently did not discuss the AT&T case in any detail before he was selected. AT&T, of course, was fully aware of Baxter's philosophy and deeply concerned when word leaked out that he might be the appointee. Brown contacted Edwin Meese, President Reagan's chief domestic advisor, and told him about Baxter's views. Brown quoted a 1977 speech by Baxter commending the Justice Department for bringing the case.[1] But Brown's intervention failed, and the administration went ahead with the appointment.

Like many senior members of the new administration, Baxter had to move from the West Coast to the East Coast. He eased into Washington slowly, coming in for a few days during February while he finished his teaching at Stanford. By the end of the month, he was beginning to exert influence on the decision-making process at the Department of Justice, and he was in Washington full time thereafter. The only questions on the government's AT&T case during his confirmation hearings before Senator

---

[1] Howard J. Trienens, "Chronology of Negotiations"; William F. Baxter, "How Government Cases Get Selected–Comments from Academe," *Antitrust Law Journal*, Vol. 46 (Spring 1977), pp. 586–601.

William F. Baxter, Assistant Attorney General, Antitrust Division, U.S. Department of Justice from 1981 through 1983, when he returned to Stanford University Law School.

Strom Thurmond's Judiciary Committee concerned possible conflicts of interest.[2]

Baxter moved into a third-level position in which he served under the Deputy Attorney General, who, in turn, was under the Attorney General. In the Carter administration, where the political strategy had been to decentralize authority as much as possible, Shenefield and Litvack had operated quite independently. Although they had dealt largely with procedural and technical issues and had confronted a possible settlement only once, it seems clear that in these matters the Assistant Attorney General had had a large amount of discretionary authority. So too with the Reagan administration, although for different reasons. Soon after he arrived in Washington, Baxter talked to William French Smith, the Attorney General, about the AT&T case. Smith explained that he had recused himself because he had been a director of Pacific Telephone. It was bad enough to have been involved with the Bell System, but Smith's ties had been with one of the three operating companies that would have been spun off under the Litvack decree. The Attorney General therefore could not be involved in the prosecution of the case. The Deputy Attorney General, Edward Schmults, also had decided that he had a conflict of interest. His law firm had been asked to give an outside opinion on an AT&T pension matter. Although this hardly appears to be the same sort of conflict that Smith had, Schmults took himself out of the line of fire; he too recused himself. This extraordinary chain of withdrawals made Baxter the senior Justice Department official on the case, with no one standing between him and the White House.[3]

At first, Baxter also operated independently of his staff. In part because he was an academic and in part because of his strong personal desire for autonomy, he decided that he would do much better if he stood apart from the bureaucracy and decided what to do about the AT&T issue on his own. This stance was in contrast to that of Litvack, who had gathered the staff and interacted with them as he set his course. But Baxter doubted that any group that could do what the department was doing with its long-running antitrust case against IBM, then in its seventh year of trial, deserved his trust.[4] The staff's involvement normally ensures a high degree of continuity in policy even though the political appointees in charge of a department change. The new Assistant Attorney General was, how-

[2]William F. Baxter, interview, February 2, 1984, pp. 2–3; 97th Congress, 1st Session, Senate, Committee on the Judiciary, "Confirmation Hearing on Assistant Attorney General-Designate, Antitrust Division, William F. Baxter," March 19, 1981.
[3]Baxter, interview, February 2, 1984, pp. 5–6; John G. Fox, interview, November 25, 1985, pp. 19–20; "Nominee Schmults Removes Self From AT&T Antitrust Case," *The Washington Post*, February 6, 1981, p. D1.
[4]Baxter, interview, February 2, 1984, p. 6.

ever, more concerned with intellectual coherence than with administrative continuity.

Baxter's style and ideology opened the way for a dramatic change in the case, but the full extent of the change became evident only gradually. Since Baxter had distanced himself from the staff, he did not at first alter the course of the trial. As a result, the Department of Justice's case became bifurcated; the trial still embodied the staff's approach, while Baxter's emerging position took matters in a new direction. When he decided to dump the Litvack settlement, Baxter had already thrown overboard most of the intellectual and political baggage left over from the 1956 Consent Decree. To Baxter (and, for that matter, to AT&T as well), the settlement approach negotiated by Litvack and his staff seemed incoherent. It seemed to be breaking something up for the sake of breaking it up. There was no discernible theory at all; it was little more than harassment of the Bell System, punishment for its size and power.

Where Litvack had in effect asked, "What can we get in the way of relief?" Baxter asked, "What relief would eliminate the problems arising in this industry?" He decided that lopping off a few operating companies would not do the trick, and he had no sympathy with Henry Geller's concept of yardsticks or indicators of competitive prices and conditions. As Geller saw the situation, it did not matter very much which operating companies were split off; the point was to enable regulators to compare the behavior of the broken-off companies with that of the companies still in the Bell System. The FCC could then correct any abuses of market power. Baxter – deeply suspicious of all regulatory agencies – did not think that the FCC could solve the problem of AT&T's market power. Only a competitive market could do so. Baxter also had no use for the division of Western Electric or Bell Labs, the proposal that stemmed most directly from the aftermath of the 1956 Consent Decree. He was not concerned about vertical integration in the Bell System if he could separate the regulated monopoly parts of the industry from the unregulated competitive parts.

In Baxter's theory, vertical integration was generally good: Horizontal integration – like regulation – was generally bad. Vertical integration promoted efficiency; horizontal integration, illegal market power. His views on the efficiency of vertical integration, it is worth noting, paralleled those of AT&T's management and of Alfred Chandler, who had been cited in support of AT&T's earlier internal reorganizations.[5] But in regard to horizontal combination and the efficacy of regulation, the two sides disagreed entirely. Baxter wanted to take the FCC's plan as it had evolved over the previous decade to its logical conclusion and build a wall between the monopoly elements of telecommunications and the competitive elements.

[5]Alfred D. Chandler, *The Visible Hand* (Cambridge, Mass.: Harvard University Press, 1977). See also Robert H. Bork, *The Antitrust Paradox* (New York: Basic Books, 1978).

The former were to be those aspects of telecommunications that constituted a natural monopoly and that should thus be regulated. The rest of the industry, he thought, should be deregulated and subject to the currents of competition.

If Baxter had his way, all of the local telephone companies would be split off from AT&T and regulated as local monopolies, and the rest of the Bell System would be a vertically integrated, unregulated private firm roughly comparable to IBM. Baxter, of course, was giving considerable thought to IBM, since the trial in the antitrust suit against that firm was grinding endlessly on as the Justice Department acted out the myth of Sisyphus. Although Baxter had elected to deal with the AT&T case first – because the trial was starting and the Litvack decree needed a decision – he always had IBM in mind. In fact, he anticipated that the future would involve an integrated computer and telecommunications industry in which IBM and AT&T would compete with each other. His prognosis, in this regard at least, was similar to Brown's vision of the new information age.

But Brown, of course, did not envision an AT&T shorn of the operating companies, and this made an agreement on Baxter's terms highly unlikely in the spring of 1981. This was evident when Baxter and Trienens first met in their official capacities on April 7 to discuss the case. Baxter explained his views to AT&T's chief counsel and suggested how they might settle their differences out of court. Baxter said that he wanted all of the operating companies split off from AT&T. In return, he would free the telephone company from the restrictions of the 1956 Consent Decree. That would allow AT&T to make exclusive use of the technology that Bell Labs and Western Electric developed and to move as it saw fit into other industries – including computers.

Trienens was no stranger to these ideas; he and Brown had raised the possibility of divestiture along these lines before AT&T's board of directors several months earlier. The board, however, had not risen to this bait. Therefore, when Baxter suggested a settlement involving divestiture of the operating companies, Trienens knew that the proposal would not be accepted at 195 Broadway – at least not yet. Fully separated subsidiaries were tolerable; divestiture was not. So ended the preliminary fencing match between these two talented adversaries.[6]

That same day, the Department of Justice notified AT&T of a major change in its proposed relief. Despite the fact that it was formulated by the Justice Department's staff, the April proposition expressed a point of view far closer to Baxter's than to that in Litvack's proposed decree or that of the staff members still primarily concerned about Western Electric. The major recommendation was to divest all of the operating companies,

[6]Baxter, interview, February 2, 1984, p. 8; Howard J. Trienens, "Chronology of Negotiations"; Howard J. Trienens, interview, January 19, 1984, pp. 19–20.

leaving AT&T with its research and manufacturing components intact. This was the preferred relief. But the new proposition also included an alternative course: AT&T would in that case keep the operating companies, but it would lose all of Western Electric; it would give up part of Bell Labs and Long Lines; and it would bear the burden of additional injunctions and regulations designed to promote equal access by other companies to the network and to the equipment market. In either case, the requested relief was far stronger than the tentative settlement—the Litvack decree—that had almost been agreed upon in January. The department's new proposal would involve radical changes in structure. It was not a happy prospect for Brown and the rest of AT&T's leadership.[7]

Time, they recognized, was growing short. The pressure to work out a settlement steadily mounted as Judge Greene drove the case ahead. At the end of the trial both parties would lose control of the outcome, a prospect that could please neither Baxter, who wanted what he saw as a clean, logical solution, nor Trienens, who wanted a settlement with which Brown and AT&T could live. Unless they could settle or find another way out of the case, they had no guarantee that Greene would give either side anything resembling what it wanted. When Trienens and Baxter first met, the delays Judge Greene had granted for settlement negotiations had run out without producing an agreement, and he was already hearing evidence in the case.

The trial began with the presentation of the government's evidence on the equipment part of the case. AT&T, the government alleged, had refused to allow equipment owned by others to be connected to the network and had refused as well to purchase equipment from other vendors. Even though the Justice Department's proposed relief emphasized the operating companies, the initial evidence presented against AT&T centered on Western Electric and AT&T's terminal equipment interconnection policies.[8] The order in which a case is presented reflects many influences, but these opening arguments seem to have embodied Litvack's understanding of the case. It had been, in his view, a foreclosure case: AT&T had refused to buy from anyone but Western Electric and had prevented others from using their own terminal equipment, illegally restricting competition. This, of course, echoed the 1949 suit. Baxter had a different perspective on the case. He thought that AT&T was "dead" on the various interconnection issues (PCAs and MCI) but did not give much

[7]Dale E. Thomas, Sidley & Austin, to Harold S. Levy, AT&T, April 7, 1981, and attached "Relief Contentions."
[8]See, e.g., US v. AT&T, CA No. 74–1698, U.S. Dist. Ct., Dist. of Columbia, opening argument of Gerald A. Connell on behalf of the Department of Justice, Transcript of Proceedings, January 15, 1981, and testimony of representatives from ITT, Milgo, Collins Radio, and TIE Communications, March 1981.

weight to the equipment issue or matters of pricing. Soon, however, neither Baxter nor the telephone company would have to speculate about any of these issues. Judge Greene would settle them. As evidence was presented to the judge, AT&T's range of alternatives steadily narrowed.[9]

There was always the possibility that the Reagan administration would intervene, as Eisenhower's had in 1956, and allow AT&T to escape the draconian relief that the Department of Justice was requesting. The Reagan administration was favorably inclined toward big business in general and the Bell System in particular. In the spring of 1981, however, it would not be easy for Brown to convert these warm feelings into a specific measure that would terminate the antitrust suit. The trial had started, radically increasing the public visibility of the case. The Justice Department also was much more independent of the White House than it had been in 1956; the scandal provoked by the Nixon administration's intervention in the 1972 ITT case, for example, had contributed to Justice's autonomy.[10] There was no way to intervene casually in a major antitrust case, particularly one already in trial.

At this time, neither antitrust issues nor the telecommunications industry were high on the list of Reagan's priorities. There was too much else to be done, measures that required immediate and all-consuming attention. The President was launching his program for reshaping the role of the federal government in American life. One facet of this grand project was the tax bill of 1981, which dramatically lowered taxes for most Americans – especially for most American businesses. Another was a massive increase in defense spending to upgrade as rapidly as possible the nation's military power. While these policies were being formulated and appropriate legislation jockeyed through Congress, the administration had little energy to devote to antitrust policy.

Nevertheless, the early Reagan program indirectly benefited AT&T by strengthening the hand of the Secretary of Defense, Caspar Weinberger. He was the spokesman for the expanding Defense Department, and he adopted the familiar military view that AT&T, in its current structure, was an integral part of the national defense. The defense establishment relied on AT&T for its communications, and the department was leery of changing the integrated national network – or, at least, of changing it very rapidly.[11]

[9]Baxter, interview, February 2, 1984, p. 7; Sanford Litvack, interview, June 21, 1984, p. 13.
[10]ITT purchased a consent decree with an offer to underwrite the 1972 Republican National Convention, a deal that was engineered in the Oval Office and came to light in a memo by a colorful ITT lobbyist named Dita Beard. The resulting scandal made the point that antitrust cases and consent decrees were the province of the Justice Department, not the rest of the administration. See, "Testimony in Deepening ITT Antitrust Case Links Controversy Directly with Nixon," *The Wall Street Journal*, March 10, 1973, p. 4.
[11]97th Congress, 1st Session, Senate, Committee on the Judiciary, Hearing, "DOJ Oversight: U.S. v. AT&T," Testimony of William Howard Taft IV, August 6, 1981, pp. 45–6.

Within Weinberger's sprawling fiefdom, there were some dissidents who welcomed rather than resisted change in telecommunications. These young turks argued that competition was already a fact of life in the industry and that dependence on AT&T was rapidly becoming inappropriate, if not dysfunctional, for Defense. AT&T under Romnes had sharply reduced its involvement in defense procurement, weakening its ties to the nation's military establishment. The memories of World War II accomplishments had faded, and with them some of the political capital AT&T had been able to use in the 1950s.[12]

Secretary Weinberger was, however, very much in charge of his department, and he was supportive of the Bell System and negative about the antitrust case. He told a closed Senate hearing on March 23, 1981, that "the American Telephone & Telegraph network is the most important communication network we have to service our strategic systems in this country. . . . it seems to me essential that we keep together this one communications network we now have, and have to rely on."[13] Recognizing all the problems attendant on dropping the suit against AT&T, Weinberger nonetheless argued strongly for dismissal. He had sent a letter saying as much to Attorney General Smith. But Smith had recused himself from the case and Baxter had just arrived in Washington. The letter appeared to have been misplaced; Baxter said he had never seen it.[14]

He did not have to wait long before learning Weinberger's views. On April 8, the day after Trienens came to Washington to talk to the new Assistant Attorney General, Weinberger's testimony was made public. Quickly the Secretary of Defense's letter was retrieved, and Baxter noted that it did not say explicitly that the suit had to be dropped for reasons of national security. Weinberger soon clarified that matter. The Deputy Secretary of Defense, Frank Carlucci, sent Baxter a follow-up letter reiterating the Defense Department's dependence on AT&T's integrated network and concluding: "it is the position of the Secretary of Defense that the pending suit against American Telephone and Telegraph Company be dismissed."[15]

[12]When a major Defense Department project at Western Electric came to an end in 1972, it was not replaced. Western Electric billings to the Department of Defense fell in the midst of inflation from $874 million in 1972 to $300 million four years later; AT&T dropped from the third largest prime contractor to the Defense Department in 1971 to the twenty-fourth in 1981. Robert E. Gradle, interview, November 16, 1984, p. 25; Robert E. Gradle, chart, "Bell System Sales to U.S. Federal Government"; Richard B. Levine, interview, June 12, 1984, pp. 21–6.
[13]97th Congress, 1st Session, Senate, Committee on Armed Services, Hearing on S. 694, Testimony of Caspar Weinberger, March 23, 1981, pp. 21–9.
[14]Transcript of press conference with William F. Baxter, April 9, 1981, p. 9.
[15]Caspar Weinberger to William French Smith, February 21, 1981, and Frank Carlucci to William F. Baxter, April 8, 1981, Appendix 1, pp. 66–7, in 97th Congress, 1st Session, House, Subcommittee of the Committee on Government Operations, Hearing, "Departments of Justice and Defense and Antitrust Litigation," November 4, 1981.

At this point, the events leading up to the Consent decree in 1956 were being repeated, almost scene by scene. With a friendly Republican administration in the White House and a grateful Department of Defense lining up on AT&T's side, the two situations were almost identical. In the 1950s, too, the Secretary of Defense had written to the Attorney General urging that the suit against AT&T be dropped. Herbert Brownell had responded by negotiating a decree that, in the views of both participants and observers at the time, left AT&T "with no real injury."[16]

But Reagan was not a military man like Eisenhower, Baxter was not Brownell, and the trial had already begun. Baxter's response to Weinberger's powerful assault established quite clearly that the pugnacious law professor was going to be a hard man to budge on this question. At his first news conference on April 9, Baxter was confronted with the conflicting messages emanating from the Departments of Justice and Defense. Baxter might have equivocated. Instead, he dug in, insisting that the case would go on. He had rejected the Litvack settlement, he said, because, "It did not do the one thing . . . that should be done, and that is, separate all the regulated components of the enterprise from all the unregulated components of the enterprise." On his conduct of the case, he proclaimed unequivocally: "I intend to litigate it to the eyeballs."[17]

Baxter's clarion call for surgery based on economic theory created a variety of problems for AT&T's leaders. They had gone along with the largely regulatory decree proposed by Litvack and had become acclimated to the idea of living with added regulations that would encumber but not fracture the company's existing structure. The Litvack settlement would have enabled the Bell System to preserve most of its horizontal and vertical structure and–so long as the injunctive and regulatory load did not become too burdensome–would have positioned it to achieve the long-run strategic goals Brown had set for the enterprise. But the Baxter proposal was another matter. AT&T would lose entirely the close ties it had maintained with the operating companies over the past century. The integrated national network that Vail had created and his successors had perfected would be gone with one slice of the legal knife wielded by a third-level administration appointee.

AT&T's top brass was certain that this was not the way the Reagan administration should run the executive branch of the federal government. Much of the concern of the company's leaders in previous years had

[16]82nd Congress, 1st Session, House, Committee on the Judiciary, *Report of the Antitrust Subcommittee on Consent Decree Program of the Department of Justice*, January 30, 1959, pp. 51–9 and C.E. Wilson to Attorney General, July 10, 1953, pp. 339–41; Horace P. Moulton, interview, July 9, 1985, pp. 21–2.
[17]Transcript of press conference with William F. Baxter, April 9, 1981; "New Antitrust Leader Vows Vigorous Effort to Break Up AT&T," *The New York Times*, April 10, 1981, pp. A1, D3.

been with the ambiguity of the regulatory system, and Brown had said repeatedly that AT&T needed – more than anything else – certainty about its economic and regulatory context. Now Weinberger and Baxter were openly disagreeing about the case. Brown and Trienens believed correctly that there was not much support within the administration for Baxter's point of view, and Brown could not believe that the rest of the administration would not prevail. As he later explained, "I was not willing to believe that the administration would not administer."[18]

Deeply concerned about the conflicting signals coming from the administration, Brown sent Trienens to Washington to ask Meese what was happening. On the one hand, the Department of Justice under Baxter was presenting itself as an implacable foe of the existing structure of AT&T; on the other, various representatives of the administration were sending out signals strongly supportive of the existing Bell System. Weinberger had publicly proclaimed the Department of Defense's support for AT&T. Malcolm Baldrige, the new Secretary of Commerce, more interested in telecommunications than his Democratic predecessors, lined up with Weinberger in favor of a settlement involving only additional regulatory injunctions. Trienens suggested to Meese and to Fred Fielding, the President's counsel, that the administration needed to get its act together.[19]

Meese agreed to take action. He would fill the vacancy at the NTIA (caused when Geller left at the end of the Carter administration) with Bernard Wunder. Wunder had been counsel to the Republican minority of Van Deerlin's subcommittee in the House of Representatives. When Van Deerlin's chief counsel, Shooshan, left just before the 1980 election in despair about the possibility of passing a communications bill, Wunder had made an unusual move across the aisle to become chief counsel to the subcommittee. His appointment to the NTIA would bring detailed knowledge and views close to those of the House subcommittee into the administration. He and Secretary Baldrige would be able to work with the Cabinet Council on Commerce and Trade in formulating a coherent administration policy based on the slogan "If it ain't broke, don't fix it!"[20]

The time for action was growing short as Judge Greene spurred the case steadily along. During April the Justice Department presented evidence that AT&T had prevented MCI from expanding its telecommunications business in the early 1970s by denying it foreign exchange interconnec-

[18]Charles L. Brown, interview, May 29, 1984, pp. 20–1.
[19]Trienens, interview, January 19, 1984, p. 30.
[20]Bernard J. Wunder, interview, June 12, 1984, pp. 9–13, 17–18; Harry M. Shooshan III and Charles L. Jackson, interview, April 3, 1985, pp. 65–8; 97th Congress, 1st Session, Senate, Committee on the Judiciary, Hearing, "DOJ Oversight: U.S. v. AT&T," Testimony of Malcolm Baldrige, August 6, 1981, p. 5.

tion. The jury in MCI's suit had already agreed that many of MCI's accusations were justified, and the evidence in Washington was presented in that context. The Justice Department then returned to the issue of the sources of the Bell System's equipment.

With the court case sweeping steadily along, the Reagan administration struggled to resolve its internal differences. Representatives of the Justice and Defense departments held a series of meetings to discuss their positions on the trial. These meetings continued into May but did nothing to narrow the gulf that separated the two departments. Defense decided to arm itself for the internal debate with a written statement of its position. It drew upon a document prepared by its own National Communication System at the end of May, and it also asked AT&T for help. The department asked AT&T's vice president for government communications, Robert Gradle, to arrange a series of briefings, which took place at the end of May and the beginning of June 1981. The information from these two sources was combined in a document that reaffirmed the Defense Department's opposition to the antitrust suit.[21]

Defense did not mince words: "the Department of Justice does not understand the industry it seeks to restructure. . . . All that divestiture as outlined by Justice could possibly cause is a serious loss of efficiency in the manner the network operates today. For these reasons, the Defense Department totally disagrees that divestiture would have no adverse effect on the Nation's ability to rely upon the nationwide telecommunications network. Instead, we believe that it would have a serious short-term effect, and a lethal long-time effect, since *effective* network planning would eventually become virtually non-existent."[22]

The Department of Commerce also lined up solidly in support of Defense's campaign to have the case dropped. Secretary Baldrige, now urged on by Wunder, wanted a legislative, not a judicial, solution of the telecommunications problem, and Baldrige felt that the presence of the case inhibited congressional action. A new telecommunications bill had been introduced into the Senate on April 7–just at the time of the public flurry between Baxter and Weinberger–and the Commerce Department's leaders decided that the case was the prime impediment to its passage.

Baldrige and Meese met on May 20 to discuss the AT&T problem. Bearing in mind the Nixon legacy from Watergate and the ITT scandal,

[21]*US* v. *AT&T*, CA. No. 74–1698 (D.D.C.), Richard Levine, testimony, August 13, 1981, Tr. 12652–3 and John T. Whealan, general counsel, Defense Communications Agency, testimony, August 13, 1981, Tr. 12553–5.
[22]*US* v. *AT&T*, CA No. 74–1698 (D.D.C.), Defendants' Exhibit 1–141, "Department of Defense Analysis of the Effect of AT&T Divestiture upon National Defense and Security and Emergency Preparedness," June 30, 1981, pp. 22–3.

The fall of the Bell System

they did not feel that they could interfere directly with the Department of Justice's conduct of its case. They could, however, build up support for an alternate course of action: legislation. Wunder suggested to Baldrige that the administration organize a task force consisting of the Departments of Commerce, Agriculture (which wanted to keep rural telephone rates low), and Defense to deal with the Senate bill. A formal proposal along these lines went to Meese, who, on May 28, established a task force that included the heads of these three departments, plus representatives of the Federal Emergency Management Agency and the Department of Energy.

Meese obviously was sympathetic to this effort to sidetrack the antitrust case. He wanted to create a task force that was united in support of legislation and had a broad enough membership to lend some weight to its conclusions. He included the Federal Emergency Management Agency because of the concern that the telephone system be able to deal with emergencies. The Energy Department was there to preserve the ability of the country to deal with an energy crisis. The Department of Justice was conspicuously absent.[23]

The task force never actually met; instead, a working group composed of department general counsels met on June 4 and adopted a position paper that Wunder and his NTIA staff had prepared. This document analyzed the telecommunications industry and the impediments to legislation. It cited the antitrust case as a major barrier—following Baldrige's line of reasoning—and recommended that the case be dismissed so that appropriate legislation could be passed. The heads of all of the departments represented on the task force approved the position paper and sent it to Meese as the task force's report. In hearings before the Senate Judiciary Committee, when Senator Thurmond asked the Secretary of Commerce why the Department of Justice had not been involved, Baldrige replied that the task force was not addressing the merits of the case. Its purpose was to make recommendations for the President about the administration's overall policy. The Justice Department, he said, had a more narrow function.[24] In reality, of course, the task force had been created to develop an alternative to what the Justice Department was doing and to muster support for that position. It would have been foolish to invite the fox into the chicken coop.

Baxter did reenter, however, in the next act. The task force report and its recommendation were discussed at a meeting of the Cabinet Council

[23]97th Congress, 1st Session, House, Subcommittee of the Committee on Government Operations, Hearing, "Departments of Justice and Defense and Antitrust Litigation," statement of William Howard Taft IV, November 4, 1981, pp. 45–6; Wunder, interview, June 12, 1984, pp. 13–14.
[24]97th Congress, 1st Session, Senate, Committee on the Judiciary, Hearing, "DOJ Oversight: U.S. v. AT&T," Testimony of Malcolm Baldrige, August 6, 1981, pp. 4–10.

on Commerce and Trade on June 12. The President attended the meeting, as did Baxter, representing the Justice Department. Since all of the departments involved except Justice had helped to prepare the report, Baxter found himself a minority of one at this meeting. The full weight of the administration came down on his shoulders. Weinberger presented the Defense Department's position, insisting that the case should never have been brought in the first place and should be abandoned now. Baldrige also argued for dismissing the case. He said there was a consensus that AT&T's structure should be changed, but he maintained that the legislature should perform this task. In concert with most of the lawyers who worked on the case, he suggested that Congress, not the courtroom, was the appropriate place to make policy decisions about the nation's vital telecommunications system. Baldrige was wary of divesting the operating companies in order to throw the equipment market open to competing producers since many of the competitors would be foreign; many Japanese. Competition of that sort would not promote American industry, he claimed; it would simply hurt the balance of payments. Baldrige here turned the government's evidence in the antitrust suit during the previous months – testimony about the Bell System's reluctance to buy outside of Western Electric – from an attack on AT&T into a defense of American industry.[25]

Isolated but determined, Baxter countered these thrusts. He emphasized his commitment to the ideals of the administration. The radical restructuring of the Bell System would promote competition, advancing one of the administration's primary goals. It would reduce regulation, another of President Reagan's objectives. Divestiture, Baxter said, was an alternative to more regulation. If you were for competition and deregulation, as most of the people around the table were – at least in the abstract – then, he said, stay with the antitrust case.

There was little discussion by the Cabinet Council. The meeting was organized for formal presentations to help President Reagan reach conclusions about what should be done. The hope had to be that Baxter would feel the pressure from the Cabinet members and do the right thing – that is, give way on the case. But, of course, a direct command to do so was not going to be given. The ghost of Dita Beard, the ITT lobbyist, was Baxter's only ally, but the memory of that political scandal ensured that the Republican administration would not order the Assistant Attorney General to dismiss the case. The administration was anxious to avoid even the appearance of impropriety in this newsworthy case. If Judge Greene was setting the pace of events and William Baxter was providing the direction, the memory of Dita Beard enabled Baxter to keep his grip on the helm.

President Reagan listened to what the members of the Cabinet Council had to say and responded, characteristically, with an anecdote. When he was a boy, he recalled, it cost $2 to make a phone call across the country and only $0.02 to send a letter. Now, he said, it costs the same $0.20 to send a letter and to make the phone call. The point was obvious. It was the theme that Weinberger and Meese had been sounding. Private firms do better than government departments. The United States had an efficient telephone system that had been able to cut prices over the years: If it ain't broke, don't fix it.[26]

Most government officials would have bent before the wind in these circumstances, but Baxter was a man on an ideological mission. He fully understood the President's point of view—his admiration of AT&T—but he thought it misplaced and irrelevant. Telephone calls were cheaper as a result of technological progress, not AT&T efficiency. Baxter decided that he would drop the case if the administration would give him a direct order. Or it could simply fire him if it wanted to abort the suit. But until it did one of those two things, he was determined "to litigate it to the eyeballs."

With Baxter unmoved, the administration necessarily continued the dialogue after the Cabinet Council meeting. The Justice Department prepared a rebuttal to the task force report. It argued that the administration could deregulate AT&T if it followed the department's—that is, Baxter's—theory about separating the regulated and unregulated sectors of telecommunications. The NTIA replied in a counterrebuttal favoring legislation. The opponents met at the end of June, but they were unable to narrow their differences. Superficially, Baxter was arguing for a particular end result, while the NTIA was arguing for a particular process. But, of course, the heart of the disagreement was about ends, not means. The NTIA and the other agencies in the task force were adamantly opposed to the dismemberment of the Bell System. They assumed that legislation would hew to their line of reasoning.

While the administration struggled unsuccessfully to mold a consensus on preserving the Bell System, the trial in another of the private antitrust suits against AT&T had concluded. Litton Systems, Inc. had filed a suit in 1976 alleging that AT&T had monopolized various markets for PBXs and other business terminals. The trial, which had begun in January 1981, ended in June, and the jury returned at the end of the month with a guilty verdict. Litton had asked for over $500 million before trebling; the jury awarded the company less than one-fifth of that amount. It was a far smaller award than in the MCI case, but that did not obscure the fact that within a single year, two juries had found AT&T guilty of antitrust violations in the two largest areas of new competition in telecommunications:

[26]Baxter, interview, February 2, 1984, p. 10; Wunder, interview, June 12, 1984, pp. 17–23.

intercity services and terminal equipment. The outlook for the giant telephone company was bad and getting worse.[27]

The Cabinet Council met again, inconclusively, on July 15. The Senate
Commerce Committee reported out its telecommunications bill the next
day. Stimulated by this apparent revitalization of the legislative effort, a
high-level conference took place in Meese's office on the afternoon of July
27. Both Meese and James Baker, Reagan's primary political advisor, were
there, along with several representatives of the Justice and Commerce
departments. Baldrige was eager to settle the dispute between the two
departments. He came to the meeting with papers prepared for dismissing
the case. The Commerce Department had researched the issue and determined that the Justice Department had the authority to simply drop the
suit at its discretion. Baxter agreed that he *could* do it. But he again denied
vigorously that he wanted to end the suit. Baldrige reiterated his argument
that the case was impeding the progress of legislation. Baker then entered
the debate. He replied to Baldrige and Meese that the political fallout on
the President would be too great if they simply dismissed the case. Baxter
was no longer a minority of one; he had an exceedingly powerful ally. Baker
was with him and Baker spoke in the President's name, even though it is
unlikely that Reagan was actually consulted.[28]

Baldrige contended that no one was really following the case and that
only a few lawyers would notice if it were dropped. Baxter acknowledged
that this was a testable proposition and proposed an experiment: "why
don't I go to Judge Greene and propose to continue the case for eleven
months? Judge Greene will throw me out of his chambers on my ass; but
we will do it all publicly, and we'll see how much press attention it gets. If
it doesn't get any closer to page one than the obituaries, we'll review the
question whether I ought to drop the case." It was agreed to try Baxter's
test.[29]

Seen as a good-faith effort, the appeal for a delay in the trial was
designed to allow time for Congress to pass or not to pass appropriate
legislation. A continuation – as opposed to a dismissal – was desirable,
given Baxter's view of the relationship between the antitrust suit and the
pending Senate bill. Baldrige and Wunder argued that the antitrust suit
was impeding legislation; Baxter asserted the opposite: The antitrust case
was the only force propelling the legislation. If the case were dismissed,
AT&T would lose interest in a new law, Baxter argued, and congressional
activity – inconclusive as it had been – would grind to a halt.[30] It may be

[27]Judge William C. Connor, *Judgment Order*, June 30, 1981, *Litton Systems, Inc.* v. *AT&T*,
   76 Civ. 2512 (WCC), U.S. Dist. Ct., Southern District of New York.
[28]Wunder, interview, June 12, 1984, pp. 27–34.
[29]Baxter, interview, February 2, 1984, p. 13.
[30]Wunder, interview, June 12, 1984, p. 36.

232 The fall of the Bell System

doubted, however, whether a good faith rationale was needed. Baxter must have known about the attempt in January to get Judge Greene to postpone the opening of the case. The judge had shown himself to be a stern taskmaster, willing to allow only short postponements in response to explicit alternative plans. It was all too likely that Baxter would indeed be turned down, if not so harshly as he suggested.

Baxter proposed to Trienens that they join forces to argue for an eleven-month postponement. Trienens, who of course agreed with the Departments of Commerce and Defense that the case should be dropped, said that Baxter's proposal was the dumbest thing he'd ever heard of. Baxter would get his teeth kicked in. "Well," Baxter replied, "I've got strong teeth."[31] With Trienens and George Saunders, AT&T's lead trial attorney, in tow, Baxter appeared before Judge Greene on July 29 and made his pitch for a delay. He explained his reason, linking the case to the bill pending in the Senate: "If the legislation passes with the amendments that have been worked out, it would be the Administration's intention to discontinue the litigation."[32]

Baxter had conceded important ground. Although the "amendments" he mentioned to Greene (later commonly called "Baxter I" and "Baxter II") expressed specific conditions that the Assistant Attorney General wanted included in the bill, Baxter clearly preferred a more radical re-structuring of AT&T than Congress would approve. He was (he later explained) not exactly "under instructions" from the administration to take this new course, but the situation was very close to that. Consequently, he had taken the position that if appropriate legislation could be passed *first*, he would then give way on the case before Judge Greene. Given the inability of Congress to act between 1976 and mid-1981, this was not a very likely outcome. But it represented a new position on Baxter's part, and it posed an alternative that the administration and AT&T would pursue with vigor.[33]

As Baxter had predicted, Judge Greene reacted negatively to the suggestion that he postpone the case. He noted that the case had been pending for seven years. He characterized the idea of holding the trial in abeyance for almost a year in the hope that the Congress would act as "a rather unusual motion." The legislative effort clearly involved issues in the case. But, Greene continued, "that is not my business if Congress wants to pass legislation to restructure the communications industry. . . . I have nothing to do with that, . . . but to say I am supposed to hold up the trial in the middle of it . . . because in the next eleven months somebody may do something, and this may remove an obstacle to their doing something, it strikes me as peculiar."

This peculiarity was offset by another, Trienens replied. The judge was devoting his energy to the trial, knowing that if the bill passed, the plaintiff would dismiss the suit. Judge Greene repeated his position: "All I can do is sit here. I didn't file the lawsuit. I didn't pursue the lawsuit since September or November, whenever it was, 1974. I wasn't even on this court at that time. The case came here. The case was pursued by the Department of Justice. The Department of Justice and the Administration have seen fit not to dismiss it. It is here. I have heard four months of testimony. We have had two and a half years of pre-trial maneuverings, and I am ready to proceed."

"I am also ready to have the parties settle it," Greene added. "Don't misunderstand me. I am not eager to take this masochistic punishment of being here every day and absorbing a great deal of technical, economic and legal information, day after day, even as much as I like the lawyers in the case." Saunders interrupted. "I thought you were enjoying it, Judge." Greene replied, "To an extent, to an extent." He reiterated once again his obligation to the judicial process and his reluctance to suspend it in the hope that some legislators would be moved to action. It took Judge Greene only half an hour after seeing the lawyers to confirm his initial impression that Baxter's request should be denied.[34]

Everyone reassembled in Meese's office the following day. Baxter's request and Judge Greene's spirited denial made the front page of *The Washington Post*, but only the financial pages of *The New York Times* and page five of *The Wall Street Journal*. It was hardly the notoriety that Baxter had predicted, but Baker seized on it to support his fears that dismissal would hurt the President's reputation. The case would have to continue while the administration sought to guide appropriate legislation through Congress. If Congress beat the court, AT&T might get what it wanted. If not, Judge Greene would decide whether Baxter should have his way.[35]

Both Baldrige and Weinberger informed Brown that even though they still favored dismissal of the antitrust suit, it was not about to happen. Subsequently, neither Baldrige nor Baxter would confirm that there was an explicit agreement that the case would be dropped if legislation was

[34]*US v. AT&T*, CA No. 74–1698 (D.D.C.), *Transcript of Proceedings*, July 29, 1981, Tr. 4, 8–10.
[35]Baxter, interview, February 2, 1984, pp. 14–15; Wunder, interview, June 12, 1984, pp. 36–7; "U.S. Eyes Dropping AT&T Suit," *The Washington Post*, July 30, 1981, p. A1; "Bid to Delay AT&T Trial Denied," *The New York Times*, July 30, 1981, p. D1; "U.S. May Drop AT&T Antitrust Suit If Equipment Sales Can Be Regulated," *The Wall Street Journal*, July 30, 1981, p. 5.

passed and signed by the President.[36] But all of the parties involved, in the government and in AT&T, continued to behave as if the two phenomena were very closely intertwined. From August on, then, the legislative and judicial efforts were pitted against each other to see which would finish first.

The maneuvering within the Reagan administration was distressing to the leaders of AT&T. Brown briefed his directors and deButts by telephone, noting the apparent conflict between Baxter's statement that the administration would drop the suit if suitable legislation passed and the continuing progress of the trial: "As Ed Ball used to say in his nightly toast of bourbon, 'confusion to the enemy'." Brown also issued a public statement in response to the newspaper stories: "We have never offered to divest the Western Electric Company. And we never intend to because the integrated nature of the Bell System has always been essential and is even more so today."[37] Howard Trienens was equally perturbed. To his mind, the conflict between different executive departments and the implicit contest between Congress and the court constituted a breakdown of the federal government.[38] His dismay was understandable. A solid majority of the strongest members of the Reagan administration favored dismissing the case. The President himself was favorably inclined toward the Bell System and was certainly no devotee of antitrust action. Yet Baxter had been able to thwart every effort to settle the matter within the executive branch. The only paths left open were the one leading to Capitol Hill and the one leading to Judge Greene's courtroom. That was a very disconcerting outcome for businessmen accustomed to hierarchy and executive authority.

But the outcome that dismayed Brown and Trienens was less unusual than they thought. The government is not a business; public policy formation does not follow the same hierarchical rules as private decision making within a corporation. In a government as large and complex as ours has become, the simple lines of authority charted by the Constitution and elaborated in government manuals no longer describe with any accuracy the manner in which policy is actually formulated and implemented. There are multiple sources of power and multiple paths to policy formation. What Trienens saw as the breakdown of the federal government *is* the federal government.

[36]Howard J. Trienens, "Chronology of Negotiations"; 97th Congress, 1st Session, Senate, Committee on the Judiciary, Hearing, "DOJ Oversight: U.S. v. AT&T," testimony of Malcolm Baldrige and William F. Baxter, August 6, 1981, pp. 13, 23.
[37]The statement went on to deny that AT&T had ever contemplated divesting Western Electric in the 1977 discussions or in the negotiations with Litvack. Charles L. Brown, "Telephone message to AT&T Directors and JdeB," July 31, 1981; Charles L. Brown to William M. Ellinghaus, memo and attached statement, July 31, 1981.
[38]Trienens, interview, January 19, 1984, p. 5.

Admittedly, Baxter's intense dedication to a particular ideology of competitive capitalism and his willingness to stand alone against powerful opposition distinguished him from the general run of political appointees. As a result, he would have a decisive impact on the largest corporation in the world and on the telecommunications policy of the United States. William Baxter had been clearly more adamant than most appointed officials. But as he later explained, "Dita Beard had given me all the cards."[39] The Justice Department, and particularly its antitrust division, had acquired great autonomy in the decade since the ITT case. It had come to be accepted that a major antitrust suit, once begun, was supposed to be decided within the legal arena according to the Sherman and Clayton acts. It would indeed have been a political scandal simply to drop the AT&T case while the trial was underway, verdicts were accumulating against AT&T in private suits, and Congress was considering the issue. Dismissal would surely have strengthened the hand of AT&T's opponents in Congress; the outcome might well have been even less pleasant than dealing with Greene and Baxter.

It is not self-evident that it is inappropriate for a decision of this magnitude to be channeled into the judiciary. Nor is it obvious that Congress would have done a better job of policy determination than the courts. Virtually all of the lawyers in the case–whether on AT&T's side or the government's–said at one time or another that telecommunications policy should be framed by Congress. But none of the lawyers–as it turned out– were particularly pleased with what Congress actually did in 1981.

Congress in motion: the Senate

The 1980 election had changed Congress in ways that would impinge decisively on telecommunications policy. Lionel Van Deerlin unexpectedly failed to win reelection, and Timothy Wirth took control of the subcommittee. In light of the debacle at the end of the previous Congress, Wirth launched his staff on a thorough study of this entire area of policy. Wirth wanted to step back from the congressional fray to restudy the issues, but at the same time he needed to stay involved in the developments in Washington if he was to achieve his long-run goals. He went on record in July with a letter to President Reagan urging him to resist the pressure to drop the suit. Noting that the arguments against prosecution of the suit did not deal with the question of AT&T's liability, Wirth claimed that by backing away from the case, the administration would

[39]Baxter, interview, February 2, 1984, p. 42.

"undermine the credibility of antitrust enforcement" and weaken the drive to increase competition.[40]

Since the Republicans had gained control of the Senate for the first time since Eisenhower's first term, the Reagan administration had an opportunity to work with Senator Packwood, the new chairman of the Senate Commerce Committee, to fashion a bill that would sidetrack the antitrust suit and preserve the Bell System. On April 7, 1981, Packwood introduced "The Telecommunications Competition and Deregulation Act of 1981," S. 898, which was taken directly from Van Deerlin's bill of the previous Congress. The House bill had elicited considerable support for its overall framework. It was the natural place for a new legislative effort to start, even if Wirth was loath to use it. Bernard Wunder was, moreover, ideally placed to facilitate the transition from House to Senate. Like Van Deerlin's bill, the Senate bill put increased reliance on competition to ensure that the nation would have adequate telecommunications services and continuing technological improvements. Competition was also to be relied upon as much as possible to keep rates low and to make certain that the industry met America's national security needs. But although the aim of promoting more competition was identical to Baxter's, the means by which competition was to be obtained were very different from those proposed by the Assistant Attorney General. Instead of breaking the Bell System into separate competitive and monopoly elements, Packwood proposed to divide AT&T into parts that would still be formally connected by common ownership. AT&T would be compelled to establish "fully separated affiliates" to divide these two elements, with the competitive units being completely deregulated and the monopolistic ones under the control of the FCC and state regulators. Although Baxter would achieve this bifurcation by creating separate companies that would be wholly in the regulated sector or wholly in the competitive sector, the Senate bill envisioned an AT&T that continued to straddle this boundary. S. 898 did not mandate any divestiture.

Instead, the bill defined AT&T as a "dominant regulated carrier" and provided extensive new rules for it. Most of the rules involved the boundary between the monopolistic and competitive sectors of the firm. AT&T would conduct its main business inside the regulatory boundary. Outside, its fully separated subsidiaries or affiliates could engage in a variety of activities, but they could not offer services similar to those in the regulated domain for two years (a period that could be extended for an additional two years by the FCC if effective competition had not arisen). The affiliates could have no more than one director in common with AT&T and

[40]Timothy E. Wirth to President Ronald Reagan, July 2, 1981, with attached July 7, 1981, press release, "Wirth Urges President Not to Drop AT&T Antitrust Suit."

no common officers or employees. They would have to have entirely separate books and records. There were rules about property and rules about joint ventures. There were rules about contracts, about information flows, about patent licensing, and about the flow of products and components between AT&T and its affiliates and between one affiliate and another.[41]

These elaborate requirements and structural changes were contrived to solve the cross-subsidy problem. In its suit, the Justice Department had accused AT&T of subsidizing its competitive activities in two distinct ways. The first was by pricing its competitive services too low, a practice allegedly permitted by regulation. The fully separated affiliates of the new bill were designed to stop this cross-subsidy. The second was by anticompetitive conduct of various sorts not directly related to pricing. This part of the government's case was dealt with in the Senate bill by the myriad injunctions and rules imposed on the dominant regulated carrier and its affiliates. Here was the crux of the Senate bill and the center of the controversy about it.

The Department of Justice, as it became involved with the bill, wanted to separate the affiliates as much as possible. It wanted to build, in the expression current at Justice, "a Chinese wall" between AT&T and its subsidiaries. Baxter, of course, was suspicious of the Chinese wall, no matter how formidable the regulations were. He insisted that even if AT&T separated the affiliates' books and manpower, they would still have incentives to cooperate with other parts of the company. The path to promotion in the dominant carrier, AT&T, would continue to be a successful tour through the subsidiaries, climaxed by a promotion to AT&T headquarters at 195 Broadway. Managers who had this goal in mind could not be expected to run their subsidiaries in a "fully separated" way, regardless of the rules. The Department of Justice consequently insisted—almost neurotically—on ever more separation when in reality no amount could achieve Baxter's goal. Obsessively, the Justice Department wanted more and more.[42]

The danger for AT&T was that the burden of the regulations would become so great that the firm's managers would be unable to run the company successfully. Brown wanted the company to be able to explore those new, competitive markets that had been forbidden to it by the 1956 Consent Decree. But to do so successfully, he maintained that it needed the technological edge that Bell Labs and Western Electric would give. He preferred Packwood's bill to Baxter's divestiture proposals because the legislation would leave the structure of AT&T intact. But he and Trienens

[41]97th Congress, 1st Session, Senate, S. 898, "The Telecommunications Competition and Deregulation Act of 1981," April 7, 1981.
[42]Baxter, interview, February 2, 1984, pp. 44–6.

were well aware that there could be so many restrictions on the relationship between AT&T and its various affiliates that the victory over divestiture would be a pyrrhic one. If the Chinese wall were high and truly
impregnable, the benefits of integration would be lost. At some point,
Brown would have to decide whether the bill was in fact a workable
measure.

The initial tug of war over Packwood's bill, however, took place within
the Reagan administration. When Senator Packwood opened hearings on it
on June 2, Secretary of Commerce Baldrige and William Brock, the United
States trade representative, were scheduled to testify for the administration. But when their draft testimony was circulated in advance, Baxter
objected strongly to what Baldrige had to say. In a letter to David Stockman, Director of the Office of Management and Budget, Baxter reported
that he and his department had substantial objections to the bill and therefore to the administration's position as expressed in Baldrige's statement.
Baxter wrote: "S. 898 will enhance, rather than diminish, the complexity of
Federal Communications Commission regulation, without offering any
prospect of effectively dealing with the potential for anticompetitive abuses
present in AT&T's participation in regulated and unregulated markets. As
such, S. 898 is fundamentally at odds with the deregulatory philosophy of
this administration." The bill, he said, would "as a practical matter, seriously diminish the likelihood that the trial court will be willing, if the
government prevails, to award effective structural relief. For these reasons, we believe it most unwise for the administration to support, even in
general terms, S. 898."[43] Confronted with this opposition, Meese decided
that he could not let Baldrige and Brock testify and have Baxter's opposition
surface. They abruptly canceled their appearances. Senator Packwood, like
Judge Greene, was not sympathetic to the Reagan administration's internal
problems. He opened his hearings on schedule with a pointed reference to
the missing spokesmen. It was not his doing that they were not there: "This
is not a bill we sprung on the administration last Friday."[44]

Mark Fowler, chairman of the FCC, was the lead witness in support of
the bill. He was clearly pleased by the Senate's adherence to the FCC's
model, as outlined in the *Computer II* decision; he was worried only that
the FCC might actually be getting more responsibility than it could exercise in a reasonable fashion. Henry Geller (now the head of Duke University's Washington Center for Public Policy Research) also supported the

[43]William F. Baxter to David Stockman, May 27, 1981, Attachment 8 of "Department of
Defense Analysis of the Effect of AT&T Divestiture Upon National Defense and Security
and Emergency Preparedness," June 30, 1981, *US* v. *AT&T*, Defendants' Exhibit D-1–
141.
[44]97th Congress, 1st Session, Senate, Hearing on S. 898, June 2, 1981, Opening statement
by Senator Packwood, p. 3.

bill, commending the Senate for emphasizing competition and deregulation. He was pleased that the bill freed AT&T from the strictures of the 1956 Consent Decree and allowed it to enter markets outside basic telecommunications services (albeit through fully separated affiliates). Like Baxter, he applauded the goal of allowing AT&T to use its substantial resources to promote progress and competition in those areas. But unlike the Assistant Attorney General, he wanted fewer rather than more restrictions put on AT&T's affiliates.

Geller supported the proposed access charge system that would, under this bill, gradually replace the existing separation procedures. The FCC would control exchange access fees, which would be paid by interexchange carriers to the operating companies for access to the local network. The charges were to be cost-based, and they were to be set at a level that would provide the local carriers with the revenue that they had received in 1980. The ENFIA agreements, which in effect provided subsidies for the specialized common carriers, would be replaced by a uniform charge to all interexchange carriers. This part of the bill, paradoxically, eliminated the differential pricing that was *helping* the competitors – that was, in fact, their economic lifeline.[45]

On June 11 Secretary Baldrige made a belated appearance, but with Baxter still refusing to back the bill, Baldrige was visibly restrained. The Reagan administration, he said, supported the "thrust" of the proposed legislation. He could not, however, formally endorse Packwood's bill. When asked whether the bill was a better structural solution for AT&T than divestiture, Baldrige answered affirmatively, but he added that the bill should have no effect on the ongoing antitrust suit. Even though he supported legislation, he would not rule out relief along the lines requested by the Department of Justice.[46]

MCI's McGowan showed no restraint in opposing the bill. He said that it would decrease rather than increase competition in telecommunications. He insisted that AT&T was using scare tactics in an effort to convince people that local rates were being subsidized by long distance rates. The reverse, he claimed, was actually the case. McGowan was particularly skeptical of the proposed equal access charges for all carriers. He did not believe that AT&T would give MCI the same quality of interconnections that AT&T's Long Lines had. As usual, the best defense is a strong offense, and McGowan used these arguments to mask his concern about losing the cost advantage MCI received from the ENFIA agreements.[47]

Brown testified that the Bell System was happy to have competition as long as Congress articulated reasonable ground rules. He was pleased

[45]Ibid., statements of FCC Chairman Mark Fowler and Henry Geller.
[46]Ibid., June 11, 1981, statement of Malcolm Baldrige, pp. 83, 94, 108–9.
[47]Ibid., June 15, 1981, statement of William G. McGowan, pp. 290–1, 293–4.

with the bill's provision for access charges. Contradicting McGowan and the Justice Department's expert, he claimed that competing long distance carriers were currently undercutting AT&T's rates because they did not pay their share of separations under the compromise ENFIA tariff. The Senate bill would correct that situation.

Although generally supportive of the bill, Brown was concerned about the inefficiencies that would be produced by the Chinese wall separating AT&T from its affiliates. He did not want to trade the actual divestiture proposed by Baxter for de facto divestiture through regulation. But when asked by Senator Cannon whether AT&T would tend to favor a fully separated affiliate as "a parent favors a child," Brown insisted that this was hardly possible. Most of AT&T's business would be closely regulated, he said, and the company would be precluded from favoring its affiliates in the unregulated part of its activities. AT&T would be foolish to jeopardize its regulated activities, its bread and butter, for the sake of its affiliates. In fact, given the bill's strong restrictions on favoritism, Brown thought that the leadership of AT&T would be vulnerable, much as the corporation would be, if they favored an AT&T affiliate. In his words, "I think we'd go to jail if we did."[48]

Brown pointed out one major inconsistency in the bill. Although generally promoting competition, it barred AT&T from providing electronic information services. Newspaper publishers had argued that competition from AT&T would diminish their First Amendment protection and their revenues, and they had convinced Packwood's committee – as they had earlier convinced Wirth and Van Deerlin's subcommittee – to exclude the telephone company from this market. Brown said that the connection between this issue and the First Amendment was tenuous, at best; the opposition to AT&T's competition was understandable instead as a device to preserve the economic viability of the newspapers. But if it was Congress's will to preserve these activities, he concluded ruefully, AT&T would agree to limit its provision of electronic information in the future.

Despite these reservations, Brown publicly allied himself with the Senate bill and the majority position in the administration. He commented on the contrast between the ongoing antitrust suit and Baldrige's support of legislation. The Department of Justice, he said, appeared to be a group of "lawyers without any client." At that moment, of course, he was right. But neither AT&T nor the Reagan administration would be able to turn that situation to their advantage and derail the antitrust suit so long as Congress was deciding what to do.[49]

The Commerce Committee reported out Packwood's bill on July 16,

[48]Ibid., June 16, 1981, statement of Charles L. Brown, p. 439.
[49]Ibid., p. 442.

and Baxter, who had not been able to kill the legislative effort, decided that he would have to make a serious effort to reshape the bill. Even though he opposed the very notion of fully separated subsidiaries, he took the committee's action as a signal that he should become actively involved with the measure. If the antitrust suit was to be undercut by the legislation, he had better make certain that the bill came as close as possible to achieving his objectives for the industry. He joined with Sherman Unger, general counsel of the Commerce Department, in calling Trienens to ask if he would be willing to discuss an amendment dealing with AT&T's procurement from Western Electric. Trienens replied in the spirit of Brown's testimony to the committee. He was interested in negotiating about the bill, but there was a limit to the restrictions that AT&T would accept.

During the following week, Baxter, Trienens, and AT&T Executive Vice President Morris Tanenbaum met almost daily at the Commerce Department to draft the amendment, called "Baxter I." They reached agreement by July 24. Baxter I was designed to ensure that Western Electric's prices to Bell System purchasers – on its so-called Bell business – were competitive. Baxter wanted a yardstick for measuring those prices, but unlike Geller, he did not want to leave that task to the FCC. Instead, Baxter wanted binding legal constraints. He came up with an amendment dictating that Western Electric could have no greater market share in its Bell business than it had in its non-Bell business. That is, if it wanted to supply 75 percent of the Bell System's need for a certain type of equipment, then it also had to supply 75 percent of the independent telephone companies' needs for that same equipment. This was termed the "market test."[50]

This was a very stiff requirement. It meant that established suppliers in independent markets would have to be displaced if Western was to continue supplying the Bell System. Some independent companies – like the Bell System – were vertically integrated, and their suppliers would have to be outcompeted. One might presume that the same antitrust rules that applied to AT&T would apply to these other firms and that they would have to be very careful about their relations with their suppliers. But that was not the case. These companies played a small role in the American market (although in some cases they were a larger factor on the international scene), and therefore did not pose either to the FCC or to the Justice Department the threat of monopolization that the Bell System

[50]Administration's Proposed Amendment to S. 898 on "Special Procurement and Open Market Sales Requirements," July 30, 1981; The ratios were complicated by the worldwide character of telecommunications. The required market shares were calculated on the basis of the U.S. telephone market, but the shares of sales compared with this standard were calculated on the basis of Western's worldwide sales (which gave Western a little more latitude than the strict ratios might imply).

presented. This situation was recognized in Packwood's bill by defining AT&T as the dominant carrier and applying the provisions of the act to it rather than to the telecommunications industry as a whole.[51]

The market test assumed that the Bell System would be supplying exactly the same kind of service as other telephone companies. But consider, for example, what would have happened under this amendment if AT&T, through Bell Labs, were to develop a new kind of equipment, a new way of doing things, that offered a slightly different service than other companies were providing. Assume that it was competing, as everyone was hoping the telecommunications companies would compete, by advancing the technology. Then, in an integrated firm like AT&T, the research people would work with production personnel, who would coordinate their activities with the operations staff. New equipment would be designed, a new service would be offered, and a competitive advantage would be secured by being first in the market.

But to do this under the Baxter amendment, Western Electric would either have to sell some of the new equipment to AT&T's competitors – eschewing the competitive advantage from its research – or else increase its sales of other, older equipment outside the Bell System. Even in the latter, more attractive situation, Western Electric would be in the schizophrenic position of increasing its efforts to sell older equipment outside the System at the very moment it was introducing improved equipment inside the System. Leaving aside the probable antitrust implications of this behavior, it would have been a manager's nightmare.

Nevertheless, Brown and Tanenbaum accepted Baxter I in the hope that it would move the Justice Department toward support for the Senate bill and an end to the antitrust suit. For a time, it appeared that this gamble would pay off. It was at this point in the negotiations that Baxter and Trienens visited Judge Greene to request a postponement, and Baxter agreed that he would drop the case if the bill were passed "with the amendments that have been worked out."[52] One amendment was the one on which agreement had been reached (Baxter I); the other – Baxter II on equal access – still had to be drafted in a form acceptable to both Justice and AT&T. Even so, Baxter seemed to have assumed at the end of July that agreement was imminent.[53]

---

[51]For a discussion of the conditions in this market, see *International Tel. and Tel. Corp.* v. *General Tel. & Elec. Corp.*, 351 F. Supp. 1153 (D. Hawaii 1972), *Modified*, 518 F.2d 913 (9th Cir. 1975), *on remand*, 449 F. Supp. 1158 (D. Hawaii 1978).

[52]*US* v. *AT&T*, CA No. 74–1698 (D.D.C.), *Transcript of Proceedings*, July 29, 1981, Tr. 3.

[53]Baxter responded to pressure from Sherman Unger of the Commerce Department by calling Trienens shortly after Judge Greene turned down their joint request. Baxter inquired if Trienens would be interested in working up a draft consent decree on the basis of the Senate bill concepts that would terminate the antitrust suit. Trienens was always responsive to such calls, and he asked his assistants in the Litvack negotiations, Jim

Complications soon arose, however, in the Senate. Baxter's appearance before Judge Greene had brought a new set of players into the congressional game. Strom Thurmond, chairman of the Senate Judiciary Committee, had been watching with some distress while Packwood's bill made its way through the Commerce Committee. Like Congressman Rodino a year earlier, Thurmond did not want a bill with strong antitrust implications to be passed without input from his committee, input that was needed both to refine the bill and to preserve the influence of the Judiciary Committee. Thurmond held hearings in July to establish a record that would support referral to his committee. Then when Baxter asked Judge Greene for a continuance of the case so that Congress would have time to act, the connection between the Senate bill and the antitrust case became visible to all. Baxter's maneuver to neutralize his opponents within the administration had provided Thurmond with the grounds he needed to take a more active role. The Judiciary Committee promptly called Baxter to testify.[54]

Baxter explained his rather complex point of view to Thurmond's committee in early August. He disavowed the firm connection between the Senate bill and the antitrust case that he had announced to Judge Greene the previous week, although he acknowledged their intellectual link: "there is a trade-off between a clean solution to the cross-subsidization problem and sacrifice of the economies of vertical integration."[55] The clean solution was the Justice Department's divestiture proposal. It would substantially decrease the integration of the Bell System, risking a loss of efficiency. To avoid this loss—which Baxter, of course, thought small—one could adopt the approach of the Senate bill: Keep the existing structure of AT&T while regulating the company to make sure that cross-subsidization did not take place. The risk in the Senate approach (as Brown was all too aware) was that the rules to avoid cross-subsidization might be so onerous as to negate the advantages of any economies of vertical integration.

Baxter summarized the differences of approach as follows: "If one argues for divestiture, one argues that the cross-subsidy problem is terribly important, that the vertical integration economies probably are not very great, and that regulatory supervision is unwanted and more deregulation

Kilpatric and Robert McLean, to prepare a draft decree. They combined the opening of the 1956 Consent Decree, parts of the last internal AT&T draft based on the discussions with Litvack, and portions of the Senate bill. This draft was given to Baxter's lieutenants, Ronald Carr and Richard Levine, on August 7 but lay dormant until negotiations began again in October. Baxter had made the call he was asked to make, but in reality he was not yet interested in negotiating a settlement.

[54] 97th Congress, 1st Session, Senate, Committee on the Judiciary, "Hearing on Monopolization and Competition in the Telecommunications Industry," July 23–24 and 29, 1981.
[55] 97th Congress, 1st Session, Senate, Committee on the Judiciary, Hearing, "DOJ Oversight: U.S. v. AT&T," August 6, 1981, testimony of William F. Baxter, p. 27.

244 	The fall of the Bell System

is possible. If one argues for the S. 898 [Packwood's bill] approach, one says that the fully separate subsidiary device does not sacrifice significantly those economies of vertical integration, that the FCC will be able adequately to police that line, and therefore the cross-subsidy problem can be solved."[56] For his part, Baxter was convinced that the primary problem of AT&T, from an antitrust perspective, was cross-subsidization. He clearly distrusted regulation, a point of view he had articulated to the Cabinet Council and made evident once again before the Judiciary Committee. Still, at this point, he was adhering to the general (although increasingly vague) understanding worked out in the administration and articulated to Judge Greene. Baxter was supporting Packwood's bill. He was hesitant and unenthusiastic, but he supported the amended form of the bill.

Despite the importance Baxter assigned to cross-subsidization, he too was inconsistent in his perception of this problem. In answer to a question at the hearing, he said: "Historically, AT&T has subsidized local telephone service with Long Lines revenues."[57] He was here referring to the separations charges. But if Long Lines was subsidizing the operating companies, why did this create problems for competition? The cross-subsidy did not hurt the fledgling competitors; it helped them. In addition, any help that the operating companies were giving to equipment sales through their support of Bell Labs was more than offset by the far larger support the operating companies were receiving from Long Lines.

Both Baxter's proposed divestiture and the Senate bill's subsidiary would separate AT&T's Long Lines from the operating companies. This presumably would eliminate any subsidy from the operating companies to Long Lines. But as Baxter and McGowan certainly understood, there was no cross-subsidy flowing across this boundary that hurt the specialized common carriers. Quite the reverse. The competitors had actually been called into being by the gap that had long existed between the prices and costs of board-to-board, long distance telephone service. On that basis, there was a large and growing cross-subsidy that went from Bell's competitive message toll service to the local companies. If this was the target of these proposals, they would obviously miss their mark.

To say that Baxter had misconceived the problem, however, does not say that a problem did not exist. Baxter, like everyone else connected with telecommunications legislation, was using cross-subsidization symbolically to stand for all of the problems the industry was experiencing with new competition. But these problems were different for telephone equipment and for intercity telephone service. Either divestiture as pro-

[56]Ibid.
[57]Ibid., p. 37.
[56]Ibid.
[57]Ibid., p. 37.

posed in April or, less effectively, Baxter I would open up more of the equipment market to the forces of competition. The industry's experience in recent years strongly suggested that this would be good for everyone except Western Electric. But this solution would not address the second problem, that of the new competitors in intercity service. This was a thorny situation because the competitors had been called into existence by the peculiar structure of regulated telephone prices. Paradoxically, Packwood's bill would eliminate the cross-subsidy that was sustaining these specialized common carriers. Equal access would be a hollow victory for the competitors if access charges were high and AT&T's prices were low. They might find it impossible to stay in business under these conditions. The confusion over cross-subsidies made it extremely difficult to resolve the problem that Baxter thought they created. Instead, the confusion promoted superficial agreement but masked deeper disagreements that would ultimately emerge and complicate the process of framing public policy.

For the moment, however, these issues were avoided as Thurmond's committee churned ahead with its probe. Thurmond asked Baldrige to explain the administration's position as expressed in the appeal to Judge Greene. Leading him through the history of the Cabinet Council, Thurmond exposed the administration's attempt to isolate Baxter and the Justice Department. The result, as Thurmond insisted through question after question, was that the Senate bill had been drafted without any explicit consideration of its antitrust implications. These implications, of course, lay just below the surface of every move that Baldrige and Meese had made. But because they were implicit and not explicit, Thurmond had the grounds to make his committee a major force in shaping Packwood's bill.[58] The Judiciary Committee did not want to start over and write a new version of the bill Commerce had already reported out; it just wanted to fine tune the antitrust implications of S. 898. So Thurmond did not request referral to his committee. He and his staff organized a clearing house for proposed amendments from all sources. They tried to negotiate agreement on the amendments they thought had merit to ease the way to adoption on the Senate floor.[59]

Foremost among these amendments was the still unwritten Baxter II. Trienens and Tanenbaum met with Baxter and Wunder on August 7 to discuss this amendment. It was intended to ensure that all interexchange carriers – that is, AT&T's Long Lines and its competitors – interconnected with local exchanges on the same basis. Baxter II required every carrier offering regulated services – that is, local telephone services – to intercon-

[58]Ibid., testimony of Malcolm Baldrige, pp. 2–16.
[59]Marcy J. K. Tiffany, interview, October 24, 1985, pp. 54–60.

nect with all interexchange carriers and not to discriminate between them. The regulated local companies were to be common carriers for any interexchange competitors that met standards set by the FCC. They could not discriminate between them either in their technical arrangements or in the pricing of their services.

Baxter II made a significant change in the bill reported out by the Commerce Committee. The original measure contained provisions for equal access that mirrored the FCC's existing policies. The criteria to be satisfied were phrased in standard regulatory language, and a joint state-federal board was to have binding authority over the Commission on matters of equal access. Baxter II reduced the authority of the joint board and made provisions for equal access much more specific.

AT&T did not strongly oppose the intent of Baxter II; the disagreements between the Justice Department and the company involved the actual wording of the amendment. In fact, AT&T had been working on this problem for a long time. The firm had decided to reprogram its switches to provide equal access in the aftermath of *Execunet*. The amendment thus would require them to do something they were already doing. They had long sought, through the ENFIA tariff and other means, to have the pricing of all interexchange carriers on an equal basis. Still, the two sides could not agree on the precise wording of the amendment, and the discussions dragged on for two months. The amendment finally went to the Senate without the full support of either AT&T or the Department of Justice.[60]

While this was happening, Baxter was maneuvering even harder to make the measure more onerous to AT&T. He tried to extract every possible concession from the telephone company. Brown had indicated that AT&T could live with the initial Senate bill; he had agreed that the Bell System could live with Baxter I, and as summer turned into fall, he had finally decided that the wording of Baxter II "was burdensome but workable."[61] These were the only two amendments on which the administration – and particularly the Justice Department – had conditioned its support for the bill in midsummer. Brown and Trienens consequently thought they had satisfied Baxter's requirements for legislation that would obviate the lawsuit – even though the understanding was not "firm." Brown expressed this view to Meese, Baldrige, and Donald Regan, the Secretary of the Treasury, in mid-September.[62]

Almost immediately after these conversations, however, AT&T was

[60]"Interconnection for Exchange Access," September 22, 1981, proposed Baxter amendment to S. 898; Trienens, interview, January 19, 1984, p. 31.
[61]Unsigned "Memorandum" with attachments, ca. October 5, 1981.
[62]Unsigned memorandum, September 16, 1981; Howard J. Trienens, "Chronology of Negotiations."

jolted by some unexpected amendments to the Senate bill. The main problem was Baxter II. The Assistant Attorney General now insisted that all carriers be accessible by dialing the same number of digits. But, as Trienens reminded Brown, if AT&T was to continue to have primary responsibility for the telephone network and remain the carrier of last resort, it was only fair that it be accessible by dialing somewhat fewer digits than its competitors required.

In addition, Baxter wanted all interexchange traffic to go to Bell's intercity switches on a common, shared group of circuits and to be divided up at each switch. This requirement was madness to AT&T. Brown listed the problems. First of all, it would force the local companies to reengineer their networks in ways that Brown thought were close to impossible from an engineering perspective. Second, the provision was far too specific for legislation. The purpose of the law should have been to set the principles for connection with the network, not design its actual configuration. Third, it ignored the many ways in which the network was actually designed to take account of special circumstances. It provided no leeway to deal with concentrated traffic or other special needs. Fourth, it would have involved Bell in expensive rearrangements and the construction of additional switches for handling the new burden of first collecting all of the intercity traffic and then distributing it again among competing companies. Fifth, it would make any future changes in the network – whether in response to new technology or changing demand – the subject of regulatory or legal conflict. The competing carriers had to take their signals from Bell's intercity switch, and a change, say, in the switch's location would require the carriers to provide new connections to this location. Bell's motives in any such change would be open to question. Finally, the new requirement presupposed that Bell would somehow find ways in a system under its control to disadvantage its competitors. This, Trienens told Brown, was fantasy. "The reality is that a statute which required the quality be no less for the competing intercity carriers would guarantee them somewhat better quality because the engineers would have to lean over backwards to avoid violating a statute in relations with competitors who have always been alert to litigate at the slightest provocation."[63]

Also unacceptable to AT&T was the reappearance of the Chinese wall. A new amendment required that the results of all research or engineering studies whose costs were included in the base for setting the rates of local carriers be made available to an AT&T affiliate only if they were simultaneously made available to all other manufacturers. This, in AT&T's view, would prohibit contact between the scientists and engineers in Bell Labs who were funded by the telephone companies and those who were funded

[63] Howard J. Trienens to Charles L. Brown, Morris Tanenbaum, Alfred C. Partoll, and Irwin Dorros, September 18, 1981.

by Western Electric. In Trienens's words: "It would erect a wall through the middle of Bell Laboratories creating intolerable restrictions in its activities."[64] It would eliminate the benefits of the vertical integration on which AT&T prided itself and would inhibit innovation. It would constitute de facto vertical divestiture.

AT&T was stung by this flurry of last-minute activity and uncertain about its genesis. Trienens and Brown suspected, with good cause, that Baxter was undercutting the administration-backed bill by overloading it with amendments he knew would be unacceptable. It was possible to conclude, on the other hand, that the Assistant Attorney General was merely ensuring that the bill, if it passed, would come as close as possible to the results he hoped to achieve by way of Judge Greene. The evidence on this point—like the administration's understanding with Baxter—was vague. But AT&T's top officers had every reason to believe that Baxter was a tough, politically astute opponent, and in this case their suspicions appear to have been right. Nevertheless, they could not be certain exactly what was happening in Washington, and that was disconcerting to the managers of the largest company in the world.

It was certain, however, that passage of the amendments would render Packwood's bill unacceptable to Bell. Floor debate on the bill began on Thursday, October 1, at which time Senator Thurmond announced his intention to propose Baxter's amendments to the bill. A very upset Brown got word to Baxter through the White House that AT&T would not agree to these new changes, but efforts to negotiate with the Justice Department proved unsuccessful.[65] AT&T managed to block adoption of the Chinese wall amendment and remove Baxter's explicit design for equal access on the floor of the Senate. The rest of the amendments were adopted on Tuesday, October 6, and the Senate passed the whole bill on the following day by a vote of 90 to 4. After considering the issue for six years, one house of Congress had finally passed a telecommunications bill.[66]

Brown issued a statement saying that the bill as passed was "tough" but acceptable to AT&T. It left the Bell System intact, and Brown thought he could live with Baxter I and II as adopted by the Senate. It was far better

[64]Unsigned "Memorandum" with attachments, ca. October 5, 1981.
[65]Howard J. Trienens, "Chronology of Negotiations."
[66]"Telecommunications Competition and Deregulation Act of 1981 (S. 898)," Amendments to bill, *Congressional Record – Senate*, October 6, 1981, S11124–43; S. 898 as passed by the Senate on October 7, 1981, *Congressional Record – Senate*, October 14, 1981, S11443–60.

   Sherman Unger, still eager to promote a consent decree, called Trienens on October 5 to ask if AT&T would sign a decree identical to S. 898 with Baxter's proposed amendments. Trienens consulted with Brown and called back to say no. Howard J. Trienens, "Chronology of Negotiations."

than the ongoing antitrust suit and the possibility of a court-ordered divestiture. His statement was, of course, redundant. No bill opposed by AT&T could have received 90 votes in the Senate.[67]

But, unhappily, what made the bill acceptable to Brown rendered it unacceptable to Baxter. He told reporters that he would *not* recommend that the antitrust suit be dismissed if the Senate bill became law. He explained that the bill lacked two necessary ingredients. The amendment restricting the use of Bell Labs research had been eliminated. The equal access amendment – Baxter II – still left "an enormous amount of discretion" to both AT&T and the FCC, neither of which Baxter trusted to do the right thing. The bill would produce, Baxter said, "endless hassles" before the Commission. Agreement on the wording of Baxter II had eluded the negotiators during the summer, and the final version leaned toward AT&T's, not Baxter's, point of view.[68]

Brown and Trienens felt double-crossed. Baxter had said clearly in the summer that he would dismiss the suit if legislation passed with his two amendments. Baxter I, on procurement, had been drafted by that time and posed no problem. Baxter II, on equal access, had not reached a final form, but its outlines were known. The version passed by the Senate clearly was in the spirit of the July discussion; the bill Baxter had described to Judge Greene and Senator Thurmond's committee had received support from AT&T and been passed. The Senate vote in fact showed overwhelming congressional support for its approach. Yet Baxter had refused to follow through. He had, it appears, been working all of that time not to achieve a new law but to derail the legislation. He had come very close to achieving that objective, and he would soon get another shot in the House of Representatives, where he could look to Timothy Wirth for support.

The telephone book

While the legislative gambit was being played to its inconclusive ending, Judge Greene was prodding the antitrust suit along to what threatened to be for the telephone company an all too conclusive decision. Shadows of the forthcoming decision were thrown on the wall in the fall of 1981. The government had presented its case in the first six months of that year. AT&T would have the last half of the year for its defense. But even while that process was going on, Judge Greene expressed an intermediate view

[67]"AT&T Measure Passes Senate on 90-to-4 Vote," *The Wall Street Journal,* October 8, 1981, p. 3; Trienens, interview, January 19, 1984, p. 24.
[68]"Baxter Discloses Potential Split Over AT&T Suit; Antitrust Chief Wouldn't Urge End to U.S. Suit as Deregulation Bill Stands," *The Wall Street Journal,* October 9, 1981, p. 5.

that stimulated Brown to try once again for a settlement. To understand the context for Greene's opinion, we must look briefly at the case the government had presented.

The government attacked AT&T on several fronts. One line of assault related to Western Electric and the Bell System's procurement of equipment and supplies. Another related to AT&T's behavior toward the specialized common carriers and stemmed largely from MCI's complaints in the early 1970s. A third involved interconnection, terminal equipment, and AT&T's requirement that its customers use PCAs. In each of these areas, the government's case had a pricing and a foreclosure component. The pricing arguments were less important. The accusations that Western Electric had overcharged the Bell Operating Companies for its products were so insubstantial – and the government's witness so unbelievable – that Judge Greene dismissed these charges even before hearing AT&T's rebuttal.[69] The allegations about predatory pricing of intercity services echoed the arguments about TELPAK, Hi-Lo, and other Bell tariffs that had been before the FCC for twenty years, but it had a new twist. The Justice Department's argument that AT&T's private line prices were predatory was based on a novel legal theory saying that prices not based on costs were anticompetitive. The government's witness on this point, Bruce Owen, maintained that there is no explanation other than anticompetitive intent for prices unrelated to costs. But the history of regulated prices in telecommunications provided another justification that was all too plausible: regulatory insistence on rate averaging, value of service, rate of return, and fully-distributed-cost prices. Owen's doctrine of "pricing without regard to cost" was both undeveloped as a matter of theory and history and quite different from the standard theories of competitive pricing. Its meaning was unclear, and it would have been a slender reed indeed on which to base a major antitrust decision.[70]

The foreclosure arguments were more serious. Both Litvack and Baxter saw them as the guts of the government's case. On the equipment side, AT&T was accused of buying only Western Electric products, even when respectable alternatives were available, and of using PCAs to bar other firms from the terminal equipment market. PCAs, the government argued, were often unavailable and too expensive when they could be ob-

[69]Judge Greene, *Opinion*, September 11, 1981, *US* v. *AT&T*, CA No. 74–1698 (D.D.C.), 524 F. Supp. 1336 at 1380–1.
[70]*US* v. *AT&T*, CA No. 74–1698 (D.D.C.), Bruce M. Owen, testimony, Tr. 10961–3. For some reason, AT&T's cross-examination of Owen did not attack this theory. See also Paul W. MacAvoy and Kenneth Robinson, "Winning by Losing: The AT&T Settlement and Its Impact on Telecommunications," *Yale Journal on Regulation*, Vol. 1, 1983, pp. 1–42; William A. Brock and David S. Evans, "Predation: A Critique of the Government's Case in U.S. v. AT&T," in David S. Evans (ed.), *Breaking Up Bell* (New York: North-Holland, 1983).

tained. On the side of services, AT&T was accused of refusing to interconnect its lines with those of the specialized common carriers in order to preserve the entire long distance market for Long Lines. The government presented many examples in support of its arguments, but it directed attention particularly at two: AT&T's insistence that customers using their own terminals employ an expensive PCA, and AT&T's abrupt disconnection of MCI's foreign exchange lines when the court stayed the FCC's interconnection order in April 1974.

This line of attack was serious because AT&T clearly had monopolies in these markets until the FCC began to permit the entry of competitors after 1959. The Bell System was, moreover, comfortable with its monopoly positions and with the technical aspects of end-to-end responsibility in a unitary network. When the FCC changed the rules and competitors appeared, they had been greeted by Bell's engineers and managers with something considerably less than enthusiasm. Judge Greene now had the opportunity to decide if this attitude had led AT&T to violate the Sherman Antitrust Act's injunction against monopolizing behavior.

Leaving aside the question of intent – which cannot be resolved here in any case – it is noteworthy that the foreclosure accusations involved actions that had been resolved by regulatory authorities and courts long before the time of the trial. The PCA controversy had passed into history in 1975 when the FCC instituted its registration program for terminal equipment. The issue of MCI's right to compete had been resolved definitively by Judge Wright's 1977 *Execunet* decision. By late 1981, juries had found AT&T guilty of antitrust violations in both of these areas and had awarded substantial damages to Litton and MCI. Given that these were completed events, what basis would they have furnished for injunctions on future behavior? The government argued that these acts showed permanent features of AT&T's behavior, dictated by its structure.[71]

This, in essence, is the case that Greene had to consider on an interim basis in the summer of 1981. When the government finished presenting its case, AT&T filed a motion to dismiss the suit before the defendants' witnesses were heard. This is a reasonably standard motion in large cases and typically is denied. In this instance, however, AT&T presented a brief of over 500 pages in support of its motion, which may be less typical, and

---

[71]AT&T replied, in words used by Brown in a June speech: "The trial grinds on. But the suit makes no more sense today than it did the day it was filed. Indeed, it makes less sense. It makes less sense because most of the controversies that gave rise to it have long since been resolved by regulatory commissions and the courts." In a more personal vein he added, after mentioning the ever-present FCC and Congress: "By now you will begin to understand why it is that from time to time in recent months I have found myself yearning for the simple pleasures of running the telephone business." Charles L. Brown, "National Security and National Telecommunications Policy," speech to the Armed Forces Communications and Electronics Association luncheon, Washington, D.C., June 18, 1981.

the Department of Justice presented an extensive rebuttal of that brief. In reply, Judge Greene wrote an elaborate opinion rejecting AT&T's motion. His document, delivered on September 11, was not encouraging to the Bell System's leaders. The judge did not simply deny the motion. He also went through the case in some detail, rejecting some of the government's claims but keeping most of them and indicating to AT&T what it had to prove to establish its innocence. It was not going to be easy. The judge had formed the preliminary opinion that "the testimony and the documentary evidence adduced by the government demonstrate that the Bell System has violated the antitrust laws in a number of ways over a lengthy period of time." This statement and others like it, although reflecting only the plaintiff's evidence, did not suggest that at this time there was much doubt in Greene's mind that AT&T was in violation of the antitrust laws.[72]

In addition to demonstrating Greene's confidence in the reliability of the government's witnesses, the opinion had two critical aspects. The first involved a construction of the evidence and the second an interpretation of the legal framework into which the evidence fit. On the first issue, AT&T had argued that the individual examples described in the government's case should be regarded as simply that: isolated incidents. There were only a limited number of episodes. If AT&T could cast aspersions on several of them, it would bring into serious question the pattern of behavior that the Justice Department claimed they represented. What kind of relief could be justified by reference to a small set of isolated historical incidents, some of which were of doubtful relevance?

The government had argued that these incidents were examples of a general trend and that it was impossible to document all of the manifestations of this trend. Against the backdrop of the IBM trial, in its seventh year and still going strong, Judge Greene was not likely to insist on a larger sample, that is, on a more elaborate description of the pattern. Indeed, he accepted the government's argument, indicating that although the witnesses were talking about specific episodes, he could see the pattern. In his words: "While it has been represented that defendants manufacture over 200 thousand different products (many of which do not have high cross-elasticities of demand), and while it is true that the government offered proof specifically with regard to only a small fraction of that number, it is also true that much of the anticompetitive conduct described by the government's witnesses transcends individual products and broadly applies to the whole equipment spectrum."[73]

In addition, the judge, quoting a government memorandum in support, rejected AT&T's claim that the rule of reason should be applied to the

[72]Judge Greene, *Opinion*, September 11, 1981, *US* v. *AT&T*, CA No. 74–1698 (D.D.C.), 524 F. Supp. 1336 at 1381.
[73]Ibid., 1376–7.

Sherman Act in this case. The telephone company's argument was not that the FCC's jurisdiction supplanted the antitrust laws—Greene had already rejected that approach—but rather that the context in which entry was denied was an appropriate one, that is, a reasonable one, given the regulatory framework. In particular, AT&T maintained that the potential providers of intercity services were cream skimming or aspiring to do so. This was an inefficient arrangement, and AT&T was acting in concert with the FCC to prevent inefficiency. But Judge Greene responded: "Regardless of whether or not the FCC has ordered interconnection with Bell facilities, and regardless of how AT&T appraises the public interest under the Communications Act, AT&T has a continuing obligation under the antitrust laws to permit interconnection, if failure to interconnect is inconsistent with Sherman Act requirements. Compliance with the standards of the Communications Act does not in any way relieve defendants (or anyone else) of the obligation to comply with the antitrust laws."[74]

Although Judge Greene did not rule on this issue (he deferred his decision on whether the government's or the telephone company's interpretation of the law was accurate), his approach did not bode well for the Bell System. He pointed out, for instance, that the defendants would have to demonstrate that the entrants actually were cream skimmers in order even to raise the issue of whether AT&T's action was legal. The telephone company could not argue that it believed that entrants were cream skimming or that the FCC so believed. It had to demonstrate that they were, in fact, cream skimming. As the judge said in a parenthetical remark, "the existence of the economies of scale, general cost differentials, or threats of cream skimming have yet to be proved, as they must be if defendants are to show that their struggle against interconnection has in fact been reasonable under the standards of the Communication Act."[75]

Greene's opinion was intermediate and narrow, simply an argument that the government's case was not so weak that it could be rejected out of hand. AT&T had yet to have its chance to rebut the government's contentions. But the opinion demonstrated that the judge had shaped the case in his own mind and that he found important aspects of the government's charges congenial. Although he could no doubt be persuaded to reject the view of the telecommunications industry that he had developed, AT&T's task obviously was going to be difficult. The judicial path to a resolution was looking almost as thorny as the legislative trail. Trienens and Brown remained confident that if Judge Greene were to order a radical divestiture, his decision would be reversed on appeal. This process, however, would take years, during which time AT&T would be subject to uncer-

[74]Ibid., 1359.
[75]Ibid., 1360.

tainty about the eventual outcome. Uncertainty would inhibit planning within the firm and, equally important, would limit its ability to raise funds in the capital market. In addition, if the judge were to impose injunctive constraints on the Bell System that precluded its efficient operation, they might be more onerous than Packwood's bill without being vulnerable on appeal.[76]

Concerned about these unpleasant alternatives, Brown looked again to the executive branch for a possible solution. In a September 17 memorandum to Secretary Baldrige, he reiterated AT&T's distress at the administration's apparent inability to pursue a single course: "Despite a valiant effort in July, the administration does not yet have control over its own policy for the telecommunications industry." After reviewing briefly the events that had led to the current situation, Brown offered "a way out" of the administration's "dilemma": a consent decree based on the bill nearing passage in the Senate. This, he said, would enable the Reagan administration "to attain control over the destiny of telecommunications policy." Hence began what came to be known in the company as "Quagmire II," the second major effort to settle out of court the differences between AT&T and the U.S. government.[77]

Brown's proposal soon found its way to the Justice Department. Baxter called Trienens on October 1, in the midst of the final negotiations over amendments to Packwood's bill, to suggest that they discuss a consent decree along the lines of the amended bill. Baxter said he could not be involved in negotiations before December 1. He needed to spend October and November on his other big case–the IBM suit–but he was willing to have his staff work on a draft. A preliminary meeting was held on October 6, at which both Trienens and Baxter were present, to discuss procedures for the negotiations. A working meeting between Kilpatric and McLean for AT&T and Ronald Carr and Richard Levine for the Department of Justice was held on October 9, but they did not have a copy of the Senate bill, and they agreed to meet the following week.

At the next meeting and at weekly meetings thereafter, these four men labored to produce a decree that would be acceptable to both sides. Even though Brown had found the Senate bill in its final, much-amended form to be at the outer limit of what AT&T could tolerate, Kilpatric and McLean tried to use the bill as a bulwark against even harsher restrictions that the Department of Justice might want to impose. Their concern turned out to be well founded. Carr and Levine did not want to be bound by the bill or by prior negotiations. They began to generate new provi-

[76]Trienens, interview, January 19, 1984, pp. 66–7.
[77]Charles L. Brown to Malcolm Baldrige, September 17, 1981. The discussions during August and September about a possible decree had hardly begun. The Senate bill had become the center of attention, and the August 7 draft by AT&T had languished.

sions that they insisted would be essential. Quagmire II grew deeper and more impenetrable. Kilpatric and McLean felt like Alice facing the Queen of Hearts: It was necessary to run very hard just to keep from falling behind.

Brown tried to prevent the quagmire from getting worse, working again through Baldrige. His memorandum to the Secretary of Commerce on October 21 said, "Negotiations for a Consent Decree are getting nowhere, initially because there is no priority of commitment by DOJ. But even if progress were being made toward drafting a document embracing the substantive provisions of S. 898, [Packwood's bill] negotiations would soon reach an impasse because Baxter, in a new split with the Administration, has attacked S. 898 as unsatisfactory in important respects." Brown reminded Baldrige of Baxter's testimony on August 6 that he was "content, enthusiastic even" about the pending legislation. Yet Baxter had announced on October 8 that he would not dismiss the case even if the Senate bill as amended was signed by the President. "Why?" asked Brown. "Because the interconnection amendment which the Administration sent to the Senate, and was adopted, was incomplete. And, of greatest significance, because a third amendment dealing with the inner workings of Bell Laboratories and AT&T's General Departments was limited to relations with the Fully Separated Affiliate and thus did not affect technological integration (as between AT&T, Bell Labs and Western Electric) on the regulated side of the business. This third amendment, in the form advocated by Baxter, would have erected a wall through the middle of Bell Labs, destroyed the technological integration of Bell's regulated activities and had the practical effect of divestiture."

The outlook, Brown said, was disheartening. "There is no basis for believing that Baxter will not generate more and more amendments beyond the Administration position." Quagmire II might then be even less acceptable than Packwood's bill – or even Judge Greene's decision. Brown ended his memorandum with a scenario that accurately forecast the course that the quagmire negotiations would follow: "If there were a single Administration position on telecommunications policy and the structure of AT&T, the substance could readily be taken from S. 898 and placed in Consent Decree form. But if Baxter continues to play his own game, it will imperil, if not destroy, hopes of either legislation or a Consent Decree containing substantive provisions consistent with the Administration position."[78]

The quagmire negotiations ground ahead on this course during October and November while AT&T presented its case to Judge Greene. Both McLean and Kilpatric were involved in the trial, and the negotiations

---

[78]Howard J. Trienens, "Chronology of Negotiations"; Charles L. Brown to Malcolm Baldrige, October 16, 1981.

generally were held in the late afternoons after the court sessions were over. It would have been difficult for AT&T to select a separate negotiating staff: Kilpatric, in particular, had been engaged in this process from the beginning, and it would have been impossible to replace him with someone equally knowledgeable. Although the Justice Department's representatives, Carr and Levine, were not directly involved with the litigation, they were reading testimony and helping their colleagues with cross-examination. The descent into Quagmire II was thus conducted at a stately pace.[79]

As the negotiations pushed along, the situation grew ever more hazardous for AT&T. Morris Tanenbaum, AT&T executive vice president, was the apostle of integration within AT&T's top management. Suggestions from the Justice Department were taken to him for technical advice and suggestions for compromises that would preserve the advantages of the Bell System's integrated structure.[80] AT&T was struggling to keep both its vertical and its horizontal integration. But since that structure was responsible, Carr and Levine thought, for abuses of power, the Justice Department negotiators kept trying to draft injunctions that would, in Levine's words, "prevent . . . all meaningful possibilities of abuse." The resulting draft for a decree soon threatened to be so restrictive that it would deprive AT&T of any of the advantages of integration. Levine felt very uncomfortable with this situation. He imagined that his brain waves were going out to the AT&T representatives, saying, "Put the company out of its misery. Do the right thing. Agree with the Justice Department [and accept divestiture]." But Kilpatric and McLean did not respond, and the decree became so long that it resembled a telephone book.[81]

Levine would have been surprised to know just how seriously AT&T was considering that option. The bind on the Bell System was getting tighter every day. The "telephone book" decree was becoming so bulky and so restrictive that Brown had to doubt whether AT&T could accept it and successfully enter the information age to compete with such corporate powerhouses as IBM and Xerox. Meanwhile, the trial was winding down. AT&T had begun to present its case on August 3. It had been at it for four months by the end of November and, under Greene's prodding, was substantially finished. There were more witnesses to come, primarily those from the Department of Defense and Brown himself. But the main structure of the company's defense was clear, and the Bell System's leaders had good reason to believe that the judge's final decision would be even less appealing than Quagmire II. Nor did the legislative route look promising. The Senate bill went to the limit of what Brown thought AT&T

[79]Jim G. Kilpatric, interview, May 9, 1984, pp. 43–5.
[80]Brown, interview, September 5, 1985, pp. 58–9.
[81]Levine, interview, June 12, 1984, pp. 37–8.

could accept, and the House was not yet even considering a counterpart. When it did, the odds were that the measure would become more, not less, cumbersome to the telephone company.

In September, before the Senate bill was passed, Trienens had outlined for Brown the four options that he and the company faced. The first was a consent decree along the lines of the telephone book decree. This decree would not require any divestiture but would contain the injunctive provisions that were of such concern to Brown. It would replace the 1956 Consent Decree and result in the dismissal of the antitrust suit. The second alternative followed the lines of Trienens's suggestion to Brown and the CEO's presentation to the board of directors a year earlier. It was a consent decree similar to the Department of Justice's April relief contentions: Divestiture of the local exchange network; abandonment of the prior Decree and the current suit; and provision that the decree would terminate if a bill restructuring AT&T was signed by the President before divestiture actually began. The third alternative was to have the trial go on, but with a stipulation, agreed upon with Baxter, that relief would be all or nothing—either the divestiture requested by the Justice Department or no divestiture at all. The stipulation would keep Judge Greene from choosing his own course and ordering the divestiture of Western Electric or imposing operating restrictions. The fourth alternative was simply to let the trial proceed and for AT&T to take its chances with Judge Greene and the appellate courts.

The alternatives seem to have been listed in the order of Trienens's preference, but he noted that any suggestion that the company might accept the second option, divestiture, would destroy AT&T's bargaining position on the first alternative—the telephone book decree. Trienens thought this was the right way to play the poker game, not revealing your hand, but he wondered if the stakes were so high that the company dared not play it right. The firm had already drafted for internal study a consent decree based on Baxter's style of divestiture, but no hint of this had been given to the Justice Department.[82]

One of the alternatives, the Quagmire II negotiations, was becoming steadily less appealing to AT&T. Typical of the questions that seemed threatening to Brown was the debate over equal access. Baxter wanted to be able to specify in physical terms the precise point at which connections would take place. Like most people who have an intensely ideological orientation, he wanted to be absolutely certain that the policy adopted was logical, precise, and set in stone. But as Irwin Dorros, an AT&T assistant vice president, pointed out to Tanenbaum when he analyzed this

---

[82]Unsigned "Memorandum for Mr. Brown," September 27, 1981; Jim G. Kilpatric and Robert D. McLean, "*Outline*," March 21, 1984, p. 19; Discussion Draft—Not a Proposal 5/1/81, "Final Judgment."

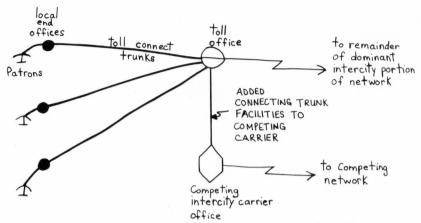

Figure 11. Connection at toll office. (Source: AT&T memorandum, "Equal Access by Intercity Carriers to Its Patrons," October 27, 1981.)

problem from a technical point of view, Baxter's proposal was unworkable. It simply would not fit the way the telephone system actually operated. Dorros prepared a memorandum – containing three hand-drawn figures that are reproduced here – that analyzed the difficulties.[83] Figure 11 shows Baxter's proposed arrangement. The toll office noted in that figure is the lowest-level toll switch, also referred to as a "Class 4" switch. Baxter wanted only a single connection between the individual exchange offices and the Class 4 switch. Traffic would be divided between AT&T and other carriers as it reached the Class 4 switch. In Baxter's terms, this was at the back of the switch, that is, before the switching function took place. He wanted the connection at this precise point because he thought that the other common carriers would have insufficient traffic on each of the trunks connecting to the local end offices to enjoy the economies of scale that benefited AT&T. In order to promote competition, he wanted to make the connection at the point where the traffic was heavy enough for all of the carriers to have roughly equal costs.

But as Dorros and others at AT&T knew, the Class 4 switch was not an isolated physical entity. It was only one function of a complex computer that provided tandem switching of local calls as well as higher-order processing of intercity calls (that is, Class 3 and above switching functions). It would be difficult to allocate the common costs for the switch, its mainte-

---

[83]Irwin Dorros, memorandum, "Equal Access By Intercity Carriers to Its Patrons," October 27, 1981.

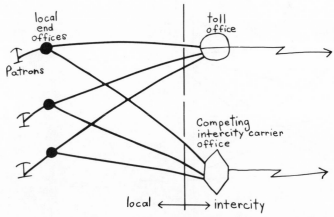

Figure 12. True equality: each carrier connects to each end office. (Source: AT&T memorandum, "Equal Access by Intercity Carriers to Its Patrons," October 27, 1981.)

nance, and its housing. Any allocation scheme would generate controversy among the several carriers. In addition, it would be difficult to improve a shared switch because agreement on any changes would have to be negotiated among the parties jointly administering the equipment.

These problems of shared control were joined by another: Dividing the network within the Class 4 switch would make it difficult to distinguish between the activities of AT&T and those of its competitors. In Dorros's words, "It forever blurs our attempt to define a bright line between local access and intercity networks." The specter of uncontrollable service degradation was horrifying to the engineers of the Bell System. If, for example, one of the competitors were to have a promotion that increased its traffic to the toll switch and the company had not made appropriate arrangements in advance, the resulting congestion would create trouble both for its own customers and for those of AT&T. AT&T's engineers would be powerless to avoid such service difficulties for its patrons.

How was this problem to be solved? Dorros proposed that equal access could be handled as shown in Figure 12, in which each interexchange carrier connects to each end office. This would create true equality between the carriers because it would provide a truly symmetrical arrangement. But since Baxter had already contended that this setup would penalize smaller carriers, another possibility had to be explored. The Bell solution was to add the option, shown here as Figure 13, in which a carrier could connect to a tandem office instead of or in addition to connecting to local end offices. But Baxter objected to this latter solution on the grounds

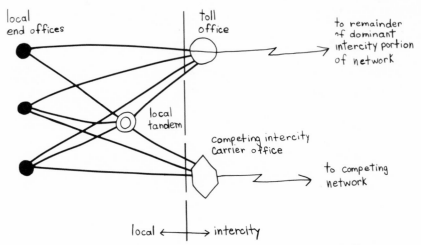

Figure 13. Added option: connection at local tandem. (Source: AT&T memorandum, "Equal Access by Intercity Carriers to Its Patrons," October 27, 1981.)

that connection through a local tandem would cost more than the facilities AT&T would enjoy. He also worried that the local companies would provide an inferior quality of access to competing carriers if the linkups were not required to be identical for all intercity carriers. It was this concern that led Baxter to want to specify the details of interconnection.

Dorros and his staff, mindful of the complexity of the intercity network and the rapidity with which the technology was changing, wanted a maximum degree of flexibility in the rules. There was, Dorros said, no "technical solution which will assure all intercity carriers equal treatment so long as one carrier is allowed to use a switch jointly for local and intercity service." As long as AT&T and the operating companies shared the use of these toll switches, no technical formula could cover the variety of situations that would arise. Dorros concluded, "An attractive solution appears to be the specification of price and quality equality rather than the constraining of technical serving arrangements." But Baxter and his staff were unwilling to approve this sort of flexible arrangement, suspicious that it would be used to AT&T's advantage.

Quagmire II began to generate a reaction within AT&T. A member of Dorros's staff, Joseph Weber (director of technical standards and regulatory planning), reviewed a variety of the provisions in the proposed decree and concluded, "I think at this point the warning must be raised that we may be heading into a massive straight-jacket which will make the network almost inoperable in the future and weigh this against the penalties to the public and to ourselves of some degree of divestiture." Weber

Reaching agreement

outlined what he thought a solution along those lines should be. Trienens
thought it was important enough to forward the proposal to Brown.[84]

In his accompanying memorandum to Brown, Trienens reviewed the
two items that were still bones of contention in Quagmire II: the interconnection restrictions analyzed by Dorros and Weber and the rules that
would erect the Chinese wall through Bell Labs. Trienens was not sanguine about the future course that these negotiations were likely to follow.
Without giving up on Quagmire II, Trienens wanted to consider what
would happen if the discussions failed to produce a consent decree with
which AT&T could live. In effect, two of Trienens's four options were
being eliminated, leaving a choice between divestiture of the operating
companies and whatever decision Judge Greene might reach.

The judge–AT&T's lawyers thought–was continuing to lean against the
company. The defense had been painting a picture of a recent history far
different from the one described by the Justice Department. Regulation–
by the FCC and state commissions–not AT&T, was the dominant feature.
The regulators had first barred competition, then admitted it, and had
proceeded to make life so confusing and difficult for the telephone company
that a reasoned response was almost impossible. AT&T did have difficulty
learning to live in its new environment–and found it hard even to learn
exactly what its changing environment was–but these problems were transitional and by 1981 past history. Surely it was not illegal for deButts and
other Bell System executives to have expressed their opinions about these
changes.[85] Surely the actions of the past provided no reason to restructure
AT&T for the future. Judge Greene heard all of these arguments, but his
treatment of the Bell witnesses did not suggest that he was adopting them.
As AT&T's lawyers tried to read the outcome of the trial in the tea leaves,
they became increasingly depressed. They doubted that Greene would
break up the telephone network or that the Supreme Court would sustain
him if he did. Instead they became increasingly concerned that he would
order the divestiture not imposed in 1956: Western Electric and some or all
of Bell Labs. Brown and Tanenbaum considered that the worst possible
outcome.

The lawyers tested their perception of the courtroom drama by asking
Michael Boudin of the Washington law firm Covington and Burling to
review some of the legal materials generated by the case, the trial transcript, and the experience of the trial attorneys. Boudin, sifting the clues to
Judge Greene's intentions, reported back that the judge could easily find

[84]Joseph H. Weber to Irwin Dorros, November 4, 1981; Howard J. Trienens to Charles L.
Brown, November 14, 1981.
[85]They were protected under the Noerr-Pennington doctrine, as Judge Greene had ruled in
his interim opinion. Judge Greene, Opinion, September 11, 1981, US v. AT&T, CA No.
74–1698 (D.D.C.), 524 F. Supp. 1336 at 1363.

for the plaintiffs and order divestiture of Western Electric and Bell Labs. As a result, the trial attorneys presented increased evidence of the benefits of AT&T's vertical integration to Judge Greene, but they were not sanguine about its effects. Greene seemed to have decided that big is bad and foreclosure of opportunity is bad. AT&T was on trial, not the FCC. He was not responsive to the ideas about the efficiency of vertical integration that animated both Brown and Baxter.[86] This was troublesome enough, but the lawyers for AT&T also had to consider the prospect that Greene's decision would be accompanied by restrictive legislation or FCC regulations that would further impede the operation of a truncated AT&T. Faced with this unpalatable possibility, Trienens again turned his thoughts to a negotiated divestiture. The Assistant Attorney General, he said, would jump at a consent decree along the lines of the April 7 relief proposals.[87]

How could such a position be reconciled with AT&T's interests? As Trienens saw it, ever since deButts's NARUC speech in 1973, AT&T had maintained that telecommunications policy should be made in Congress. A divestiture consent decree would facilitate congressional action by terminating the legal process and by providing a specific alternative to which a congressional bill could be compared. Trienens had in mind a decree that would no longer apply if legislation was signed into law before divestiture actually began. It would set a deadline for congressional action.

Although he didn't express it this way, the divestiture decree, in Trienens's view, would terminate the separations process and return telephone accounting to a board-to-board basis. AT&T would structure the operating companies to conform to state boundaries. The FCC's jurisdiction would be limited to interstate service (not to interexchange service, as the Senate bill had provided). With the end of separations charges and with state telephone companies, each state's public utility commissioners could choose the kind of service they wanted. Weaning the local companies away from their dependence on AT&T as the source of equity capital, Trienens believed, would force the state utility commissioners to allow the companies to earn enough to attract capital on their own. This would increase substantially the returns to AT&T's stockholders on their local exchange investment.

A consent decree of this sort would also prevent the fragmentation of local companies envisaged by the Senate bill. Instead of trying to split the activities of the local companies between regulated and unregulated activi-

[86]Robert D. McLean, interview, September 19, 1984, pp. 66–70; Jim G. Kilpatric and Robert D. McLean, "Outline," March 21, 1984, p. 30–31.
    After the trial, Judge Greene maintained that he had not made up his mind. See Stuart Gannes, "The Judge Who's Reshaping the Phone Business," Fortune, April 1, 1985, p. 134.
[87]Howard J. Trienens to Charles L. Brown, November 14, 1981.

ties, it would provide for unitary operating companies completely within state jurisdictions. These companies would be able to provide communications services and customer premises equipment. Because of their limited geographic scope, they would not raise questions about a monopoly of customer premises equipment.[88]

Perhaps because it was unnecessary to do so, Trienens did not point out to Brown that an AT&T that no longer owned the operating companies and was no longer encumbered by the 1956 Consent Decree or by the complex rules in the telephone book decree – the "new" AT&T – would be well positioned for competition in the information age. It would be a vertically integrated corporation with significant research and manufacturing capabilities. AT&T in this form would be somewhat removed from the public policy spotlight because it would no longer be the largest corporation in the world. It would be able to look forward to even further deregulation and might at last be able to compete as it had wanted to for some years "on a level field." Brown and Trienens had discussed all of these aspects of the decision on previous occasions. Now they began to edge toward the conclusion that Brown should opt for divestiture, accept the trauma of surrendering responsibility for the national network, and abandon forever the Bell System that Theodore Vail had created.

Brown and Baxter play the final hand

As AT&T's list of alternatives grew shorter, Howard Trienens – the man who was unfazed by gordian knots – again developed the options. In December 1981 he presented a "status quo option" to the Office of the Chairman. That was the fourth and final possibility Trienens had described in his September memo to Brown. It called on AT&T to follow the case to its conclusion. Legislation for the industry might be passed in the meantime, but AT&T would merely stay on course and await the outcome. Trienens argued for a short time horizon. AT&T could run for another five years just as it was. No one knew what Judge Greene was going to do, but his decision could be appealed in any case, and the more drastic the decision was, the more likely that an appellate court would "goof around with it" for another year or two. Then the Supreme Court would review it. So, Trienens concluded wryly, "We've got a five year pass."

Looking around at the men in the room, the general counsel made the point that none of them were going to be there for more than about five years. Why not, like Louis XIV, operate for the present? The idea was not

[88]Ibid.

presented as reasonable or responsible; the objective was to move forward the consideration of the firm's alternatives. The proposal certainly achieved that goal. Brown, Olson, and the others went up like a sky-rocket. Everything was changing, they said. Markets were changing, technology was changing, AT&T was under all kinds of pressure. The present situation was intolerable. The status quo option was unacceptable.[89]

Trienens's first option, a decree or a law embodying regulation without divestiture, looked by December even less promising than it had in the fall. The House had yet to act, but position papers written by Congressman Wirth's staff that fall suggested strongly that the House measure would be far less acceptable to AT&T than the Senate's. Billed as the "first comprehensive review of competition in the telecommunications industry ever undertaken by the Committee . . . or any other Federal agency in recent years," the papers identified the Bell System as the primary barrier to entry in the industry. Woven through the specific issues was a central concern about the sheer size of AT&T. The size and power issue had been implicit in many of the congressional pronouncements; it was explicit among Wirth's staff.[90] The telephone book decree had meanwhile become so detailed and onerous to AT&T that even though the two sides were within striking distance of a final decree, Trienens thought that the complex document promised more trouble than relief. Brown agreed.

Then, on December 10, Wirth dropped the other shoe. He introduced a bill into the House for consideration in early 1982. This proposal tipped the scales for Brown, leaving him virtually no choice but to pursue the divestiture option. In addition to the constraints already in the Senate bill, Wirth's bill gave the FCC regulatory authority over the Bell System's competitive as well as its monopoly activities. Bell would be forced to buy 30 percent of its equipment outside the System, and users of Bell-embedded terminal equipment would have new rights. In short, AT&T would have far less room to compete than under the Senate bill.[91] AT&T's competitors promptly endorsed the measure, but Brown decided that Wirth's bill slammed the door on the legislative option. Any bill that Congress might pass would be a compromise between the House and Senate measures. The results, Brown thought, would leave the Bell System encased in an unwieldy regulatory system that would make it

---

[89]Trienens, interview, January 19, 1984, p. 21.
[90]97th Congress, 1st Session, House, Committee on Energy and Commerce, "Telecommunications in Transition: The Status of Competition in the Telecommunications Industry," a report by the Majority Staff of the House Subcommittee on Telecommunications, Consumer Protection, and Finance, November 3, 1981, pp. III, 130–31.
[91]97th Congress, 1st Session, House, Committee on Energy and Commerce, Subcommittee on Telecommunications, Consumer Protection, and Finance, H.R. 5158, "Telecommunications Act of 1982," introduced December 10, 1981.

impossible to run the company efficiently. Harsh as it was, Baxter's divestiture was now the best option.[92]

At Brown's request, Howard Trienens went to Washington to test the water on a divestiture consent decree. He needed to approach this task with caution. The only possibility worse than divestiture was to have that option go the way of Quagmire II. Trienens called Baxter on December 10, the same day Wirth introduced his bill, and asked if the two of them could meet. They got together in Baxter's office the following day, but moved to Trienens's suite at the Madison Hotel to escape the bedlam at the Justice Department. Over club sandwiches sent up to the suite, they held the only meeting they had outside the Department of Justice.[93] Because the telephone book decree was almost completely drafted, they talked about the logistics of implementing it. This would involve some careful legal dancing. An essential function of any new consent decree was to supersede the 1956 Decree. But while the current case was in a Washington court under Judge Greene, the 1956 Decree was in a New Jersey court under the jurisdiction of Judge Biunno. Judge Biunno had recently – September 23 – decided that it was legal under the 1956 Decree for AT&T to offer enhanced services and customer premises equipment in accord with the FCC's *Computer II* decision. The Justice Department had appealed, and the appeal was currently pending in the Third Circuit. The appeal had removed the 1956 Decree from Judge Biunno's jurisdiction, making it impossible for him to do anything with it. The legal situation was a tangled mess.[94]

The Justice Department was not eager to have Judge Biunno active in the settlement because it disagreed with his handling of the *Computer II* decision. Baxter also did not want to appear to be running away from Greene, and AT&T agreed to locate the new decree in Judge Greene's court. The questions of how to do this and what latitude Judge Greene would have after it was done occupied Baxter and Trienens as they ate their club sandwiches.

Finished with lunch, Trienens casually reminisced with Baxter about Quagmire II. They talked about how they had entered those negotiations, and Trienens remarked that he supposed Baxter still preferred his original idea of complete divestiture. Baxter made it perfectly clear that he did. As recently as November 4, Baxter had reiterated this point of view before a

[92]"New Coalition of AT&T Competitors, Users Gather Funds to Campaign for Wirth Bill; AT&T Says Bill Permits FCC to Manage Competition; Rodino Comments on 1980 Referral," *Telecommunications Reports*, Vol. 48, No. 1 (January 4, 1982), pp. 4–5.

[93]Baxter, interview, February 2, 1984, p. 20; Trienens, interview, January 19, 1984, pp. 36–8.

[94]*US v. Western Electric Co.*, CA No. 17–49, U.S. Dist. Ct., Dist. of New Jersey, Judge Biunno, *Order Regarding Motion for Construction*, September 23, 1981; *Notice of Appeal of United States of America*, No. 81–2837 (Ct. of App., 3rd Cir.), October 30, 1981.

House subcommittee.[95] He told Trienens that he of course preferred divestiture, but, he added, that was just too bad – the telephone book decree might work. Trienens asked, if they agreed on divestiture, would the 1956 Consent Decree go, "lock, stock, and barrel?" Baxter said that as far as he was concerned, yes. The brief discussion ended on that note.[96]

This short, seemingly incidental exchange heralded a startling shift in the case of *United States* v. *AT&T*. Howard Trienens was not making idle conversation. Brown and he had planned the question to be sure that the clear-cut divestiture option was still available and completely separable from Quagmire II. It was, and Trienens and Baxter had in effect begun their negotiations. AT&T's message was received. Baxter did not try to alter the negotiations on Quagmire II, but he held himself in readiness for AT&T's next move.

Brown pondered Baxter's response over the following weekend. He had a very hard choice to make. He recalled that he had never heard a single elected government official advocate breaking up the Bell System. The Presidents under whom the case had been brought and continued had never taken that position, and Congress had dealt with a series of bills that, with one early exception, all tried to introduce competition into telecommunications while leaving AT&T's integrated structure intact. Even Congressman Wirth, whose staff identified AT&T's size as a major barrier to entry, had not advocated divestiture. It was bizarre, Brown reflected, that a policy choice of this magnitude would be made without active support from officials higher than the Assistant Attorney General for Antitrust. Given the magnitude of the decision he was about to make and its importance to the nation, Brown could not believe that the top officials in the United States government had defaulted to a political appointee at Baxter's level.[97]

He could not be certain what would happen in Judge Greene's courtroom, but the news from that front was not encouraging. The judge had become testier and testier as the company presented its defense and its corporate leaders.[98] He seemed to have received with favor the government's contention that AT&T had foreclosed the market for telecommunications equipment (both within the Bell System and at customers' premises), and Brown thought that Greene would probably deal with this problem simply and directly, by forcing AT&T to divest Western Electric. There was no way to know if that decision would be upheld by the Supreme Court,

[95] 97th Congress, 1st Session, House, Subcommittee of the Committee on Government Operations, Hearing, "Departments of Justice and Defense and Antitrust Litigation," statement of William F. Baxter, November 4, 1981, pp. 4–5, 37.
[96] Baxter, interview, February 2, 1984, p. 20; Trienens, interview, January 19, 1984, pp. 38–39.
[97] Brown, interview, June 9, 1984, pp. 2–6.
[98] N.B.: *US* v. *AT&T*, CA No. 74–1698 (D.D.C.), Transcripts of Proceedings; Kilpatric, interview, May 9, 1984, p. 73.

but that possibility might pose a major threat to Brown's plans for the corporation's future. He had no doubt that the key to AT&T's success over the previous century had been its vertical integration. He had opposed the early relief proposals from the Justice Department on the grounds that Western Electric and Bell Labs were vital to AT&T. The negotiations on Quagmire II were stalled, largely on the issue of internal communications between Bell Labs and the rest of AT&T. Brown did not want Greene to have the opportunity to endanger AT&T's technological capabilities when the Labs and Western were vital to the firm's long-run strategy.

The issue was immediate for AT&T's CEO. He was scheduled to testify for AT&T after the Christmas holidays, and his testimony was going to be that the divestiture proposed by the government would be a disaster. In effect, his own testimony would foreclose the divestiture option, since Brown was not about to contradict his own testimony by later accepting Baxter's terms. The approaching testimony of witnesses for AT&T from the Defense Department also posed problems. Baxter was extremely sensitive to what he regarded as the incestuous relations between AT&T and the Department of Defense. Although AT&T wanted Judge Greene to hear the Defense Department's view that the structural integrity of AT&T was vital to the nation's security, it had reason to be concerned about how the Department of Justice and the judge would react to that testimony. Earlier, when AT&T had introduced in evidence the Defense Department's June report, Judge Greene had inquired closely into the report's origins. After all, the government – not just the Justice Department – was the plaintiff in this suit, and divisions within the government were not appropriately resolved in the courtroom. There was every prospect that Defense Department witnesses testifying for AT&T would be cross-examined roughly on the suspicion that their views had been ghost-written by AT&T.[99]

Hugel reported back to Brown at this time that the company could handle divestiture along Baxter's lines. Drawing on his original consideration of an inter–intra split and his planning for Van Deerlin's bill and *Computer II*, Hugel had analyzed the management problems that would be posed by spinning off intrastate service. Three years earlier, he had considered the costs of a complete split to be prohibitive; in 1981 he assessed them as reasonable. Then he had kept his work secret; now he talked to the chairman of the board. Hugel assured Brown that the divestiture option was within Bell System's managerial capability.[100]

Brown then made the biggest single decision that an American business-

[99]*US* v. *AT&T*, CA No. 74–1698 (D.D.C.), August 6, 1981, Tr. 12070–9; Baxter, interview, February 2, 1984, pp. 24–6 and December 12, 1985, p. 40; Brown, interview, May 29, 1984, p. 45.

[100]Anticipated costs were lower in 1981 because Hugel allowed the separated companies to use some facilities jointly, a possibility not considered earlier. In addition, Brown was not deButts, and 1981 was not 1978. Author's conversations with Howard J. Trienens and Charles L. Brown, August 1986, and telephone call to Charles Hugel, October 1986.

man has had to make in the last century. With his back against the wall, he decided, after a weekend of pondering the issue, to deal with Baxter on his terms. He accepted the fact that his best option was to break up the Bell System. He spent the first few days of the next week walking the idea around his top leadership. He talked individually with the members of the Office of the Chairman: Cashel, Ellinghaus, Olson, and Tanenbaum. Then he gathered them with Hough, Hugel, and Whalen at the company's facility in Basking Ridge, New Jersey, for a collective discussion. They were not happy, but they supported Brown's decision.[101]

A choice as important as this clearly had to be presented to the board of directors, which was meeting that Wednesday. Brown scrapped the prepared agenda–a report on marketing–and presented his decision to accept Baxter's terms and to divest the operating companies. The board had been carefully prepared for this possibility by extensive prior discussions over the previous year and a half. Nevertheless, the reality of Brown's decision was sobering. He was peppered with questions, which he took his customary care in answering. After a meeting that lasted no more than the normal two hours, the board approved the course Brown had selected. The unthinkable was about to happen. No one had much to say, but one new director emerged from this, his first meeting, and asked: "That was terrific; what are you going to do for excitement next month?"[102]

Trienens phoned Baxter that afternoon. He recalled their conversation of the prior Friday and a claim Baxter had made that even though the telephone book decree had grown to be a hundred-page document, a divestiture decree could be written in two. Trienens expressed interest in a two-page document and asked Baxter if he would draft one. Yes, Baxter could do that.[103] In fact, that very afternoon, while the Justice Department's press corps was giving a Christmas party, Baxter plowed into the room looking for his deputy, Ronald Carr. Baxter is not the kind of person to look frantic, but Richard Levine thought he appeared more purposeful than a Christmas party warranted. He was. Baxter found Carr, and they disappeared from the party. As the party began to break up, Levine followed them to Baxter's office and asked what was happening. Baxter and Carr replied that they were glad Levine had come: Trienens had said it would be worthwhile to draft a divestiture decree. Levine then typed a one-page prospectus, and the three men put together a draft agreement over the weekend.[104]

[101]Brown, interview, September 5, 1985, pp. 64–5; William M. Ellinghaus, interview, June 13, 1985, p. 49. Trienens, of course, was also a member of the Office of the Chairman.
[102]"AT&T's Accord–How the Bell System, Government Reached Divestiture Agreement," *The Wall Street Journal*, January 19, 1981, p. 1; Trienens, interview, January 19, 1984, p. 44; Donald S. Perkins, interview, November 25, 1986, pp. 16–17.
[103]Trienens, interview, January 19, 1984, pp. 46–7.
[104]Levine, interview, June 12, 1984, p. 42.

Since Baxter had boasted that a divestiture decree could be done in two pages, Levine tried to keep the draft within that limit. He almost succeeded. The decree was only three pages long, if you did not count the two separately numbered appendices of five and six pages. Who would niggle about the appendices, given the momentous nature of the decision that was being made in this modest document? Baxter sent his draft of the divestiture decree to Trienens on Monday, December 21. An accompanying hand-written note said,

> A draft, as promised. Everything is negotiable except the concept of separating the local exchange function and then confining the BOC's [Bell Operating Companies] to local exchange functions. The biggest problem I see is how to handle the CPE [customer premises equipment] installed base. I believe this is a substantial political problem for us both as well as a technical problem for me. Regards, Bill.[105]

The decree was titled a "Modification of Final Judgment," that is, a modification of the 1956 Final Judgment (Consent Decree). It consisted of two short sections. After a brief statement that the Consent Decree of January 14, 1956, "is hereby vacated in its entirety and replaced by the following terms and provisions," the first section dealt with AT&T's reorganization. It required the company to file a plan of reorganization that provided for the transfer from AT&T to the Bell Operating Companies of the physical plant, personnel, and rights to technical information needed to provide local exchange telephone service.[106] The license contracts and the standard supply contracts between the operating companies, AT&T, and Western Electric were to be terminated. Ownership of the operating companies was to be transferred to AT&T's stockholders. AT&T was required to take all of the steps needed to ensure that the operating companies would be able to provide equal access to all interexchange carriers.

The second section required the operating companies to provide equal access. It stipulated that they could not discriminate between AT&T and other firms in a wide variety of activities – including purchases and interconnection. It restricted the divested operating companies' activities: They could not provide interexchange long distance service or electronic information services, nor could they manufacture or provide telecommunications products or customer premises equipment (except that they could service the customers' equipment that was already installed). The first

[105]William F. Baxter to Howard J. Trienens, memorandum transmitting a draft of the divestiture decree, December 21, 1981.
[106]The decree allowed shared use of some buildings and switching equipment when a complete separation of function would have meant extensive duplication of facilities. The possibility of contracting for joint use avoided a huge capital expense that had made divestiture seem so impractical to Hugel in 1978 and to the Defense Department in 1981.

The fall of the Bell System

appendix defined the terms used in the document, and the second described in greater detail the equal access requirements.

Although most of these provisions (including the one on equal access) had already been the subject of extensive negotiations, Trienens had wanted the Department of Justice to write the decree for several reasons. Because AT&T was essentially agreeing to the Justice Department's prayer for relief, there was a certain logic in having the department write its own solution. It was also preferable, from a political point of view, to have the agreement based on a document written in the first instance by the Department of Justice. Trienens was not eager to evoke any echoes of 1956. Finally, given AT&T's earlier experiences with Quagmire II, it is understandable that Trienens would want to have the Justice Department initially committed on paper to a relatively simple agreement.[107]

Although the decree was indeed simple, the path to final agreement was complex. Trienens, Levine, and some of the other negotiators had their second Christmas vacation in a row ruined by the attempt to settle the case. Trienens started by marking up Baxter's draft and sending it back the same day. His suggested changes provided the topics for negotiation over the next week. Paradoxically, these negotiations coexisted with the continuing Quagmire II discussions. Levine was consequently in the position of negotiating with McLean and Kilpatric on the regulatory decree during the day and then getting together with Carr, Baxter, and Trienens on the divestiture decree in the evening. He was like an actor who plays in one play at night and rehearses for another during the day.[108]

As the divestiture negotiations gathered steam, they focused on two substantive issues. The first involved the treatment of existing terminal equipment. Baxter had suggested that the operating companies maintain the existing equipment, even though they were barred from selling or servicing new terminals. Trienens countered that this bifurcation of responsibility to existing customers made no sense. AT&T should service all of the equipment. Baxter readily acceded.

The second and knottier problem involved equal exchange access. Agreement had never been reached on the wording of Baxter II, which the Assistant Attorney General insisted be incorporated in any decree. There was an issue of substance: Where and at what cost did you cut the network? There was also an issue of process: How much control should

[107]Trienens, interview, January 19, 1984, pp. 46–7.
[108]Levine, interview, June 12, 1984, pp. 43–4. AT&T's last witnesses in the trial appeared on December 18, 1981, the last trial day before a two-week holiday recess. Some AT&T witnesses had presented testimony on the importance of the Bell System's integrated structure prior to the recess, but several key witnesses on this point were to appear after the trial resumed. These witnesses included Brown, AT&T network engineering vice president Irwin Dorros, AT&T treasurer Virginia Dwyer, and economists Paul MacAvoy and David Teece. Dorros had submitted extensive written testimony on the costs of a breakup of the Bell System.

the federal government have over the operation of the telephone system, and how much control should the telephone company have? The discussions took place at the first level, but the question of control inevitably lurked behind the negotiations. Friday was Christmas, and AT&T's representatives spent their weekend talking about the access issue. Trienens and Baxter spoke on the telephone on Monday without reaching agreement. They met on Tuesday, again without striking a deal. Brown interrupted his Florida vacation to attend a meeting on Wednesday, December 30, to try to settle the access matter and to deal with the restrictions Baxter wanted to impose on the operating companies' activities.

These provisions went to the heart of Baxter's theory, which was based on the separation of regulated and competitive activities into different firms. It was vital to him that the operating companies provide only regulated services. If they provided competitive services as well, they would then be back in the position that the Justice Department was accusing AT&T of occupying. They would have the opportunity and the motive to cross-subsidize their competitive activities with revenue from their regulated services. Brown returned to Florida without being convinced of the wisdom of restricting the operating companies in this manner, but he understood that this provision was an integral part of Baxter's theory. There was no way to have the divestiture decree without that restriction, and Brown wanted a decree.[109]

Equal access, however, continued to present serious problems. Brown explained to Baxter that he, Baxter, was very close to getting everything he wanted, but that he was fooling around with something he really did not understand. Brown said that a precise physical specification of where and how access would take place was impossible to implement. Although time was running out on the negotiations, the two men were unable to bridge their differences on the access problem.[110] Baxter was about to go skiing in Utah, and he prepared to leave with this issue unsettled. The final version of the telephone book decree had been served on AT&T, and on December 31 the Department of Justice issued a press release saying that it was negotiating with the company.[111]

But it was unclear at this juncture whether the final roadblock could be cleared. Baxter's draft of the proposed divestiture decree incorporated the language of the Senate bill, which referred to specific facilities, defined as including a point of concentration above the local end office. The draft stated that the "point of concentration of interexchange traffic above local end offices . . . shall be located at those switches referred to by defendants as Class 4 switches, and the trunking used to transmit interexchange telecommunications between end offices and a point of concentration

[109]Trienens, interview, January 19, 1984, pp. 47–8; Brown, interview, May 29, 1984, p. 27.
[110]Brown, interview, May 29, 1984, p. 61.
[111]Department of Justice press release, December 31, 1981 (DOJ 1982-01).

specified in this paragraph shall be shared by all carriers."[112] This was the physical boundary and traffic mixing that AT&T's Dorros had analyzed two months before when Packwood's bill was being considered. It was no more workable now than it had been then, and Brown would not impose an unmanageable requirement on the divested operating companies. When Levine tried his hand at drafting a more acceptable provision, he too struck out. His revisions reached Brown and Trienens on January 1, 1982, the same day the newspapers reported that negotiations were taking place. As both men quickly determined, Levine's proposal was still written in terms of physical facilities. It would not do. Brown called Baxter, who was about to depart for his week-long skiing trip, to say that the revised draft was unacceptable. Baxter, true to the form he had displayed since his first day on the job, replied, "Fine, see you in court." He left town for Utah and the ski slopes.[113]

Although Baxter seemed unwilling to blink, his position was in reality weaker than Brown's. Baxter did not want the trial to end and Judge Greene to decide how the telecommunications industry should be structured. That seemed likely to result in a resolution that would be far less attractive to Baxter than the divestiture decree. If the judge made his decision and the case was appealed, Baxter would probably not be around for the conclusion. Moreover, Baxter and his staff at the Justice Department were at a distinct disadvantage when it came to technical matters involving the way the network operated. Brown had spent most of his career in Long Lines and the operating companies. He spoke with a technical mastery Baxter could not hope to match.

Although the Assistant Attorney General was in Utah, he, Brown, and Trienens continued to discuss the access knot by phone. Brown pointed out yet again that there was no simple rule that would indicate how to draw the line where equal access should begin. The local companies should not be required to undertake a hopelessly difficult reengineering of their networks. There were too many local offices, too much geographical diversity, too much variation in the size of exchanges and metropolitan areas, for any simple rule like Baxter's to work. Brown wanted the decree to define equal exchange access in terms of service quality, not hardware: "Equal quality of transmission and equal probability of blocking." The decree should leave the decision on how to provide that service in the most efficient way to the individual operating companies.[114]

Baxter demurred. He insisted on his plan to specify the much discussed Class 4 switch as the point of entry. But the calls continued; one famous

[112]U.S. Department of Justice, December 21, 1981 draft, *Modification of Final Judgment*, Appendix 1, para. O.
[113]Brown, interview, May 29, 1984, pp. 61–3; Baxter, interview, February 2, 1984, p. 31.
[114]Brown, interview, May 29, 1984, p. 64.

call was made from a warming hut halfway down the mountain.[115] Brown assured Baxter that service would be supplied to all interexchange carriers on an equal price basis, and Trienens proposed legal language to guarantee it. If it were more expensive for the other common carriers, the operating companies would average the cost differences and charge all carriers the same. Whatever the physical facilities, all interexchange carriers would face the same charges for access. This would provide an incentive for the operating companies eventually to engineer the Bell System along lines similar to those that Baxter wanted. This was not as satisfying to Baxter as engineering the network himself, but it was an offer that he found difficult to refuse.

At last Baxter gave way. If it was impossible to define the rule in terms of hardware, then equal access would be defined in terms of service. He had so many misgivings about his concession that he could not sleep that night, but the agreement was completed. The offending references to the point of concentration above the local end office and the Class 4 switches were replaced in the draft decree by a statement that followed the exact lines – on the quality of service – that Brown had outlined. With other less significant changes, this was the Modification of Final Judgment that Baxter and Trienens would sign.[116]

At this point in the negotiations, only a small number of company and government officials knew what was happening. Brown set out to correct that situation, meeting secretly with the Bell Operating Company presidents on January 5. The traumatic meeting, held at AT&T's facility in Basking Ridge, New Jersey, was the first news the presidents had of the decree. They were sworn to secrecy and pointedly not provided with any written record of the proposed decree. They were being informed, not consulted. The presidents went into shock. Their System – almost a family – was being torn apart. They reacted as to the death of a close relative – with numbness, replaced over time by anger and frustration. Initially the presidents took the harsh news calmly, but their agitation spilled out into the corridors.[117]

Baxter received the redrafted decree on January 6. He called Trienens that morning from Utah to advise him that the papers were satisfactory and would be retyped for signing on January 8. Brown then headed to

[115]"How the Bell System, Government Reached Divestiture Agreement," *The Wall Street Journal*, January 19, 1982, p. 1. Baxter, interview, February 2, 1984, pp. 31–3.

[116]Levine, interview, June 12, 1984, p. 49; Baxter, interview, February 2, 1984, pp. 32–3; *US v. AT&T*, CA NO. 74-1698, *Modification of Final Judgment*, January 8, 1982, Sec. IV, F.

[117]Brown, interview, June 9, 1984, pp. 5–6 and September 5, 1985, p. 65; Ellinghaus, interview, June 13, 1985, pp. 48–50; Sharwell, interview, July 10, 1985, pp. 33–5. Sharwell remembers angry discussions at that meeting. John L. Clendenin, interview, November 22, 1985, p. 12a; Delbert C. Staley, interview, February 25, 1986, p. 4; William L. Weiss, interview, November 20, 1985, pp. 19–22.

Washington to tell the Reagan administration what happened. His first call was to Caspar Weinberger at the Department of Defense. Weinberger's office had informed Brown that the Secretary was busy, but Brown called from the airport. Weinberger came to the phone and said that he had someone important there.

Brown replied, "Cap, I've got to talk with you."

Weinberger explained, "You know I've done all I can on this case," and started to elaborate.

Brown interrupted. "Cap, I've settled this thing."

There was a long silence, and then Weinberger invited Brown over to talk.

Brown explained the settlement, emphasizing to Weinberger that there would be a central point of contact between the Defense Department and the operating companies. He assured Weinberger that AT&T would do everything possible to meet Defense's needs and provide for coordination in times of emergency. His intention was to make the new arrangement work.

Enjoining Weinberger to silence, Brown went off in search of Baldrige and Meese. The Secretary of Commerce was in New York, and Brown was unable to see him until the following day. He went to the airport in Baldrige's car and described the settlement as they were driven back into town. Baldrige had done everything he could to avoid this outcome; he said he was surprised and very sorry at the news. Later in the day, Meese reiterated these sentiments. Brown did not try to see President Reagan. Everyone assumed that the President was opposed to such an agreement, but a visit from Brown would have appeared to be a last-ditch attempt to get the government to drop the case. By that time, it was in no one's best interest.[118]

Baxter told Fielding about the settlement by phone that same morning, January 7. He called Fielding from the Salt Lake City airport and said that he proposed to settle the AT&T case. After only a respectable pause, Fielding said, "Is that what you recommend?" Baxter interpreted the question as the administration's effort to distance itself from his proposed settlement; that would protect both Baxter and the rest of the administration in the event of an inquiry into any political pressures behind the consent decree. He replied, "Yes." Fielding said, "Then that's what we'll do," and the conversation ended.[119]

When he arrived back in Washington late on the evening of Thursday, January 7, Baxter reviewed the papers that his staff had drawn up in conjunction with AT&T's lawyers. Everything was put in place for the

[118]Brown, interview, June 9, 1984, pp. 2–5.
[119]Baxter, interview, February 2, 1984, pp. 33–7.

intricate legal ballet of the following day. Baxter and Trienens met in Baxter's office at 8 A.M., signed the decree, and shook hands like tennis players who had just finished a match. McLean and Carr then flew with the signed decree to Trenton, New Jersey, where Judge Biunno still had jurisdiction over the 1956 Consent Decree. His previous decision – on AT&T's ability to operate a competitive subsidiary under *Computer II* – was under appeal in the Court of Appeals, limiting his ability to act. Consequently the lawyers arranged for three simultaneous filings. First, a Justice Department representative in Philadelphia would file in the Third Circuit for dismissal of the department's appeal of Judge Biunno's interpretation of the 1956 Consent Decree. Second, McLean and Carr would file the new decree with Judge Biunno and request the judge to transfer the 1949 case to Washington, that is, to Judge Greene's court. Third, the trial lawyers for AT&T and the Justice Department would take the stipulation dismissing the 1974 case to the District of Columbia courthouse and file it with Judge Greene. On cue, activated by phone calls from Washington to Philadelphia and Trenton, the Byzantine deed was done.[120]

This very complicated set of maneuvers was designed to accomplish a number of goals. It would give Biunno the power to make a decision about the 1956 Consent Decree so that the new decree could be substituted for it. It would move the new decree (which was entered as a revision of the 1956 Decree and therefore appeared to belong in Judge Biunno's court) down to Washington and to Judge Greene's court. It would dismiss the 1974 suit in a way that made the revision of the 1956 Decree serve as a settlement of that case – a settlement that logically should reside in Judge Greene's court.

But this arrangement was far too complicated. Judge Biunno did not wait for the remand from the Third Circuit to give him the authority, nor did he transfer the proposed modification of the 1956 Decree to Judge Greene's court with the issue of its acceptance open. He simply approved the modification in New Jersey. His actions, apart from their vulnerability on appeal, made a mess of the intricate legal dance.[121]

Jerry Connell, the Justice Department's lead counsel, was to explain to Judge Greene on that same day, Friday, January 8, what all of these steps involved and to assure the judge that the aim was to give him jurisdiction over the modified decree. Judge Greene, however, turned out to be vacationing in the Caribbean! Anticipating some action while he was gone, he had left instructions that filings could not be filed with his court, only "lodged." He had not, however, anticipated the intricate legal maneuvers of January 8, about which he was told over the phone. It seemed that

[120]Kilpatric, interview, May 9, 1984, pp. 52–3; Ronald Carr, interview, June 13, 1984, pp. 33–6.
[121]Carr, interview, June 13, 1984, pp. 36–7.

his case had been dismissed and that Judge Biunno had accepted a settlement in an apparently unrelated proceeding. It looked as if the parties were trying to flee his jurisdiction. He was furious.

Judge Greene's temper notwithstanding, the basic agreement that Brown, Trienens, and Baxter had forged would remain intact. Neither the judge nor the Congress of the United States, nor the FCC, nor, for that matter, President Reagan would intrude in any dramatic way on the political process that these three men had come to dominate in its final stages. All of the other potential participants in the judiciary, legislature, and executive branch had played important roles in guiding the settlement toward the particular form that it had taken. But none had been able to control that process. If any one person had the major responsibility for the outcome, it was William Baxter. He had stood against the pressure of his own administration, maneuvered carefully in his dealings with Congress, and guided the Quagmire II negotiations to a fruitless but telling conclusion. He had played his hand as well as a man could and won from Brown and Trienens a settlement that embodied his basic economic theory and his understanding of the industry. All that remained to be seen was whether this settlement could be successfully implemented and – eventually – whether the nation's new telecommunications system would work.

VII

Creating the new order

Defending the agreement

The unthinkable had become thinkable, then possible, and finally – relative to Brown's view of the alternatives facing AT&T – unavoidable. Brown had agreed to abandon the Bell System and its integrated national network in order to get out from under the judicial, regulatory, and legislative guns aimed at AT&T. His acceptance of Baxter's plan was a total surprise to the ordinary citizen and the shocked members of the Reagan administration, and even to the officers of the Bell Operating Companies who were given a day or two's advance warning by Brown. It was, as well, a decision embodying a new theory of the industry. Everyone inside and outside the Bell System had grown up under Vail's theory of a consolidated, universal network furnishing end-to-end service. The edges of this concept had been nibbled away over the previous decade as the *Carterfone*, *Specialized Common Carriers*, and *Execunet* decisions were implemented and extended, but the basic structure of the Bell System had remained largely intact. Divestiture dethroned the national integrated network in favor of competition.

According to Baxter's theory, divestiture was complete in itself. In one fell swoop, it eliminated not only the opportunities but also the incentives for anticompetitive cross-subsidization. Judge Greene, the Congress, and the FCC had been preempted; they had nothing to do but step aside gracefully and let the market work. This implication of the Modification of Final Judgment was clear to Brown and Baxter. It was less clear to the stunned observers. Brown's first task after announcing the agreement was thus to defend it against interference, modification, or even annulment by the many interested parties who had a stake in telecommunications. Baxter would help by making statements to the court and Congress, but alas, he was now only a passing comet in the telecommunications sky. Lawyers in the Justice Department's Antitrust Division had been reassigned to other cases as soon as the AT&T trial ended. The staff dedicated to implementing the decree was only one-tenth the size of the staff supporting the trial. The brunt of the defense had to be borne by Brown.[1]

[1]Jim G. Kilpatric, interview, May 9, 1984, p. 65.

Baxter, Brown, and Howard J. Trienens announcing the agreement to break up the Bell System at the press conference in Washington, D.C., on January 8, 1982.

The network operations center in Bedminster, New Jersey, the principal control point of AT&T's nationwide network as it looked after divestiture.

Brown's task was threefold. He had to publicize the agreement and clarify its legal status, tangled now by the unanticipated events of January 8. He had to convince Congressman Wirth and the House of Representatives that they had indeed lost the horse race and should return to the paddock. He had to persuade the FCC to let the new, divested Long Lines compete on equal terms with its competitors. Two of these three problems would turn out to be difficult to solve. One of them would ultimately prove intractable.

Brown and Baxter met the press together in Washington at noon on January 8. Trading in AT&T stock had been halted that morning, and news of an agreement was beginning to leak out. Baxter opened the press conference by praising the decree; it fulfilled the objectives of the Justice Department as Baxter had explained them in countless forums. Brown followed, taking the tone of a commander laying down his sword. He called the agreement "historic" and reaffirmed the correctness of his decision to settle the lawsuit. He insisted, however, that "clearly it was not the solution that we sought."[2]

Brown's approach had been carefully and discreetly planned. Almost as soon as negotiations over divestiture had begun in December, he had called in Edward Block, AT&T's vice president for public relations and employee information, to ask whether such a decree could be explained as being in the public interest. Block commissioned a small public opinion survey, satisfied himself that the task was feasible, and submitted a publicity plan to Brown. Among the many other items, it included a proposal for Brown's statement at the Baxter-Brown press conference, press materials for the Bell Operating Companies, information releases to be distributed simultaneously to the Bell System's one million employees, letters to share owners and other key constituencies, and advertisements for the major media. All were developed in great secrecy before January 8 by a small group from AT&T's public relations staff. The initial ad was set by a trusted typesetter, who had his employees prepare and proofread different parts of it so that they would not discover the whole story.[3]

On Monday, January 11, lawyers from AT&T and the Justice Department appeared before Judge Biunno. He began over again, approving the Modification of Final Judgment, interpreting it solely as a modification of the 1956 Consent Decree, and postponing action on the request for a transfer to the Washington court.[4] Judge Greene, who had returned to

[2]"U.S. Settles Phone Suit, Drops I.B.M. Case: AT&T to Split Up, Transforming Industry," *The New York Times*, January 9, 1982, p. 1.
[3]"Public Relations and the Business Story of the Decade," November 30, 1984 (revised November 30, 1985).
[4]*US* v. *Western Electric Co.*, CA No. 17–49, U.S. Dist. Ct., Dist. of New Jersey, Judge Biunno, *Opinion*, January 11, 1982.

Washington still extremely annoyed, held a hearing on Tuesday that was at best confusing. George Saunders, AT&T's lead attorney, kept insisting that the current antitrust case—the one in front of Judge Greene—was over, both parties having agreed to dismiss it. But Greene, trying hard to see his way through the thicket of legal maneuvers, was not convinced. He would not be frozen out of the case he had kept on schedule with difficulty and had been hearing for a year. He simply refused to accept the government's dismissal of the case. Although it was not clear that he could do this legally, no one objected very strenuously. On January 12, therefore, Judge Greene "lodged" the government's dismissal without accepting it. This new legal status was a state of suspended animation. On Thursday, January 14, Judge Biunno finally transferred the 1949 case against Western Electric, the 1956 Decree, and the current modification of that decree to the Washington, D.C., District Court in a hand-written order (sent from a hospital bed). All of the actions were at last together in one court.[5]

At this point, Judge Greene faced a crucial decision. If he chose to consider the several actions confronting him as merely modifications of an old decree coupled with an unrelated dismissal of the current suit, nothing further had to be done. But if he determined that all of the maneuvering was a single action, if the modification of the 1956 Decree was in fact a new consent decree settling the current 1974 case and vacating the 1956 Decree, then the Brown-Baxter agreement fell under the jurisdiction of the Antitrust Procedures and Penalties Act of 1974. This law, known ubiquitously as the Tunney Act, had been passed in the aftermath of the 1972 ITT Consent Decree—that is, the Dita Beard imbroglio. The scandal in the Nixon administration had stimulated Congress to mandate public disclosure of the steps leading up to the settlement of a major antitrust case and of the government's motivation for its actions. The statute was designed to ensure that the government would air the steps leading up to a consent decree, as Congressman Celler had done in the 1950s in his hearings on AT&T's 1956 Consent Decree.[6]

In the current action, of course, AT&T had abandoned its prior position,

[5]*US* v. *AT&T*, CA No. 74–1698, U.S. Dist. Ct., Dist. of Columbia, Judge Greene, *Order*, January 8, 1982, and Transcript Vol. 134, January 12, 1982; *US* v. *Western Electric Co.*, CA No. 17–49 (D.N.J.), Judge Biunno, *Order*, January 14, 1982.
[6]The Tunney Act required that any proposal for a consent decree submitted by the United States in an antitrust proceeding be filed by the court and published in the *Federal Register* at least 60 days prior to the effective date of the judgment. Any written comments relating to the proposal and responses by the government also had to be filed with the court and published in the *Federal Register*. At the same time that the proposed consent decree was published, the government was obligated to file a Competitive Impact Statement describing the circumstances giving rise to the antitrust case, the proposal at hand, anticipated effects on competition of the proposal, and alternative proposals considered by the United States. The statement also had to describe the procedures available for modifying the proposal if it was accepted. *The Antitrust Procedures and Penalties Act*, 15 U.S.C. §16(b)-(h) ("Tunney Act"), December 1974.

not the Justice Department. The issue of public policy consequently was quite different from the one the Tunney Act had anticipated. That could easily be handled within the framework of the act, but the unusual legal form in which the case was settled raised more serious questions. Use of the Tunney Act in these circumstances, its first important application, could substantially broaden its applicability. Consent decrees are modified all the time as conditions change and as parties convince judges that measures agreed upon at one time have become unsuitable for another time or have failed to achieve their promised objectives. The current situation involved precisely that kind of action. Application of the Tunney Act might set a precedent for use of that law in myriad cases where it was neither wanted nor desirable. AT&T and the Justice Department, anticipating this problem, filed a joint statement with the court saying that even though both parties were willing to submit the settlement to Tunney Act scrutiny, their acquiescence would not – they hoped – set a precedent for other legally similar but different circumstances.[7]

When Judge Greene invoked the Tunney Act on Thursday, January 21, the bargaining process that had been narrowly confined to two parties was suddenly opened up to all of those who had a stake in the industry. Greene's decision ensured that an already complex process would become far more complicated, with the former antagonists allied in defending the agreement against all comers – and against Judge Greene. The judge vacated Judge Biunno's order approving the modification of the 1956 Consent Decree and said that the proposed modification needed to be published in the *Federal Register* as soon as possible. The government needed to file a Competitive Impact Statement within 15 days and would receive comments on the proposal during the following 60 days. At the end of that time, the court would consider all of these factors and might also hold hearings on them. For the moment, however, all of the motions to intervene were denied. All motions and the comments received over the following two months were sent to the Department of Justice, which filed them with the court in the context of its comments.[8]

<hr/>

[7]William F. Baxter and Jim G. Kilpatric letters to Judge Harold H. Greene, January 18, 1982.

[8]The Tunney Act (Sec. 2(g)) also required "each defendant in an antitrust suit settled by consent decree to file with the court a description of any and all written or oral communications, by or on behalf of such defendant . . . with any officer or employee of the United States concerning or relevant to such proposal, except that any communications made by counsel of record alone with the attorney general or the employees of the Department of Justice alone shall be excluded from the requirements." The judge was informed about the meeting between Brown, Trienens, and Baxter on December 30; about the telephone conversation on January 1, in which the disagreement about the equal exchange access provision came to a head; and about Brown's conversations with Weinberger, Baldrige, Meese, and Fielding on January 6 and 7. With the exception of those meetings, all discussions of the proposed consent decree had been conducted by the lawyers. Earlier, Brown had spoken extensively with members of the administration about legislation and about the case, but not about the proposed decree. *US* v. *AT&T*, CA No. 82–0192 (D.D.C.), *Defen-*

The Department of Justice filed its Competitive Impact Statement on February 10. The department summarized its position succinctly: "The basic theory of both the *Western Electric* and *AT&T* cases was that, as a rate base/rate of return regulated monopolist, AT&T has had both the incentive and the ability through cross-subsidization and discriminatory actions, to leverage the power it enjoys in its regulated monopoly markets to foreclose or impede the development of competition in related, potentially competitive markets. . . . the proposed modification removes, clearly and efficiently, the structural problems that have given rise to the controversies between the United States and AT&T over the last three decades." Not only was the agreement well justified, it was–the statement implied strongly–the only measure needed to cure the ills of the telecommunications industry. It followed directly that the 1956 Consent Decree was no longer needed.[9]

The FCC was not convinced by the Justice Department's logic. The agency had lost a considerable amount of turf, and it now mounted a strong counteroffensive. Despite the assertions of previous heads of the FCC's Common Carrier Bureau that AT&T could not be effectively regulated, the bureau was not about to stop trying. Baxter had successfully imposed his views on the administration. He had not bothered with the FCC–they had not been involved in the case–even though they were part of his plan. Having separated the competitive and monopoly parts of the industry, Baxter's theory required that regulation be confined to the monopoly part. It was in fact to get the FCC out of the impossible position of regulating competitive industries that Baxter had pursued his grand strategy. His aim, as he kept repeating during 1981, was to substitute divestiture for regulation.

This aim was part of Baxter's larger vision as well. He had not only settled the AT&T case on January 8, he also had dismissed the long-running IBM case on the same day. Although these actions appeared antithetical–the government achieved its aims in telecommunications and appeared to abandon them in computers–they were integrated in Baxter's mind and those of the other Justice Department strategists. As Richard Levine succinctly explained: "The best relief in the IBM case was to release AT&T from the 1956 Consent Decree, so that AT&T could provide a significant competitive challenge in computers."[10] To be an effective competitor, Brown had long argued, AT&T needed to be freed

dants' Description of Written or Oral Communications Concerning the Modification of Final Judgment, February 5, 1982; *US* v. *AT&T*, CA No. 74–1698, 82–0192 (D.D.C.), Judge Greene, *Order*, January 21, 1982.

[9]*US* v. *AT&T*, CA No. 74–1698, 82–0192 (D.D.C.), *Competitive Impact Statement*, February 10, 1982, pp. 3–4, 8, 38.

[10]Trudy E. Bell, "The Decision to Divest: Incredible or Inevitable?" *IEEE Spectrum*, Vol. 22 (November 1985), p. 49.

as well from the regulation that had grown up since and under the 1956 Decree.

But the FCC was not about to go out of business, or even out of the business of regulating AT&T, just because the Department of Justice had restructured the industry. Whatever the views of prior commissioners and staff members, the FCC in 1982 still believed in the efficacy of regulation. It was unconvinced by a theory premised on its ineffectiveness. Baxter notwithstanding, the FCC was responsible for the legislatively mandated aims of universal service and nondiscrimination, goals not addressed directly in the new consent decree. Business would go on as usual at the FCC. In fact, the Commission submitted an *amicus* brief to Judge Greene, asking that its authority be explicitly recognized and, indeed, extended in the Modification of Final Judgment to cover the limitations on the divested operating companies.[11]

Nor did the agency stop with those stiff counterassaults. Although one might think that the fully separated subsidiary mandated by the FCC's *Computer II* decision was now unnecessary, the FCC did not agree. The Commission's Common Carrier Bureau concluded in February that the decree enhanced its previous decision. By superseding the 1956 Consent Decree, the new decree eliminated the legal confusion surrounding *Computer II*. But it did not obviate the need for it. To the FCC – although not to Baxter – the toll transmission network was a bottleneck facility. AT&T Long Lines dominated long distance service, and it would be able to leverage its power into other markets. In addition (although the rationale was not the same), a separate subsidiary was still needed for terminal equipment. "Even with the divestiture of local exchange operations," the Common Carrier Bureau said, "the potential for significant cross-subsidization still exists through AT&T regulated intrastate interexchange services and its interstate communications services."[12]

The FCC had an important intellectual ally in Congress. Congressman Wirth agreed that the sun was not about to set on the telecommunications regulatory system – not if he had anything to do with it. Predictions that local telephone rates would double were floating about, raising congressional hackles.[13] Wirth disagreed with the Justice Department's claim that

[11]*US* v. *AT&T*, CA No. 74–1698, 82–0192, Misc. No. 82–0025 (PI) (D.D.C.), *Brief of the Federal Communications Commission as Amicus Curiae, On Stipulation and Modification of Final Judgment*, April 20, 1982; William R. Stump, interview, November 30, 1984, pp. 67–9.

[12]FCC, Common Carrier Bureau, "Consent Decree Analysis," February, 1982, pp. 52–5. *Computer II*, was also needed until the new consent decree took effect if AT&T was to offer enhanced services. Even AT&T therefore did not ask the FCC to vacate *Computer II* before divestiture was accomplished.

[13]For example, "U.S. Settles Phone Suit, Drops I.B.M. Case: AT&T to Split Up, Transforming Industry," *The New York Times*, January 9, 1982, p. 1.

divestiture would end all cross-subsidies and produce fair competition. The bill Wirth had introduced in December 1981, after a year of study, had become obsolete overnight, but the congressman remained certain that there still was a need for new legislation. Wirth set his staff to rewrite his bill in light of the divestiture agreement. The new bill, like the old, had the twin aims of promoting competition and preserving universal service. Wirth had maintained from the beginning that competition was the best way to promote service expansion and innovation. He did not differ from Baxter in this view. But he, like the FCC, considered even the divested long distance services of AT&T to be a monopoly. After all, his staff calculated that the Bell System had had 96 percent of the long distance market in 1980. It therefore had "the incentive to engage in anticompetitive conduct – particularly cross-subsidization – in any nonregulated industry it is permitted to enter."[14] He and his staff refashioned his bill to deal with this problem.

The revised bill did away with most of the fully separated subsidiary requirements of the measure already passed by the Senate, but it mandated that AT&T form such a subsidiary for its long distance service. Free to enter any competitive business it chose, AT&T was not to be allowed to use revenues from its monopoly to do so. Since Wirth and his staff still viewed long distance service as a monopoly, the House bill extended the FCC's jurisdiction instead of reducing it, as Baxter wished. Nothing in the consent decree shook Wirth's opinion that the hopelessly outdated 1934 act needed to be improved – not supplanted by market forces. Thus, in the new bill, the Commission was given the right to prescribe tariffs, not just to respond to carrier-initiated tariffs. It was given authority over all transmission equipment, not just transmission lines, and over all interexchange services (not just interstate service). It was given other new powers as well, including the power to strengthen the requirements of the act if it found violations of its provisions.[15]

Wirth also embodied in his revised bill the continuing congressional desire for low-cost, universal service. Consumer groups, state regulators, and the operating companies themselves came to the subcommittee with pleas to preserve low local rates. One possible source of income was the lucrative Yellow Pages business. The operating companies seemed unconcerned about provisions in the decree allocating the Yellow Pages to AT&T, and the subcommittee decided that it needed to protect them

[14]U.S. House, Committee on Energy and Commerce, Subcommittee on Telecommunications, Consumer Protection, and Finance, Majority Staff, to Timothy E. Wirth, re "Competitive Issues – Remaining Problems and Legislative Options," March 2, 1982, citing "Telecommunications in Transition: The Status of Competition in the Telecommunications Industry," a report by the majority staff, November 3, 1981, p. 58.
[15]97th Congress, 2nd Session, House, Amendment in the Nature of a Substitute to H.R. 5158, March 23, 1982 (committee print).

from themselves, as well as from AT&T. The revised bill restored the Yellow Pages to the divested operating companies. It also gave them all of the embedded base of installed telephones and permission to sell new telephone equipment after five years. For that five-year period, AT&T was also barred from "bypassing" the operating companies' local transmission network and connecting its long distance lines directly to large customers (thus depriving the operating companies of needed revenues). To keep AT&T from taking operating company assets in the process of divestiture, the bill proposed that divestiture take place before those assets were valued. That would take the valuation out of AT&T's hands.[16]

Wirth was clearly the guiding spirit behind this new bill, but his efforts soon began to win support from other representatives because the measure touched some long-standing congressional concerns and deep-seated suspicion about Baxter's agreement. The bill was discussed extensively within the subcommittee, picking up support as it was modified. As a result of Wirth's attention to his colleagues, the subcommittee was able to report the bill out unanimously on March 25, 1982.[17]

Brown was incensed. He had entered into his bargain with Baxter after Congress had failed to act. The legislature, having lost the horse race with the trial, should, he thought, hang up its colors. Brown had no desire to be subject to both a new consent decree and a new communications act. More importantly, the House bill undercut the agreement. Brown had given the Department of Justice everything it wanted, and now Congress was trying to take even more. The bill was particularly distasteful because Wirth was challenging Brown's good faith in implementing the divestiture. There was no shred of evidence indicating that Brown would fail to do everything possible to send the operating companies successfully on their way. But Wirth clearly did not trust AT&T to protect the interests of either the firm's stockholders or ratepayers.

Brown pulled out all the stops. He marshaled all of the Bell System's considerable political power against Wirth's bill. There was no longer anything to be gained from restraint. The Bell System would shortly cease to exist and its political clout would disappear, along with the integrated network. Brown appealed to his employees and his shareholders to write Wirth and his colleagues in protest against the bill. In sharp contrast to 1976, many of them did. The Bell System, fully activated, could generate

---

[16] 97th Congress, 2nd Session, House, Committee on Energy and Commerce, Subcommittee on Telecommunications, Consumer Protection, and Finance, Hearing, "H.R. 5158 and Proposed AT&T Antitrust Settlement: The Impact on the Bell System," February 23, 1982; David K. Aylward, interview, September 26, 1985, pp. 64–5.

[17] Aylward, interviews, September 26, 1985, pp. 58–9, 67–9, and October 17, 1985, pp. 7–9; 97th Congress, 2nd Session, House, Committee on Energy and Commerce, Subcommittee on Telecommunications, Consumer Protection, and Finance, "Consensus Agreement," March 25, 1982.

political concern in every state and congressional district in the United States. As the campaign went into motion, Wirth received a torrent of letters in opposition to his bill; more importantly, he began to get calls from other members of Congress who were receiving similar complaints. His staff began to work frenetically to answer these calls and then to answer editorials from around the country in support of the Bell System's position.[18]

AT&T also worked with the Commerce Committee, which had received the bill from its subcommittee, to block passage. Members supporting AT&T insisted on carefully reading the bill and proposing amendments at every juncture. There were new amendments, more every day. Committee members continued to receive rumblings from back home: Who are you representing? Us or Timothy Wirth's Colorado? Why are you attacking the Bell System? Gradually, the committee process ground to a halt as more and more time was spent on this single measure.[19]

Although Wirth thought he had the votes needed to report the bill out of the committee (which was heavily Democratic), the process was clearly going to be slow and painful. The chances for House passage were dim. Reluctantly, he withdrew the bill rather than fight to the death for what was likely to be a losing cause. He had let the country know that Congress had not been a party to the bargain that had destroyed the Bell System. He had found considerable support for measures to curb AT&T's power, even though the legislators disagreed over the specific measures to be used. Congress, unlike Baxter and the Justice Department, wanted to enhance competition while preserving low local rates, and many congressmen seemed prepared to channel resources to the Bell Operating Companies to do so. Wirth expressed these concerns in a letter to Judge Greene,

[18]Aylward, interview, October 17, 1985, pp. 14–19; James E. Olson, remarks at press conference in Washington, D.C., March 25, 1982.

   Brown included a personal note in a special mailing to shareowners: "This is an unusual message from the management of AT&T. I urge you to read it carefully and then take action. Let your voice be heard. It is very important to you as a shareowner of AT&T. (signed) C.L. Brown," March 25, 1982.

   "The Divestiture Papers: I, A Plea for Orderly Policy-Making," a Bell System advertisement that appeared in newspapers across the country on Sunday and Monday, March 25–6, 1982.

   "Congress Flooded with Letters Opposing H.R. 5158 as Bell System Ends Second Week of Campaign," *AT&T Management Report*, No. 13 (April 9, 1982).

   "An Urgent Message to AT&T Shareowners: The Anti-Bell Bill Continues to Move Through Congress. The Time to Speak Out Is Now," a Bell System advertisement that appeared in a number of major newspapers across the country on Friday and Sunday, June 18 and 20, 1982.

[19]The committee held mark-up sessions on June 22, 23, and 24, 1982. R.L. McGuire and Michael Baudhuin, interview, November 16, 1984; Aylward, interview, October 17, 1985, pp. 19–26; Edward M. Block, interview, December 3, 1985, pp. 68–9; John G. Fox, interview, November 25, 1985, pp. 55–9; Kenneth J. Whalen, interview, July 18, 1985, pp. 49, 58–60.

urging him to revise the Modification of Final Judgment's provisions on
the Yellow Pages, asset assignment, and the role of the operating companies in planning the divestiture. Without these changes, Wirth said, "certain ancillary elements of the parties' agreement could unnecessarily
weaken the Bell Operating Companies and otherwise threaten the most
fundamental requirement of the Communications Act – universality of service at reasonable rates."[20]

This rolled the ball back into Judge Greene's court, where in May the
Department of Justice and AT&T filed their responses to the public comments. Well over 600 comments had been received. None of them seriously opposed divestiture. There seemed to be no loyalty to the Bell
System outside the System itself. Even so, many states, firms, and industry organizations thought that they could benefit from some change in the
proposed decree. AT&T and the Justice Department consequently found
themselves fighting hard as allies in defense of their handiwork. Having
come this far, neither wanted Congress or the court to disturb the fundamental bargain framed in the new decree. For Baxter, amendments
would inevitably weaken the logic of the surgical divestiture. For Brown,
amendments would make an already harsh solution even more difficult to
accept and the fractured system more difficult to operate.

The Department of Justice took the position that the court could not
modify the agreement without concurrence from both AT&T and the
Department of Justice. The purpose of the Tunney Act was to assure the
public and its representatives in the government that the settlement was
in the public interest. The act did not, however, specify what judges could
do if they found that the settlement was not in the public interest. Presumably they could reject it and return to the courtroom, letting the process
of litigation continue as if the voluntary settlement had never existed. It
was arguable whether a judge could also modify a decree to ensure that it
protected the public interest, and the Justice Department argued that the
court's discretion here was very limited. Greene could not, for example,
implement the FCC's requests, which Justice opposed on substantive as
well as procedural grounds. The department wanted an industry that
would work with a minimum of regulation. Its aim was precisely to freeze
the FCC out of the action and let competition rather than regulation
determine the behavior of firms. Greene accepted the view that he could
not order changes *tout simple;* instead, he insisted that AT&T and the
Department of Justice accept certain modifications in the decree.[21]

[20]Timothy E. Wirth et al. to Judge Harold H. Greene, July 27, 1982.
[21]*US* v. *AT&T*, CA No. 74–1698, 82–0192, Misc. No. 82–0025 (PI) (D.D.C.), *Brief of the
Federal Communications Commission as Amicus Curiae*, April 20, 1982; *Response of the
United States to Public Comments on Proposed Modification of Final Judgment*, May 20,
1982, pp. 5–6, 15–19; Judge Greene, *Opinion*, August 11, 1982, 552 F. Supp. 131 at 153
(D.D.C. 1982), *aff'd mem. sub nom. Maryland* v. *US*, 103 S. Ct., 1240, 1983.

AT&T, which supported the Justice Department, leveled most of its arguments against submissions from the states (which had maintained that federal actions had preempted the authority of the states). State regulators wanted Judge Greene to amend the decree to ensure the continuation of low local telephone rates, to preserve at least this benefit of the integrated Bell System after it was gone. But AT&T insisted that the states had no standing. They were not entitled to intrude on this transaction. Even though the consent decree involved actions in every state, it was a matter of federal antitrust, not state regulatory, jurisdiction. As Trienens had noted earlier, this was one of the primary objectives to be gained by a court-ordered divestiture compared to a voluntary one. AT&T also presented to the court the same face it had presented to Baxter on the equal access question, insisting that technical decisions about how to accomplish this objective should be left in the hands of those who provided telephone service.[22]

Henry Geller, former head of the NTIA, and Chip Shooshan, former chief counsel of Van Deerlin's subcommittee, opposed most of the agreement's restrictions on the operating companies. They acknowledged that barring the companies from offering long distance services was integral to the theory of the decree; otherwise the companies would have the same incentives to favor their own affiliates that AT&T previously had. They even understood why the operating companies should not manufacture terminal equipment. But Geller and Shooshan questioned the logic of prohibiting the companies from engaging in all unregulated activities, including the sale of terminal equipment. They maintained that communications technology was changing so rapidly and new firms were entering the field in such numbers that the exercise of market power by the operating companies would be quite difficult. Separate subsidiaries would eliminate cross-subsidies. The constraints would simply re-create all of the difficulties experienced under the 1956 Consent Decree.[23]

Judge Greene responded to these and other arguments he received by requesting additional information and comments in eight general areas, ranging from the powers of the court in public interest proceedings to the division of assets and liabilities among the divested companies. A hundred and fifty-nine interested parties filed comments on these eight areas of inquiry. AT&T, the Department of Justice, and forty others then replied to the comments, and at the end of June, the judge held two days of

[22]*US* v. *AT&T*, CA No. 82–0192 (D.D.C.), *Reply Comments of the American Telephone and Telegraph Company*, May 21, 1982.
[23]*US* v. *AT&T*, CA No. 74–1698 (D.D.C.), *Comments On Proposed Modified Decree*, April 20, 1982, submitted by Henry Geller, Harry M. Shooshan III, et al.

hearings. On August 11, he issued an opinion accepting the agreement with certain modification, and proposing ten amendments to the decree.[24]

He believed that the operating companies should be allowed to provide, although not to manufacture, customer premises equipment. This was the first breach of the boundary the Justice Department had tried to draw between regulated and competitive activities. The supply, repair, sales, and manufacture of customer premises equipment clearly were part of the competitive realm. One of the primary arguments against AT&T in the antitrust suit was that it had tried to impede competition in that market, one that the FCC had opened to competition long before the settlement had been negotiated.

Judge Greene was in sympathy with the arguments by Geller and Shooshan and with the operating companies' contention that they should be able to service equipment as well as lines. Greene noted that the Tunney Act standards required the imposition of restrictions on the operating companies only if there was a substantial possibility that they would use their monopoly power to impede competition. He agreed with the FCC that the operating companies would not be able to do so in the market for terminal equipment. He nevertheless retained the prohibition on manufacturing.

Following Wirth's plea, Greene would also give the operating companies the right to issue the Yellow Pages. This was yet another breach in the wall between regulation and competition. No one had argued that there was any natural monopoly in the business of issuing advertising directories. There are all kinds of directories and all kinds of people issuing them. But in this instance, Judge Greene was not concerned about competition; he, like Timothy Wirth, was worried about the effect of divestiture on local rates. The issue was whether profits from the Yellow Pages would be used to subsidize local rates. In this modification, Judge Greene was in effect accepting the position that AT&T had held during the case; local regulated rates were receiving subsidies rather than generating them. He wanted to give the Yellow Pages to the operating companies in an effort to preserve universal service.

Greene decided, too, that the operating companies should not be permanently barred from nonregulated activities. He provided a mechanism that companies could use to petition the court for a waiver if they could show that there was no substantial possibility that they would impede competition in the market they sought to enter. This again breached the wall Baxter had so carefully erected, although it was unclear at this time

[24]*US* v. *AT&T*, CA No. 74–1698, 82–0192 (D.D.C.), Judge Greene, *Memorandum*, May 25, 1982; *Reply Brief of American Telephone and Telegraph Company*, June 24, 1982; *Reply Brief of the United States*, June 24, 1982; Transcript of Proceedings, Vols. 135–6, June 29–30, 1982.

how significant a break this would become. This move, more than any other, transformed the court into a second regulatory agency and created a crack in the Justice Department's wall that the operating companies would be sorely tempted to pry open.[25]

Using language taken from Wirth's revised bill, Judge Greene proposed to bar AT&T from the field of electronic publishing for seven years. This was justified on First Amendment grounds, but–as with the legislative initiatives on this subject–it is very hard to see what the First Amendment had to do with the decision. There was nothing in the antitrust case that related to freedom of speech, and the Justice Department's aim in proposing divestiture was precisely to enable AT&T to enter new fields of endeavor. This modification ran directly counter to the Justice Department's view of the decree. It was pure and simple protectionism. Just as the decision on the Yellow Pages was designed to protect the local customer, so this one protected the local newspaper–including such politically potent newspapers as *The Washington Post*. [26]

By contrast, Greene introduced modifications to promote competition in the interexchange market. One resembled the warnings required on cigarette packages. If an operating company provided billing services for AT&T's interexchange service, it had to include a legend indicating that it was a distinct company: "This portion of your bill is provided as a service to AT&T. There is no connection between this company and AT&T. You may choose another company for your long distance telephone calls while still receiving your local telephone service from this company." Another provision related to a transition period, much as the original draft of the decree had done. It said that less than equal access for interstate carriers should carry less than equal charges. This technical provision was designed to open competition by speeding the transition in the field of interexchange telephone service.[27]

[25]Judge Greene, *Opinion*, August 11, 1982, *US* v. *AT&T*, CA No. 74–1698, 82–0192, Misc. No. 82–0025 (PI) (D.D.C.), 552 F. Supp. 131.

[26]Ibid. at 225–6; Ronald Carr, interview, June 13, 1984, pp. 42–4; Lionel Van Deerlin, interview, December 11, 1985, pp. 42–4; see also Fox, interview, November 6, 1985, p. 48, November 25, 1985, p. 39, and Harry M. Shooshan III and Charles L. Jackson, interview, April 3, 1985, pp. 37–45.

[27]Still other modifications dealt with divestiture and procedural problems. One said that shared assets should be given to the operating company or to AT&T on the basis of predominant use. Another specified debt ratios of approximately 45 percent for separated operating companies except for Pacific Telephone which was to have a debt ratio of approximately 50 percent. The court also insisted that it could act on its own, *sua sponte*, to enforce compliance with the decree or to punish any violation of it. Finally, AT&T's plan of reorganization had to be accompanied by approving affidavits from the CEOs of the regional holding companies and had to be approved by the court. Judge Greene, like Wirth and many commentators, worried that divestiture might provide the opportunity for AT&T to strip the operating companies of resources. He did not want their protests to surface long after the deed was done. Judge Greene, *Opinion*, August 11, 1982, *US* v. *AT&T*, CA No. 74–1698, 82–0192, Misc. No. 82–0025 (PI) (D.D.C.), 552 F. Supp. 131 at 225–6.

The Department of Justice tried to persuade the judge not to breach the wall between monopoly and competition. It sought reconsideration of the modification that allowed the operating companies to provide, although not to manufacture, customer premises equipment. The Department of Justice argued that this be limited to residential or single-line items. This echoed the FCC's attempts to distinguish between basic and enhanced services; it would keep the operating companies out of the latter field. It took the judge only a few days to reject this request.[28]

The Department of Justice and AT&T nevertheless accepted Greene's ten amendments, and the judge entered the final version of the Modification of Final Judgment. The parties involved signed the decree, as did Judge Greene, on August 24, 1982. Civil Action 74–1698, *US* v. *AT&T*, was dismissed. The case was closed.[29]

The acceptance of Judge Greene's modifications and the defeat of Wirth's bill left the decree largely as Brown and Baxter had agreed to it. The judge had nibbled at the edges, making some changes that would have significant effects on AT&T, the operating companies, and their actual and potential competitors. In drafting the original agreement, the Department of Justice, following Baxter's lead, had sharply differentiated between the new AT&T, which was to be wholly in the competitive arena, and the independent operating companies, which were to be wholly regulated. Judge Greene's modifications had blurred that line. On balance, however, neither Baxter nor Brown could be terribly disappointed with the Tunney Act proceedings. Working together, the company and Justice had defended their basic agreement from the assaults of a large number of interested parties. Dispossessed regulatory agencies, aspiring competitors, powerful publishers who feared competition, and many others had managed to persuade Judge Greene to compromise the logic of the agreement on a few points but not to overturn the basic premises of the Modification of Final Judgment.

The Plan of Reorganization

Defending the Modification of Final Judgment was only one of Brown's activities at the start of 1982, arguably the least of them. He had only two years in which to implement the decision to divest the operating compa-

[28]*US* v. *AT&T*, CA No. 74–1698, 82–0192 (D.D.C.), *Memorandum of the United States in Response to the Court's Opinion of August 11, 1982*, August 19, 1982; *US* v. *AT&T*, CA No. 74–1698, 82–0192, Misc. No. 82–0025 (PI) (D.D.C.), Judge Greene, *Memorandum*, August 23, 1982.

[29]*US* v. *AT&T*, CA No. 82–0192 (D.D.C.), *Modification of Final Judgment*, August 24, 1982; *US* v. *AT&T*, CA No. 74–1698, 82–0192 (D.D.C.), Judge Greene, *Order*, August 24, 1982.

nies, a tight deadline he himself had chosen to minimize the disruption it would impose on the Bell System. For the national network had to operate even as its dissolution was being planned and effected. It was, one participant said, like converting a Boeing 727 into a 747 in mid-air. From a manager's point of view this was an incredibly difficult task, rife with potential conflicts of interest. Billions of dollars of assets had to be divided; hundreds of thousands of employees had to be kept working effectively while their future roles were being decided. While all of this was being accomplished, AT&T had to ensure that when customers picked up a phone they would have a dial tone, and when they placed a call they would be reasonably certain to get the party they wanted.[30]

Brown's decision to manage this transition had important implications for the company. He placed John Segall (vice president, planning and financial management) in charge of divestiture planning, James Olson (vice chairman of the board) in charge of structuring the new AT&T's unregulated activities, and Morris Tanenbaum (executive vice president – intercity network development) in charge of planning for the new AT&T's regulated actions. The appointments were far from symmetrical; Brown kept firm control of the divestiture process. As he saw it, he was completing a transformation he had initiated. The problem was that he had a dual role: divestiture czar and future AT&T CEO. There was never any doubt in his mind or in those of his close associates that he was above any conflicts of interest; he worked for the shareholders, all the shareholders. To outsiders, however, there could have been a problem, and Brown bent over backward to be fair. Had he appointed a senior divestiture head who would retire at the start of 1984 – like the widely respected president of AT&T, William Ellinghaus – or announced his own retirement as of that date, the problem would have been eliminated. Instead, to maintain absolute probity, Brown tended to favor the operating companies.

In addition to making Segall head of divestiture planning, Brown brought the operating companies into the heart of the process from the start. He selected six major areas that required immediate attention and formed study groups composed of operating company presidents to deal with them. The presidents were asked to list their preferences among the study groups, and they were assigned to one or another of the groups in the last half of January.

As the groups got underway, it quickly became apparent that Brown was able to marshal one resource that had not figured in the divestiture agreement or in any of Baxter's or Judge Greene's calculations: the culture of the Bell System. The values and traditions deeply ingrained in the

---

[30]Charles L. Brown, interview, June 9, 1984, p. 11; William M. Ellinghaus, interview, June 13, 1985, pp. 54–7.

minds of thousands of managers and hundreds of thousands of workers favored cooperative behavior to maximize the efficiency of the entire network. Coordination and technical integration were as natural to the Bell System as were careful staff work and systems engineering. Among those to whom the mystique and daily performance of the network were overriding concerns, Brown's call to cooperation had a powerful appeal.

This became apparent as the study groups got underway. One of the most important groups, chaired by William Cashel, vice chairman and financial officer of AT&T, dealt with corporate structure. Bolger and Whalen, both executive vice presidents of AT&T, chaired study groups on exchange boundaries, access charges, and the projected centralized staff for the operating companies. Two additional study groups considered personnel matters (under Whalen) and asset assignment (under Cashel). Within two weeks of their formation, all of these groups were able to set out the basic lines on which AT&T would proceed, and the company took these directives to the Department of Justice for a briefing. The processes of divestiture planning and restructuring were done under the scrutiny of the Department of Justice and the court, and AT&T kept in particularly close touch with Baxter's two lieutenants, Carr and Levine.[31]

The corporate structure study group quickly made a crucial decision about the framework for the operating companies. The decree said that the operating companies were to be divested by AT&T, but it did not say how they were to be divided or combined. One option had been proposed by Garlinghouse in 1972 and Trienens in 1980: Create a company for each state and allow the jurisdictional boundaries for regulation to be the corporate boundaries. But this would have meant breaking up many of the existing Bell Operating Companies and was never seriously considered. Alternatively, the companies could have been aggregated into one large holding company or maybe just an eastern and a western holding company, but Brown had visions of another antitrust suit in the year 2000 against such giant companies and refused to contemplate that large an aggregation.

Even the option of retaining the existing 22 companies as separate firms was not considered very long. It was not rejected for any consideration of technical feasibility, but to avoid financial weakness. Brown and Trienens wanted to bring the link between service and revenue as close to the state regulators as possible, but not at the expense of having an unsound financial structure. The operating company presidents thought that the new firms needed to have assets of between $15 and $20 billion. They wanted companies of roughly comparable size, and they decided to create seven

[31]Reports of Bell Operating Company Presidents' Study Groups, Presidents' Conference, May 10–14, 1982, La Quinta, California.

regional holding companies to consolidate the operations of the 22 operating units into firms of the proper size. This was almost exactly the number Hugel had proposed in his Case B planning exercise two years earlier. How did they arrive at the $15 to $20 billion figure? Two Bell Operating Companies, Pacific Telephone and Southwestern Bell, were of that size. The study group decided that they were large enough to be financially viable, that is, able to attract at reasonable rates the extensive capital that any utility needs.[32]

Brown announced his appointment of the CEOs of the seven regional holding companies at the May Presidents' Conference. He chose six existing Bell Operating Company presidents and Bolger, who had been the youngest president of any company at age 39. The six presidents were Zane Barnes (Southwestern Bell), Wallace Bunn (Southern Bell), Donald Guinn (Pacific Telephone), Jack MacAllister (Northwestern Bell), Delbert Staley (New York Telephone), and William Weiss (Illinois Bell). All were men who had compiled outstanding records as they came up through the ranks; they were proven managers who could have looked forward to continued advancement in the Bell System. Far from denuding the operating companies of managerial talent, as Wirth and others suspected he might, Brown had given them the cream of the crop.[33]

With the appointment of the CEOs, the planning for divestiture moved into high gear. The executive officers picked names and designed logos for their projected companies, ranging from the traditional (Bell Atlantic, BellSouth, Southwestern Bell) to the exotic (Ameritech, US West, NYNEX, Pacific Telesis). They each picked regional directors of planning and general counsels. These men, with loyalties now directed to their future company, took their place with the AT&T representatives in the planning process. The independence of the fledgling chicks from the mother hen – a factor that Baxter had eagerly anticipated in his negotiations for the decree – quickly began to emerge. After Brown had appointed these prospective CEOs, he could hardly afford to fire them. That would have been interpreted as evidence of attempted theft from the operating companies and would have created a political storm for AT&T. The executives were "fireproof" and could champion the causes of their prospective companies at will. They did exactly that. Brown had his hands full keeping this collection of vigorous managers on one course. His guiding role was to

[32]Occupied as they were with the network and with raising capital for it, the operating company presidents gave little attention to the threat of corporate takeover. Given the time at which they made this decision (early 1982), they could not have known what a popular corporate sport this was to become. Nonetheless, a side effect of their decision to create large companies is that the regional holding companies are reasonably well insulated against takeover. William S. Cashel, interview, March 26, 1986, pp. 37–42.

[33]W. Brooke Tunstall, interview, May 30, 1984, p. 41; Brown, interview, June 9, 1984, pp. 12–13; Brown, "Remarks," Annual Meeting, April 20, 1983.

make decisions – and to ask others to do so too – that best served all of the stockholders, to make divestiture the last act of a unified Bell System.[34]

The decision to have multiple holding companies raised an immediate question: how to preserve the central coordination for the divested operating companies mandated by the decree? Brown also had personally assured Secretary Weinberger on January 6 that there would be a single point of contact for the Defense Department; both men had been determined to maintain central network planning as it related to national defense. To serve this and other integrating functions, Bolger's presidential study group drafted plans for a Central Service Organization, later named Bell Communications Research or "Bellcore." It would take over some of the functions that had been performed by the AT&T General Departments.[35]

Another question requiring quick resolution was how to continue doing business under the old structure until the date of divestiture and then begin operating as a series of separate firms the very next day. It was decided to establish two subsidiaries within each operating company: one for the interexchange business destined to be transferred to AT&T under the decree and another for the embedded customer premises equipment business to be transferred to AT&T's separated subsidiary under the FCC's *Computer II* ruling. The directors and officers of these new subsidiaries would continue to be employees of AT&T after the divestiture. The transition would be made by a transfer of stock in the new subsidiaries.

The study groups reported to the Presidents' Conference in May. The asset assignment and personnel groups had similar problems. They had to decide how much of AT&T's resources should stay with the parent firm and how much should go to the divested companies or the Central Service Organization. They had to divide the same overhead expenses that had defied assignment to a specific activity in the seemingly endless twenty-year debates over cost allocation. They adopted a rule that a person's or an asset's disposition should be determined by his, her, or its predominant use. They started with the people and assets whose functions could be classified easily and then dealt with more complicated questions as they gained experience. The personnel question, as it turned out, was relatively straightforward. Nine out of ten Bell System employees stayed in the same job after divestiture, working for the same supervisor. Three-quarters of the employees stayed in the same company as well.[36]

[34]William L. Weiss, interview, November 20, 1985, p. 45; Thomas E. Bolger, interview, September 27, 1985, p. 8.
[35]At the time of divestiture, Bellcore employed 2,400 of the 12,000 employees at AT&T's corporate headquarters. W. Brooke Tunstall, *Disconnecting Parties: Managing the Bell System Break-Up: An Inside View* (New York: McGraw-Hill, 1985), pp. 102, 131–42. See also Tunstall, interview, May 30, 1984, pp. 9–10; Brown, interview, June 9, 1984, p. 15.
[36]John L. Segall, "Dealing with Change: Cosmic, Corporate, and Personal," speech to the Human Resources Conference, Hong Kong, January 8, 1986.

The access tariff group identified the issues involved in changing from separations procedures to access charges, analyzed various alternative tariff structures, and selected one to recommend to the operating companies. It was designed to be cost based, efficient, and conducive to good relations between the operating companies and the interexchange carriers. It was also consistent with a future introduction of measured local service and with reform of jurisdictional separations. Despite these attributes, the recommendations of the access tariff study group were headed for far more controversy than those of the other groups. Access charges involved the interests of many persons and organizations outside of the Bell System; they would complicate the transition by fighting to protect their stakes.[37]

While these decisions were being made, the lines of the actual division were being determined. Even though divestiture was spoken of as a separation of the operating companies from Long Lines, there was no thought that it would follow the lines that existed within the Bell System on January 8, 1982. The existing organizations had been generated by historical processes too complex to specify simply; there was no reason to think that the resulting divisions were appropriate for the new structure of the industry. New lines had to be drawn before detailed divestiture plans could be drafted.

Setting these boundaries was particularly important because the Modification of Final Judgment restricted the divested operating companies to providing services within exchange areas; AT&T and its competitors would serve interexchange traffic. The exchange areas thus also mapped the boundary between monopoly and competitive services central to Baxter's theory. If the exchange areas were too small, there might not be enough traffic to exhaust economies of scale. It could easily happen, then, that only one carrier – presumably AT&T – would have the facilities to serve some rural communities. In that case, consumers would face only one interexchange carrier or perhaps multiple carriers who leased facilities from AT&T. In neither case did this situation correspond to Baxter's idea of competition. If exchange areas were too large, there would be symmetrical problems; the operating companies would have monopoly rights (at least temporarily) to services that ought to be competitive.[38]

[37]Presentations at the Presidents' Conference, May 10–14, 1982, La Quinta, California. See the discussion in the next section of this chapter.

[38]Although the Justice Department did not think that the operating companies' local monopolies would survive long in the face of technological progress, it was not ready to introduce competition everywhere just yet. The decree prevented the operating companies from offering interexchange services but did not restrict entry into the local business. *US* v. *AT&T*, CA No. 82–0192 (D.D.C.), *Response of the United States to Comments Received on BOC LATA Proposals*, November 23, 1982; Delbert C. Staley, interview, February 25, 1986, p. 7.

The process of defining exchange areas was also complicated by the issue of control that had arisen in the negotiations over equal access. Brown and his colleagues did not think that a group of amateurs could redesign the telephone system and make it work effectively. It was appropriate for the government to set principles; it was equally appropriate for the telephone company to decide how to implement them. The Justice Department, however, was hesitant about relying on the Bell System's good offices. Baxter's troops had just emerged from a complex lawsuit in which they had endeavored to prove that AT&T had tried to destroy its competitors. Baxter and Levine once again asked for an explicit rule that would specify the hardware to be used, while Brown and Trienens insisted on a rule that emphasized service.

All of these concerns had been present in the negotiations over the Senate bill, and the results of the debate were much the same. In fact, the decree took over the language that had been worked out there with only a few modifications. The most obvious change was in terminology. In order to avoid confusing the new exchange areas with the old ones, a new term was introduced: "Local Access And Transport Areas," or "LATAs." These areas had to be defined in specific terms before the rest of the reorganization plan could be compiled, but all that the decree set forth were the principles for defining those crucial geographical units. According to the decree, each one had to be based in an area serving a common social, economic, or related purpose, even if it crossed governmental boundaries. Every point served by an operating company had to be within a LATA. And the units could not include substantial parts of two or more standard metropolitan statistical areas (SMSAs) or cross state lines without court approval. As with equal access, AT&T had prevailed in the process: The units were defined in terms of service, and it was the job of the telephone company to propose specific LATAs for the Justice Department's approval.[39]

One of the presidents' study groups had taken up this task. The study group and its staff met with representatives of the operating companies, who in February presented preliminary proposals for their respective LATAs. The study group discussed and revised the proposals, working in conjunction with the operating companies and the Justice Department. They were on their fourth iteration by the time of the Presidents' Conference in May. This plan contained 204 LATAs, including 69 "exemptions" that had to be cleared by the court. The number of LATAs per operating company ranged from over thirty (Southwestern Bell) to three (New Jer-

[39]William F. Baxter to Patrick J. Power, California administrative law judge, October 20, 1983.

sey Bell). Ten operating companies were to preside over more than ten LATAs, three of them over more than twenty.[40] These proposals were presented formally to the Department of Justice at the end of May, and Carr and Levine reacted negatively. Some of the LATAs were just right, but others, they said, were too big and some were too small. More explicit criteria were needed to permit the discussions to continue. Levine asked AT&T to generate some traffic statistics for those LATAs covering small areas and for independent companies in the same vicinity, with each one treated as its own LATA (AT&T had been using only its own data). The reply gave Levine information on about 40 LATAs in some midwestern states, and he tried to find a pattern in them. Using his Apple computer, he plotted the number of messages leaving the LATA per month per subscriber – the number of times someone inside the LATA called someone outside it – against the geographical size of the LATA. Not surprisingly, he found that the larger LATAs had fewer calls per subscriber to the outside. This made sense. Even if people simply called a constant distance, no matter where they were located, larger LATAs would have a larger proportion of internal calls.

Could one go further? Were there breaks in this relationship? Levine inspected his graph. The relationship between outside calls per subscriber and the number of subscribers was not a straight line; it appeared to change direction after about 100,000 subscribers. For smaller LATAs, the number of outside calls rose sharply as the geographical size of the LATA fell. For larger units, the number of outside calls responded far less to the size of the LATA. Levine presented his conclusions to the AT&T representatives, who were impressed by his computations. With their approval, the Justice Department adopted a minimum size for LATAs of 100,000 to 125,000 "main and equivalent main stations."[41] Levine's method of analysis was casual and questionable, but there was no time for detailed study. The parties wanted a reasonable rule that would allow the divestiture process to continue.[42]

[40]Sam R. Willcoxon, "LATA Boundary Status Report," Presidents' Conference, May 10, 1982, La Quinta, California.

[41]Carr, interview, June 13, 1984, p. 52; Richard B. Levine, interview, June 12, 1984, pp. 51–5; *US* v. *AT&T*, CA No. 82–0192 (D.D.C.), *Response of the United States to Comments Received on BOC LATA Proposals*, November 23, 1982, p. 18.

[42]Levine's simple summary of the data represented an impressive accomplishment, and it is perhaps churlish to suggest its limitations. It is well, nonetheless, to remember that a highly sophisticated network was being altered in this instance by a lawyer using a rather casual approach to its operating statistics. There are many smooth curves that look like a combination of straight lines, particularly when they are approximated by a scattering of points. Levine's graph could have been of a single hyperbola rather than two straight lines. If so, there would have been no reason to prefer any one point along it to any other. But no thought was given either to the manipulation of Levine's numbers or to the creation of a model that would predict the number of outside calls from a LATA of a given size.

LATAs covering large areas posed a rather different question. Once in a substantial metropolitan area or even a conurbation, the economies of scale for local transmission were quickly exhausted. It appeared to make sense from the competitive point of view, therefore, to break up service in these areas into separate LATAs and allow competition in the extensive local communications. But, as the AT&T technical people had insisted in the negotiations over equal exchange access, the network is not that simple. Just as any language has a series of rules for declining verbs and a set of irregular verbs for which the rules do not apply, so there were exceptions to the standard way of engineering the telephone network. Just as irregular verbs tend to be shortcuts for the most common verbs, the exceptions in telephony tended to cluster in the areas of densest usage. In large SMSAs it made sense to engineer special trunks, tandem switches, and other custom-made switching arrangements to deal with the high volume of local calls. The sharp distinction between local and long distance calls was blurred for engineering, if not for billing purposes. Even the distinction between toll and local switches was ambiguous where switches were performing both kinds of activities.

Drawing a division at any piece of hardware, such as the Class 4 switch, or at any given size of LATA measured by subscribers, would have required the whole system to be reengineered. To force the telephone network in these dense areas to conform to the abstract plan of a network would be doubly bad. The cost of reengineering the switches, laying new trunks, and rerouting the traffic would be enormous, and the new system would sacrifice the economies that had been gained by the special arrangements. It is precisely because special arrangements are more efficient in particular cases that the engineers of the Bell System departed from the rules and took advantage of local conditions. When these considerations were set forth, the Department of Justice went along with AT&T's argument that it was hopeless to make a general definition in terms of hardware and absurd to break up the concentrated areas. A LATA always included the whole of a SMSA. Concern arose when a LATA proposed by AT&T contained more than one SMSA. Even in this case, the Department of Justice adopted a rule that emphasized geography and population, rather than switching hardware.

By the fall of 1982, AT&T and the Bell Operating Companies were ready to propose a plan for dividing the country into LATAs. There was substantial agreement between the companies and the Justice Department, although it was expected that some modifications would still have to be made. Court approval was required for a variety of state-line crossings and for two so-called corridor exceptions.[43] AT&T submitted the proposed

---

[43]In October 1981, Senator William Bradley of New Jersey had introduced an amendment to
   S. 898 excepting consolidation of SMSAs in densely populated states from the requirement

plan (161 LATAs) to the court on October 4. As always, comments were invited, and AT&T and the Department of Justice filed their responses on November 23.[44] Justice concurred with 152 of the proposed units and reserved judgment on the remainder. This provided a basis on which to formulate the plan of reorganization, and Judge Greene finally settled the details of the LATAs in 1983. Greene ordered eight LATAs combined into four and six LATAs divided – more or less a wash, although the totals were not really as important as the specific changes made in local arrangements.[45] More ominous was the manner in which the court was being subtly transformed as it took on functions that traditionally had been reserved to regulatory agencies.

In the fall of 1982, with the LATA plan approaching completion, AT&T's lawyers began to concentrate on the difficult task of drafting a Plan of Reorganization. Under the terms of the decree, the company had only six months after its final acceptance (August 24) to file a plan with the court. The plan had to specify exactly how the Bell System was to be torn apart. Howard Trienens and John Zeglis of Sidley and Austin spearheaded this crash effort to translate the "two-page" decree into a specific proposal. Drafts were written and then sent for comments to operating personnel at AT&T and the designated officers of the seven regional holding companies. Olson and Tanenbaum continued to map out the new AT&T. Communications between the lawyers and the operating personnel often were strained. The reorganization was a legal document, and the lawyers had to write language that would hold up in court. But divestiture involved the reorganization of a series of functioning companies, and the plan had to make commercial and technical sense as well. Conflicts were inevitable. Brown reorganized the planning operation to deal with the increased volume of questions. He placed Sharwell in charge of divestiture implementation under Ellinghaus, his long-time boss and friend, freeing Segall for divestiture planning.

There were many channels for conflict resolution, of which the close

for court approval. But since S. 898 was only a Senate bill and not law, court approval was still needed for two "corridors" that crossed state lines – New York City and northern New Jersey, and Camden, New Jersey, and Philadelphia – where the network had been configured to use large local trunks for what was conceptually interstate toll traffic.

[44] *US v. AT&T*, CA No. 82–0192 (D.D.C.), *Application of the American Telephone and Telegraph Company and the Bell System Operating Companies for Approval of Exchange Areas or Local Access and Transport Areas (LATAs) Established Pursuant to the Modification of Final Judgment*, October 4, 1982; *Response of the United States to Comments Received on BOC LATA Proposals*, November 23, 1982; *Response by AT&T to Comments and Objections Relating to the Proposed LATA Configurations*, November 23, 1982.

[45] Judge Greene, *Opinion*, April 20, 1983, *US v. AT&T*, CA No. 82–0192, Misc. No. 82–0025 (PI) (D.D.C.), 569 F. Supp. 990. Even at this late date, the court requested more information on over half a dozen LATAs, preserving a residual uncertainty about the final LATA plan that continued almost up to the date of divestiture.

contact between Brown and his general counsel was the most important. Typical of procedures at lower levels was the Restructure Implementation Board chaired by Brooke Tunstall, director of divestiture planning, and Robert Dalziel, representing the regional holding companies. Dalziel had dinner with the seven regional company representatives on the day before each biweekly meeting, dissipating some of the tension generated in the process of negotiation. When the representatives met with fifteen or so AT&T officers the following morning, they were able to present a much calmer and more coherent point of view than would have been possible the night before.[46]

The divestiture organization functioned like a series of terraces, each of which resolved some disputes and allowed others to go to the next level. Everything that could be settled at a lower level between the appropriate staffs was taken care of without intervention by top management. As one AT&T officer later explained, he did not become involved with many of the issues that arose because he was responsible only for those questions involving assets of $1 billion or more. In this case, the Bell System's traditional style of management, with its emphasis on precise definition of responsibility, worked to minimize friction. The process was well designed to achieve consensus among those managers of the respective companies best qualified technically to settle the various disputes. But even then, some issues did not yield to more manpower of greater expertise. These issues traveled up the levels, even, if need be, to Brown's office for resolution. Brown normally would invite the contending parties to confer with him and would persuade them to work out an acceptable solution. He also decided some matters himself; until the date of the actual divestiture, he was still the boss.

Dispersed among the important decisions were some minor ones that were nonetheless memorable. Sharwell proposed to Brown that AT&T continue to maintain its service indexes for the entire telephone network. This was not a major activity. It would not cost a great deal to keep it going. But Brown nevertheless turned down the proposal. He worried about the size of the headquarters staff of the new AT&T; besides, the government had decided that AT&T should no longer be the steward of the national network. The indexes harked back to Vail's concept of the corporation. Brown was pointing AT&T toward a different future.

Another small but thorny problem involved an outside test yard in New Jersey. Operated by Bell Labs, it was the area where tests were run on outdoor equipment like telephone poles and cables. Despite the triviality of the issue, lower levels of the divestiture group could not resolve the

[46]Tunstall, *Disconnecting Parties*, pp. 42, 54; Tunstall, interview, May 30, 1984, pp. 23–30.

dispute over who should get the yard. The argument finally became so heated that Brown went out and looked at the test yard. Then he, like Solomon, split it down the middle.[47]

Throughout all of these negotiations and planning efforts, of course, Brown and the other Bell System personnel had to keep the nation's telephones operating. Despite the massive diversion of manpower to divestiture planning, America's telephones rang and were repaired if they did not. Consumers did not bear the cost of divestiture; instead, AT&T paid for it in the coin of foregone planning for the postdivestiture world. Divestiture consumed an inordinate amount of the company's planning energies; even so, some problems could not be resolved.

When Brown could not settle an issue, it went to the Justice Department or Judge Greene. One of these troublesome matters involved the ownership of blue public telephones. Pay phones clearly were the province of the operating companies, but the blue Charge-A-Call telephones that do not receive coins were intended for toll calls, most of which were interLATA calls. According to the rule of predominant use, they belonged to AT&T. But it seemed absurd to have the operating company servicemen worry about the black phones and the AT&T servicemen handle the blue ones in a bank of mixed phones. The plan was amended at the request of the Justice Department and the regional holding companies to give both sets of phones to the operating companies.[48]

A problem more significant – and partly symbolic – to most of the telephone managers involved the use of the Bell name and logo. All parts of the Bell System that was being broken up seemed to be appropriately termed Bell. The *Bell Telephone Hour* had been AT&T's venture, the operating companies frequently had the Bell name in their title, and, of course, Bell Labs used the name as well. Brown took the position that AT&T owned the Bell name and logo, but that it would allow the operating companies to use it; there was no sense in depriving them of this traditional identification. Although Brown saw no reason why the name and logo had to go either to the operating companies or to AT&T, he insisted that AT&T owned the name.

The Tandy Corporation, which owns Radio Shack, objected to Brown's proposed joint use of the Bell name on the grounds that it would create confusion. Tandy wanted to sell its telephones to Bell companies and to the customers of those firms. Tandy said that it would be unfair to have to

[47]Ellinghaus, interview, June 13, 1985, pp. 58–9; William G. Sharwell, interview, July 10, 1985, pp. 56–61, 81–3; Staley, interview, February 25, 1986, p. 18. AT&T also decided to stop publication of the *Bell Journal of Economics*, a decision undoubtedly made at a lower level of the organization. See Tunstall, *Disconnecting Parties*, pp. 52–3, for a list of difficult issues.
[48]John D. Zeglis, interview, May 23, 1984, p. 68.

compete against Bell telephones sold by AT&T, an unrelated company; consumers would give unwarranted preference to AT&T's products. The judge, impressed by Tandy's argument, awarded the Bell name exclusively to the operating companies. As with his decision on the Yellow Pages, Judge Greene had no qualms about taking assets from AT&T and awarding them to the operating companies.[49] Brown quickly accommodated to Greene's decision. He asked his people to design a new AT&T logo, and they came up with the now familiar globe. Until this was done, however, some of AT&T's managers who had spent a lifetime working under the distinctive Bell rubric expressed strong feelings about this decision on Greene's part.[50]

Far larger and more complex problems were posed by Bell Labs's patents, Western Electric's support for existing operating company equipment, and the matter of embedded wire. Patents were a problem because the combined revenues of the Bell System had paid for them and it was questioned whether the new, competitive AT&T should have exclusive rights to use them. As long as the Bell System was still intact, support for existing equipment had been implicit in the sale; the problem was how to continue and finance servicing after divestiture. The debates between Western Electric and the operating companies over these issues raced out of control. They generated bad feelings that would poison relationships after divestiture.[51] Embedded wire – that is, wire already installed in customers' houses and businesses – was a problem partly because regulatory rules had required their installation to be capitalized rather than expensed. The operating companies had been prevented from recovering the installation costs through revenues, and they were left with a large account that did not correspond to any usable asset. Each of these problems was disputed at great length and finally resolved, but in the meantime the sense of a common effort within the Bell System was weakened. The vital energy that was making divestiture work began to ebb.[52]

[49]Brown, interview, June 9, 1984, pp. 20–2; *US* v. *AT&T*, CA No. 74–1698, 82–0192, Misc. No. 82–0025 (PI) (D.D.C.), *Comments of Tandy Corporation*, April 20, 1982. Baxter and Carr disagreed on this issue; Baxter favored Judge Greene's view, but Carr thought that there would be a social cost in depriving AT&T of the Bell name. Given a choice, he would have given it to AT&T, but his preferred solution was to allow everyone to use it. Carr, interview, June 13, 1984, pp. 58–9.
[50]Block, interview, December 3, 1985, p. 76.
[51]Weiss, interview, November 20, 1985, pp. 32–3.
[52]The Justice Department asserted that the operating companies had an equity in the patents. Since they referred largely to the manufacture of equipment, which the operating companies were barred from doing, AT&T did not agree with this position. The company nevertheless gave rights to technical information to the operating companies in order to help ease them into their independent existence. But since the operating companies would no longer be part of an integrated system, these rights came with many strings attached. The companies could freely allow outsiders to make products for their use but not to

In spite of the mounting tension, AT&T was able to file a Plan of Reorganization on December 16, 1982. Ten thousand copies were printed and distributed, first to those most intimately involved and then to anyone who asked for one. The plan was accompanied by the court-ordered affidavits by the heads of the regional holding companies and AT&T. With one exception, these officers described the process by which the plan had been put forward, agreed that it had been formulated cooperatively, and stated that their concerns had been incorporated into the proposal. They also asserted that their enterprises would be viable entities with the resources needed to perform the functions assigned to them in the Modification of Final Judgment. Running through these affidavits, however, were some still unresolved issues, which would have to be settled by the judge.[53]

Donald Guinn of the Pacific regional holding company was the only CEO to declare that he was not "in a position to express an opinion on the subject of financial viability . . . under the Plan." The Pacific firm said that it was not in a sound financial position because it would have postdivestiture debts substantially higher than those of the other compa-

replicate a Western Electric design. Such an amorphous goal has – as one might have anticipated – provoked endless wrangling.

The operating companies were assured that they would continue to get support for their equipment from Western Electric, and they were given "a golden parachute" as well if Western abandoned them. Whenever they were dissatisfied with their support from Western, the operating companies could move the support function and its personnel from Western Electric to the Central Service Organization. They were therefore assured, one way or another, of getting the service that was needed to maintain the network.

The embedded wiring, valued at $12 to $15 billion, was assigned to the operating companies. After 1982, investment in new inside wiring was expensed in the form of an upfront, one-time charge to subscribers who required its installation. The existing or embedded investment in inside wiring installed before 1982, which previously had been capitalized, was to be amortized over a ten-year period.

Another arrangement allowed the operating companies to amortize their expenditures in reengineering the network for equal access over ten years. If they had not recovered their costs after ten years because regulators had not allowed them to earn a rate of return sufficient for this purpose, AT&T would be liable for the balance.

AT&T saw the possibility of getting a bill for billions of dollars on January 1, 1994, and went back to the government. Additional conditions were inserted requiring the operating companies to file tariffs each year designed to recover the balance of the costs then remaining and also requiring the regulators to allow all of these costs as rate-making costs. If those conditions were not met, that amount of the guarantee would not be valid. In other words, AT&T was not to be held liable either for the laxness of the operating companies in attempting to recover their costs or for regulatory stringency that prevented them from doing so. They were protected instead from a failure of demand or from other commercial problems that prevented recovery even under favorable regulatory circumstances. Zeglis, interview, May 23, 1984, pp. 61–77.

These and other operating relationships between AT&T and the Bell Operating Companies were ultimately covered by the multitudinous contracts negotiated between the companies.

[53]*US* v. *AT&T*, CA No. 82–0192 (D.D.C.), *Plan of Reorganization*, December 16, 1982; see Tunstall, *Disconnecting Parties*, pp. 60–2, for a list of the outstanding issues in the POR.

nies. An exception had been made for Pacific in the consent decree. But Pacific still felt financially jeopardized by its debt burden. Guinn argued that nonvoting preferred stock should be counted as debt. This would increase the company's debt-equity ratio from 50 percent, as promised in the decree, to 54 percent. As he pointed out, too, Pacific Telephone faced a unique tax liability of over $1.5 billion because of the way in which the California Public Utility Commission insisted on handling certain deferred investment tax credits. The company's financial position was thus doubly hazardous.[54]

Brown's affidavit anticipated Guinn's objections and sought to explain the extraordinary condition of Pacific Telephone by reference to the unfavorable regulatory climate in California during the 1970s. In a period of strongly accelerating demand and high interest rates, California regulators had held Pacific Telephone's earnings to a minimum. Pacific Telephone, as a result, had been forced to finance expansion by debt. In addition, Brown estimated that Pacific Telephone had suffered an after-tax shortfall in earnings amounting to $1.5 billion over the same period, roughly the size of the outstanding financial liability. Finally, Brown said, preferred stock is preferred stock, not debt.[55]

On December 23, Congress helped to resolve this dispute when it passed the Surface Transportation Act of 1982, one section of which eliminated most of Pacific Telephone's extraordinary tax liability. Guinn then certified that the reorganization plan would provide his company with the resources necessary to be financially viable (although he still maintained that his preferred stock should rightly be seen as debt and that the plan was not in conformity with the guidelines on Pacific's debt structure).[56]

On this note, the planning process initiated by Brown when he appointed the six presidential study groups at the beginning of 1982 came to a conclusion at the end of the year.[57] The implementation of the consent decree was an effort that dwarfed the reorganization of 1978, also planned

[54]*US* v. *AT&T*, CA No. 82–0192 (D.D.C.), *Sworn Statement of Donald E. Guinn*, December 15, 1982.

[55]*US* v. *AT&T*, CA No. 82–0192 (D.D.C.), *Affidavit of Charles L. Brown*, December 15, 1982.

[56]*US* v. *AT&T*, CA No. 82–0192 (D.D.C.), *Supplemental Statement of Donald E. Guinn*, January 13, 1983.

[57]Comments were invited on the Plan of Reorganization, and 54 parties responded. AT&T responded in March, and there were further inquiries, comments, and responses throughout the first half of 1983. Judge Greene issued a major opinion on the plan at the beginning of July. But with a petition from AT&T and other outstanding matters, it was not finally approved until August 5, 1983, less than five months before the date of actual divestiture. Only in July did Judge Greene settle the cost of providing equal access, the use of the word "Bell," and the arrangements for licenses from AT&T to the operating companies.

Judge Greene, *Opinion*, July 8, 1983, and *Order*, August 5, 1983, *US* v. *AT&T*, CA No. 82–0192, Misc. No. 82–0025 (PI) (D.D.C.), 569 F. Supp. 1057 (D.D.C. 1983), as amended July 28, 1983 and August 5, 1983.

in a single year, as well as the changes stemming from *Computer Inquiry II*. This time also AT&T would have little opportunity to test the new structure; it had only another year to make the new plans fully operational. Contracts to keep the Bell System running had to be negotiated and signed by AT&T and the regional holding companies. AT&T would have to open for business on January 1, 1984, without any other formal connection to the operating firms or their regional holding companies. Brown and his colleagues had much to do before that transition could be made.

Access charges

One of the most difficult problems facing Brown – thornier than the questions involving assets and personnel – was the division of revenues. Ever since the wartime agreement on separations, revenue from long distance service had been shared between the suppliers of local and long distance service. The steady rise in the proportion of local costs assigned to long distance had made separations a major feature of telephone pricing. Over $7 billion was involved in 1981, compared to total interstate revenues of $20 billion.[58]

The Modification of Final Judgment forced everyone in telecommunications to confront this issue because the Bell System would no longer exist to pay separations charges as internal transfers. The agreement, however, said only that the separations charges were to be replaced by a set of cost-justified tariffs for the provision of access to the local network. Like all other tariffs, these were to be nondiscriminatory. Nothing was said about the level of the new tariffs. Both Brown and Baxter testified to a suspicious Congress in early 1982 that divestiture had no implications for the subsidy from long distance to local service. The senators questioning Brown left no doubt about their desire to preserve the subsidy; Brown replied that the regulators still had the power to continue it. The regulators agreed. The FCC saw no reason why the decree should affect local rates.[59]

The operating companies were not so sure. They responded to the announcement of the consent decree by filing or threatening to file for higher rates to replace the separations subsidies that they claimed they

---

[58] Peter Temin and Geoffrey Peters, "Cross-Subsidization in the Telephone Network," *Willamette Law Review*, Vol. 21 (Spring 1985), pp. 199–223.
[59] 97th Congress, 2nd Session, Senate, Committee on Commerce, Science and Transportation, "Hearing on AT&T Proposed Settlement," Charles L. Brown, testimony, January 25, 1982, and Committee on the Judiciary, Hearing, "Oversight of Recent Actions of DOJ in *US v. IBM*," William F. Baxter, testimony, January 25, 1982; *US* v. *AT&T*, CA No. 74–1698, 82–0192, Misc. No. 82–0025 (PI) *Brief for Federal Communications Commission as Amicus Curiae*, April 20, 1982, pp. 17–19.

would soon lose. Their actions spooked the media and heightened congressional anxiety, some of which was embodied in Wirth's revised bill.[60] Whatever the merits of their immediate actions, Wirth and the operating companies were good prophets. The old price structure was not viable given the new structure of the industry. Just as regulatory prices had created incentives for entry into private lines and then message toll service in the old structure, they would induce "bypass" in the new setting, that is, direct connection between large telephone customers and interexchange carriers. If the subsidy to local service was to continue to depend on interLATA traffic going through the operating companies, it would accelerate efforts to bypass the local firms. Competition had come to the center of the telephone network, and the stakes were much higher than before. The price structure would have to respond faster.

Brown expressed the process succinctly. After noting that 40 percent of interstate revenues were used to keep local rates down, he continued: "With competition, this subsidization of local rates by AT&T's long distance service is no longer possible and will be gradually phased out. Long distance rates will come down, and local rates will rise." He clearly identified the separations charges from the operating companies as subsidies. He attributed the pressure for their elimination to competition, not the Modification of Final Judgment. But divestiture markedly increased the intensity of competition in long distance service and therefore the pressure for rate reform.[61]

For a change, the problem was relatively simple. The tariffs for exchange access mandated by the Modification of Final Judgment were to be paid to the operating companies (by the interexchange carriers, including AT&T)–in proportion to the use made of the local facilities. If an interexchange carrier used fewer lines or had fewer calls into the local exchange, then it would pay less to the operating company. But if a customer was big enough to be, in essence, its own local exchange, it could request an interexchange carrier to connect directly with it, bypassing the local company and reducing the interexchange carrier's payments to the local company. There would be added costs: The physical connection between a large firm and the interexchange carrier would have to be made and maintained. But these costs were small relative to the exchange access charge, and the firm and the carrier could divide the gain. Local rates would rise, therefore, whether the tariff for exchange access was

[60]"Members of Two House Units Reflect Constituents' Concerns About Impact on Local Rates in Three-Hour Session with AT&T Chairman; Need to Pursue Legislative Route Emphasized," *Telecommunications Reports*, Vol. 48, No. 5 (February 1, 1982), pp. 11–12; Levine, interview, June 12, 1984, p. 63.
[61]Charles L. Brown, "Remarks of the Chairman," AT&T Annual Meeting, Atlanta, Georgia, April 20, 1983.

decreased or not. If it was lowered, then the local companies would lose revenues directly. If not, the operating companies would lose revenues due to bypass. The companies were in the situation AT&T had been in after the *Specialized Common Carriers* decision, except that the revenue in question was much, much larger by 1982.[62]

Throughout the years of the debates, these charges (resulting from separations, not tariffs) had been called "contributions" by AT&T. Under Bell's board-to-board theory, they were cross-subsidies as well. The FCC, Congress, and the government's expert witnesses in the Justice Department's antitrust suit had adhered to the rival station-to-station theory, in which the definition of cross-subsidies was much more elusive. It was not possible, using that theory, to say convincingly either that separations charges were or were not cross-subsidies. Most adherents of the station-to-station theory held that they were not. But divestiture broke the telephone network apart along board-to-board lines. Theory frequently follows reality, and the station-to-station theory began to fade almost immediately. As more and more people came to think in terms of board-to-board accounting, separations charges or exchange access tariffs commonly came to be viewed as cross-subsidies. Fully distributed costs began to seem as inappropriate to rate making as they had become to evaluating cross-subsidies. The developments of 1982 made the arguments of 1981 almost incomprehensible, and in 1984 the FCC would abandon its insistence on the use of fully distributed costs.[63]

This did not happen overnight, but the FCC began to hear talk of bypass as early as 1982. It began to ponder what it could do to avoid the problem and to preserve the financial condition of the operating companies. That year it was not yet ready to abandon its fully distributed cost pricing standards. It was already willing, however, to moderate the impact of separations charges as they had grown since the Second World War and particularly in the 1970s.[64] At the end of 1981, when divestiture was still a Justice Department pipe dream, the joint NARUC-FCC board on separations recommended that the formula used to calculate separations charges be capped at its 1981 level. The joint board also advocated phasing terminal equipment already on customers' premises out of the

[62]AT&T was not happy about its role in this process. It preferred to work through the operating companies to get the services they offered, but it was not about to refuse the requests of large customers. Even though the customers came to AT&T with a professed concern about service quality, not price, the prices they were paying obviously affected their decisions—and, as a result, AT&T's actions as well. Morris Tanenbaum, interview, May 23, 1985, pp. 54–5; Donald E. Guinn, interview, December 12, 1985, p. 48.
[63]FCC, *Notice of Proposed Rulemaking*, FCC CC Docket 84–1235, "Guidelines for Dominant Carriers' MTS Rates and Rate Structure Plans," adopted November 21, 1984, released January 9, 1985, 100 FCC 2d 363.
[64]See Figure 4.

separations process altogether. The FCC adopted the joint board's recommendations in February 1982, shortly after divestiture had been announced. Then, instead of raising the access charges that the other common carriers paid to 65 percent and then 75 percent of AT&T's (as that firm had anticipated when it agreed to the ENFIA compromise in 1978), the FCC froze ENFIA charges at a rate highly favorable to the other common carriers.[65]

How, then, would the operating companies regain the revenues lost from both capping the rate and removing terminal equipment from cost sharing? The Commission considered this question as part of its long-running investigation of competition in long distance markets. Started in response to Judge Wright's *Execunet* decision in 1977, the study had concluded in 1980 that competition in ordinary long distance service was here to stay. The agency had not, however, terminated its investigation at this point.[66] With Congress considering proposals for access charges to replace the separations process, the Commission moved on to consider the way in which operating companies would be paid for their services in a competitive long distance market. It announced its plan at the end of 1982. The FCC's new study worked from the obvious to the unexpected, proclaiming that "the monopoly telecommunications environment of the past has ended." Starting from this bald acknowledgment, the Commission signaled its adaptation to competition. Quoting economics textbooks, it said that marginal cost pricing was the appropriate standard for competitive markets. This set the stage for its startling conclusion.

As the agency recognized, bypass was a growing problem. AT&T in particular now seemed to have an incentive to bypass the independent operating companies, bringing the danger from the fringes of the long distance market to its center. Even if AT&T's management was reluctant to bypass its former partners in the Bell System, it could hardly turn away business from a large firm that wanted direct connections. The Commission could deal with this problem either by denying authorization to firms that wanted to construct bypass facilities or by changing its prices to remove the incentive. Wirth's bill favored the former approach, but the FCC embraced the latter course by way of marginal cost pricing. Expanding the meaning of the term "access charge," it proposed to lower the charge to interexchange carriers to cover only the marginal costs their traffic imposed on the operating companies. The rest of the operating

[65]FCC, *Decision and Order*, FCC CC Docket 80–286, "Amendment of Part 67 of the Commission's Rules," February 26, 1982, 89 FCC 2d 1.
[66]The FCC's announcement came virtually contemporaneously with the jury's finding that AT&T had illegally interfered with MCI's competitive efforts. FCC, *Report and Third Supplemental Notice of Inquiry and Proposed Rulemaking*, FCC CC Docket 78–72, "MTS/WATS Market Structure," August 25, 1980, 81 FCC 2d 177.

companies' costs – its fixed or non-traffic-sensitive costs – would have to be recovered from their subscribers.[67] This was an amazing about-face. The FCC had proclaimed at the beginning of 1982 that the Modification of Final Judgment would not affect its behavior, but it had completely reversed its position on pricing by the end of the year. Instead of using the traditional regulatory solution to the bypass problem – continuing average-cost pricing while barring entry – it proposed to work through prices. Ever since the *Above 890* decision, the FCC had been allowing entry without allowing, or at least without approving, competitive price responses. Having dropped one shoe in 1959, it finally dropped the other 23 years later. It would not only allow regulated companies to charge the same prices that they would have offered in an unregulated competitive market, it would order them to do so.

AT&T, of course, had been arguing for this permission since the early 1960s. Its unsuccessful and long-lasting campaigns for incremental cost pricing had carried through the debates over TELPAK, Hi-Lo, and successor tariffs, but AT&T had been unable to convince the FCC to allow it to charge competitive prices for telephone service. Finally, the FCC adopted a new policy. But not until divestiture was breaking up the Bell System along board-to-board lines, severely crippling the arguments behind *Smith v. Illinois Bell* and traditional regulatory pricing. And not until the Modification of Final Judgment had reduced AT&T's size and market power enough to make its claims to be an ordinary competitive firm more plausible.

The FCC's decision was also an extension of agency jurisdiction as audacious as anything Wirth had proposed. The Commission wanted to increase local rates, but it had no jurisdiction over those rates and did not try to assert any. All it did was to expand the concept of access charges to cover charges to end-users. Nevertheless, the proposed access charges would be part of the bill that subscribers would pay to their local operating companies. It would be a local telephone rate in everything but name. The FCC was up to its ears in local rate making.

Trienens had foreseen a similar development as he contemplated divestiture in 1980 and 1981. AT&T knew well how the existence of 50 separate state jurisdictions impeded change at the local level. The company had been charged – reasonably – with using this regulation as a barrier to competition in terminal equipment and network interconnection. Now the Modification of Final Judgment was effecting by a single stroke changes in the industry that could not have been achieved in a dozen years at the state level. Trienens had talked mainly about firm structure, which felt

---

[67]FCC, *Third Report and Order*, FCC CC Docket 78–72, adopted December 22, 1982, released February 28, 1983, 93 FCC 2d 241.

the direct impact of divestiture, but the argument extended to prices as well. It would have been a long, costly, painful war to fight through rate increases in every state jurisdiction in order to replace the lost separations payments. How much cleaner and easier to have the FCC impose access charges on end users.[68]

The Commission, bold with concepts, was cautious about numbers. The total amount of money involved was "immense." Revenue requirements for non-traffic-sensitive interstate exchange plant were estimated to be $8.5 billion in 1984, the first year of the Commission's plan. Divided by an estimated 100 million subscriber lines, this meant that an access charge of about $7.00 per month was needed to cover these costs, plus an additional $2.00 to $2.50 per month for traffic-sensitive costs. The FCC was so impressed by these numbers that it calculated the $7.00 monthly charge incorrectly (as $8.50) and failed to say that the traffic-sensitive costs undoubtedly would continue to be covered by long distance charges.

Understandably, the FCC proposed to slowly phase in this large increase in end user charges. The agency hoped to make this radical change in telephone pricing over seven years, increasing access charges on end users in small steps. It ordered a charge of at least $2 a month for residential customers and $4 a month for businesses, preserving the two-to-one price discrimination introduced by Bell a century earlier. As with Jacob and Esau, the words referred to interstate commerce, but the charges were local rates. The Commission issued the full text of its decision in February 1983, spelling out the details of its plan. At about the same time, the joint NARUC-FCC board considering separations recommended that the freeze on separations and ENFIA charges imposed by the FCC the previous year be continued so that the amount of non-traffic-sensitive local plant allocated to the interstate jurisdiction would continue to move toward a goal of 25 percent.

These actions went on independently, but the actors kept a careful eye on each other. The clear intent of the FCC's access payments was to reduce ENFIA charges. There were two political problems in this complex maneuver. End-user access charges raised the price of service to consumers, arousing congressional indignation. Lowering the ENFIA tariff threatened the preference rates for AT&T's competitors that had been set "temporarily" in 1978. Under the Modification of Final Judgment, the preference would essentially vanish in 1986; the access charge plan was consistent with this planned phaseout. The other common carriers, faced

[68]Trienens recognized, however, that even FCC actions would be traumatic and politically explosive. Howard J. Trienens before the FCC, March 24, 1982 (transcribed from an audio cassette).

with the imminent loss of their preferential charges, were, of course, strongly opposed to the FCC's plan.[69]

The FCC's move toward higher end-user charges consequently generated intense opposition. In April, Judge Greene loosed a blast at the FCC in his opinion approving the new LATAs. He railed against the FCC's decision to "saddle" local subscribers with the costs of access; this, he said, was "directly counter" to the consent decree's intent. He was horrified at the Commission's effort to "unjustifiably" assign responsibility for its decision to the Modification of Final Judgment. He restated his objectives to be "achieving fair competition, on the one hand, and the protection of rates which will permit all segments of the population to enjoy telephone service, on the other." Following in the long tradition from President Johnson's 1968 task force through many, many FCC decisions, he did not spell out how the conflicts between these contradictory goals were to be resolved or who, exactly, would pay the tab.[70]

"Troubled" by this attack, the Commission reminded Judge Greene that its access charge decision was on appeal before the circuit (appeals) court, "which has exclusive jurisdiction to review the decision."[71] The FCC, content to let the courts decide AT&T's antitrust liability, was not eager to have them take over telephone rate setting. But that was what Judge Greene was doing. He apparently did not want to be known as the man who had doubled telephone rates. He was already extending his control over industry structure through his supervision of the consent decree; he was now edging toward control over prices as well. AT&T, far from finding relief from regulation in divestiture, was actually acquiring more regulators.

Congress was also up in arms over the proposed access charges to end users, stimulated both by consumer groups and by the other common carriers. Sparked by a press conference by Senator Packwood, who voiced his concern about residential telephone rates, congressional interest gathered steam throughout the early summer. Bills limiting the amount by which local rates could rise or explicitly terminating the FCC's access charges were introduced in both houses. At the end of July, in a rare display of unified congressional power, Senator Packwood held a joint

[69]FCC, *Third Report and Order*, FCC CC Docket 78–72, adopted December 22, 1982, released February 28, 1983, 93 FCC 2d 241; FCC, *Decision and Order*, FCC CC Docket 80–286, February 26, 1982, 89 FCC 2d 1; FCC, *Second Recommended Decision and Order*, FCC CC Docket 80–286, adopted April 15, 1983, released September 26, 1983; FCC, *Order on Reconsideration*, FCC CC Docket 78–371, "ENFIA," April 5, 1983, 93 FCC 2d 739.
[70]Judge Greene, *Opinion*, April 20, 1983, *US* v. *AT&T*, CA No. 82–0192, Misc. No. 82–0025 (PI) (D.D.C.), 569 F. Supp. 990, at 998, 1000.
[71]*US* v. *AT&T*, CA No. 82–0192 (D.D.C.), *Motion of Federal Communications Commission for Leave to File Response*, June 13, 1983.

news conference with Congressmen Dingell and Wirth to announce the introduction of compatible bills in the House and Senate to preserve inexpensive local telephone service. Significantly, these measures would also preserve the ENFIA discount for other common carriers. Both houses would hold hearings at the full committee level in the next few days and mark up the bills when Congress reassembled in September.

The thrust of the bills was to "use long distance rates to subsidize rural and residential service," according to Packwood, and "maintain the status quo," according to Dingell. If there was a difference between the two, Dingell said, it was that he preferred to call Packwood's subsidy a "fair allocation of costs." Consistent with this view, the House bill specifically required interexchange carriers to pay the direct cost of local connections, a share of joint and common costs, and a surcharge for a universal service fund.[72]

Congressmen and senators rushed to associate themselves with these and similar bills, but dissenting voices also began to be heard. The joint hearings held the following week brought opposition to the bills from the heads of several interexchange carriers, from the designated CEOs of all seven regional Bell holding companies, and from FCC Chairman Mark Fowler. These witnesses supported the FCC's access charge and decried the haste with which Congress was rushing to the attack. It was obviously going to be hard to get agreement on a bill specifying proper telephone pricing; talk of a bill that simply postponed the access charges began to be heard in the halls of Congress.[73]

The mood was similar when Congress reassembled in the fall. The Senate Commerce Committee first adopted a weak Democratic substitute for Packwood's bill (which appeared to have little chance of passage by the full Senate) and then a compromise measure. Wirth's subcommittee sent the House bill to Dingell's committee, which scheduled its markup for October. Curiously, the banner of universal service was supported by Democrats in the House, partly as an expression of anti-Reagan senti-

[72]"Packwood to Ask Other Senators for Input on Legislation Addressing Need for Subsidy and Local Telephone Rate Issues; May Distribute Draft Bill Aimed at Keeping Exchange Rates Down," *Telecommunications Reports*, Vol. 49, No. 21 (May 30, 1983), pp. 1–2; "Senate, House Commerce Unit Leaders, Displaying Unity in Thrust and Purpose but Variation in Specifics, Hold Joint Press Conference to Announce Introduction of Bills to Block FCC Access Charge Order, and Maintenance of 'Subsidy' and Access Status Quo," *Telecommunications Reports*, Vol. 49, No. 29 (July 25, 1983), pp. 1–6. 98th Congress, 1st Session, Senate, "Universal Telephone Service Preservation Act of 1983," S. 1660, introduced July 21, 1983; 98th Congress, 1st Session, House, "Universal Telephone Service Preservation Act of 1983," H.R. 3621, introduced July 21, 1983.
[73]"Some Steam Appears to Be Out of Prospect for Universal Service/Access Charge Bill This Year, as Specific Problems Arise at Hearings and Numerous Witnesses See Major Problems with Proposals, but Strong Impetus and Support Remains for New Legislation," *Telecommunications Reports*, Vol. 49, No. 30 (August 1, 1983), pp. 1–3, 16–24.

ments, and by the Republicans in the Senate on party-line votes. The unity expressed by Packwood, Dingell, and Wirth was holding.[74]

Alarmed by the prospect of legislation that would extend the differential ENFIA pricing that favored AT&T's competitors, Brown wrote to all of the members of both the House and the Senate early in October. "It is too late," he said, "for Congress to have second thoughts about whether or not, and at what pace, competition should be encouraged – or," he added for emphasis, "whether the Bell System should have been broken up to begin with." AT&T urged its shareholders, employees, and customers to write their congressmen in opposition to these measures. It was a repeat, on a slightly smaller scale, of the blitz against Wirth's bill the previous year.[75]

AT&T also announced a price reduction in response to the FCC plan. This too aroused hostility, which Dingell and Wirth expressed on the Op-Ed page of *The Washington Post*. They started with the now familiar complaint about the rise in local rates that would follow from the FCC's new access charge. They went on to say that the Commission's decision would transfer more than $4 billion from the pockets of local rate payers to AT&T – a sum that AT&T had promised would be passed back to customers by means of reduced long distance rates. But AT&T proposed to cut rates by only about 10 percent, turning back less than $2 billion to the rate payers. Where, Dingell and Wirth asked, would the other $2 billion go, if not to the company's corporate coffers? Most of it, in fact, went to the operating companies to bring their earnings up to authorized levels; the congressmen had forgotten them. But some of it ($0.6 billion) went to AT&T to lift its earnings to the level authorized by the FCC. AT&T, by its own lights, had ample reasons for its actions – the earned rates of return for it and the operating companies were below the allowed rates – but solicitude for the rate payer was not highly visible among them. AT&T, still the responsible utility, was pilloried for adhering to the rules for regulatory pricing, as it had been assailed for attempting to use competitive pricing in the 1970s.[76]

AT&T, acting like a regulated monopolist, found itself under attack from all quarters. While Dingell and Wirth were assaulting the company for not lowering prices enough, the other common carriers were complain-

[74]"Proposed Universal Telephone Service Legislation Quickly Reaches Cliffhanger Status on Both Sides of Capitol; Senate Committee, in 9–6 Vote, Moves to Substitute Simple Year's Moratorium on Residential End-User Access Charges for Entire Packwood Measure," *Telecommunications Reports*, Vol. 49, No. 38 (September 26, 1983), pp. 1–5; "Senate Committee, House Subcommittee Approve Compromise Versions of New Legislation to Enhance Prospects of Some Bill This Year Substantially; Senate Bill Heads Toward Floor, While Full House Committee Schedules Markup Sessions to Begin in Mid-October," *Telecommunications Reports*, Vol. 49, No. 39 (October 3, 1983), p. 1.
[75]Charles L. Brown to all members of Congress, October 5, 1983.
[76]James R. Billingsley to Mark S. Fowler, October 3, 1983; John Dingell and Timothy Wirth, "The Great Phone Robbery," *The Washington Post*, October 26, 1983, p. A27.

ing that it had lowered them too far. The smaller firms were faced with stiffer competition as a result of AT&T's lower prices; they had higher costs as a consequence of increased charges by the operating companies. The heads of eight common carriers wrote to FCC Chairman Mark Fowler that the "very survival of the OCC [other common carriers] industry was threatened." They acknowledged that they had been allowed to underestimate their usage of local lines and were enjoying an even larger discount from AT&T's charges than the ENFIA tariff specified. Unfazed by their admission that they were in fact enjoying 65–75 percent discounts from Long Lines' charges, the new carriers insisted that the loss of their preferential prices would be devastating.[77]

The FCC, alarmed by the growing conflict, postponed the proposed access charges from January to April 1984. Fowler also wrote to Packwood that the Commission opposed legislation. Like Brown two years earlier, however, he added that anything was better than uncertainty. Despite this added opposition, Dingell's committee reported the Dingell-Wirth bill to the House, which passed it by voice vote in short order.[78] The bill was based on the premise that universal service was threatened by increased local rates. It forbade access charges for residential customers and single-line businesses. Yielding to the pressure for bypass, it limited the proportion of local costs that could be allocated to the interstate carriers to the level reached at the end of 1983 and imposed a penalty on firms bypassing the local companies. And, continuing the House's solicitude for the other common carriers, the bill froze the ENFIA discounts at their July 1983, level.[79]

For the most part, the bill missed its mark. It is unlikely that universal service was threatened to any significant degree by the FCC's cautious approach to end-user access charges. As the FCC explained, the penalty for bypass was too small to have any effect, so that local rates would have to rise to compensate for lost revenues in any case. The most effective part of the bill, therefore, was the provision maintaining preferential pricing for AT&T's competitors. Presumably it was this feature that endeared the bill to the House Democrats.

---

[77]US Transmission Systems, US Telephone, Satellite Business Systems, EMX Telecom, MCI, GTE, Western Union, and Lexitel, to Mark S. Fowler, October 4, 1983, in FCC, Common Carrier Docket 78–72.

[78]FCC, *Memorandum Opinion and Order*, FCC CC Docket 83–1145, "Investigation of Access and Divestiture Related Tariffs," October 19, 1983; Mark S. Fowler to the Hon. Robert Packwood (R., Ore.), October 19, 1983. See also the letter from the FCC (W.J. Tricarico, secretary) to Reps. James T. Broyhill (R., N.C.) and Don Ritter (R., Pa.), November 9, 1983. "House Adopts Largely Unchanged 'Universal Telephone Service Preservation Act' by Voice Vote After Opponents Lose by Nearly 2–1 Margins on Key Rollcall Tallies; Reagan Administration Announces Opposition to Pending Legislation," *Telecommunications Reports*, Vol. 49, No. 45 (November 14, 1983), pp. 1–6.

[79]98th Congress, 1st Session, House, "Universal Telephone Service Preservation Act of 1983," H.R. 4102, October 6, 1983.

Thirty-two senators, led by Majority Leader Robert Dole, wrote to the FCC in January, stating, "We feel it would be preferable for the Commission to revise its orders rather than for Congress to enact legislation at this time." The senators wanted the charges to end users postponed beyond 1984, made voluntary for small telephone companies, and capped until 1990. They also asked the Commission to "substantially reduce the amount of increase in the interconnection charge that must be paid by Other Common Carriers." Their solicitude too extended beyond consumers to AT&T's competitors.[80]

The FCC had learned a lot since its resistance to the senate majority leader in 1950. It had taken Senator MacFarland two letters to get the Commission to preserve low local rates by raising separations charges. Senator Dole's letter, by contrast, generated immediate FCC action. Access charges were delayed and reduced, although the concept of shifting the fixed costs of the local exchange plant to the end users was not abandoned. Access charges of $1 and $2 – half of the original charge – went into effect in mid-1985, eighteen months later than the FCC had first ordered. They would be doubled a year later if the protests were not too loud. The agency's clever compromise was enough to kill the moribund Senate bill.[81] It was almost enough to kill AT&T as well. AT&T Communications claimed that its earnings would fall from its authorized 12.75 percent to less than 5 percent. The company withdrew its announced price reduction. The FCC, caught in the middle, rolled back the increased access charges that the operating companies were planning to charge the interexchange carriers and ordered AT&T to institute a smaller price reduction. The Commission was struggling to recover its political position – at considerable cost to AT&T and the operating companies.[82]

The FCC, however, was trapped. On the one hand, the operating companies claimed that a low access charge to end users would encourage bypass. On the other, Congress asserted that raising local rates would eliminate universal telephone service. There was no way to resolve the issue, although the quantitative estimates made to date suggest that the former danger was more pressing than the latter. A March 1985 study by former Van Deerlin staff member Charles Jackson and Jeffrey Rohlfs for

[80]Robert Dole, U.S. Senate et al., to the Hon. Mark S. Fowler, January 18, 1984.

[81]FCC, *Memorandum Opinion and Order*, FCC CC Docket 78–72, adopted February 3, 1984, released February 15, 1984, 97 FCC 2d 834; "Phone Access Fee Delayed Until '85," *The New York Times*, January 20, 1984, p. 1; "Further Rate Reductions for MTS and WATS, and Cutback of Overall Private Line Charges Foreseen by AT&T if Access Charges go Into Effect as Filed; Company Says That Access Charge Costs Were Overestimated, and That Added Rate Slashes Could Result if Allowed," *Telecommunications Reports*, Vol. 50, No. 4 (January 30, 1984), p. 1.

[82]Richard H.K. Vietor and Dekkers L. Davidson, "Economics and Politics of Deregulation: The Issue of Telephone Access Charges," *Journal of Policy Analysis and Management*, Vol. 5, 1985, pp. 3–22.

Bell Atlantic looked at the costs, risks, and potential profits in bypass to determine the estimated speed of adoption for bypass. The report concluded that the expected profits of bypass were high and growing and that the risks were low. Adoption of bypass would be rapid under the FCC's proposed $2 access charge. If the access charge to end users was not raised, the report predicted that Bell Atlantic would lose almost 40 percent of its business switched access revenue within five years. It would lose half by 1995.[83]

Another study noted that the proportion of households with telephones had risen from 37 percent in 1940 to 93 percent in 1980 at the same time that the relative price of telephone service (the ratio of telephone rates to all consumer prices shown in Figure 5) had fallen by half. But the study attributed much of the rise to the effect of larger incomes. It estimated that the proportion would have been 88 percent – only 5 percent less than the actual proportion – if the relative price had remained unchanged, that is, if local rates had been twice their actual level in 1980. Relative residential telephone rates were almost as low in the late 1940s, when separations charges were first introduced, as they were twenty years later, even though the number of households with telephones had changed dramatically. The growth of telephone service could not have been due solely to price. And, even if prices were raised sharply, the projected fall in the number of households with telephones could be avoided in part by "lifeline" services that would provide low telephone rates for targeted demographic and income groups.[84] The risk to universal service of high end-user access charges is far smaller than the risk to operating company finances of low access charges.

These complex changes are all part of the unfinished struggle to complete the settlement worked out in the Modification of Final Judgment. At present the future is unclear, but the prospect is for further reductions in the payments from interexchange carriers to local operating companies and increases in the charges to end users. FCC authority will be extended to local rates through the legal fiction of end-user access charges, and state regulators will be able to turn away complaints about rising rates by directing consumer attention to the federal agency. The Modification of Final Judgment has changed the political climate, perhaps enough to allow federal regulators to override the concerns of Congress and state regulators for low local rates. If so, we will have come a long way since the 1950 struggle over separations.

---

[83]Charles L. Jackson and Jeffrey H. Rohlfs, "Access Charging and Bypass Adoption," (Shooshan and Jackson, Inc., Washington, D.C.), March 1985.
[84]"Residential Demand for Telephone Service 1983," prepared for the Central Services Organization, Inc., of the Bell Operating Companies by Lewis J. Perl, NERA, December 16, 1983.

AT&T reborn

Access charges and divestiture planning related mainly to the operating companies: how they would be organized and how they would be paid for their services. But they were only part of the new world of telecommunications. If AT&T was to emerge like a phoenix from its trials, it too needed to be reorganized to deal with its new environment. Planning for a new AT&T had begun in the aftermath of the FCC's 1980 *Computer II* decision; the process was accelerated and transformed by the Modification of Final Judgment. Once the agreement was reached, Brown concentrated on the division of the old company, while Olson and Tanenbaum took charge of structuring the new, smaller AT&T. The planning process for AT&T never slowed, despite the extensive staff needs of the divestiture effort. As a result, a new type of firm was ready to open its doors on January 1, 1984.

To understand the postagreement planning for AT&T, it is necessary to glance again at developments prior to the divestiture agreement. The market segmentation reorganization of 1978 had barely been completed when the outlines of the FCC's *Computer II* decision became known. Despite the rapidity with which the Bell System's second reorganization had been implemented, it was being overtaken by events within months of its conclusion. Brown quickly decided to move farther and faster down the path outlined in 1978, realigning AT&T more closely to the markets in which it operated.

Brown had started by reorganizing the EPC again. In February 1981 it was combined with another planning group and renamed the Executive Management Committee. In addition to the duties it had acquired in the previous reorganization, it was to monitor the company's entire planning effort to ensure consistency among its many programs. The Office of the Chairman was unchanged. It remained the locus of decision making. It also remained small, comprising only half a dozen members, including its secretary, John Segall, and Morris Tanenbaum, who chaired the new Executive Management Committee.[85]

Further changes followed in rapid order. Segall described an extension of market segmentation to meet the requirements of *Computer II* at the spring 1981 Presidents' Conference (even as the Justice Department was presenting its case to Judge Greene). AT&T would reorganize again along lines of business, with the structure adapted in this case to the Bell System's need to deal with both competition and regulation. A line of business is normally defined in terms of products or markets, but regulatory constraints were at least as important as market clusters in the estab-

[85]Charles L. Brown, memo, "To All AT&T Officers," February 26, 1981.

lishment of AT&T's fully separated subsidiaries. It was clear, for example, that AT&T would not be permitted to structure itself to market and deliver its communications services and equipment through the same organization, even if customers wanted to buy both from the company. The degree of autonomy conferred on each strategic business unit of AT&T was also restrained. Other firms, like GE and Texas Instruments, had adopted a decentralized structure in which the individual business units had significant autonomy. Their central management appeared to view themselves largely as strategic and financial administrators of a portfolio of discrete assets. Brown and his managerial team were following their lead, but they did not want to go as far down the path of divisional autonomy as these other companies. They believed strongly in the synergies between AT&T's various activities; they were not tempted by the portfolio model – and indeed, at this time many corporate managers were becoming deeply concerned about the failure of that approach to provide enough coordination among highly diversified but related activities. Brown was certain that close management control was needed to maintain the effective coordination that would yield operating efficiencies and competitive advantages.[86]

AT&T used the business plans emerging from the several lines of business to maintain central control of its varied operations. The detailed business plans incorporated descriptions of the market opportunities, the business strategy, the timing of innovations, and cost and revenue objectives for several years for each line of business. AT&T's central management reviewed these plans, using them to allocate available resources among the various units. The plans constituted the building blocks for AT&T's long-run corporate planning.[87]

The plans from the lines of business – or at least their quantitative elements – were to be fed into a management system known as the Integrated Planning and Resource Allocation Process (IPRAP) for synthesis into an overall corporate financial plan. IPRAP was designed to show the capital requirements, risks, and expected returns for various projects at the line of business level. It could not be implemented in 1981 because this early form of the line of business framework was at variance with the primary structure of the Bell System, which was still ordered along the geographical lines of the operating companies. After the consent decree, however, Edward Goldstein, by then in charge of IPRAP, pressed ahead with its introduction. Recognizing that the new AT&T would need a

[86]John L. Segall, "Integrated Planning/Resource Allocation," Presidents' Conference, Hot Springs, Virginia, Spring 1981; Philippe Haspeslagh, "Portfolio Planning: Uses and Limits," *Harvard Business Review*, Vol. 60 (January-February 1982), pp. 58–74.
[87]Paul M. Villiere to Morris Tanenbaum, March 27, 1981.

better system of financial controls for its reorganized operations, Goldstein pushed hard to accelerate IPRAP's development.[88]

The transition to IPRAP and the lines of business would constitute a fundamental change in AT&T's internal operations and culture. The transformation started with a period of planning under the existing structure and rules, a phase in which relations between the operating companies and AT&T were still emphasized. The preliminary period from 1983 to 1985 would be followed by operation in the full line of business format by 1986. It was recognized at the outset that the transition would involve new forms of motivation and corporate relationships, not simply revised reporting rules. Planning in Bell's traditional regulatory environment had been mostly bottom-up and construction oriented. In AT&T's new competitive mode, authority would need to be exercised top-down and would emphasize the company's cash flow. Technological development, long a distinguishing feature of the Bell System, had emphasized the internal needs of the network and the special role of R&D in satisfying those needs. Now AT&T would need to refocus its technological resources to satisfy the specialized demands of particular customers. AT&T's corporate culture, based on consensus management, steady promotions, and thorough staff planning, would have to give way to one based on increased risk taking, rewards for results, and faster action.[89]

The long-standing reliance on engineering excellence as the means for improving corporate performance in the Bell System had increasingly been challenged – as we have seen – by an emphasis on marketing. When the marketing department was first established in 1973, Whalen had tried unsuccessfully to dethrone the engineers. The 1978 market segmented reorganization had advanced the marketing cause without fully achieving Brown's goals; reorganization had generated internal resistance from the engineers, whose exalted status within the Bell System was at risk. The line of business organization would crush that resistance, clearly subordinating the engineers to the marketing specialists, who, in turn, were beholden to the firm's customers. Just as knowledge of geographic markets had been deemphasized relative to knowledge of product or service markets in 1978, so engineering excellence would increasingly be seen as a means of satisfying customer needs rather than the technical needs of the switched network. Service, the hallmark of the Bell System, was still a major theme in Brown's business creed, but he now reinterpreted service to emphasize customer satisfaction instead of operational or technical imperatives.

The first stage in the line of business realignment dealt with the

[88]Paul M. Villiere, "Integrated Planning/Resource Allocation," Presidents' Conference, Hot Springs, Virginia, Spring 1981; Edward M. Goldstein, interview, April 25, 1985, pp. 87–91.

[89]Tunstall, *Disconnecting Parties*, pp. 175–86.

detariffed activities to be handled by the new, fully separated subsidiary, soon to be designated "American Bell." AT&T filed a capitalization plan for the subsidiary with the FCC in the summer of 1982, as required by *Computer II*. According to the plan, American Bell would be launched on January 1, 1983, with its own separate engineering and design staff, software capabilities (transferred from both Western Electric and Bell Labs), corporate staff, board of directors, and marketing and sales forces. Later it would obtain installation and service maintenance corps from the operating companies. Until mid-1984, however, these two functions would be performed by the operating companies themselves. American Bell was allowed to purchase from Bell Labs some R&D services, including the engineering of custom-designed integrated circuits, power supplies, and other components. Western Electric would then manufacture products for American Bell according to specifications established by the subsidiary's own engineering and design staff.[90]

Of the $158 million in net plant transferred to American Bell, $88 million represented buildings, leasehold improvements, furniture, fixtures, and other miscellaneous assets belonging to the Bell Operating Companies. Each company filed a petition describing the reorganization to its own state commission, just as AT&T did with the FCC. The transfer of the remaining assets, primarily from Bell Labs, did not require state approval.[91]

Charles Marshall, the designated CEO of American Bell, set up two separate lines of business in his new subsidiary. The first, the Consumer Products Division, would handle small business and residential terminal equipment. It would employ about 6,500 people at its inception, over half of them at American Bell's new Phone Center stores. The other division, Advanced Information Systems, would market equipment and enhanced services to large business customers. Archibald McGill, now a vice president, headed this division. It would employ about 18,000 persons, and there would be an additional 4,000 in research, support, and management jobs. McGill at last had a chance to test his ideas as head of a large business operation. Although American Bell was not a truly vertically integrated strategic business unit (as McGill would have liked), its marketing function was structured according to the tenets he had long advocated within AT&T. After years of intense struggle, the master marketeer was at last in charge of an important wing of the business.

Before McGill had an opportunity to test his ideas, however, the Modification of Final Judgment was signed, and Brown set James Olson to the task of planning for the unregulated parts of postdivestiture AT&T. Olson was as

[90]Alfred A. Green to William J. Tricarico (Secretary, FCC), July 1, 1982, forwarding "Supplement to Plan of Company for Capitalization of American Bell, Inc.," July 1, 1982.
[91]Ibid.

different from Brown as two men could be. Although they had both come up through operations, Olson was a kinetic, vocal administrator – a man who leaned forward in his chair and punctuated his sentences with vigorous gestures. He was less inclined than Brown was to mold consensus – more inclined to move quickly to cut his losses and get on to the next job. He would need to move quickly and forcefully if AT&T was to succeed in developing a corporate structure that would coordinate the operations of Long Lines, Western Electric, and Bell Labs, as well as the new arm's-length subsidiary, American Bell. It would be Olson who would decide how the new AT&T would manage the inevitable tradeoff between synergy within these several organizations and autonomy at the line of business level.

Had he gone the full way along the path advocated by McGill, Olson would have divided up Western Electric and Bell Labs among the various lines of business. Internal communications would have flowed largely along product or market lines within each line of business, instead of going through a centralized planning and coordinating staff. The manager of each strategic business unit would have been given direct control over the resources required to achieve all of the goals of that line. Since he would have control over the identification of consumer needs, product development, manufacturing, sales, and service, he could be held responsible for the company's fortunes in that area. His career and the resources upper management allocated to his business unit would mirror the success his unit achieved. But as McGill and Olson both knew, the traditions of the Bell System leaned toward a quite different view, one that emphasized the advantages of integrated manufacturing and R&D on a company-wide basis. Within both Western Electric and Bell Labs, there was a free flow of ideas and people, cross-pollination of diverse activities, and synergy between different endeavors. Each firm also had its own accounting, cost, and business systems in place. Was it worth giving up these programs and advantages for greater accountability on the part of the managers of the lines of business?[92]

"Western Electric's 'Line of Business' management control system is as sophisticated and mature a system as exists in industry today," said a report from AT&T's corporate planners. "This system has taken years to develop and is now fully computerized. And it cannot be transferred to a newly formed LOB [line of business]." The price of a radical change seemed to be very high.[93]

---

[92] A study completed earlier in 1982 had outlined some of the consequences of each course. Charles E. Hugel (E. Wayne Weeks), "Technical Resources Committee Restructuring Plan," presentation to the Office of the Chairman, May 4, 1982.

[93] W. Brooke Tunstall, "AT&T Corporate Structure and Management After Divestiture," August 6, 1982, presentation to the Office of the Chairman, August 19, 1982.

Still, Western Electric's fate as a separate organization hung in the balance. The strengths of Western were increasingly irrelevant to the markets it would face. It clearly lacked the marketing capability for operating in the new environment. In the new PBX market, it had not recovered from the marketing problems of its Dimension system. In 1981 the Bell System had had only one-quarter of the market for new small PBXs (fewer than 100 lines) and one-half of the market for new mid-sized PBXs. The trend was down. Only in large systems (more than 400 lines) had AT&T regained some of its old share – although even here the gain was short-lived. Northern Telecom had introduced a digital PBX only a year after AT&T's Dimension went on sale, and it still led the ranks of AT&T's new PBX competitors, followed closely by Rolm, General Dynamics, and others. As Brown recognized, AT&T's domination of the market for telecommunications equipment was gone forever. Western Electric was fast becoming one of several competitors in its markets, and not even a large one relative to the size of many of the markets.[94]

Nevertheless, Olson opted at first to leave Western intact, except where *Computer II* forced AT&T to assign units of the manufacturing company to American Bell. Concerned that many of AT&T's operations were already being radically transformed, Olson decided to maintain the well-functioning manufacturing company largely as it was. It would provide some stability in the shifting sands of reorganization. Western Electric organized its manufacturing activities along product lines. Terminal equipment, for example, was already under a single vice president. It was easily transferred to American Bell, but the remainder of Western Electric remained a single organization as 1983 began.[95]

Bell Labs was also kept together as a single, unified R&D organization. It was reorganized internally so that its activities could be reoriented to the needs of the new line of business units. But it was not carved up – except for those parts assigned to American Bell. Again Olson concluded that the interactions within Bell Labs were more valuable than the benefits derived from the enhanced accountability that would have come from vertically integrating its parts into new strategic business units. Communication between the Labs and the business units took place on a dotted-line basis through a project budget process.[96] This form of matrix management was designed to maintain the existing synergy of an integrated organization while achieving a higher degree of communication between Bell Labs and the lines of business – and thus the firm's markets.

[94]Richard Gilbert and Jeffrey Rohlfs, "Forecasting Technology Adoption," Appendix A of Jackson and Rohlfs, *Access Charging and Bypass Adoption;* Brown, interview, June 9, 1984, p. 46. Arthur D. Little, Inc., *World Telecommunications,* Vol. 2, *The Americas and Oceania* (Cambridge, Mass.: Arthur D. Little, n.d.), pp. 22, 92.
[95]Donald E. Procknow, interview, December 19, 1985, pp. 31–4.
[96]Ian M. Ross, interview, April 3, 1986, pp. 38–40.

The internally reorganized Western Electric, Bell Labs, and American Bell, along with AT&T International, became the building blocks of the AT&T Technologies Sector, the group of businesses and related activities that was to be managed without regulatory restraints following divestiture. A report sent to the Office of the Chairman from Olson's staff proposed a six line of business structure for this sector: two lines (business and residence) in American Bell, two lines (equipment designed primarily for telephone operating companies and specialized equipment for other customers) from Western Electric, and two others: Bell Labs and AT&T International.[97] Olson convened meetings of the involved executives, including the prospective heads of AT&T's new lines of business and the presidents of Western Electric and Bell Labs, to discuss matters relating to this sector structure, and their advice greatly influenced his decision to maintain Western and Bell Labs intact.

Setting forth a viable, market-oriented structure for the new AT&T represented the first step in preparing the company for divestiture. Hugel wrote to the heads of Bell Labs and Western Electric, warning both organizations that they had to cut costs in order to bring them in line with those of AT&T's competitors. He demanded that outside people be hired to create a dynamic sales force. He tried as well to integrate the leaders of Bell Labs and Western into AT&T's structure planning process. He insisted that "we first must have a full commitment from all of our senior officers . . . unequivocal and clearly articulated to our people." Concerned that his views would be overlooked in the rush to meet divestiture deadlines, Hugel then lobbied Brown to spend less time on divestiture and more on planning for the new AT&T.[98] He was not the only company officer who was concerned at this time that divestiture was preempting AT&T's transformation into a competitive company.[99]

On January 1, 1983, one year before divestiture of the Bell Operating Company operations would take place, American Bell opened its doors. Despite that official act, the composition of its assets was still not settled. Its management was in charge of marketing all new enhanced services and terminal equipment, but the FCC had not been willing to free the existing installed base of terminal equipment from regulatory control. AT&T warned the FCC that if its installed base was not detariffed and transferred to American Bell by the end of the year (when divestiture took place), AT&T would have to organize an entirely new entity to manage it,

[97]Victor Pelson, "Sector Structure Planning Project," report to the Office of the Chairman, March 18, 1983.

[98]Charles E. Hugel to Donald E. Procknow and Ian M. Ross, April 23, 1982; Charles E. Hugel, interview, March 18, 1986, pp. 40–41. The regional holding companies would have similar problems after divestiture in pulling their new organizations together. Staley, interview, February 25, 1986, pp. 24–7.

[99]Donald S. Perkins, interview, November 25, 1986, pp. 32–3.

file tariffs in fifty different jurisdictions, and develop new billing procedures and programs for the varying rules in the states. This, AT&T estimated, would cost the company unnecessary billions of dollars. In order to allay the Commission's fears about the subsidiary's entrenched market power over the great mass of existing telephones, AT&T offered to give customers the option of purchasing their telephones. It would also guarantee to those who chose not to buy that its rental prices would not rise faster than the Consumer Price Index for a two-year transition period. Persuaded at last, the FCC approved the transfer of existing terminal equipment to the separated subsidiary on November 23, 1983, the eleventh hour of divestiture.[100]

Throughout this period of controversy, AT&T did not enjoy total discretion over how its new subsidiary would be organized – or even over what it would be named! In the midst of these deliberations, the court ruled on July 8 that the Bell name and logo would belong to the Bell Operating Companies after divestiture. AT&T's plans to use the familiar Bell symbol – and exploit the advantages attached to it – to leverage itself into new markets suddenly had to be abandoned. A new designation would have to be found, not only for American Bell but also for the remnants of the Bell System that would remain with AT&T. The company decided, as already noted, to launch itself into the postdivestiture era as AT&T; its fully separated subsidiary was named AT&T Information Systems.[101] But deciding on a new name and logo was far easier than making it clear to customers that these units were in fact parts of the traditionally reliable Bell System. That was a task that would take many years, several subsequent reorganizations, and many advertising dollars to accomplish. The reorganized and renamed organization is shown in Figure 14. Figure 15 illustrates the matrix structure for a single line of business. Note that although the computer line of business was located within AT&T Technologies, it had several dotted-line connections with Information Systems and Bell Labs. It was not a fully integrated strategic business unit.

The creation of a new sector organization and the renaming of its various components involved, as Olson pointed out, far more than a change in nomenclature. It represented, he said, "a change in organizational philosophy." AT&T was now giving the line of business heads effective control over the functions needed to serve their markets, along with responsibility for their effective deployment. "In the past," Olson remarked, "we had at least three voices who thought they knew what was best for the customer. . . . Now, instead of tri-company committees and a General Departments organization trying to figure out what our priorities should be,

---

[100]FCC, *Report and Order*, FCC CC Docket 81–893, "Second Computer Inquiry," adopted November 23, 1983, released December 15, 1983, 95 FCC 2d 1276.
[101]AT&T news release, August 3, 1983.

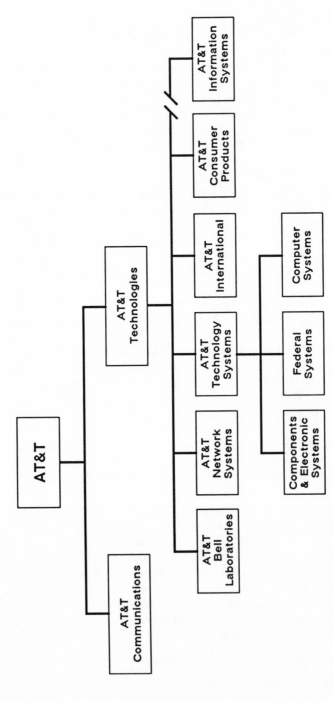

Figure 14. Postdivestiture AT&T.

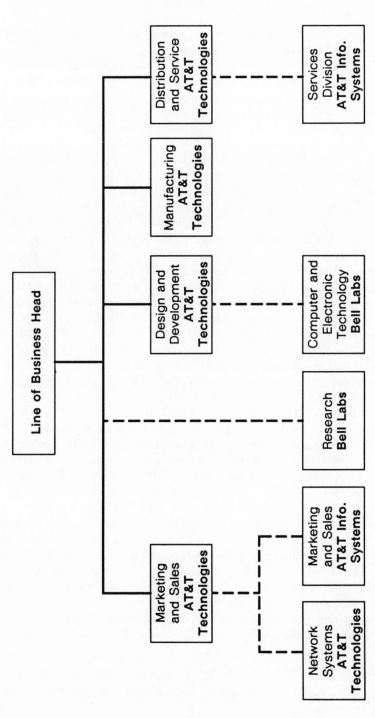

Figure 15. Example of AT&T's line of business matrix structure in 1984.

the responsibility–and accountability–for such decisions rests with one person, the LOB [line of business] head."[102]

The R&D functions performed by Bell Labs remained the major exception to this rule. Matrix management, initially employed in the market-segmented units of the operating companies in 1978, survived in the new AT&T in 1983. But even in the renamed AT&T Bell Labs, operations were realigned and decision-making authority was modified to give the line of business heads the major influence over the Labs's priorities and projects. In this type of organization, the head of each line of business had a measure of authority over the researchers deployed by Bell Labs to his line of business. The lines of business did not yet have the power of the purse, but they were approaching that point.

On the communications side of the business, the task of reorganization was less formidable but the stakes were even higher. This regulated sector was initially designated, for planning purposes, as the "AT&T Interexchange Entity (ATT-IX)." Brown and Tanenbaum knew that the future of the corporation depended on the success ATT-IX would have in retaining its customer base during the vigorous competition that was to be the hallmark of equal access. Since all customers would be asked to designate a primary long distance company during the two-year period following divestiture, the whole market was up for grabs. Early surveys, moreover, showed that few customers thought of AT&T as a long distance company. Clearly, there was a large job ahead in creating a market image for this end of the business.

The new ATT-IX faced other problems as well. It would inherit that portion of the interstate toll business that had once been provided by the operating companies and that crossed LATA boundaries. The rates for this service had been set by the individual operating companies as part of their overall intrastate rate structure. State regulators, like their federal counterparts, had pursued objectives that had nothing to do with relating the rates for particular services to their costs. ATT-IX therefore had to establish relations with state commissions–something Long Lines had never had to do–and to reformulate the intrastate toll rate structure within the context of interexchange service. Only on the technical side was life easier. The long distance facilities by and large were already in place, enabling management to concentrate on formulating marketing, pricing, and business strategies for competition with its discount rivals.

Tanenbaum presented plans for AT&T's regulated communications business to the Office of the Chairman in early 1983.[103] The new organiza-

[102]"Olson at Management Forum: AT&T's Lines-of-Business Sector Approach Signals a Fundamental Change in Organizational Philosophy," *AT&T Management Report* (May 13, 1983).

[103]Morris Tanenbaum to Charles L. Brown, January 18, 1983; Office of the Chairman meeting, January 21, 1983.

tion would be operated as a single entity and would be organized to minimize both the tax liabilities resulting from the transfer of operating company toll assets and its exposure to state regulation. An Interexchange Management Corporation would be established to handle the transfer of assets from the operating companies. This corporation, which would own no assets, would merely sell its services to both AT&T and its new long distance communications unit. Later, ATT-IX would be named "AT&T Communications." It would launch a sweeping, expensive, and apparently effective campaign to ensure that the public knew who had given them reliable and ubiquitous service for the better part of a century.

Although it was evident that a number of holdovers from AT&T's predivestiture days had survived and even prospered, this would not be the case with Archibald McGill, who lasted for less than a year as head of Advanced Information Systems. He left AT&T in June 1983. He had been given his own organization to run, but as it turned out, he was a far better planner and staff revolutionary than manager of a large organization. He found the pace of change in AT&T still too slow—as he always had. The Vail ideals were tenacious. Divestiture changed the structure of AT&T very quickly but the culture lagged, as it almost always does. Frustrated and disappointed, McGill left AT&T.[104]

Although the pace of change was too slow to satisfy McGill, it was fast enough by 1983 to destroy many of the communication channels that AT&T's corporate management had used in the past to monitor and control the company. Brown instituted the "AT&T Management System," of which IPRAP was an important element, but while the new system was being worked out, AT&T experienced serious problems of adjustment. The information needs of the new Office of the Chairman were still in the process of definition in 1983. It would need different kinds of messages in its new coordinating role. Programs to resolve conflicts between different lines of business and to communicate corporate decisions were still in the formative stage. "Some progress" had been made in defining the role and structure of corporate headquarters, in setting line of business boundaries, and in establishing accountability within the lines. But little progress had been made in the all-important task of setting ground rules for the new style of operation, for the continuing transition from AT&T's old corporate culture to its new competitive mode.[105] Brown was also putting AT&T's central headquarter's staff on a severe diet. He was determined to have a leaner corporate headquarters, and some existing groups were disbanded entirely in an effort to achieve that goal.

[104]Frederick W. Gluck, interview, September 23, 1985, pp. 55–6, 62–3; Archibald J. McGill, interview, June 20, 1985, pp. 29, 41, 52–3; Sharwell, interview, July 10, 1985, p. 102.
[105]"The Case for a Revised Management System," presentation by W. Brooke Tunstall to Office of the Chairman meeting, June 16, 1983.

It was going to be a tough job. Brown was determined to complete the transformation quickly, but the attempt to shift the values of the Bell System had been going on for close to a decade, and the old culture was still deeply implanted. Brown at least no longer had to worry about the orientation of the operating companies; they were the responsibility of the regional holding company CEOs he had appointed. But the parts of the Bell System that were left in AT&T still seemed slow to change, hesitant to abandon a technological orientation for a market-centered view. With McGill gone, who was going to throw the bombs? Could the managers who had grown up within the Bell System communicate to the new AT&T that the values of the old steward of the network were to be replaced by those of an aggressive competitor? Time and the market would eventually tell, but at the end of 1983 an unambiguous message had not yet been received.

In 1983, time was certainly at a premium for AT&T. The divestiture process went on "yellow alert" in March. There were just too many tasks to do before divestiture could take place. One of the most contentious involved the ever-troublesome Class 4 switches. Many of them were No. 4 Electronic Switching Systems (4ESSs), the largest, most modern and sophisticated switches in the Bell System; each one was worth about $20 million.[106] Under the predominant use standard being employed for the assignment of assets, it seemed at first as if all but two of these critical switches would be assigned to AT&T. A few operating companies were up in arms. The network, they reminded the AT&T representatives, had been designed as a unit, and the 4ESSs provided many or, in some cases, all of their local tandem switching functions. They cited the phrase in the Modification of Final Judgment ensuring them facilities for "switching traffic within the exchange area above the end office."[107] AT&T responded in essence that the control over its own network that Brown had won in hard bargaining with Baxter was not about to be given away now. The negotiations were complicated, in addition, by pressure from competing long distance companies for connections to the digital 4ESSs instead of the analogue local switches through which they had entered the network. AT&T, emerging from a decade of litigation with these entrants, was reluctant to share its equipment with them and provide the opportunity for new allegations.

After considerable hard bargaining, agreement was finally reached on

[106]R. F. Rey (ed.), *Engineering and Operations in the Bell System 1982–83* (Murray Hill, N.J.: AT&T Bell Laboratories, 1984), pp. 425–8; Joseph H. Weber, "Network Reconfiguration: Dividing the Indivisible," AT&T internal study of divestiture.

[107]*US* v. *Western Electric Co.*, CA No. 17–49 (D.N.J.), *Modification of Final Judgment*, January 8, 1982, Sec. IV, F.

the basis of an "aggregate use" concept. The contested switches were assigned on the basis of the aggregate use of 4ESS capacity by the operating company, not by its use of each switch. AT&T increased its offer from two to ten 4ESSs. It ultimately agreed to construct three additional ones to be assigned to operating companies. But the issue was not settled finally until Judge Greene reassigned one additional 4ESS from AT&T to New England Telephone in response to that company's appeal.[108]

Once ownership was decided, an arrangement for leasing shared switches had to be devised, and the bargaining began again. Each asset of the Bell System, not just the 4ESSs, had to be identified, documented, and assigned either to AT&T or to an operating company by the end of March 1983, to allow enough time before December 31 for contracts for these shared assets to be written. Tensions mounted. Subject matter experts on rotational assignment from operating companies found themselves caught between their loyalties back home and the injunctions from Brown to work together for the good of all. Conflict was inevitable as these tired men played out a series of zero-sum games with their counterparts at AT&T.[109] The wonder is not that there was conflict, but rather that the problems were in fact resolved in time to meet the deadlines.

At this point, the Securities and Exchange Commission (SEC) also became involved in the divestiture process, negotiating with AT&T and the regional holding companies over the terms under which their stocks would be traded. Seven entirely new companies, each of which would be among the largest American corporations, would appear, full grown, on January 1, 1984. But first the Commission had to approve what the public was to be told in advance about these new firms. It had to be determined exactly how the 3 million stockholders of AT&T were to be prepared to make informed decisions about their shares when the markets opened.

Agreement with the SEC on filing requirements was not reached until August 1983. In early November the agency gave AT&T its review of the company's proposed information statement and prospectus, and the company printed the revised material a few days later. Two vans filled with AT&T's SEC filings were parked in a garage near the agency's Washington, D.C., office on the night of November 15. The next morning, after AT&T's board approved the filings, the vans delivered them to the SEC, which approved them within the hour. Trading in the stocks of the seven regional holding companies on a "when issued" basis began on November

---

[108]Joseph H. Weber, "Network Reconfiguration: Dividing the Indivisible," AT&T internal study of divestiture.

[109]The assignment of Bell System patents to the soon to be independent companies also posed problems that defied easy resolution. The bargaining continued through 1983, poisoning future relations between Western Electric and its best customers.

21; each of them started its financial life with many, many more stockholders than General Motors. In fact, when each of AT&T's 3 million stockholder accounts became eight accounts, they comprised close to half of the stockholder accounts in the United States. The transition was amazingly smooth. The market's valuation of these stocks strongly suggested that Brown had done exactly what he had told his fellow executives to do—preserve the interests of all of the stockholders by putting the new regional firms on solid financial and managerial bases.

Any stock exchange of this magnitude must involve the Internal Revenue Service as well, and the IRS ruled that the exchange of AT&T stock for stock in the new AT&T and seven regional holding companies would not be treated as a sale of one and a purchase of the other. It was, in other words, not taxable. (An exception was made for Pacific Telephone, as always a troublesome exception. The exception was appealed and eventually overruled.)[110]

In the midst of this hectic activity, in August 1983, the Bell System's workers went on strike to gain assurances of fair treatment after divestiture. The two-week strike put even more strain on AT&T's management during this critical period. Long-range planning was the hardest hit; the company had to operate on autopilot. Sharwell, in charge of administering AT&T's Plan of Reorganization, was put in charge of the strike control center. As always, he was an excellent fire fighter. Telephone service in the short run was unaffected; the cost of the strike would be felt only over the long term.[111]

When AT&T conducted its first trial run of divestiture implementation on the West Coast the next month, the results were, at best, mixed. It was evident that much remained to be done when the network went into a "divested mode" on October 1. But enough operational changes had been made, business records revised, and personnel retrained for Sharwell (back from his strike duties) to decide that the rest of the job could be finished piecemeal before the end of the year. Field trips by staff members in charge of operations produced some "chilling disappointment," but they also uncovered "in many locations a heartening transformation of plans into reality."[112] By late December, operations were stabilizing throughout the country. On New Year's Day, 1984, dial tones greeted those who picked up their phones and calls to distant locations were routinely completed. This was the truest test of what had been accomplished by a Bell System that had approached the unpleasant tasks of

[110]U.S. Tax Court Decision, April 17, 1986, Docket No. 32031–85, 86 T.C. No. 46; 86 T.C. 745.
[111]Sharwell, interview, July 10, 1985, pp. 71–9; Tunstall, interview, May 30, 1984, pp. 31–5.
[112]"Managing Divestiture in Operations," ca. July 1984, pp. 84–5.

divestiture in the spirit it had developed in running the nation's telephone network for a century. This was a tribute to the corporate culture that had been tested in the service crises of 1969. That same culture had served deButts well as he had pumped up the Bell System's earnings and improved its performance in the early 1970s. Now it had performed its last service to the company and the country.

One casualty of the rush during 1983 was private line service. Private line applications had always been processed through a system of personal contacts across the operating companies and Long Lines. The organized communication paths for handling this business varied from company to company, and managers long familiar with each other used their personal connections to smooth over these differences and keep up with demand. But divestiture suddenly and unexpectedly destroyed these informal networks; nothing had been set up to take their place. This was one of the unanticipated outcomes of the corporate transition; an informal, unplanned social system had not made its way into the divestiture planning process. Long Lines argued for the use of uniform procedures, but the companies said no. January 1, 1984, came without the imposition of uniform procedures for handling this part of the service. Each operating company reverted to its own procedures, and each private line had to be treated as an individual problem.[113] Private line installations fell far behind orders as the time needed to process each order grew. Long Lines and the operating companies belatedly acknowledged the importance of revising their procedures, and agreement was reached. Uniform procedures were instituted, and Long Lines worked night and day to reduce the backlog. Long Lines personnel even became heroes of a sort as they overcame this situation and the impediment of the strike.[114]

Balanced against this kind of problem were some AT&T antitrust victories halfway through the divestiture process. The private suit brought by Southern Pacific on behalf of its Sprint service was decided in AT&T's favor in December 1982. Judge Charles Richey, a former state regulator, took a very different approach than had the juries in the MCI and Litton trials. He decided that it had been the FCC, not AT&T, that had blocked entry into private lines, and that the delays attendant on Southern Pacific's attempts to offer service had come from the agency's inaction, not AT&T malfeasance. Unlike Judge Greene, he was convinced by AT&T's argument that it was trying during the 1970s to understand the FCC's evolving, and frequently confusing, policies. Any mistakes, or at least the important ones, by AT&T were just that, not evidence of a larger

[113]"Service Under Scrutiny," AT&T *Outlook*, Vol. 1, No. 2 (February 29, 1984), p. 1; "Some Good News, Some Bad News About Our Service," AT&T *Outlook*, Vol. 2, No. 3 (March 30, 1984), p. 10; Sharwell, interview, July 10, 1985, pp. 76–9.
[114]Sharwell, interview, July 10, 1985, pp. 78–9.

anticompetitive pattern. It was a cheering opinion to AT&T – with more than a little legal significance – but it came too late to affect either the divestiture decision or its implementation.[115]

The following month brought a decision on AT&T's appeal from the huge MCI award in 1980. The Court of Appeals upheld some of the jury's findings but denied others. In particular, the appeals court found that AT&T had not engaged in predatory pricing, but agreed that it had illegally refused to connect MCI to its switched network. This was an important decision. In addition to vindicating some of AT&T's contentions in the suit, it sharply reduced the scope for damages. Although the issue of MCI's damages would not be settled for another two years, there was every prospect that the huge sum initially awarded in 1980 would not actually change hands.[116]

The news for AT&T was thus mixed on the eve of the breakup of the Bell System. From 1978 to the end of 1983, Charles Brown had labored hard to prepare AT&T to become a central competitor in the information age he saw dawning. Where he had succeeded, the reorganized firm was slimmed down, moving more quickly, and operating more efficiently. But much remained to be done before the new line of business structure was perfected, IPRAP thoroughly operational, and Western Electric and Bell Labs brought into the new style of operations in spirit as well as form. Those tasks might in fact have been closer to completion had he and most of the firm's management not been preoccupied with getting the new regional holding companies launched and the final steps in severing them from AT&T completed by the end of 1983.

Brown announced one final realignment of the company at the end of the year. Under Olson's initiative, AT&T Technologies would assume Western Electric's corporate charter at the point of divestiture, combining R&D, manufacturing, and six lines of business. "This is the last structural step necessary to get us ready for 1984," Brown said. "It positions us squarely for future growth." "This puts us in the fast lane," added Olson, named chairman and CEO of the new company. "The resources of the two companies whose names have been synonymous with the Bell System's reputation for leadership in science and for the introduction of technology on a massive scale – Bell Laboratories and Western Electric – become the centerpiece of this new organization. Integrating manufacturing with our lines of business will translate customer needs into products and systems in the fastest, most efficient way. The head of each business unit will now

[115]Judge Richey was so impressed by AT&T's position that he incorporated John deButts's NARUC speech into his opinion. *SPCC* v. *AT&T*, CA No. 78–0545, U.S. Dist. Ct., Dist. of Columbia, *Memorandum Opinion of United States District Judge Charles J. Richey*, December 21, 1982, 556 F. Supp. 825 (D.D.C. 1983).

[116]*MCI* v. *AT&T*, 708 F.2d 1081 (7th Cir. 1983).

have control over all the resources necessary to be successful, and will be accountable for the profitability of that business worldwide."[117]

On the eve of this new era, just before the divestiture took place, AT&T's managers and the Bell Operating Company presidents had one last opportunity to toast the values and accomplishments of the Bell System. The final Presidents' Conference took place at Litchfield Park, Arizona, in the fall of 1983. It was a nostalgic and untraditional gathering. The presidents were invited to bring their wives, shattering the almost exclusively male business fellowship that the conferences had long fostered. There was a photographer taking candid shots – also unheard of – and Brown sent everyone a portfolio of pictures after the meetings. The wives put on a skit on the last night, and the mood was bittersweet as their husbands pondered the dissolution of an organization that had been their professional home for many decades. Competitive tensions had already emerged. Not all of their personal friendships would survive divestiture. Whatever the future would bring, they knew it would be far different from the past for them, for their industry, and for the millions of Americans who had been accustomed to the unique services of the Bell System.[118]

[117]AT&T news release, December 14, 1983.
[118]Sharwell, interview, July 10, 1985, pp. 98–9.

VIII

Reflections

The process of change

The Bell System ceased to exist on December 31, 1983. On January 1, 1984, a new, smaller AT&T and seven new regional telephone holding companies made their debut. The world went on. Telephones worked, and the FCC and state commissions still regulated them. Congress was still interested in local telephone rates. To the telephone user, continuity seemed far more apparent than change.

But, of course, the divestiture was a momentous change. Occurring at a time of marked shifts in the relationship of government and business, it climaxed the largest single corporate reorganization in history. It spawned eight new companies that would evolve consonant with the Modification of Final Judgment, with their prior histories, and with the shifting nature of this complex industry. Divestiture greatly accelerated the painful movement toward competitive telephone pricing. It set up a contest between the FCC and Judge Greene for control of the changing telecommunications industry. The question of how soon or even whether the industry would approach the conditions envisaged by Brown and Baxter as they forged their final agreement in the early days of 1982 would not be answered for many years.

How had this dramatic change come about? The preceding pages have detailed the particular events leading up to the Modification of Final Judgment. The time has now come to stand back and survey the entire process, to ask what deeper meaning this story has for the United States, for business-government relations, and for the history of this country. What can a businessman learn from this episode? What lessons does it suggest for our potential leaders? and for the public, for consumers of the industry's services?

Looked at from this perspective, three major characteristics of the path to divestiture stand out. First, the growth of competition in intercity telecommunications services was an unstable, cumulative process. Once the FCC started down the road with its *Above 890* decision, the interaction of the discrepancy between regulatory and competitive prices and the pattern of FCC rules created ever-increasing pressure for change. This does not mean that the pressure could not have been resisted and the path altered. Close and critical decisions were made on the road to divestiture, but as the process continued, the forces pressing for a major shift in public policy grew ever stronger, the likelihood that the process could be stopped ever smaller.

Second, the accelerating movement was supported by a pervasive change in ideology that dictated both the government's decisions on entry and AT&T's choices on its internal structure. The new ideology gave rise to both the deregulation movement and the growth of new forms of management and competition in the 1970s.

Third, implementation of this change in telecommunications was complicated by Theodore Vail's legacy: the Bell System's powerful internal culture. By comparison, the federal government, riddled with inconsistencies and frequently at odds with itself, found it easier to shift direction than did the meticulously organized, rigidly hierarchical Bell System. Bell's rigidity—most notable with respect to terminal equipment—hurt AT&T in the political process. It also complicated and retarded the company's attempts to adjust to its rapidly changing markets and regulatory settings.

These attributes of the process can be generalized to suggest some widely applicable lessons. For one thing, the unstable process was clearly a joint economic and political phenomenon that revealed how closely intertwined these two spheres have become in modern America. The growth of government since the Second World War has created opportunities for companies to make profits by focusing more closely on their interaction with the polity than with their customers. In other words, for many firms, economics is politics. This flies in the face of American tradition, contradicting several centuries of experience in which the private and public sectors were separate and distinctly unequal. But the United States has acquired a powerful administrative state. Public and private life have blended together, even though the belief in and desire for limited government has yet to give way.[1]

The role of ideology, of course, is startling in a society that was supposed to have transcended ideology.[2] We have bet our telecommunications future on an openness to domestic and foreign competition unheard of throughout the world. This microeconomic adventure—like those in macroeconomic planning in recent years—may turn out well for the United States over the long haul. But the risks are great and the institutional changes involved are terribly expensive. The consequences of this ideologically grounded transformation will have ramifications that will

[1]Charles A. Reich, "The New Property," *Yale Law Journal*, Vol. 73 (April 1964), pp. 733–87.
[2]Daniel Bell, *The End of Ideology*, rev. ed. (New York: Free Press, 1962).

extend throughout our society and reach deeply into the international economy.

Finally, this experience demonstrates how profoundly our private and public institutions differ. Government is not a business. Organizations – public and private – are adapted to their function, differing from each other in structure as much as in mission. They cannot shake their histories, and in some circumstances our corporations in this century may be less flexible than government in adapting to change.[3]

These observations deserve more detailed discussion. The FCC, which played a crucial role in this history, is the logical place to start. The Commission embarked on a cumulative process with almost no understanding of the forces it was setting in motion. It failed to see prices – particularly the gap between regulatory and competitive prices – as incentives. It therefore did not see that granting permission for entry into a corner of the telecommunications market would create intense pressures for further entry. The FCC resolutely refused to recognize the nose of the competitive camel as it pushed into the government's regulatory tent. Nor did the agency understand what the camel was likely to do.

Regulatory prices in telecommunications differ from competitive prices in three important dimensions, as noted in Chapter 2. They are based on historical costs, averaged nationally, and shaped by the separations process.[4] Each of these characteristics created discrepancies between regulatory and competitive prices. Where the latter were lower – often dramatically lower – firms that could have made normal profits with competitive prices could make far more money under the umbrella of the Bell System's regulatory prices. They naturally used any avenue open to them – and tried to create new paths as well – to take advantage of this inviting situation. Each characteristic of regulatory prices was important in turn.

In the *Above 890* proceedings, Motorola and others tried to take advantage of the opportunity created by the gap between historical and current costs. Granted the opportunity, they were frustrated in the attempt to make a killing by AT&T's TELPAK tariff. MCI received permission a decade later to exploit the discrepancy between national average and route-specific prices. It was confronted by AT&T's Hi-Lo tariff. After the *Execunet* decision, MCI, Southern Pacific, and other specialized common carriers tried to take advantage of the gap opened up by the separations process – the spread between station-to-station and board-to-board costs.

---

[3]Philip Selznick, *Leadership in Administration: A Sociological Interpretation* (Berkeley: University of California Press, 1984 [first published 1957]).

[4]As shown in Chapter 2, the first characteristic comes from rate-of-return regulation; the second, from the Postmaster General in World War I; the third, from the federal nature of the U.S. government.

Here the entrants were successful. The fateful ENFIA compromise as-sured them of a substantial price break, even if they had the same operat-ing costs as Long Lines. AT&T agreed in 1978 to what it thought was a short transitional discount, only to discover that the price differential had enduring political staying power. As Henry Kissinger demonstrated in international affairs, incomplete bargains can be hazardous.

The FCC did not seem to understand, or at least it did not admit that it understood, this process. When AT&T responded to *Above 890* by filing its TELPAK tariff, the Commission opposed it. The ensuing proceedings were long, tangled, and inconclusive. Dockets, hearings, and pronouncements continued for well over a decade. The confusion they created could be seen in the contrast between the approval on Strassburg's desk, when he retired in 1973, of the use of long-run incremental costs for pricing and the final decision in favor of fully distributed (average) costs three years later. A decision sympathetic to the pro-competitive thrust of Commission policy was rejected in favor of a requirement that the Bell System use regulatory pricing in a setting for which it was never intended – competition.

The FCC regarded its approval of MCI's application as an experiment to test the competitive waters. Strassburg appreciated neither the profit opportunity the Commission was creating nor the personality of Mc-Gowan, who rushed to occupy this profitable corner as completely as possible. The *MCI* decision was followed only two years later by *Special-ized Common Carriers*, which hurriedly converted the "experiment" of allowing MCI to construct a single facility on a single route into national policy for all applicants.

The FCC claimed in *Specialized Common Carriers* that the expansion of competition posed no threat to the Bell System. It affected only a small corner (private lines) of AT&T's business. The agency failed once again to see the cumulative nature of its decisions. It did not see the incentive for MCI and others to offer ordinary long distance services (switched message toll services). It did not even recognize immediately that MCI's Execunet service was a type of message toll service! It did not realize that its loosely written decision in *Specialized Common Carriers* would create the oppor-tunity for a judge to carry competition from a corner of the Bell System's business to its very center. With Judge Wright's decision in *Execunet*, the camel was fully in the tent.

Could the tent hold it? Both MCI and the Justice Department had filed their antitrust suits by this time – as had many others. Neither the FCC's adoption of its registration program for terminal equipment in 1975 nor *Execunet* terminated these antitrust proceedings. Several of the private suits resulted in payments by AT&T in compensation for costs it had imposed on its fledgling competitors during this tangled process. The Justice Department, however, took AT&T's actions as signs of its continuing predatory intent – not as transitional behavior. Justice wanted to tear down the tent, not feed the camel.

The government's suit, nominally insulated from politics, was a thoroughly political act. Started in the ruins of the Nixon administration, protected in subsequent years by the memory of the Dita Beard affair, continued in mid-trial on the grounds that dismissal would look bad for the President, and ended in a manner that implemented a new telecommunications policy – the government's antitrust suit culminated a political drive against the ubiquitous phone company. Unable to obtain entry into telecommunications markets through Congress, AT&T's opponents had found an alternative forum in which to make their move.

The federal government that implemented that new policy is in reality a loose collection of policymaking bodies. Coordination between these bodies is the exception, disagreement the rule. It follows that the political system was more open to new ideas than was the Bell System – not because a government bureaucracy was more flexible than a private one, but rather because a plurality of political power created a marketplace for ideas. This is particularly true in a government as large and complex as ours has become in recent decades. Control over this far-flung set of institutions has diminished in rough proportion to its size. As a result, an important action – like breaking up the Bell System – could be undertaken with very little political support.

In particular, court proceedings, although very much part of the political process, have acquired an independence from interference that lets legal proceedings maintain a life of their own. The two most important decisions in this cumulative process involved courts. Judge Wright's *Execunet* decision opened up the Bell System's national message toll service network to all comers. The judge was not compelled to take this action. In fact, as seen in Chapter 4, the FCC opposed him, wanted to appeal, and cooperated with AT&T's moves to blunt the decision's impact. Congress at that time was stalemated; no directions came from the Hill. Nor was the law compelling. Even if Wright's reasoning is accepted as valid, he could have remanded the case to the FCC. The agency would then have controlled its own destiny while it followed a "correct" procedure to determine if competition in ordinary long distance service was in the public interest. The judge, in short, had a choice, which he exercised with a fine political sense. Aside from the FCC and AT&T, no one protested Wright's decision.

The independence of the legal process is both its strength and its weakness: Judicial decision making can be swift, but it need not be informed. Wright called for analysis of the effects of his decision, but the resulting investigation by the FCC took place after competition had become a political and economic reality. The possibility that the decision might then be reversed was negligible. The ENFIA discounts were in place, acquiring the political solidity that subsequent events have revealed. The FCC's investigation was academic. Wright's decision was made, therefore, without any analysis of its public policy implications.

The other important decision, of course, was the Modification of Final Judgment. This was Brown's rather than Judge Greene's decision, but it was made in an isolation similar to that which characterized *Execunet*. Like Judge Wright's decision, it followed the logic of the political process to a conclusion that no elected official seemed to desire. Indeed, there was ample high-level opposition to divestiture within the Reagan administration. Had there been an easy way to stop the antitrust suit, the Reagan administration would have used it. AT&T maneuvered hard to persuade the White House to adopt that course. It was the Bell System's bad luck that Judge Greene kept his trial date firm, and William Baxter could thus deal with the company in the context of a trial nearing completion.

Once Brown had decided that Baxter's terms were the best of a bad lot, the isolation broke down and the political process again became complicated, inclined toward compromise, and tense with conflict. Judge Greene, the FCC, the various members of the refashioned telecommunications industry, and the industry's customers and competitors declined to play the roles assigned to them by Baxter and Brown. They had not been consulted in reaching the decision; they did not necessarily subscribe to its theory; they felt no obligation to implement Baxter's particular view of the industry and competition. The fact that these political struggles continue today indicates how incomplete the consensus was when the fundamental decision for divestiture was made.

Congress had ample opportunities to create a consensus, but it failed to design a compromise measure that would give the legislature the leading role in managing change. Congress became involved in the 1970s soon after the FCC had begun to explore new terrain. The government's looseness, its pluralistic character, made multiple approaches to political power possible. Interested parties could approach that part of the government most sympathetic to their cause. AT&T, frustrated at the FCC, turned to Congress. MCI, temporarily blocked by the FCC, went to the Justice Department and to the courts. Equipment vendors, business customers, and consumers all found ways to make their presence known in the political process as well as the marketplace. Political competition went hand in hand with competition in telecommunications markets. The checks and balances of the founding fathers have become entry ports for alternative points of view, forces making for change more than stability.

Small companies frequently had an advantage over the mighty Bell System in the political free-for-all. It has been said that small groups have more veto power in the political process than in the economy and more innovative power in the market than in politics.[5] It appears here that small groups had a greater chance to innovate through politics than through markets. AT&T's political power was frequently criticized, but the Bell System was unable to build a constituency and push through a solution to the industry's problems. AT&T had too little veto power to prevent change. It could block action in one specific forum – Congress, for example, or the FCC – but it could not prevent the damning end runs that other interests kept mounting against it. In that sense, the vaunted political power of the Bell System was largely illusory.

In fact, from a political point of view, AT&T was too big. It had grown rapidly in the 1960s and 1970s and appeared to have overwhelming power, equal almost to that of the federal government. But the underlying fear of AT&T's political punch paradoxically reduced its ability to influence events. The size and power issue could not be escaped; it was always in the background, creating a general presumption that change was needed when more specific issues were being discussed. Although no one in power ever said so, the United States found it difficult to tolerate any company quite as large and omnipresent as the old AT&T.

The Bell System's size also reduced its political clout indirectly. The System's top leaders – with the notable exception of Trienens – typically had spent their entire working lives in the Bell System. They responded to the tides within this populous community, not to new currents in the national political arena. DeButts, for example, had formed his views of national politics during his Washington service in the halcyon 1950s. Neither he nor any of his (or Crosland's) advisors were in touch with the political realities of the 1970s and the pressures they generated on AT&T.

But why did AT&T's opponents keep coming back for more? MCI, of course, wanted to make money. So did the equipment vendors, other specialized common carriers, major telephone customers, and the newspapers. From their point of view, public policy was a means to a private – not a public – end. It was their good fortune to be able to clothe their self-interest in the public interest. Erik Erikson has written that the difference between a madman and a prophet is not whether one of them is monomaniacal; they both are. The difference is that the prophet is in tune with his times; he finds responsive audiences.[6] So too with businesses in the political realm. The difference between the Bell System and its opponents was not whether one side sought profits; they all did. But the opponents were in tune with their times. The aspiring entrants were able to turn their private efforts into an ideological crusade that resonated in Washington.

[5]Charles E. Lindblom, *Politics and Markets* (New York: Basic Books, 1977), pp. 347–8.
[6]Erik H. Erikson, *Young Man Luther; A Study in Psychoanalysis and History* (New York: Norton, 1958); ibid., *Gandhi's Truth: On the Origins of Militant Non-Violence* (New York: Norton, 1969).

Even though the process was dominated by practical men – engineers, entrepreneurs, lawyers – those who did not have an immediate stake in the outcome responded more to theoretical constructions and to their related ideologies than to the dictates of technology or of law. A key element of the emerging new ideology was a fundamental shift in the relationships between business and government. This change has been much discussed in recent years. Often it is associated with the Reagan revolution, but as the telecommunications story shows, Reagan's appointees – important as they were – entered only late in the drama. Long before 1981, the active government that had originated in the late nineteenth century and received a great boost from Franklin D. Roosevelt's New Deal and then from Lyndon Johnson's Great Society was under siege. This was particularly so where the government's regulatory powers were concerned. The balance between regulation and competition was shifting, as liberals and conservatives alike condemned the manner in which regulated industries had performed.

In the specific case of telecommunications, the Bell System's economic performance was not the issue; the concern was whether the industry's structure had closed off opportunities for others. The boundary between regulation and competition became all-important. As both economic and political advisors to AT&T kept saying, and Baxter kept repeating, a strict separation – a bright line – between the two was needed. Both price determination and the conditions of entry into a market are different in the two regimes. Regulatory prices can exist only with restrictions on entry; free entry compels firms to charge competitive prices. It is no surprise, therefore, that prices and limitations on entry – "foreclosure," in the Justice Department's language – were the core of the government's case in the antitrust suit.

These issues had existed since the early twentieth century. The integrated Bell System, molded into its modern form in the full flower of the public utility concept, had created controversy from its earliest years. The Kingsbury Commitment described in Chapter 1 had followed hard on the heels of the breakup of Standard Oil. The rise of the large corporation had generated substantial fear in the United States that economic opportunity would be foreclosed to individuals and small businesses, that prices would be pushed up for the profit of the monopolists, and that the state itself would be controlled by giant enterprises like Standard Oil, American Tobacco, and AT&T. The governmental response to these concerns included both antitrust policy and regulation, two different means of achieving the same end: controlling monopoly.

In the Progressive era, fear of the new, large firms was opposed by another view, originally expressed by businessmen themselves. They argued that rationalization of industry, now called "horizontal integration," promoted efficiency. J. P. Morgan consolidated the railroads in order to create large, efficient railroad systems. Theodore Vail gave expression to this philosophy when he called for "One System, One Policy, Universal Service." He cooperated with various public authorities to create a single regulated telephone network for the country. The Bell System could thus achieve economies of horizontal integration and operate the network as a common carrier, a form of public utility. On this basis, Vail created a symbiosis between AT&T and the government that functioned well, in sharp contrast to the fate of the railroads, for over half a century of rapid technological change.

During those several decades, the division between regulation and competition varied over time, but not enough to threaten the integrity of the Bell System. The federal government was more sympathetic to business in the 1920s than in the 1930s, but even under the New Deal, the reform of telecommunications regulation stopped short of giving the new Federal Communications Commission authority over AT&T's corporate structure. There was pressure for change in the telephone equipment market, but the subsequent effort to use antitrust action to split off Western Electric was turned aside in the 1950s by the Eisenhower administration. Vail's bargain with the government endured.

Not so in the 1970s. The boundary between regulated and competitive activity was redrawn. It shifted for many reasons, and it changed throughout the economy, not simply in telecommunications. Alfred Kahn, who has made his appearance in these pages, argued, as the Bell System was being dismantled in the 1980s, that the public utility concept itself was dead.[7] AT&T's divestiture was, in his view, only one expression of an economywide change that was embodied in the deregulation movement. Competition, so said the new policy, was to replace regulation as the means of controlling railroads, airplanes, trucks, banks, and security dealers – as well as the suppliers of telephone services and equipment. The market, not the government, would set prices, control entry, and ensure that consumers received good service. At this writing, the process of change has not gone as far as Kahn predicted. The public utility concept seems far from dead, especially in telecommunications. But there can be no question that the general deregulation movement helped to undercut the Vail accommodation and bring about the breakup of the Bell System. Ideology, not technology, triumphed in the 1970s and 1980s.

The deregulation movement gained impetus from the increased international competition American firms have faced. Intense competition from firms in Asia and Europe has focused attention on the inefficiencies stemming from the regulation system. Both regulation and antitrust measures

[7] Alfred E. Kahn, "The Passing of the Public Utility Concept: A Reprise," in Eli M. Noam (ed.), *Telecommunications Regulation Today and Tomorrow* (New York: Harcourt Brace Jovanovich, 1983).

were developed when the U.S. economy was still largely self-contained; both policies were framed with this domestic economy in mind. But global competition in the last two decades has undercut the premises of these policies, accelerating the deregulation movement and bringing into serious question the application of antitrust theory to large U.S. corporations that have shown themselves to be efficient, innovative competitors. Seen in this light, the breakup of the Bell System may well mark the beginning of the end of the antitrust experiment, as Americans look increasingly to the global market for the forces that will control even the largest U.S. firms and prevent them from taking advantage of their monopoly or near-monopoly positions in the domestic economy. Global competition, the new outlook says, erodes market power and disciplines companies in all countries.

As a result of these developments, the structure of the American telecommunications industry is now far different from the industry's structure in any other country. It is open, both to foreign equipment and foreign services, to a degree unheard of in other major countries. Great Britain and Japan have started tentatively to follow the United States down the road to competitive telecommunications, but they have eschewed actions as dramatic as the Modification of Final Judgment. The American openness may well be good policy in the long run; industrial policies elsewhere in the world have not been very successful.[8] But divestiture was coupled in the short run with an overvalued dollar that placed domestic suppliers at a distinct disadvantage. Secretary of Commerce Baldrige seemed to be thinking primarily of the balance of payments when he argued within the administration that the benefits of competition would flow to foreigners. If AT&T is replaced by foreign suppliers of telecommunications equipment in the long run, divestiture may have other costs as well.

Dramatic as the destruction of the Bell System was, divestiture did not, of course, signal the end of government influence in the economy, and certainly not in telecommunications: Divestiture, as seen in Chapter 7, has not meant deregulation. Instead, there has been a shift at the margin; the line between public and private activity has moved. AT&T, skating close to the line for the better part of a century, found itself in the 1980s on the wrong side. Martha Derthick and Paul Quirk therefore overstate their case when they describe divestiture as merely one more episode in the ideologically driven deregulation movement. In their excellent discussion of why two other deregulation bills passed Congress, Derthick and Quirk seem almost to imply that a telecommunications bill also passed. This curious impression comes from their attempt to place changes in

[8]Paul R. Krugman, "The U.S. Response to Foreign Industrial Targeting," *Brookings Papers on Economic Activity*, Vol. 1, 1984, pp. 77–121.

airlines, trucking, and telecommunications in one bag. Steve Coll, by
contrast, understates the case in his popularization of the story. He sees
the world as a seething mass of personal grievances that find expression in
public policy. Jordan J. Hillman, too, avoids ideology in his careful review
of the legal process leading to divestiture, tracing the origins of the "con-
vulsive shift in institutional structure and ethos" in telecommunications to
technological forces.[9] This view – widely held within the telecommunications industry – is respectable but wrong.

New policies came from new ideas. New economic theory applauded
vertical, not horizontal, integration. The benefits that Progressive era
businessmen saw in horizontal integration under the aegis of public authority were seen in the 1970s as anticompetitive.[10] Vietnam, Watergate,
rampant inflation, and intense international competition combined to
weaken the legitimacy of government and the concept of regulated public
utilities. Regulators, who had been seen as servants of the public, were
attacked as lackeys of the firms they regulated.[11] How could a regulatory
commission deny entry to an aspiring firm just to maintain a public
utility's monopoly? The FCC's first steps toward competition were supported by a presidential task force even before 1970. Congress sustained
the FCC's initiatives in the late 1970s. The Department of Justice, and
particularly William Baxter, mounted increasingly sharp assaults on the
Bell System's horizontal integration as the antitrust suit progressed. Despite faith in the Bell System from within and from the bulk of the public,
too many important actors in the world at large viewed the mammoth
institution as a present or potential threat.

The changes that took place were expressed in terms of the technology
of communications, but the pervasiveness of deregulation in the late
1970s demonstrates clearly that technology was not the prime mover. The
introduction of transistors and computers led to pressure for entry into the
business of making and selling terminal equipment. But although new
entrants naturally used the new technology, entry had been barred previously by agreement between AT&T and the federal government and by
regulatory rules, not comparative costs. Non-Bell telephones, in particu-

[9]Martha Derthick and Paul Quirk, *The Politics of Deregulation* (Washington, D.C., Brookings Institution, 1985); Steve Coll, *The Deal of the Century: The Breakup of AT&T* (New
York: Atheneum, 1986); Jordan Jay Hillman, "Telecommunications Deregulation: The Martyrdom of the Regulated Monopolist," *Northwestern University Law Review*, Vol. 79,
1984–5, p. 1183.

[10]Robert Bork, *The Antitrust Paradox: A Policy at War with Itself* (New York: Basic Books,
1978); Oliver Williamson, *The Economic Institutions of Capitalism* (New York: Free Press,
1985).

[11]Henry J. Aaron, *Politics and the Professor: The Great Society in Perspective* (Washington,
D.C.: Brookings Institution, 1978); Seymour Martin Lipset and William Schneider, *The
Confidence Gap: Business, Labor, and Government in the Public Mind* (New York: Free
Press, 1983).

lar, had always been easy to make; it was AT&T's tariffs, as approved by regulators, that forbade their attachment to the network. Microwave radio similarly encouraged the growth of independent private line facilities and then interexchange systems, but the inducement for entry was created by the structure of regulated prices, not the costs of microwave radio. It was ideology, not technology, that translated improvements in long distance transmission and switching into cheaper local service, as shown in Figure 5. And it was a change in ideology that allowed the increasing gap between AT&T's prices and the board-to-board costs of long distance service to be seen as profit opportunities for AT&T's would-be competitors and its largest customers (who could avoid paying to support local service by using these competitors or forcing a change in the Bell System price structure).

The point can be stated more strongly. If the Bell System was destroyed because it was unsuited to the new technology, then a gigantic mistake was made. The new technology was different; that was what made it new. But there is precious little evidence that the fundamental technological forms of telecommunications have changed. People still gain access to the system through a device that can be widely made. Long distance service of all sorts is still carried most inexpensively through a cable, and the rush to install optical fiber indicates that this will continue to be true for many years. To the extent that the Bell System was broken up to usher in the age of microwave radio, the government forced a permanent shift in the industry's structure to take advantage of a temporary technical opportunity – which has already been superseded for most high-density uses.

A new technological argument has surfaced in the aftermath of divestiture. Citing the fall in switching costs relative to transmission costs, the new approach denies that there are compelling reasons for there to be either a hierarchical architecture or bottlenecks in the new "geodesic" network.[12] This argument from technology, like its predecessor, must be treated with caution. Over time the costs of transmission have fallen rapidly as a result of coaxial cables, microwave radio, and fiberoptics; it is unlikely that the decline in switching costs has been faster. The hierarchical network has not disappeared. In fact, new methods of transmission like packet switching have increased the efficiency of operating a single, hierarchical network in ways not normally captured in cost comparisons. And if technological progress is eliminating all bottlenecks, then – even if reasons to destroy the Bell System can be derived from this change – the theory

---

[12]Peter W. Huber, *The Geodesic Network* (1987 Report on Competition in the Telephone Industry), prepared for the Department of Justice in connection with the court's decision in *US v. Western Electric*, 552 F. Supp. 131 (D.D.C. 1982) (Washington, D.C.: GPO, 1987), Chapter 1.

actually used to prosecute and then break up the Bell System has again already been superseded.

Just as changing views of vertical and horizontal integration informed public policy, new concepts of business strategy informed AT&T's internal decision making. The modern ideology of competition stressed the importance of vertical integration and decentralization of authority in business firms. Historian Alfred Chandler provided the classic statement of this view in his historical studies of the rise of big business. Chandler saw business leaders as efficiency enhancers, not robber barons.[13] He described the manner in which some of America's largest and most successful industrial corporations had integrated vertically so that they could control efficiently the flow of goods and services through their various steps of manufacturing and distribution; as their operations became more diverse and widespread, they learned how to manage them through relatively autonomous divisions. Chandler chronicled the changes that had been made at DuPont and GM in the 1920s, changes that were very much like the ones AT&T instituted in the 1970s. The "multidivisional structure" pioneered by these firms and by Standard Oil, Sears Roebuck, and GE was widely adopted by industrial firms in the 1940s.[14]

In the 1970s, many companies went farther down the path of extreme business segmentation along product lines. In the words of a recent management text: "This concept originated in 1970, when Fred Borch, then Chairman of General Electric, decided to break the G.E. businesses into a set of autonomous units, following a recommendation made by McKinsey and Company."[15] McKinsey, of course, gave the same advice to AT&T, citing GE's actions in support. At the time that GE adopted this new structure, it was not faced with a change in public policy. It was, however, a large corporation faced with the problems of conducting business in a series of rapidly changing industries. "Confronted with this

[13]Alfred D. Chandler, *Strategy and Structure: Chapters in the History of American Industrial Enterprise* (Cambridge, Mass.: MIT Press, 1962); ibid., *The Visible Hand: The Managerial Revolution in American Business* (Cambridge: Harvard University Press, 1977).

[14]The Bell System always had a multidivisonal structure of sorts. It was too large even in Vail's days to be operated as a unit, and the history of local companies militated against it as well. Like the railroads that Chandler described, AT&T's functional organization was a pioneer in business organization. But it was not a division of the business by product. It divided up markets geographically, not by products or customer groups. As the nation was pulled together in the twentieth century by improved means of transportation and communication, the geographic division came under more and more strain.

Transportation and communication were facilitated, of course, by new technology. To the extent that improvement in the economy's infrastructure gave rise to greater competition and – at least in theory – less need for regulation, it affected the deregulation movement. But that is far different from the argument that the Bell System's structure and dissolution were determined primarily by telecommunications technology.

[15]Arnaldo C. Hax and Nicolas S. Majluf, *Strategic Management: An Integrative Perspective* (Englewood Cliffs, N.J.: Prentice-Hall, 1984), p. 14.

formidable task, G.E.'s answer was to break down the businesses of the firm into independent autonomous units that could be managed as viable and isolated business concerns. Those entities were labelled Strategic Business Units, or SBUs for short."[16] AT&T adopted this same approach to corporate reorganization, although it never went as far along the path of divisional autonomy as GE. The strategic business units were called "lines of business" in AT&T; they were an adaptation of the general model to the particular synergies that existed in the telecommunications business. AT&T under Brown thus moved toward the mainstream management structure of American industry.

As their environment changed, AT&T's leaders thus decided to move away from the unique aspects of the company's history and mission toward the common pattern of industrial firms. The company gradually had more and more reason to see itself, in other words, as just another industrial firm–"competitors among competitors" in Brown's words–not as the steward of the nation's telecommunications network. Brown and Baxter both anticipated a grand economic joust between AT&T and IBM.

This company view, of course, had a profound impact on public policy. Brown and Baxter–approaching the problem of AT&T's future direction from widely divergent conceptual frameworks–nevertheless found themselves in substantial agreement about one thing: Neither man thought that the firm's vertical integration should be disrupted, and Judge Greene seemed likely to do exactly that if he were allowed to decide the case. The area of agreement between Brown and Baxter was no accident. Management science and economics were in complete agreement about the nature of competition in the 1970s. This joint view, which stimulated the deregulation movement in other industries, made possible the resolution in telecommunications embodied in the Modification of Final Judgment.

AT&T's self-image had also affected earlier events. As Alfred Partoll insisted, the firm's intense desire to hold on to the terminal equipment market against enormous regulatory and competitive pressure had affected its ability to retain the intercity communications market. The demand for telecommunications was expanding too rapidly and becoming too complex to be supplied completely by the Bell System, despite deButts's comments to Congress in 1976. But the Bell System's traditional concept of itself as the "One Policy" in Vail's "One System" made it impossible to trade off the equipment sales and focus on the network. Spinning off Western Electric, as the Justice Department wanted in the 1950s and again under Griffin Bell, was never considered a viable possibility. Western not only supplied the Bell System, it also supported most of Bell Labs's development work. Abandoning Western Electric, and thus

[16]Ibid., p. 15.

much of Bell Labs, would have meant abandoning AT&T's long-standing emphasis on technical excellence. As Brown looked to the future, moreover, he thought that vertical integration would become even more important as AT&T competed for business in the information age.

There was, of course, an alternative path that would have followed the lines of Partoll's recommended public stance and Sharwell's scenario for the division of Western Electric. The early negotiations with the Justice Department had raised the possibility of a division of Western Electric, although the lines of this division were never drawn explicitly. Let us suppose that AT&T had chosen early to withdraw from the terminal equipment market (telephone sets and PBXs), while retaining its strong position in network switching technology. Those parts of Western Electric that produced terminal equipment (and the part of Bell Labs that supported them) could then have been relinquished without destroying AT&T's technological edge or its ability to provide the central switching capacity for its network.

Movement toward this end in the early and mid-1970s might have blunted the impact of PCAs, made the FCC's registration program more palatable to AT&T, and increased the chances for passage of the CCRA (the Bell bill). If AT&T had left the terminal business, the small firms rushing to take advantage of the *Carterfone* decision in the early 1970s would have become AT&T's partners rather than its competitors. AT&T's unions would not have retained a stake in the production of Bell terminal equipment. AT&T's opposition to certification would not have infected its opposition to intercity competition in the process that Partoll saw so well. If the CCRA of 1976 had acknowledged the legitimacy of competition in terminal equipment, it would have stood a reasonable chance of passage. Congress was not willing to overturn the whole of FCC policy, but there was a feeling there, as well as at AT&T, that the Commission had gone too far in *Specialized Common Carriers*.

If AT&T did not provide new terminal equipment, the PCA or any other coupling arrangement would not have been anticompetitive. AT&T's arguments that it feared for the technical capacity of its network might have been taken more seriously – at least until experience showed them to be excessive. There would have been no grounds for an antitrust suit here. A Bell System organized along the lines just described might well have emerged from Geller's Chinese menu. It would have been far different from the current industry structure, and in that sense, using the historian's advantage of 20/20 hindsight, we can see that AT&T's internal ideology had a profound effect on the shape of telecommunications today.

This is not to say that such an outcome was ever likely. Romnes had said in the late 1960s that AT&T had less stake in the terminal equipment market than in the network. But neither he nor anyone else saw the implications of the company's stance for the next decade. Baxter and Trienens debated the advent of competition in private line service; Romnes and the presidents of the Bell Operating Companies contemplated AT&T's financial distress; but no one at that time could see the way these problems were intertwined with those in terminal equipment. What they should have been able to see – and this is not asking too much of corporate managers – was that the deButts strategy of no compromise was a losing stance.

It is, as I have said, too much to insist that people should foresee a tangled and uncertain future. But a more flexible approach by AT&T's leadership in the mid-1970s might have offered room for compromise before the pressure for change reached its climax in late 1981. For example, had deButts not been CEO or Garlinghouse his general counsel, at least the tone of AT&T's approach to NARUC, the FCC, and Congress could have been far different. A Bell System more welcoming to competitors might have been able to reach agreement with the government, possibly along the lines of Geller's menu, before congressional and antitrust pressure for radical restructuring became as intense as they were in 1981.

No observer, even one gifted with wonderful hindsight, should make the mistake of thinking that changes in direction would have been easy. AT&T did not withdraw from terminal equipment in 1970; it did not foresee the future, revise its corporate plans, and abandon its original product. It tried instead to make an internal change that was in the spirit of current management practice. This effort tapped into the support that any mainstream activity can acquire – consultants' reports, experts hired from other companies, conversations with high-level executives from other firms. Still, as the preceding pages have shown, this change was exceedingly difficult to consummate. Decades of technological and business success had reinforced the corporation's culture and made change difficult to implement.

Businessmen contemptuous of government would do well to contemplate AT&T's institutional rigidity and the role it played in the fall of the Bell System. AT&T's modern corporate structure had been created by Vail in 1909. His geographical organization of operating units and his division of these units into three functional departments (Plant, Traffic, and Commercial) lasted for over sixty years. This stability reflects Vail's genius. It also reveals that the creation of a corporate structure and its supporting values can be a durable investment, no less than the construction of a plant. In fact, few plants are used the same way for over half a century. But like a plant, with its sunk costs, a successful structure and its supporting culture can become formidable impediments to change.

AT&T consequently spent the 1970s in almost continual turmoil over its internal structure. Starting with concern over the marketing of terminal equipment, the reorganization impulse gradually spread throughout the entire Bell System. The increasing pace of reorganization in the 1980s shows how much was left to do and how hard it was for AT&T to escape its own history. AT&T's internal trials – less well known than its external problems – should provide an object lesson for any CEO or government official who thinks it is easy to make dramatic changes in the mission of a large, well-established corporation.

Resistance to change was most visible in AT&T's public dealings. The company moved too slowly to catch the political process. Far from abandoning the terminal equipment market, deButts could not bring himself to accept the FCC's registration program until it was fully in place. Brown accepted the idea of fully separated subsidiaries in 1979, and in the heady days of 1980 and 1981 it appeared that this gambit might succeed. But Congress was too suspicious of AT&T by then, and the separation of subsidiaries became a form of divestiture with added restrictions. Time had run out on the Bell System.

Institutional rigidity also retarded internal change. The company leadership, unable to reach agreement with AT&T's critics, pressed ahead with its internal reorganizations. DeButts replaced Vail's tripartite organization with a compromise between Vail's structure and a truly competitive one. The CS/NS/OS organization never had a name or a compelling identity. Brown instituted a competitive organization, but the changes he initiated were not welcome. Any large organization generates positions for the people who run it. Reorganization threatens some of these positions and gathers opposition in proportion to the number of persons affected. Brown pushed through a reorganization that tightened the reins from 195 Broadway in the interest of better competitive responsiveness. Small wonder that it aroused resistance and resentment.

There was much internal planning during the ferment of the 1970s. Boettinger was a gadfly in the early years of the EPC, arguing, for example, for a more accommodating stance toward other companies' terminal equipment. Partoll understood well that the opposition to terminal equipment registration was politically intertwined with the opposition to competition in interexchange communication. Sharwell's Friday Committee struggled to find a path through the growing legal, political, and business jungle. The Friday Committee grew into the Planning Council and then into a revised EPC. Reports from internal and external advisors were considered widely. But none of this planning had much effect. In the absence of a clear signal from the top, no organized planning could go on. Authority can flow from the bottom up under stable conditions, including those stabilized by regulation, but structure and goals must be defined from the top down during periods of rapid change. This type of central direction, in fact, is one of the essential tasks of leadership.[17] Romnes articulated the desire to compete without showing the company how to accomplish that goal. His statements did not penetrate the organization in any meaningful way. DeButts gave mixed signals to his troops; only with Brown did effective communication of a new corporate goal emerge. But by then the company's options were severely circumscribed.

The federal government, as already described, shifted direction with less strain. Leaderless or unconcerned with telecommunications through much of the 1970s, the federal government nevertheless articulated and implemented a coherent change in policy. Opponents of AT&T shopped for government bodies sympathetic to their aims, appealing from one forum to another to get their way. AT&T also selected its arena, albeit with less skill. The federal government was moving inexorably toward more competitive telecommunications. The election of Ronald Reagan signified the collapse of any opposition, both in his general stance toward the role of government and in the appointment of William Baxter.

It is possible to argue, in fact, that the government reacted too fast. For all its checks and balances, the federal government rushed pell-mell into a giant experiment with no controls. Broadly speaking, we are engaged in a trial of modern competition: less government involvement; big, vertically-integrated business. The government, at least under the theory of the Modification of Final Judgment, should be withdrawing from telecommunications; AT&T has retained its vertical integration (at considerable cost). In telecommunications, therefore, perhaps more than anywhere else, we are testing whether vertical integration promotes efficiency and furthers progress more than horizontal integration.[18]

The impact of divestiture

What, then, are the effects of divestiture? In the three years or so since the Bell System came to an end, only the dim outlines of the transition have appeared. Nevertheless, it is possible to discern some of the results, some part of the impact this major reorganization has had.

[17]Chester Barnard, *The Functions of an Executive* (Cambridge, Mass.: Harvard University Press, 1938); Kenneth R. Andrews, *The Concept of Corporate Strategy*, rev. ed. (Homewood, Ill.: Richard D. Irwin, 1980).
[18]MacAvoy and Robinson, after first congratulating AT&T on pulling off a great coup through divestiture, have come around to this less sanguine view. In their more sober second look, they declare flatly: "Breaking up AT&T was a mistake." Paul W. MacAvoy and Kenneth Robinson, "Winning By Losing: The AT&T Settlement and Its Impact on Telecommunications," *Yale Journal on Regulation*, Vol. 1, 1983, pp. 1–42; ibid., "Losing By Judicial Policymaking: The First Year of the AT&T Divestiture," *Yale Journal on Regulation*, Vol. 2, 1985, pp. 225–62, at 247.

Already it is clear that there was at least one thing that divestiture did *not* accomplish. It did not separate the monopoly and competitive parts of telecommunications. This was Baxter's primary aim: to draw a bright line between those parts of the industry in which competition could flourish and those in which it could not – and for which, therefore, regulation was needed. The bright line, according to this theory, could not run through any corporation. If it did, there would be no way to avoid cross-subsidization of competitive activities from monopoly revenues. Unhappily, the clean theory on which the Modification of Final Judgment was based described the complex real world only tenuously. There is no bright line today, and we can now see that if cross-subsidies flowed across the line drawn by Baxter, they flowed from the competitive to the monopoly services.

Consider the divested operating companies first. They clearly have local monopolies in exchange telephone service to households and small businesses. They probably still have extensive market power in the local market for large businesses, although the growth of bypass threatens to erode it.[19] Judge Greene expanded their mandates in order to strengthen their financial condition, allowing them to pursue the competitive businesses of marketing terminal equipment and Yellow Pages and to file waivers in his court for permission to engage in other competitive activities. Geller and Shooshan predicted that the restrictions on the operating companies in the new consent decree would re-create the regulatory problems of the 1956 Decree; Judge Greene's modifications compounded this problem. Instead of a bright line between competition and regulated monopoly, there is a murky, shifting shadow. Judge Greene's court and the Justice Department were overwhelmed by waiver applications by the end of 1986.[20]

Postdivestiture AT&T falls astride this boundary as well, although for very different and more complex reasons. The case for competition in telecommunications equipment seems clear. In fact, that case has been valid since the beginning of telephony a century ago. Alexander Graham Bell had been granted patents on a machine that anyone could build, once the central idea was explained. He and his associates chose to manufacture all Bell telephones themselves – and purchased Western Electric to do so – primarily for commercial reasons, albeit with some technical advantages as well. End-to-end responsibility originated as a commercial con-

[19]Much of the current and threatened bypass, to be sure, involves the choice between switched and private line services, both connected through operating companies, rather than the construction of independent facilities. It is less of a threat to the local monopoly than a replay of the regulatory history of interstate private lines in the 1960s and 1970s.
[20]"AT&T says Justice is 'Overwhelmed' with Routine Line-of-business Waiver Issues, Cannot Properly Address Enforcement of Decree's Core Prohibitions," *Telecommunications Reports*, Vol. 52, No. 50 (December 15, 1986), pp. 3–6.

cept, designed initially to protect the Bell patents in the absence of advantages to large-scale production. The Bell interests were first protecting their patent and second enhancing the network.

The concept of end-to-end responsibility gradually acquired other meanings as the telephone network was engineered on the basis of Bell's practice. By the post-World War II era, it had acquired a mystique within the Bell System, a hold that was hard to break in the 1970s. The struggle to break it down has obscured some benefits that were gained by this integrated planning and the prospect of similar benefits that have been foregone by divestiture. The lack of these benefits from integration may slow technical progress in the future, but there does not seem now nor has there been in the past an economic argument explaining why competition could not exist in the sale of telecommunications equipment.[21]

By contrast, it is far from clear that the provision of intercity telecommunications services has the cost characteristics needed to sustain active competition – as opposed to an oligopoly of a few dominant firms. No one expects that there will be many national networks approximating the competitive conditions of farmers, gas stations, or telecommunications equipment manufacturers. It is becoming clear that it may not even be reasonable to expect the market to be composed of a few similarly sized firms.[22]

Microwave radio was the innovation that was thought to have destroyed Bell's natural monopoly in intercity telecommunications. Instead of a continuous right-of-way between two endpoints, an independent entrepreneur needed only to set up microwave towers on hilltops, tall buildings,

---

[21]The historical argument cannot include large electronic switches, which are as new as electronic computers. They are, in fact, a particular kind of electronic computer. And the Justice Department agreed with IBM that this market has been and is competitive. For arguments in support of this position from IBM's economic experts, see Franklin M. Fisher, John J. McGowan, and Joen E. Greenwood, *Folded, Spindled, and Mutilated: Economic Analysis and U.S. v. IBM* (Cambridge, Mass.: MIT Press, 1983).

[22]The attempts to use econometric techniques to uncover the presence or absence of economies of scale have not been successful. Econometricians themselves are not convinced by their econometric studies. Evans and Heckman note charmingly in their econometric study of the Bell System's cost subadditivity, that is, declining costs, that they "resoundingly reject" the assumptions their estimates are based on. They conjecture that the same logical inconsistency plagues other econometric studies as well. They therefore conclude in a survey of econometric studies that "none of these studies can provide decisive evidence that the telephone industry is or is not a natural monopoly." David S. Evans and James J. Heckman, "A Test for Subadditivity of the Cost Function with an Application to the Bell System," *American Economic Review*, Vol. 74, 1984, 620n; David S. Evans and James J. Heckman, "Natural Monopoly," in David S. Evans (ed.), *Breaking Up Bell: Essays on Industrial Organization and Regulation* (New York: North-Holland, 1983), p. 149.

A recent report to the Justice Department goes further, acknowledging that competition in interexchange service is illusory. The report suggests, in fact, that the smaller carriers continue to exist "only at the combined grace of AT&T itself and the FCC." Peter W. Huber, *The Geodesic Network*, pp. 3.6–3.7.

or towers at thirty-mile intervals. But the age of microwaves was short-lived. The growing use of fiberoptics is altering the industry and the potential for competition dramatically. Although fiberoptic cables are smaller than coaxial cables, they share the same necessity of obtaining a continuous right-of-way. The future of common carrier transmission thus appears to be with "wire" transmission. Fiberoptics are the low-cost means of long distance telephone service, and there is every indication that they will continue to be so for quite a while. Electronic signaling has been using more and more efficient cables and higher and higher frequencies for the better part of a century. It is more accurate to view light-guide technology as the contemporary expression of that trend than to see it as a process with a totally different technology and cost structure than its predecessors. Technical factors, therefore, suggest that AT&T is still likely to have a natural monopoly in intercity telecommunications or at least be the dominant member of a very small oligopoly.

The other common carriers have grown in the shade of the price umbrella held over them first by the Bell System's regulated prices and then by differential ENFIA and access charges. Their growth consequently shows the difference between regulatory and competitive prices. It carries no information about the viability of competition. This central fact has been obscured by the long, tortuous, and largely vacuous debate over cross-subsidies.[23] It is probable, in short, that consideration of the costs of intercity telecommunications leads to the same conclusion as analysis of the technology.

There were two reasons to separate the competitive and regulatory parts of the Bell System. One was to eliminate the Bell System's ability to foreclose access to its local service bottleneck monopoly in order to stifle competition in its competitive markets. This has been accomplished only in part. The lines of divestiture do not follow the lines of any bottleneck monopoly; each of the regional Bell companies has in effect been left in the monopoly position that AT&T formerly held. Divestiture nevertheless has decreased the opportunities to favor a Bell System company by foreclosing entry and refusing another firm access to a bottleneck facility. It has thereby increased competition.

The second reason to separate the competitive and regulatory parts of the Bell System was to eliminate cross-subsidies from the latter to the former. This was not accomplished. Divestiture separated the regulated operating companies from the putatively competitive AT&T. The cross-subsidy to be eliminated, therefore, must have flowed from the operating

---

[23]Even without cross-subsidies, it is not possible to infer from the entry of new firms into a part of a natural monopolist's market that the natural monopoly does not exist. John C. Panzar and Robert D. Willig, "Free Entry and the Sustainability of Natural Monopoly," *Bell Journal of Economics*, Vol. 8, 1977, pp. 1–22.

companies to Long Lines, Western Electric, or Bell Labs. But as the preceding pages have shown, it did not.

The notion that the operating companies subsidized Long Lines had its origin in FCC accounting rules. Under Hinchman, the FCC defined cross-subsidies in terms of fully distributed costs. By this definition, telephone rates that were nonsubsidizing contained a cross-subsidy of local rates both in terms of the FCC's earlier 1950 definition and in board-to-board accounting. The Commission has now abandoned fully distributed costs as a basis for rate making, and the definition of cross-subsidies based on them must be abandoned too. With it surely also goes the long, hopeless task of trying to allocate the costs of the non-traffic-sensitive local plant in a "correct" way. It simply cannot be done; there is no reason to prefer any one allocation of a fixed cost – even SLU – to another.[24]

Instead, it is fitting to acknowledge the divestiture by returning to board-to-board analysis. The telephone network was broken up along board-to-board lines; it is time to bring the definition of cross-subsidies in line with reality.[25] On a board-to-board basis, Long Lines has been heavily subsidizing local service since the separations process was initiated during the Second World War. The size of the subsidy has grown steadily over time, exceeding $7 billion in 1981.[26] Whether or not they are called subsidies, this extensive use of interstate revenues to support the local plant has been a pivotal fact of telecommunications history.

The Justice Department followed the lead of the ill-informed congressional discussion when it chose to disregard this transfer in its antitrust case against AT&T. The department asserted that there was "no basis for claiming that changes in jurisdictional separations procedures caused disparities between the cost and price of Bell's interstate rates because the fundamental thrust of the changes . . . has been to arrive at reasonable and equitable cost allocations between interstate and intrastate telephone services."[27] This statement is disingenuous to the point of being dissembling. It is true that separations did not create a disparity between prices and station-to-station costs, because the FCC changed the definition of station-to-station costs to correspond to separations. But separations did create a large and growing discrepancy between interstate rates and

[24]John R. Meyer et al., *The Economics of Competition in the Telecommunication Industry* (Cambridge, Mass.: Oelgeschlager, Gunn & Hain, 1980); Leland L. Johnson, *Competition and Cross-Subsidization in the Telephone Industry* (Santa Monica, Calif., Rand Corp. 1982).

[25]The network, of course, was not broken up along the lines of existing "boards" in 1981. The whole LATA discussion was designed to draw new boundaries between the separated parts of the network.

[26]Peter Temin and Geoffrey Peters, "Cross-Subsidization in the Telephone Network," *Willamette Law Review*, Vol. 21 (Spring 1985), pp. 199–223.

[27]*US* v. *AT&T*, CA No. 74–1698, U.S. Dist. Ct., Dist. of Columbia, *Plaintiff's Third Statement of Contentions and Proof*, January 10, 1980, p. 1865.

board-to-board costs. A firm that could effect board-to-board entry and then avoid the impact of separations charges could practically print money. MCI did just that. It benefited from separations charges when it subscribed to local service at normal business rates and then from differential ENFIA payments after *Execunet*. One suspects, in fact, that MCI made all of its money from the discrepancy between the prices it paid for local services and the price paid by Long Lines – and none from any differences between its costs and Long Lines' costs of intercity services.

The Justice Department referred to the search for "reasonable and equitable cost allocations" as if separations were a small, technical process of no particular importance. But this is a totally untenable position. The rapid growth of separations charges could not have escaped the attention of even the densest regulator. Everyone connected with telecommunications in the 1970s knew that local telephone service was being supported more and more by revenues from interstate traffic. Anyone who thought about the amount of money involved must also have understood that this was hardly the unintended fallout of a jurisdictional decision in 1930. It was instead the result of an ongoing political process that can be seen in the pressure Senator McFarland put on the FCC in 1950, as well as congressional pressure on the Commission not to impose end-user access charges in 1983. Some interested parties chose to disregard all of these factors, sowing confusion among the uninitiated and impugning AT&T's attempts to explain it. But the fact of the giant subsidy remained.

The Justice Department also argued that the operating companies subsidized Western Electric by paying too much for its products. Judge Greene thought so little of that argument and the government witnesses who presented it that he dismissed it without even waiting for AT&T to reply.[28] Ironically, a subsidy of this sort might have been growing in the 1970s as Western Electric's position as the low-cost supplier of telecommunications equipment eroded. If so, however, the subsidy did not flow to Western Electric's profits, never notably high, but instead to the workers at Western Electric. This story gains plausibility from union insistence on the terminal equipment portions of the CCRA and the strike on the eve of divestiture, as well as from the declines in employment at Western Electric and then AT&T Technologies in the past decade.

Finally, regulated local service was said to subsidize the competitive sale of terminal equipment and network services through R&D at Bell Labs. Bell Labs research activities, of course, were supported by the operating companies through their License Contract payments to AT&T. This was never considered a subsidy by the members of the Bell System;

[28]Judge Greene, *Opinion*, September 11, 1981, *US* v. *AT&T*, CA No. 74–1698 (D.D.C.), 524 F. Supp. 1336 at 1380–81.

it was a normal business expense. Indeed, to Brown and other believers in the importance of vertical integration, it was the heart of an effective, innovative corporate organization. Bell Labs provided the knowledge to improve all aspects of telecommunications services, both local and long distance. But to Congressman Wirth and possibly to Baxter, research at Bell Labs on network design represented a subsidy to the competitive, long distance service from the monopoly local service.

However this research is labeled, it was far smaller than the separations charges in the reverse direction. License Contract payments in 1981 were about $1 billion, and payments from AT&T to Bell Labs were less than half of that amount.[29] Even if all of Bell Labs's charges to AT&T were for interexchange services and were paid from License Contract revenues, the transfer from the operating companies to Long Lines would have been only one-tenth the size of the transfer from Long Lines to the operating companies. A definition of cross-subsidies that makes the net flow run to – not from – Long Lines is contorted indeed.

Divestiture therefore did not eliminate cross-subsidies to Long Lines; the subsidies simply ran the other way. It did eliminate Bell Labs as the virtually exclusive source of network R&D. Bell Labs still continues to operate, of course, but it is connected to only one part of the telecommunications market. It has been joined by Bellcore and other companies performing similar functions for other firms. AT&T's leaders championed the benefits of synergy between the Bell System's myriad activities, what economists have come to call "economies of scope."[30] They thought them most evident in Bell Labs's astonishing and wide-ranging productivity during the years that AT&T's monopoly was intact. No estimates have been offered for the size of these economies, but if AT&T is in the future unable to sustain the budget of the Labs at its traditional level, their loss could well be a significant cost of divestiture.

Bell Labs engaged in both pure and applied research, as well as product development. The basic research part of this activity threatens to erode as a result of divestiture. It is not only that AT&T's revenues are smaller, but also that Bell Labs no longer serves the entire telephone network. Discoveries basic to telecommunications will benefit many people and firms external to AT&T. There is no reason for AT&T to search for discoveries that do not earn a return for the firm, no matter how valuable they may be. If AT&T is to be "a competitor among competitors," to use Brown's phrase, it will do no more.

As a result, a great national resource has been lost, or at least has had its

[29]Bell Labs billed slightly more of its expenses to Western Electric than to AT&T. *Bell System Statistical Manual, 1950–1981*, AT&T Comptroller's-Accounting Division, June 1982, pp. 1002, 1311.
[30]Oliver Williamson, *The Economic Institutions of Capitalism* (New York: Free Press, 1985).

wings clipped. The research no longer done at Bell Labs should be done, so the theory goes, elsewhere. But if the gains are external to any one telecommunications firm, no one will undertake basic research. No one, that is, except the government. Divestiture was, in this sense, only one-half of a rational policy: To be fully rational, the government should support the kind of basic research that has been done at Bell Labs. Critics of the Bell System argued that a national resource should not be paid for by private revenues. If so, the proper remedy was not to destroy the resource; it was to revise its financing. But the Reagan administration and Baxter saw only the first half of the policy. The administration seems not to take kindly to arguments for a government that helps the peacetime economy in this direct way.

Technical changes in the network also will be harder to introduce. The interconnections between the Bell Operating Companies and the interexchange carriers are made according to a set of protocols. Changes in the technology that suggest new protocols will be hard to implement. Agreement among all of the parties involved will not come easily. There is a real danger that the antitrust effort to ensure an efficient network today through competition may bring an outmoded network tomorrow as new technology is introduced more easily in more integrated national systems.

Given all of the confusion that attended the controversy over this industry, it would be surprising indeed if the Modification of Final Judgment had eliminated most of telecommunications regulation. It has not. Baxter's argument for pursuing the antitrust case within the Reagan administration – that it was a policy of deregulation – was based on a misreading of regulatory history. The FCC did not retire from the field. AT&T may now consider itself to be a competitor among competitors, but the FCC has taken a different approach. Judge Greene, in addition, threatens to become another regulatory agency as he tries to keep up with the flood of waiver requests from the operating companies.[31] *Telecommunications Reports* has found just as much to write about in a postdivestiture world as it did in the tumultuous 1970s.

Divestiture, therefore, did not succeed in creating a simple competitor among competitors or end cross-subsidies. The nature and extent of competition in telecommunications services are far from clear, and regulation has not withered away. AT&T still occupies, somewhat unwillingly, a special place in the roster of interexchange common carriers. Cross-subsidies to the new AT&T were never a problem; cross-subsidies from it continue to pose dilemmas for the FCC and state commissions.

Even after divestiture, AT&T carries the bulk of interexchange telecom-

---

[31]See a recent speech by Judge Greene as reported in *Telecommunications Reports*, Vol. 53, No. 6, February 9, 1987, p. 1.

munications traffic, although its share of this market is falling over time. AT&T has three-quarters of the market today; it is forecast to have only two-thirds by 1991.[32] It is tempting to view the path of this market share as a good test of the competition that Baxter sought in 1970, no less than in 1981. But doing so ignores the effects of the differential access charges that are the legacy of ENFIA and the separations process. The future division of the market will be affected at least as much by the tangled regulatory future of these charges as by the construction and operating costs for intercity telecommunications services.

Nor did the consent decree foment a great commercial contest between the new AT&T and IBM. IBM has reached an agreement with MCI that gives the latter firm financial backing and gives IBM entry into the interexchange telecommunications markets. AT&T has purchased part of Olivetti and gone into the commercial computer field.[33] But neither company has changed its primary focus. IBM is a full-line computer manufacturer with an interest in telecommunications. AT&T manages a national telecommunications network and sells computers primarily to perform switching functions in that network. The notion that the AT&T settlement was a remedy in the abortive IBM case is chimerical. It has no possible legal basis; AT&T was not a party to the IBM case. The statement of this position only demonstrates yet again how little autonomy the antitrust trial had.

The view of two technological giants slugging it out for control of the giant computing and telecommunications field reveals a total lack of understanding of the internal operations of the two firms. They have had far different, almost opposite histories, and their internal operations differ radically as a result. AT&T was set up – under Vail's enduring influence – to respond to regulators. It was not the fleet-footed competitor that could catch IBM in a race for the general computer market. IBM, for its part, has no expertise in the operation of a national network and no desire to get involved in the tangled regulatory arena of telecommunications in the 1980s. The result should have been predicted. The two firms overlap to some extent but are almost completely in separate markets.[34]

This has been a long list of negatives. But it is necessary to dwell on the changes not realized by divestiture because they include so many of the

[32]The Yankee Group, "Long Distance Update," December 1985. Other predictions are roughly similar. See the predictions of the Gartner group in *The Wall Street Journal*, February 24, 1986, Sec. 3, p. 5D, and comments in Huber, *The Geodesic Network*.

[33]"IBM Agrees to Acquire Initial 16% Holding in MCI; Alliance Would Create Powerful Challenge to AT&T," *The Wall Street Journal*, June 26, 1985, p. 3; "AT&T to Buy 25% of Olivetti For $260 Million," *The Wall Street Journal*, December 22, 1983, p. 2.

[34]For another failure to understand the legacy of AT&T's past, see Paul W. MacAvoy and Kenneth Robinson, "Winning by Losing: The AT&T Settlement and Its Impact on Telecommunications," *Yale Journal of Regulation*, Vol. 1, 1983, pp. 1–42.

anticipated benefits. The advertising for the Modification of Final Judgment, like much advertising of consumer products, promised more than it could deliver.[35]

Still, divestiture delivered a great deal. It dismantled the Bell System. The large monopoly that seemed to be such an affront to the antitrust laws is gone, as is the integrated telephone network of the United States. The end of the Bell System is a boon to competitive firms, even though the boom in message toll service may be short-lived and the equipment suppliers that gain may be European, Asian, and Canadian. The end of the integrated network will slow the pace of technical improvement in telecommunications if the economies often cited by the leaders of AT&T turn out to have been important.

In brief, divestiture may well have sacrificed long-run gains in the quest for short-run goals. Competition has replaced the (regulated) monopoly provision of many telecommunications services. It has brought many new choices of terminal equipment. It has brought a range of possible new equipment to the Bell Operating Companies. It has brought a choice of suppliers with different prices and – to the casual observer – different qualities to consumers. Competition among the alternative suppliers can be expected to result in lower prices and product improvement.

There are, however, offsets to this rosy scenario. Many consumers find the new choice bothersome rather than helpful. They have discovered after the fact that they liked the telephones that lasted forever and the utility that took responsibility for the entire network. Consumers have more choices, but the option of remaining under the old Bell System is not one of them. The stimulus to other U.S. firms was blunted by the strength of the dollar in the early 1980s and the growth of telecommunications imports. In addition, the improvements in products and services under competition may not be as great as they would have been under monopoly. If the interconnections between the different parts of the network and the externalities from new discoveries are anywhere as large as AT&T claimed in the government's antitrust suit, then competition will be inferior in this regard too. Alas, there are no measures of these offsets and no way to know if they will wipe out the theoretical advantages of competition. The possibility, however, is worrisome.

[35]Even the Department of Justice appears to have abandoned the theory underlying the *Modification of Final Judgment*. In its triennial report to the court on the Consent Decree, the Justice Department recommended that almost all the constraints on the Bell Operating Companies be removed, allowing them to straddle regulated and competitive markets, as AT&T did in the 1970s, and to enter interLATA communications. Baxter, Carr, and Levine, of course, are long gone from the government. The Justice Department, apparently happy to have a smaller AT&T, harbors no loyalty to the now discredited theory of divestiture. *US* v. *AT&T*, CA No. 82–0192 (D.D.C.), *Report and Recommendations of the United States Concerning the Line of Business Restrictions Imposed on the Bell Operating Companies by the Modification of Final Judgment*, February 2, 1987.

The consent decree sharply reduced AT&T's size. Baxter and others denied that AT&T's size rather than its market power was of concern. But the effect of the Bell System's vast size on the political history of divestiture cannot be overestimated. The FCC constantly complained that it was overwhelmed by AT&T's submissions. The telephone company was too large, it stated, to be regulated. Congress was receptive to arguments for special privilege advanced by AT&T's small competitors. The several judicial decisions that were important to this history also seem likely to have been affected by AT&T's great size (although there is no way to prove this). To the extent that the Bell System did have a substantial amount of political power – and I believe, as noted before, that Bell's power has been exaggerated – the problem no longer exists.

I have commented already on the effects of changing ideology on telecommunications policy. It is important to acknowledge changes in the objects of policy as well. The Bell System was the largest private corporation in the United States at the end of World War II. It continued to grow rapidly thereafter, as shown in Tables 1 and 2, doubling its size in each decade. AT&T more than kept pace with the expanding American economy, riding on the increasing scale of telecommunications. DeButts anticipated that AT&T would continue to supply essentially all of this rising market; Brown regarded Bell's expansion in the 1970s with the satisfaction of a successful corporate executive. But outside observers watched this growth with both political and economic apprehension. They doubted that the country could stand a single control over so large and important an aspect of the American economy. The growing suspicion of AT&T, in other words, was stimulated both by the growing distrust of government and utilities and by the rapidly expanding size of the Bell System.

To the extent that the expansion of telecommunications and AT&T was due to technical progress, technical change reenters the story. And rightly so. The astonishing expansion of computing power, data transmission, and switching capability of the modern information age stands behind this tale. But it must be remembered that the telecommunications industry has expanded in part due to the rise in demand. And this acknowledgment of the effect of technology on the growth of AT&T should be distinguished from stories that see the end of the Bell System as the result of a specific innovation, whether the transistor, microwave radio, touchtone dialing, or electronic switching.

Divestiture also changed sharply the internal workings of the members of the former Bell System. The regional holding companies and the Bell Operating Companies were invigorated by their new independence. Far from becoming the water companies or railroads of the telecommunications industry, they have become the centers of new activities and aggressive growth. AT&T, by contrast, far from becoming another IBM, has had to struggle to find its new identity. The widespread failure to anticipate this contrast shows the poverty of the theory underlying the Modification of Final Judgment and the ignorance that existed about the internal structure of the Bell System.

The Bell System functioned for three-quarters of a century as an integrated service organization. Its managers were rotated throughout the System to get experience and exercised considerable operating autonomy while in the field. The operating companies were the front-line service representatives, containing the bulk of the System's managers at any moment. AT&T's Charles Brown left the operating company leadership in place, both by appointing company presidents to head the regional holding companies and by relying on the predominant use standard for allocating less senior personnel. The AT&T leadership pipeline thereby suffered a major break.[36]

Divestiture was, in this sense, a mirror image of the 1978 reorganization. Then, the shift to a market-segmented structure reduced the autonomy of the operating companies and, by eliminating the operating vice presidents, deranged the career development path. Divestiture, by contrast, greatly increased the independence of the operating company leaders and brought the top executive positions closer to each of the existing managers. Small wonder that this new independence energized the operating company leadership. The vigor shown by the regional holding companies reveals the quality of the Bell System managers; it may also indicate that the old service ethic in a monolithic organization reduced its scope.

AT&T suffered greatly from the divestiture. It resembled Vienna after World War I more than West Germany after World War II. It has had to reduce the size of its internal bureaucracy, to develop new leadership paths, and – most importantly – to define a corporate mission appropriate to its new business. As the preceding narrative has shown, redefinition of corporate objectives also requires the firm's managers to reorganize corporate structure and operations. Redefinition at the top is simply not enough. Business systems as well as missions must change.

Finally, divestiture has increased the pressure to abandon regulatory pricing completely in telecommunications. The FCC and Judge Wright had introduced competition well before the agreement between Baxter and Brown. But there can be no doubt that the extent of competition has been increased – both within the United States and internationally – by divestiture, placing further weight on the telephone price structure. The pressure on regulatory prices in the 1970s broke up the Bell System rather than the

[36]There were, of course, some prominent exceptions to this policy. For example, Thomas Bolger went from AT&T to Bell Atlantic; Robert Allen, from The Cheasapeake and Potomac Telephone Companies to AT&T.

structure of prices. Now the pressure has been focused directly on prices. The painful transition to competitive telecommunications prices has begun. It is slow; it is politically volatile; but it is inevitable.

Although it is still too early to evaluate divestiture either as public policy or as corporate strategy, some short-run indications deserve to be noted. AT&T stockholders, ever the focus of AT&T's chairman, have benefited from this change. In fact, Brown's twin aims of protection of the stockholders' interest and the maintenance of service seem to have been largely accomplished. Thus far, the gain to the regional holding companies has exceeded the problems of AT&T – at least in the view of the stock market. The widow – that inevitable widow – holding AT&T stock in 1981 gained appreciably by 1986 if she held on to the combined shares of the operating companies and AT&T she was given at divestiture.[37] AT&T employees, as indicated by the number of layoffs and strikes, did not fare so well.[38] Business customers found the available range of telecommunications services increased; residential customers found the quality of their repair services and installations impaired. Many of these problems would have emerged even without divestiture as *Computer II* was implemented, but they followed divestiture and are attributed to it. The "ordinary telephone subscriber" was, in addition, besieged by mail asking him or her to choose a long distance carrier and hit by increases in the local telephone bill. Those customers who owned – and kept – Bell System stock must have felt that the trade was worthwhile. Heavy users of long distance services should have agreed. The majority of residential customers did not.[39]

In the longer run, as I have observed, divestiture must be looked on as an enormous gamble. It is part of a general experiment in competition as a way of organizing previously regulated industries. Telecommunications was unique among these industries, both because of the dominance of a single firm and because of the presence of an interactive network. Only in the long run will we know – and possibly not even then – if the competitive market can innovate as well as the integrated Bell System. Brown also

[37]"Widows, Orphans Win!: Bell Breakup Produces Capital Gains," *Barron's*, January 27, 1986, p. 49; "Analysts Like Bell Regionals," *The New York Times*, June 3, 1986, p. D10.
[38]For example, see "AT&T and 3 Unions Hold Informal Talks as a Strike by Telephone Workers Begins," *The Wall Street Journal*, August 8, 1983, p. 4; "AT&T Is Struck, But Calls Go On," *The New York Times*, June 2, 1986, p. B12, on 1986 strike; on AT&T layoffs, see "24,000 AT&T Jobs To Be Eliminated from Systems Unit," *The New York Times*, August 22, 1985, p. A1, and "AT&T Seeks to Ease Fears on Layoff Reports," November 6, 1986, p. D1.
[39]See, for example, "Eagleton Poll," *The Star Ledger*, March 18, 1984, Sec. 1, p. 10; "Phone Users' Complaints Rising After the Bell System's Breakup," *The New York Times*, February 17, 1984, p. A1; "Jump in Local Rates Since AT&T Breakup Is Spurring Protests," *The Wall Street Journal*, September 27, 1985, p. 1; "Can you hear me?" *Forbes*, September 23, 1985, p. 186.

gambled. He bet his company on the agreement with Baxter. Today the parts spun off–representing three-fourths of the assets of the old Bell System–seem to be fine, but the jury is still out on AT&T itself. The changes chronicled here and continuing today have shaken AT&T and severely taxed its resources. There can be no question: The new AT&T is rising, phoenix-like, from the ashes of the Bell System. But no one yet knows how high it will fly.

Index

Above 890 decision, 28–31, 30n3, 85, 107, 137, 215, 310, 336, 338, 339; AT&T response to, 31; pricing effects of, 34–5; sharing, 47; significance of, 31–6, 40

access charges, 186, 239, 306–17, 361; congressional response to, 312–16; FCC decision on, 308–12; Judge Greene on, 312; postdivestiture AT&T study group on, 296; Telecommunications Competition and Deregulation Act of 1981 (S. 898) and, 239

Ad-Hoc Committee for Competitive Telecommunications (ACCT), 124, 127–8, 185

Administration D (AT&T), 115, 152

Advanced Information Systems Division (AT&T), 321, 329

Allen, Robert, 181–2, 364n36

Amendment in the Nature of a Substitute to HR 5158, 284

American Bell, 321–5

American Telephone and Telegraph Company (AT&T), *see* AT&T

Anderson, Kenneth, 200n76, 205–6

antitrust laws, 9–11, 99, 235, 253, 343–4, 362

Antitrust Procedures and Penalties Act of 1974, 280–2, 280n6, 281n8, 287

antitrust suit(s) (*see also* Justice, U.S. Department of; *United States v. AT&T*): against AT&T, 116, 131, 155, 158, 177, 188, 231, 251, 339; bottleneck monopoly basis of, 108–9; Datran, 177; by Department of Justice against AT&T, 9, 14–15, 100–101, 110–12; IBM, 252, 254, 282–3; impact of, 339–42; ITT, 177; Litton Systems, Inc., 177, 230–1, 251; MCI, 107–8, 177, 188, 207–8, 208n86, 230–31; 334; Southern Pacific Communications Company, 333–4

Arthur D. Little, Inc., 127

AT&T (*see also* Administration D; Advanced Information Systems Division; Bell System; Broadband Planning Group; Consumer Products Division; corporate planning; Executive Policy Committee; lines of business; network access pricing; Office of Chairman; Planning Council; Tariff Review Committee; Tri-Company Councils): board of directors, 68, 70, 199, 208, 216, 221, 268; budgetary procedures, 18, 145–7, 167–8; horizontal integration of, 12, 353; monopoly building by, 11–14; postdivestiture reorganization of, 318–35, 326fig, 327fig: *authority structure, 320; Bell Labs, 323–4, 328; corporate management, 329–30; deregulated activities, 320–28; divestiture press conference and public relations, 278plt, 279; leadership for, 318; lines of business strategy, 319–28; logo, 302–3, 303n49, 325, 328; management systems, 329; marketing emphasis, 320; post-agreement planning for, 318–20; regulated activities, 328–9; stock performance of, 4, 5fig, 146, 146fig;* and telephone network, 16, 44–5, 49, 53, 62, 66, 71–2, 84–5, 96, 102, 104n55, 113, 131–3, 141–2, 144, 160, 168, 175, 178, 184n44, 192–3, 227, 247, 258–61, 271–3, 277, 285, 292–3, 330, 347, 355, 360–2; vertical integration of, 12–14, 95, 322, 350, 353; Western Electric, 322–3, 334–5

AT&T Bell Labs, 323, 324, 328, 334–5

AT&T Communications, 329, 333

AT&T Information Systems, 325

AT&T Interexchange Entity (ATT-IX), 328–9

AT&T International, 199, 324

AT&T Technologies Sector, 324, 334–5

Aylward, David, 187

Baker, James, 231

Baldrige, Malcolm, 226–31, 233; divestiture decree and, 274; on global competition, 345; on Telecommunications Competition and Deregulation Act of 1981 (S. 898), 238–40, 245, 246, 255

Ball, Ed, 234

367